THE SOCIAL REBEL
in American Literature

PERSPECTIVES ON AMERICAN LITERATURE

Robert H. Woodward and James J. Clark
General Editors

THE
SOCIAL REBEL
in American Literature

———•———

EDITED BY

ROBERT H. WOODWARD
San Jose State College

JAMES J. CLARK
San Jose State College

THE ODYSSEY PRESS

NEW YORK

ACKNOWLEDGMENTS

Acknowledgment is gratefully made for permission to reprint the following material:

Daniel Aaron. From *Writers on the Left*, © 1961, by Daniel Aaron. Reprinted by permission of Harcourt, Brace & World, Inc.

Sherwood Anderson. From *A Story Teller's Story*. Reprinted by permission of Harold Ober Associates, Inc. Copyright © 1924 by B. W. Huebsch. Renewed 1951 by Eleanor Copenhaver Anderson.

James Baldwin. From *Notes of a Native Son*. Reprinted by permission of the publisher, Beacon Press, copyright © 1955 by James Baldwin.

Randolph S. Bourne. "For Radicals" from *Youth and Life*. Reprinted by permission of Houghton Mifflin Company.

Henry Steele Commager. From *The American Mind*, by Henry Steele Commager, pp. 247–250, 257–262, 267, 273–276. Reprinted by permission of Yale University Press.

Malcolm Cowley. From *Exile's Return* by Malcolm Cowley. Copyright 1934, © 1962 by Malcolm Cowley. Reprinted by permission of The Viking Press, Inc.

John Dos Passos. From *Three Soldiers*. Copyright 1921 by John Dos Passos. Copyright Renewed 1949 by John Dos Passos. Published by Houghton Mifflin Company. From *The 42nd Parallel*. Copyright 1930 by John Dos Passos. Copyright Renewed 1958 by John Dos Passos. Published by Houghton Mifflin Company. From *Nineteen Nineteen*. Copyright 1932 by John Dos Passos. Copyright Renewed 1960 by John Dos Passos. Published by Houghton Mifflin Company.

Joseph Freeman. "The Tradition of American Revolutionary Literature" from *American Writers' Congress*, Henry Hart (ed.). Reprinted by permission of International Publishers Co., Inc. From *An American Testa-*

ment by Joseph Freeman. Copyright 1936, © 1964 by Joseph Freeman. Reprinted by permission of Holt, Rinehart and Winston, Inc.

Allen Ginsberg. "America" from *Howl and Other Poems.* Copyright © 1956, 1959 by Allen Ginsberg. Reprinted by permission of City Lights Books.

Albert Halper. From *The Foundry* by Albert Halper. Copyright, 1934, 1962, by Albert Halper.

LeRoi Jones. "The Screamers." Copyright © 1963 by LeRoi Jones. From *The Moderns,* published by Corinth Books. Reprinted by permission of The Sterling Lord Agency.

Jack Kerouac. From *On the Road* by Jack Kerouac. Copyright © 1955, 1957 by Jack Kerouac. Reprinted by permission of The Viking Press, Inc.

Martin Luther King, Jr. "Love, Law and Civil Disobedience" from *Rhetoric of Racial Revolt* by Roy L. Hill, published by Golden Bell Press, Denver, Colorado.

Sinclair Lewis. From *Main Street* by Sinclair Lewis, copyright, 1920, by Harcourt, Brace & World, Inc.; copyright, 1948, by Sinclair Lewis. Reprinted by permission of the publisher.

Norman Mailer. "The Patron Saint of MacDougal Alley." Reprinted by permission of G. P. Putnam's Sons from *Advertisements for Myself* by Norman Mailer. © 1959 by Norman Mailer.

H. L. Mencken. "Duty" from *Prejudices: Third Series* by H. L. Mencken. Copyright 1922 by Alfred A. Knopf, Inc. and renewed 1950 by H. L. Mencken. Reprinted by permission. "The Icononoclast" from *A Mencken Chrestomathy* by H. L. Mencken. Copyright 1924 by Alfred A. Knopf Inc. and renewed 1952 by H. L. Mencken. By permission of Alfred A. Knopf, Inc.

Henry Miller. "Epidaurus and Mycenae" from *The Colossus of Maroussi.* Copyright 1941 by Henry Miller. Reprinted by permission of New Directions Publishing Corporation.

Michael Millgate. From *American Social Fiction* by Michael Millgate. Reprinted by permission of the publisher, Barnes & Noble, Inc., and the author.

C. Wright Mills. "On the New Left." Reprinted with permission from *Studies on the Left,* Volume II, No. 1 (1961).

Kenneth Rexroth. "The Students Take Over" from *The Nation,* Vol. 191 (July 2, 1960). Reprinted by permission of Kenneth Rexroth.

Upton Sinclair. From *Boston.* Reprinted by permission of Bertha Klausner International Literary Agency, Inc.

John P. Sisk. "Beatniks and Tradition" from *The Commonweal,* Vol. 70 (April 17, 1959). Reprinted by permission of Commonweal Publishing Co., Inc.

John Steinbeck. From *In Dubious Battle* by John Steinbeck. Copyright 1936, © 1964 by John Steinbeck. Reprinted by permission of The Viking Press, Inc.

Mark Twain. "The War Prayer" from *Europe and Elsewhere* by Mark Twain. Copyright 1923, 1951 by The Mark Twain Company. Reprinted by permission of Harper & Row, Publishers.

PREFACE

ALTHOUGH AMERICAN SOCIETY is noted for the high degree of conformity that it imposes on its members and for the materialistic values that seem often to take precedence over human ones, it is a significant fact that much of the serious literature of America has since its beginnings been one of criticism, dissent, rebellion—a double-sided mirror that reflects not only social practices but also the underlying ideals and aspirations of America. The theme of social rebellion is a fundamental one—perhaps the fundamental one—in American literature. This collection of comment on the role of the social rebel in American life and of literature reflecting the course and direction of his rebellion is designed primarily for use as a controlled-research casebook that will allow the student sufficient material to formulate and to document his own conclusions about "the subversive tradition" in American literature.

In a volume of this size we could not hope to cover adequately the multifaceted body of literature of social rebellion. We have, therefore, emphasized the recurrent tendencies that seem to us the most significantly American ones—those reflecting the continuing moral revolution against the stringent restrictions of a puritan heritage, those stemming from the democratic faith in the individual and the belief in his inalienable rights, and those in opposition to the economic structure of American society. We have had to be satisfied merely to glance at literature of dissent that is less locally American—utopian literature and the literature of bohemia, for example.

The volume contains two principal types of selections. The first section, "Perspectives," contains several authoritative assessments of or germinal statements about the literature of rebellion and the role of the rebel. These essays make generalizations and observations that can be supported—or argued—by the second type of selections, usually works of imaginative literature expressing important features of the theme of social rebellion. The organization of the three literary sections permits a chronological overview that suggests major lines

vii

of development or evolution of particular aspects of the theme.
We have kept editorial additions to the minimum necessary for
effective use of the volume in courses in American civilization, American history, American literature, and English composition. The introductions to the four divisions provide only brief generalizations
about the selections that follow. At the end of the book are questions
intended to provoke discussion and suggest topics for papers. The
volume concludes with suggestions for further reading and notes on
the authors. Bibliographical information about each selection appears in a footnote, and the original pagination is shown within
brackets. The number before the virgule (/) indicates the end of
the original page; the number after it signals the beginning of a
new page. If in the original a word is divided at the end of a page,
the page number has been placed at the end of the word.
We wish to express our appreciation to two of our colleagues,
Nils T. Peterson and Graham C. Wilson, for their suggestions and
interest; to E. R. Hagemann, University of Louisville, and the staff
of the San Jose State College Library for their cooperation; and to
Vivien Nylen for her assistance in the preparation of the manuscript.

ROBERT H. WOODWARD
JAMES J. CLARK

San Jose State College
San Jose, California

CONTENTS

THE SOCIAL REBEL

in American Literature

I

Perspectives

IT IS PERHAPS an ironic feature of American literary history that social protest literature has had a long and respectable past, that society would find acceptable the kinds of criticism which frankly attempt to subvert the values of that society. Thomas Jefferson saw the political need of "little rebellions" to keep society healthy, and, to bear out Jefferson's hopes, America's history is a chronicle of the activities of those who sought to instigate "little rebellions," the list of the instigators including famous as well as infamous names. There was the not-so-respectable Thomas Morton in the 1600's, the pious John Woolman in the 1700's, James Fenimore Cooper, Emerson, and Thoreau, to name only the best known of the critics in the early 1800's. Since the days of Emerson and Thoreau the list has progressively increased, the American critics of America speaking loudly and persistently, sometimes, it would appear, even obsessively—the English critic Michael Millgate regrets the American writer's "inescapable self-consciousness" about his society—but speaking frankly and openly, sparing no one and no institution. The American writer has been amused by or has criticized capitalism, commercialism, Puritanism, the middle class or *booboisee*, Main Street and Madison Avenue, and even himself, and in so doing has prepared a body of literature that is marked certainly by a great deal of variety and often by an impressive degree of literary excellence.

From this literature has emerged a figure, the social rebel, a person who chose in some way to oppose the world he lives in. He is the antagonist, the adversary. This rebel may be the writer himself —a Thoreau, Whitman, or Ginsberg—or he may be a fictional representation, a Huckleberry Finn, or Tom Joad of *Grapes of Wrath*, or John Andrews of *Three Soldiers*. In general these writers or characters may be viewed as social rebels rather than revolutionists; they are members of a society that is ever changing, that, in addition, has in its structure the political and social ingredients to ferment new

1

changes. They serve generally a useful purpose in a watch-dog capacity, exposing the corrupt and awakening the conscience of a busy and practical country: Mark Twain's Huckleberry Finn uncovered the hypocritical moral pretensions of a nation when he befriended a Negro named Jim; in his two-year stay at Walden Pond Thoreau made a quiet protest that capitalism and commercialism have yet to answer effectively; Sister Carrie dreamed her way past an entire culture of Puritan restrictions and inhibitions; Jack London's Martin Eden in his suicide revealed an ultimate defiance of the whole ethic of money success; Fitzgerald's flappers introduced jazz and Freud to a shocked nation, revealing the flaws of the involved Puritan and Victorian fabric of social morality. The contemporary writer-rebel, history may record, is providing an equivalent useful social purpose in reminding a conformist culture about what John P. Sisk calls the "dream of utopian freedom and innocence to be found in a commitment to instinct and feeling." All of these writers or their creations have succeeded in some measure in changing social attitudes. How profound the changes have been or will prove to be perhaps creates a separate question. Commager, for instance, argues that the social criticism of the 1920's was largely ineffectual, that "the economic hide was too thick for the barbs of the satirists." And it has been often noted by many other critics that the middle class commercial culture is able to absorb seemingly alien philosophies with no perceptible harm to its own character—that it is able to use bohemianism, for instance, for its own commercial purpose. The importance of the changes may be a matter of controversy, but the fact of the confrontations of rebel and society is not. The confrontations are a matter of record, and they therefore can be examined and analyzed.

In his article on American writing Millgate raises a basic question: what are the reasons for the American artist's seeming antipathy toward his culture? To answer his question, he suggests that the problems facing the American artist are unique (as opposed to the problems faced by the English writer), the American artist having to come to terms with the "peculiar difficulties presented by the vastness, newness, shapelessness, and instability of American society." Commager, interested also in the American artist's problems of identity with his culture, suggests that the artist "took seriously the promise of American life, expected to realize the American dream," and therefore he was critical when the ideal seemed distorted. Other critics have singled out the corrupting influences of commercialism, or the process of dehumanization in modern industry that leads to the alienation of the individual man from a realistic commitment to his work or to his fellow man.

Another simpler explanation to help account for these many criticisms by the American writer is that a writer, the serious artist, works within the context of an artist's values and speaks therefore from a biased position. The democratic message of individualism quite naturally has a strong spokesman in the artist, who of necessity has adopted an individualistic philosophy and feels that he must oppose the forces antagonistic to this philosophy. A danger rests, however, in the possibility that the artist identifies individualism with artistic expression, therefore limiting the concept of individualism, particularly as that concept may be useful in a country which does not take artistic expression very seriously, or which will accept it more often than not in order to exploit it. The problem here is not one that is concerned with the validity of an artist's message in artistic terms, but the relevance of the artist's philosophy to the philosophy of the prevailing culture. Sisk mentions the danger to literature when writers accept too seriously their positions as antagonists, positions that may allow for "a good deal of swaggering and posing as they equate literature with opposition to orthodoxy." The trouble with many of these writers, according to Sisk, is that they seem to forget that "they remain a critically engaged part of society." In some degree, then, their place as antagonists becomes only a series of roles, make-believe stances that may finally appear only comic or bizarre.

But no matter how effective or ineffectual an artist's protest may be, the observer is made aware of the fact of the protest, and he is beneficially reminded that the difference between an artist's values and the values of the artist's surrounding money culture is a comment on the culture itself. There are differences between the bohemian revolt of the 1920's and the "beat" revolt of the 1950's and early 1960's, but the similarities in the two revolts may be more significant than the differences. There is something in the artist's revolt that may give the movement a more general significance, placing the artist rebel in the same camp with the civil rights worker, to use one instance, giving him a place in the specific movements that have the moral strength of a principle behind them. Kenneth Rexroth seeks to discover a common ground for all rebellions of this nature: "What matters is the immediate realization of humane content, here, there, everywhere, in every fact and relationship in society." Rexroth sees in the present rebellions (speaking specifically of the Berkeley Free Speech Movement and the civil rights movements) "personal moral action" and "spiritual revolution." The artist can certainly claim rights to a search for this "immediate realization of humane content."

The artist and the civil rights worker—these are contemporary examples of the two major categories of social rebels we can quickly recognize in American literature. In the one category there is the writer who looks toward Emerson and Thoreau as his ancestors, taking his direction from the transcendentalist's doctrine of the uniqueness of the individual and the priority of the individual's values over the demands and values of society. A straight line can be drawn from Emerson's study or Thoreau's Walden to the Big Two-Hearted River of Hemingway, to an artist's bohemian quarters in Greenwich Village or the Paris Left Bank, or to Kerouac's "Road." The comments from each of these settings may differ profoundly in moral tone, but the posture has remained the same, and it is the individual's moral or social vision which creates criteria and judgments. The judgments may often appear subjective and arbitrary—a reaction many have for the expressed hipster values, for instance—but these judgments nevertheless fulfill a valuable social purpose. The central message of Emersonian idealism in its individualistic claims provides a basis for explicit criticisms of the culture in which the individual lives, particularly when the culture, as in America, is dominated by a doctrine of materialism opposed to the transcendentalist's idealistic vision. The vision then creates a stance, a position taken in reference to the world in which it has grown. Kingsley Widmer in "The Diogenes Style" calls Thoreau a descendant of Diogenes. The Cynic, the Outsider, the Transcendentalist, the Beat—in these we have gestures of defiance to an Enemy who has always remained the same despite his many changes of shape in time.

The second category of social rebel is the activist, the John Brown who openly contests the unjust laws of a segment of American society or of a region, protesting in the name of an ideology or a humanitarian ideal or a social cause. Samuel Adams and Thomas Paine were among the most vocal before the American Revolution, and in this group can be listed the signers of the "Declaration of Independence." There was Bronson Alcott among the Transcendentalists and John Greenleaf Whittier among the Abolitionists. After the Civil War there were Henry George, Edward Bellamy, Hamlin Garland, the muckrakers of the early 1900's, the socialists and communists in the period from 1910 to the late 1930's, and in the period following World War II the members of the various civil rights movements.

The frontier of activity for the activist rebel naturally has changed with the times, but the favorite target for the most sustained and stubborn attacks has been the country's economic structure, capitalism as it has been interpreted and practiced in the United States. Since the days of James Fenimore Cooper there has been opposition to commercial attitudes and common ethical practices in business, but the tone of the opposition has changed as the influence of business became more pervasive and as the strength of corporate enterprises developed. Optimism about the possibilities of radical changes in the capitalistic structure, and the accompanying commercial morality, persisted until the end of the Depression period. This optimism is best illustrated in the "Perspectives" section by Bourne's radical who acts in the faith that his actions can meaningfully effect some transformation of the economic system. And certainly the socialist and communist writers, Joseph Freeman, for instance, who were most active in the 1920's and 1930's, were aggressive and affirmative in their demands for social reform or social readjustment. Since World War II, however, there have been fewer objections to the system itself that arise from serious hopes of change, for whatever reasons. Perhaps the socialist gains since the New Deal days have proved satisfactory to many of the former radicals, or critics hopefully see possibilities of reform in the normal process of government activity, or the "radicals" concede now that the system is here to stay. C. Wright Mills is sharply critical of the former liberals who hesitate to act today, those who have joined what he calls the "end-of-ideology" school. The new radical still has issues and causes as vital and urgent as those of the past, so Mills claims. But Mills is seeking, somewhat defensively, to arouse an intellectual who appears atrophied in his confusion about the forces he opposes. The Enemy now is something more abstract: it is now Bureaucracy, or Bigness. Perhaps a classic, as well as one of the first, illustrations of this reaction may be found in Herman Melville's "Bartleby the Scrivener." Modern examples in literature are common. John Andrews in John Dos Passos's *Three Soldiers* was destroyed under the wheels of army bureaucracy. Kenneth Rexroth in "The Students Take Over" speaks often of the "machine" of society. The individual rebellious response of today betrays a more romantic flavor, often directs itself to an otherworldly philosophy, and more often we hear the word "alienation" to explain the contemporary predicament. There are still frontiers to conquer, old moral positions to be broken, and new routes of human behavior to explore, but certainly the activist rebel is finding his scope of activity restricted by the external pressures of a world becoming ever more highly organized.

The two groups of social rebels mentioned above are not inseparable. Henry David Thoreau is a pivotal figure in the area where the idealist, the one who rejects society, meets the activist, the one who confronts society, and it is Thoreau's "Civil Disobedience" that joins members of both camps. Martin Luther King in the essay "Love, Law and Civil Disobedience" places himself and the civil rights movement, of which he was a leader, directly in the tradition of Thoreau by his avowed indebtedness to Mohandas K. Gandhi. The moral position of Thoreau in "Civil Disobedience" and "Life Without Principle" has furnished a platform for action which has effectively created a racial conscience, has changed people's minds and profoundly affected legal and legislative decisions. More recently has been heard the militant chant of "Black Power." Whether or not black power will prove more effective in the social and political arenas is a matter history will decide, but it is noteworthy that the philosophy of nonviolence in acts of civil disobedience is being re-examined closely to determine its ultimate strategic value.

In his words about the need to keep open the possibilities of change in government, Thomas Jefferson revealed his understanding of the radical nature of the American culture that readily accepted the new and the experimental. One part of the American tradition is thus dedicated to the process of change. Society in general, however, is intransigent by nature, seeking stability and permanence. In its past, therefore, these two antithetical positions, the desire for change and the struggle to remain stable, have built into the social structure the seeds of a dynamic process, always the *status quo* faced with someone opposing it, and opposing it in the name of the process itself. As Jefferson recognized, changes are imperative, "a little rebellion now and then is a good thing, & as necessary in the political world as storms in the physical." Society must be willing and able to adapt to new human conditions; consequently, there is always the need for freedom of expression, but, even more important, for conditions that will allow the possibilities of success for the person striving to make the change. A study of the social rebel in American literature is a study of this healthy process at work.

MICHAEL MILLGATE

American Novelists and
American Society

-1-

IN ENGLISH social novels, almost without exception, society is presented in terms of human relationships, not patterned by an abstract concept. In the nineteenth and twentieth centuries, at least, there have been few examples of the "moral fable" in English fiction, and English novelists, broadly speaking, have approached society in three principal ways. Some of them have undertaken a close and comprehensive examination of society, acting on the unspoken assumption that society is interesting for its own sake, as the way men live: Dickens and Thackeray do this in *Our Mutual Friend* and *Vanity Fair*; George Eliot declares it to be her aim in *Middlemarch*; and it provides the central concern of C. P. Snow's "Strangers and Brothers" sequence. Other English novelists have presented society mainly as a background or setting for the action of their novels. Often a careful and lengthy description of the social scene in the opening pages serves to establish it for the whole book; in subsequent chapters "society" is something that can be assumed, taken as read. George Eliot uses this method in *The Mill on the Floss* and *Felix Holt*, so does D. H. Lawrence in *The Rainbow*. Finally, there are those novelists whose sense of society and its sanctions is so integral a part of their whole conception that it is almost impossible in their work to separate out any presentation of society as such. In novels of this kind, notably those of Jane Austen and Ivy Compton-Burnett, we become aware of society, almost exclusively, through the interplay of characters.

From Michael Millgate, "American Novelists and American Society," *American Social Fiction: James to Cozzens* (New York: Barnes & Noble, Inc., 1964), pp. 195–205.

With good reason, then, Richard Chase spoke of "great practical sanity"[1] as a characteristic feature of the English novel. Not only [195/196] does England lack a significant novel called *The Englishman;*[2] it also lacks novels called *The Titan, The Octopus,* and *The Turmoil.* The titles of English social novels are likely to be more factual, less metaphorical and romantic; *Hard Times, North and South, The History of Mr. Polly, The Man of Property.* The gradualness of change in England, the relative permanence of the basic social structure, the background of a long and comparatively settled history, have all made it possible for the English novelist to take society more or less for granted: that is to say, he has been able to assume that he and his readers share a large area of common knowledge about the structure of society, the nature of social relationships, and so on. For the American novelist this has not been possible to anything like the same extent, and to this fact can be traced a great many of the differences between the English social novel and the American.

It is not difficult to see some of the reasons why American novelists have lacked assurance in their treatment of society: the instability of the society itself; the extreme self-consciousness of the whole American experience; the part played by the novel in developing America's awareness of herself as a nation. American writers have repeatedly been worried, confused, or angered—rarely amused—by the irreconcilability of American ideals and American experience, and one result of this sense of the gulf between the way things should be and the way things are, has been a readiness to regard the novel as a political instrument. English reform movements have tended to be dominated by intellectuals, whose preferred media have been the essay and, occasionally, the problem play. In seeking to achieve radical alterations in society, they have not directly sought mass support; in fact, much of their attention has been directed to the problem of restraining popular unrest and of guiding it into the most profitable channels. Most American reform movements, on the other hand, have been "grass-roots" uprisings led by demagogic personalities of sincere but simple pieties and [196/197] programmes: Mary Lease's "raise less corn and more hell"[3] is typical of the slogans which have gained circulation and allegiance. And just as the stories

---

[1] Chase, *The American Novel and Its Tradition*, p. 2.

[2] Constance Rourke observes of Henry James's *The American:* "Even the title was a fulfillment. Who ever heard of a significant English novel called *The Englishman* or of an excellent French novel called *Le Français?*" (*American Humor*, New York [n.d.] p. 194.)

[3] Quoted in Frank Thistlethwaite, *The Great Experiment*, Cambridge 1955, p. 262. Mary Lease was one of the leaders of the Populist movement.

of Horatio Alger were among the most influential propagators of the American "success" myth, so in their day the novels of Ignatius Donnelly, Edward Bellamy, William Dean Howells and many others were the often unsubtle but nonetheless powerful advocates of a wide variety of political doctrines and Utopian dreams. At the end of the nineteenth century, writers such as Gustavus Myers, Jacob Riis, and Lincoln Steffens showed that straight reporting might in certain circumstances be more effective than fiction, but Jack London and Upton Sinclair, more doctrinaire in their approach to social problems, continued to preach socialism through the medium of the novel—presumably because it was wider in its circulation, simpler in its appeal, and less hampered by the discipline of observable fact.

In addition to these narrowly political writers there have been the many novelists of social protest. Early in the century there were the "muckrakers," such as Winston Churchill, William Allen White, Robert Herrick, and Ernest Poole; later came Anderson, Dos Passos, Steinbeck, the "proletarians," and Norman Mailer. For all the differences between them, such novelists of social protest have at least one thing in common: they approach society not in a responsive or sensitive way but with their minds already made up; they come armed not only with their talents but with a theory. It is of the essence of the novelist's job that he should impose a pattern upon his material, but these novelists impose a pattern not of art but, in the broadest sense, of politics.

It is often a very simple pattern. In Churchill and Poole, in Howells, Anderson, and Dos Passos, more recently in such novels as Norman Mailer's *Barbary Shore* (1951) and David Karp's *All Honorable Men* (1956), we recognise again and again the clear outlines of pastoral, morality, parable, or polemic, for the American social novel has frequently taken the form of the "moral fable." As Arnold Kettle has pointed out, one great limitation of the moral fable is that "If you start with an abstract 'truth,' even a profound [197/198] one, it is difficult to avoid the temptation to mould life to your vision": for example, in *Candide*, "it is the vitality of Voltaire rather than of the world that comes across."[4] Of course, Voltaire frankly presents *Candide* as fantasy-parable, but many American novelists who are highly "realistic" in their treatment of surface detail found their themes, quite as plainly as Voltaire, upon some entirely abstract political or economic "idea."

[4] Arnold Kettle, *An Introduction to the English Novel*, London 1951, I. 18–19. Kettle (II. 172) mentions Graham Greene's *The Heart of the Matter* as a recent example of the moral fable; to this we might add William Golding's *The Lord of the Flies*.

These generalisations apply most obviously to such "angry" and directly "intentional" novels as Upton Sinclair's *The Jungle* and *The Metropolis,* Jack London's *The Iron Heel*—though that novel is set in the future—and John Steinbeck's *The Grapes of Wrath.* In these novels a steady accretion of shocking events, a rhetoric of action, often takes the place of thought or, except at a journalistic level, even of observation. The limitations of the moral fable are equally apparent, however, in such important novels as *U.S.A.* and *The Naked and the Dead.* Dos Passos and Mailer are not so much responding to the social fact as trying to fit the social fact to their particular social "idea." Dos Passos especially shows a marvellous knowledge of American life in breadth and in detail, but we have seen that his overall portrait of America suffers severely from political stylisation and that, as in *The Naked and the Dead,* the stylisation is actually underlined by the introduction of obtrusive structural devices.

Such novels are particularly obvious examples of an extreme self-consciousness about society which has led American writers, again and again, to undertake some sort of large cultural statement about American society as a whole. Indeed, American social novelists have commonly failed not because of their timidity in the face of society but because of their temerity. Refusing to work within the social area they know, they attempt to encompass American society as a whole. Their very titles—*An American Tragedy,* for example, and *U.S.A.*—testify both to the magnitude of their undertaking and to the underlying pre-occupation with cultural definition. We may now find at once comic and tragic the [198/199] spectacle of Thomas Wolfe facing up to continental America and, like a photographer at the Grand Canyon, being frustrated into fury at being unable to get it all in, but Wolfe is only an extreme example of a tendency to grandiosity that is both widespread and continuing.

– 2 –

Most American social novelists have lacked a sense of proportion in their treatment of society, and we may relate this to the extraordinary importance in the history of the American novel of "realism" and, in the non-philosophical, literary sense of the term, of "naturalism." In America the novelists' use of "realistic" techniques has often represented a self-conscious attitude towards society rather than a genuine understanding; their preoccupation with a realistic presentation of the social surface, in which everything tends to become of equal importance, may often disguise an essential ignorance of deeper social realities. Such is undoubtedly the case with many "muckraking" novels, with most of the "proletarian" novels of the nineteen-thirties, and with a large proportion of contemporary "tough" or *exposé* novels about such subjects as politics, business, the entertainment industries, and advertising.

The most persistent tendency in American realism is for the realist to become obsessed with his material. He not only fails to shape it, he allows the novel to be shaped by it: the material takes charge. This is what happens in Abraham Cahan's *The Rise of David Levinsky*, for example, and, again, in the work of Theodore Dreiser. We noticed earlier Dreiser's preference for basing his novels on an actual incident or case-history, because of the greater sense of reality this gave him. Dreiser's immersion in the social fact is perhaps his greatest source of strength, but his failure to organise his material is his greatest weakness. His passion for social documentation becomes an obsession which, in such novels as *The Financier*, *The Titan*, and *The "Genius,"* operates in complete disregard of literary form.

Lionel Trilling, himself the author of an impressive socioeconomic novel, *The Middle of the Journey* (1947), has spoken recently of the job the contemporary novel should do "of giving us reasonably accurate news of the world, of telling us the way [199/200] things are."[5] This is, perhaps, peculiarly the job of the contemporary American novelist, and in the same essay, a review of David Riesman's *Individualism Reconsidered*, Trilling seems to suggest that it is proving too much for him: "No American novel of recent years," says Trilling, "has been able to give me the sense of the actuality of our society that I get from Mr. Riesman's book."[6] Riesman, of course, is a sociologist, and his book is a collection of essays: he does not have to face the problems of artistic verisimilitude—specifically, the problems involved in the presentation of feasible human relationships—which make it difficult for any novelist with primarily sociological ambitions to produce anything of lasting interest. In the first place he cannot hope to compete with the sociologist proper: for example, *The Hucksters*, which enjoyed a certain vogue as an exposure of advertising, in fact reveals less than a single chapter of such a journalistic survey as Martin Mayer's *Madison Avenue, U.S.A.* More importantly, it can be argued that the delineation of society as such is a dubious undertaking for any artist. Again and again the material takes charge, as it does in Dreiser; or the political intention takes charge, as in so many of the novelists of social protest; or there is a tendency for the social material, the "information," to become separated out from the ostensible action of the novel, as happens in *The*

[5] Lionel Trilling, *A Gathering of Fugitives*, p. 92.
[6] *Ibid.*

Pit and in Tarkington's *The Magnificent Ambersons*.[7] So many institutional novels are weak because their authors, having first decided to write, say, an academic novel, have only then looked round for a suitable story and characters.

The proper function of social description in a novel must be to define and illuminate the human predicament. This is something which English novelists seem almost automatically to have accepted. Many American novelists have not accepted it, and they have often squandered their powers as a result. The examples of James Gould Cozzens and C. P. Snow are relevant here. Whatever reservations we may make about their work we do not doubt that they are [200/201] both engaged in a serious attempt to see society as it is and to understand the forces which condition and motivate men as social beings. However, Cozzens favours a technique of rich and detailed social notation while Snow keeps such notation to a minimum, and these differences in approach are highly suggestive of the problems which still face the American social novelist. Even today an English novelist, such as Snow, Angus Wilson, or Anthony Powell, seems to take his society more or less for granted. Some of the best among recent American novelists, notably Saul Bellow and William Styron, attempt to do this in some of their books, but for the most part the American novelist remains highly self-conscious about his relation to society and often makes an ambitious attempt to create and sustain the whole social area in which his characters move. Hence we find the profusion of technical detail in Cozzens's books, the minute documentation of O'Hara, the emphasis on information in the contemporary "institutional" novel, in the *exposé* novels of Budd Schulberg and others, and in the "recording" novels of Marquand and Brooks.

– 3 –

In the Preface we referred to Lionel Trilling's observations, from "Manners, Morals and the Novel," on the poverty of American social fiction. We might now suggest that the social novel may be more common in America, and commonly more distinguished, than Trilling allows, and that whatever the limitations of the American social novelists, they have been astonishingly successful in evoking, recreating, and investigating many different areas of American society. What American social novelists have failed to do—and this may be partly to blame for their being so consistently underestimated by American critics—is produce impressive examples of either of

[7] Booth Tarkington, *The Magnificent Ambersons*, Garden City, New York, 1918. Chapter 28, for example, is almost entirely given over to potted social history.

the two major traditional forms of the European social novel, the picaresque novel and the novel of manners.

America, as Cooper, Hawthorne, and James long ago complained, has never favoured the novelist of manners. Except here and there for brief periods—for example, in late nineteenth-century Boston and in parts of the South before the Civil War—American society has never stood still long enough for manners to become settled and readily identifiable. Scott Fitzgerald's extraordinary achievement was that he created a novel of manners out of the material offered by a society in a state of extreme flux. Even in such American novels of manners as do exist, there is an inversion of our normal expectations of the form. These expectations, of course, were created by familiarity with European examples, although it is interesting to notice that many recent novelists of manners in England—for instance, Kingsley Amis, John Wain, and Iris Murdoch—seem to have more in common with American novelists than with most of their English predecessors. In the traditional European novel of manners, supremely exemplified by Jane Austen, defaulters such as Frank Churchill are judged according to standards which are fundamentally social. In the American novel of manners, the values of society are almost invariably rejected and the defaulter becomes the hero. We are on Gatsby's side, on Lily Bart's side. We are even, with qualifications, on the side of George F. Babbitt and Silas Lapham. We sympathise with Marquand's George Apley and H. M. Pulham when they deviate from the standards of their society rather than when they adhere to them. In his essay "On Social Plays," Arthur Miller writes:

> The fact remains, however, that nowhere in the world where industrialized economy rules—where specialization in work, politics, and social life is the norm—nowhere has man discovered a means of connecting himself to society except in the form of a truce with it. The best we have been able to do is to speak of a "duty" to society, and this implies sacrifice or self-deprivation. To think of an individual fulfilling his subjective needs through social action, to think of him as living most completely when he lives most socially, to think of him as doing this, not as a social worker acting out of conscientious motives, but naturally, without guilt or sense of oddness—this is difficult for us to imagine, and when we can, we know at the same time that only a few, perhaps a blessed few, are so constructed as to manage it.[8]   [201/202]

Although Miller is speaking of all industrialised societies, not only of America, this sense of radical maladjustment to modern society [202/203] seems peculiarly strong in American writers. Almost all

[8] Arthur Miller, "On Social Plays," Introduction to *A View from the Bridge*, New York 1955, p. 6.

American novelists have presented the relationship between the individual and society as a struggle between irreconcilables, and it has often been noted[9] that American literature is rich in images of isolation and escape: its typical figures are Natty Bumppo alone on the prairie, Huck Finn lighting out for the territory, Babbitt wanting to escape back into a safe man-world, Holden Caulfield planning to act deaf-mute and live in a hut on the edge of the woods. There seems little doubt that this situation, in part, reflects the American writer's perennial sense of insecurity in a society to which he has himself been unable to adjust—a society, moreover, which has scarcely ever been able to offer him an audience which he could confidently identify and directly address. This sense of alienation, experienced by almost all the important nineteenth-century writers apart from Mark Twain, has in the twentieth century become virtually institutionalised under such heads as Progressivism, "The Lost Generation," the Communist Party, Southern Agrarianism, and "The Beat Generation." An attitude of "protest" has become almost *de rigueur* for the American writer.

We are not surprised, then, to find the novel of manners poorly represented and the sanctions of society rejected. What is surprising, and much harder to explain, is the absence of distinguished picaresque novels. Richard Chase's observation that "the American social scene has not been so interesting, various, and colorful as the European"[10] may be true of the vertical cross-section through society, which principally interests the novelist of manners, but it hardly applies to the horizontal sweep across the land as a whole, which might be expected to appeal to the picaresque novelist. Although Whitman was the first writer to point out the richness of these horizontal contrasts of American life, Mark Twain was the first novelist really to exploit them. *Huckleberry Finn* (1884), like other books by Twain, is essentially a picaresque novel, but this aspect of Twain's work seems not to have been influential. Thomas Wolfe, of course, wrote picaresque novels and Dos Passos, [203/204] though he has not one but several main characters, often achieves a picaresque effect through sheer variety of action and scene. Few other serious writers have written novels of this kind, but recently we have had Saul Bellow's *The Adventures of Augie March* (1953), Ralph Ellison's *Invisible Man* (1952) and Jack Kerouac's *On the Road* (1957), all of which though differing greatly in quality and in their approximation to the picaresque, at least share the appealing virtue of responding posi-

---

[9] See, for example, Henry Bamford Parkes, "Metamorphoses of Leatherstocking," in *Literature in America*, ed. Philip Rahv, New York 1957, pp. 431–45.

[10] Chase, *The American Novel and its Tradition*, p. 160.

tively and often vividly to the richness and variety of American life. This virtue also distinguishes such novels as Thornton Wilder's *Heaven's My Destination* (1934) and J. D. Salinger's *The Catcher in the Rye* (1951), which both contain elements, of the picaresque, and even Vladimir Nabokov's *Lolita* (1955), though Nabokov's intentions are largely satirical.

English picaresque novelists have often had to go abroad to find material for picaresque novels; American novelists have long had such material available within their own borders, but they have made little use of it until comparatively recent years. We might have expected that the very conditions which worked against the novel of manners in America—the shapelessness and instability of society, the stress on individualism—would have made the picaresque novel a popular form. This, however, is to look at the American novel with preconceptions formed by familiarity with the European novel, and it is essential that the American novel be discussed on its own terms. It is more valuable to see it, not in relations to the European novel and European society, but in relation to the peculiar characteristics of American society and, above all, to the position of the novelist within that society.

The comparatively few American writers who have seen man and society in proper proportion, and who have had the power to realise their vision in terms of the novel, seem to have chosen two principal methods of coping with the peculiar difficulties presented by the vastness, newness, shapelessness, and instability of American society and by their own inescapable self-consciousness about it. They have chosen, as in *The Great Gatsby, The Catcher in the Rye*, and *Appointment in Samarra*, a primarily poetic method, dependent upon imagery and allusion. Or they have chosen, like Fitzgerald in *The Last Tycoon*, O'Hara in his later novels, Sinclair Lewis and [204/ 205] Howells in their best work, Edith Wharton and Cozzens in almost all their books, a technique of social saturation, of working deeper and deeper into a single, carefully delineated social area. Dos Passos in *U.S.A.* might be said to have attempted a development of this second method by putting down a series of sample borings all over the surface of America.

Sociologists, historians,[11] and even literary critics such as Bernard DeVoto[12] have complained that "highbrow" American fiction gives an inaccurate image of American life as a whole. They may very

---

[11] See, for example, John Chamberlain, "The Businessman in Fiction," *Fortune*, Nov. 1948, 134–48; Robert A. Kevish, *Businessmen in Fiction*, Hanover, N.H., 1955; and especially Allan Nevins, "Should American History be Rewritten?" *Saturday Review of Literature*, XXXVII (6 Feb. 1954), 7–9 etc.

[12] Bernard DeVoto, *The Literary Fallacy*, Boston 1944.

well be right: the popular magazines always provide a more accurate indication of what the great mass of people are thinking and doing. In the last analysis, what we ask of the social novelist is not so much that he should reflect our view of society, but that he should make us see society his way. In admiring the novels of George Eliot, we need to remember that what seems to us the accuracy of her social observation is in some degree an indication of her greatness as a novelist, of her power to make us accept the image of society she presents. It matters little whether or not William Faulkner's novels give an "accurate" picture of the South; what matters supremely is that Faulkner presents his South, the world of Yoknapatawpha County, solidly and vividly, both as a setting and as a conditioning environment. Of the American novelists we have considered in detail, perhaps only two, Edith Wharton and Scott Fitzgerald, have unmistakably achieved this kind of power in the social novel, though others have approached it in their best work, and it is in their handling of the business theme that the distinction of Edith Wharton and Fitzgerald is most clearly seen. [205]

HENRY STEELE COMMAGER

The Literature of Revolt

AMERICAN SOCIETY of Veblen's generation may have been habituated to money standards, but it found few literary spokesmen to justify those standards or even to explain them. Who, in the half-century from Cleveland to Franklin Roosevelt, celebrated business enterprise or the acquisitive society—who aside from John Hay, Thomas Bailey Aldrich, Mary Halleck Foote, Booth Tarkington, and a miscellany of contributors to popular magazines whose efforts are now buried in oblivion? Almost all the major writers were critical of those standards, or contemptuous of them; they voted, as it were, for Bryan and the two Roosevelts and sometimes even for Eugene Debs and William Z. Foster rather than for McKinley, Taft, or Hoover. Those authors who repudiated the economic system outright were few; Mark Twain, Henry James, Willa Cather, Ellen Glasgow, and others accepted it tacitly, while such lesser writers as James Lane Allen, George W. Cable, and Sarah Orne Jewett took little thought of economic affairs. But the dominant trend in literature was critical: most authors portrayed an economic system disorderly and ruthless, wasteful and inhumane, unjust alike to workingmen, investors, and consumers, politically corrupt and morally corrupting.

This all but unanimous repudiation of the accepted economic order by its literary representatives is one of the curious phenomena of American culture. The tradition of protest and revolt had been dominant in American literature since Emerson and Thoreau, but the protestants had by no means monopolized the stage, and their protests had been, for the most part, political or social rather than economic. Never before in American literature and rarely in the literature of any country had the major writers been so sharply estranged from the society which nourished them and the economy [247/248] which sustained them as during the half-century between the *Rise of Silas Lapham* and *Grapes of Wrath*. The explanation is

Henry Steele Commager, "The Literature of Revolt," *The American Mind* (New Haven: Yale University Press, 1950), pp. 247–49, 260–62, 273–76.

elusive. It can scarcely be maintained that novelists from Howells to Steinbeck were unfamiliar with the scene they portrayed. Yet their findings did not correspond with those of more popular novelists and journalists, or, later, of Hollywood producers, radio script-writers, and advertisers—most of whom pictured a society that was prosperous, vigorous, harmonious, and contented. To suggest, however, that the novelists misrepresented their society presents difficulties equally perplexing; assuredly the society that cherished and rewarded them did not regard them as alien or false.

Whatever the explanation, the facts are incontrovertible. From the mid-eighties to the second World War the literary protest paralleled the political, and both were directed toward the economic malaise. The parallel was so close as to suggest subservience, yet we know that literature was not only an echo but often—as with *The Jungle*— a trumpet and an alarm. During the Populist era it was Howells and Garland, Norris and Frederic, who set the literary tone: those who were not championing the cause of the farmer were pleading the rights of labor or designing Utopias—some fifty of them altogether during these years—to show what felicity man might achieve if only economic competition were banished. In the early years of the new century, the novelists stood with T. R. at Armageddon and battled for the Lord: William Allen White was there, and Winston Churchill and Ernest Poole and David Graham Phillips and Brand Whitlock and, somewhat uneasily in such company, Upton Sinclair. They exposed the iniquities of business, romanticized labor, lamented the slums, and denounced corruption, and they were as sure as Roosevelt himself that the promise of American life would be fulfilled if virtuous men supplanted malefactors of great wealth. Volume for volume, they echoed the muckrakers, and if the whole of that body of evidence were to be lost, it could be reconstructed from the findings of the novelists. For Jane Addams' *New Conscience and an Ancient Evil*, substitute Phillips' *Susan Lenox*; for Lawson's *Frenzied Finance*, Norris' *The Pit*; for Phillips' *Treason of the Senate*, Robert Herrick's *Memoirs of an American Citizen*; for Russell's *Greatest Trust in the World*, Upton Sinclair's *The Jungle*; for Steffens' *The Shame of the Cities*, one of Winston Churchill's New Hampshire novels; for Judge Lindsey's *The Beast*, Brand Whitlock's *Turn of the Balance*; [248/249] for Ross's *Sin and Society*, Theodore Dreiser's *The Titan*. The list could be extended interminably. . . . [249/260]

In the mid-twenties a distinguished historian described American civilization as "almost wholly a businessman's civilization." Perhaps the generalization had been valid since Appomattox, but its validity was more readily conceded in a decade when the president an-

nounced that the business of America was business and when a political campaign could substitute the promise of two cars in every ga-
rage for the more modest full dinner-pail of an earlier generation.
The advertisers, the radio, the movies, popular journals and newspapers, even churchmen, hastened to welcome the "new era," and colleges and universities were zealous to confer their honorary degrees
upon corporation lawyers and stockbrokers. A chorus of praise for
what was now, in despite of Jefferson, called the American system
ascended to the skies. No major novelist joined in the chorus: the
novelists remained unreconciled and unregenerate.

Yet the direct assault of the Populist-Progressive era was abandoned. Muckraking had been played out, and there were no successors to *The Arena* or *McClure's* or *Hamptons*, or to Herrick and
Churchill and Phillips and Whitlock. It was partly that, as William
Allen White later recalled, "the whole liberal movement . . . which
had risen so proudly under Bryan and Roosevelt and La Follette,
was tired. The spirits of the liberals . . . were bewildered." It was
partly that the public, lulled into complacency by prosperity and
disillusioned by the abortive crusade to make the world safe for democracy, was no longer interested in exposures. It was chiefly that
the triumph of business was so spectacular and its battlements were
so formidable, that it seemed invulnerable to direct assault. Protest
persisted, but the attack, in so far as that term may be used, was
oblique and insidious. It took the form of satire and of repudiation,
and satire and repudiation are confessions of defeat. [260/261]

The confession is written large in the literature of the twenties.
For as the novelists contemplated the business civilization which
reached its apogee in that decade they were uncomfortable rather
than indignant, derisive rather than rebellious; their protest was personal and their estrangement private. They looked with disapproval,
even scorn, upon the contemporary scene, but they confessed no
sense of shock, only a desire to shock. And what was perhaps most
striking about the fiction which they wrote was not its overtones of
satire and its undertones of antipathy and repudiation, but that the
satire should be directed toward the middle classes rather than toward the rich, that the antipathy should be reserved for the social
rather than the economic manifestations of the new era, and that the
repudiation should be private rather than public. What these novelists lacked was what their predecessors so conspicuously had—sympathy, dignity, and purpose. They were not deeply moved by wrong
because they had so little pity for the victims of wrong. They were
not outraged by the violation of moral standards because they themselves were so unsure of their standards. They did not embark upon
crusades because they had no program, only an attitude. They did

not stand at Armageddon and battle for the Lord—how could they
when they did not believe in the Lord?—but fled to Greenwich Village or to the Left Bank and thumbed their noses at the middle
classes or at Puritanism or at the small town. Their greatest ambition was *épater la bourgeoisie,* their greatest triumph when the bourgeoisie acknowledged the shock.

Yet that triumph was brittle and evanescent. The economic hide
was too thick for the barbs of the satirists, and the ultimate evidence
of the futility of the attack was the enthusiasm with which it was
welcomed by its victims. How completely mere satire failed of its
purpose was made clear in the case of Sinclair Lewis, for when the
public swarmed to buy his novels, when Main Street became a national shrine and Babbitt a folk hero, when the Pulitzer Committee
found that *Arrowsmith* reflected the "wholesome atmosphere of
American life," the joke was surely on Lewis himself rather than on
Gopher Prairie or Zenith. Others who took refuge in satire or in malice suffered a comparable fate: the mordant Ring Lardner was regarded as a first-rate sports writer; the profoundly disillusioned
Fitzgerald was acclaimed the spokesman for gilded youth; James
Branch Cabell, whose repudiation of contemporary life was complete, achieved popularity [261/262] because Jurgen contained passages esoterically erotic; Mencken, whose hatred of democracy was
morbid, was embraced by all the young liberals; *The New Yorker*
was welcomed as merely a humorous magazine, the fortunate successor to *Life* and *Judge.*

Of all the novelists of the twenties, it was Sinclair Lewis who
gave the most elaborate report on his society and whose scenes and
characters came most nearly to symbolize its meaning to the future.
Main Street was published the year of Howells' death, and its author was, as much as any one could be, Howells' successor. Yet the
contrasts between Howells and Lewis are more striking than the
similarities. Both were observant and shrewd, both ranged widely
over the national scene though rarely outside the middle classes they
knew so well, both were realists and critics. Both were historians of
the commonplace, but where Howells had rejoiced in the commonplace, Lewis found it intolerable. Both were interested primarily in
character, but where Howells was concerned with its inner compulsions, Lewis was content with its outward manifestations. Both
looked with skepticism upon the conventions of their day, but where
Howells acquiesced in order to achieve intellectual freedom, Lewis
battered so frantically against convention that he had no energy left
to enjoy the freedom he won. Where Howells was urbane, Lewis
was raucous; where he was judicious, Lewis was dogmatic; where

he was affectionate—or at least compassionate—Lewis was scornful. Yet Howells' quarrel with his society was deeper than Lewis', his repudiation more fundamental. . . . [262/273]

Surveying the literature of the twenties, one of the most astute critics, Bernard De Voto, charged that the major novelists were victims of a literary fallacy—the fallacy that what they saw was the whole of America and that their report on it was faithful:

> The repudiation of American life by American literature during the 1920's signified that writers were isolated or insulated from the common culture. There is something intrinsically absurd in the image of a literary man informing a hundred and twenty million people that their ideals are base, their beliefs unworthy, their ideas vulgar, their institutions corrupt, and, in sum, their civilization too trivial to engage that literary man's respect. That absurdity is arrogant but also it is naive and most of all it is ignorant. For [273/274] the repudiation was the end-product of systems of thinking, and the systems arose in an ignorance that extended to practically everything but imaginative literature and critical comment on it. (*The Literary Fallacy*, p. 150)

Mr. De Voto, in short, was pained that the novelists did so badly by American civilization, that they emphasized its harrowing aspects and ignored its admirable. He wrote in 1944 when Americans, confronted with the greatest crisis of their history, had revealed qualities not wholly ignoble, and he asked how it happened that the walking shadows who strutted and fretted their hours through the pages of Lewis and Fitzgerald and Dos Passos were able to meet that crisis.

And it was, in fact, remarkable, a reflection on the accuracy of the literary interpretation. Yet Mr. De Voto's charge is a point of departure rather than a conclusion. No major critic denied that the novelists of the twenties and the thirties were alienated from their society: it is the theme of much of the writing of Edmund Wilson, of Lewis Mumford, of Maxwell Geismar and Alfred Kazin. What is important is to ask how this situation came about. How did it happen that novelists from Lewis to Steinbeck were uniformly critical of America's business civilization? How did it happen that, after Silas Lapham, almost the only respectable businessmen in American fiction are Booth Tarkington's Plutocrat—the dubious Earl Tinker—and Sinclair Lewis' equally dubious Sam Dodsworth? Mr. De Voto is inclined to blame the novelists, and his resentment against what appears to be calculated misrepresentation is not hard to understand. Yet it is difficult to believe that all the novelists were blind except those who wrote for the popular magazines, that two generations of writers could have been led astray. It is, after all, a serious reflection on the business civilization that it was unable to commend itself to artists who were, on the whole, men of good will.

The problem is even more intriguing when we compare American with English literature of the same period. British writers from Hardy to Forster were critical enough of the class-ridden society and the raddled economy which they portrayed, but except for a few of them, like D. H. Lawrence, they confessed no such alienation from their society as Americans revealed. There is poverty and meanness in De Morgan's Hackney and in Bennett's Five Towns as in Wells's middle-class London, and Galsworthy's patricians are scarcely more admirable than Mrs. Wharton's. Yet with what tenderness does De Morgan [274/275] re-create the world of Joseph Vance, with what romance does Bennett invest the life of Edwin Clayhanger, how irresistible Wells finds his Mr. Polly, with what dignity does Galsworthy surround the austere Soames Forsyte. These writers had come to terms with their society and their economy, and when they criticized, it was like a family quarrel. Just as American literature lacks the amiable satire of the small town that we find in an E. F. Benson or an E. H. Young, the humorous attitude toward class distinctions of a P. G. Wodehouse or a George Birmingham or a Humphrey Pakington, the affection for the metropolis that permeates everything that Bennett and Wells and Priestley and Swinnerton wrote, so it lacks the quality of taking the acquisitive economy for granted and dealing with it on its own terms that is implicit in the work of such varied writers as Galsworthy and Brett Young, Forster and Priestley, Swinnerton and Walpole.

Was American society, then, so much less admirable than the British in its economic manifestations? Was its cupidity more ostentatious, its irresponsibility more reckless, its cruelty more revolting? Was it afflicted with some singular depravity, ravished by some unique immorality? No one familiar with the economic history of the two countries would so argue. Indeed the most perspicacious British observers from Bryce to Brogan, agreed that the American economy offered fairer rewards to the average man than any other in the world, and immigration statistics suggested that this opinion was widespread.

What then is the explanation of the minority report which imaginative writers filed on the American economy? It explains nothing to say that they were out of touch with reality: they had taken out a patent on realism. Perhaps it was that American economy had developed so rapidly and so spasmodically that it left little room for the amenities and the artist was more sensitive than others to ugliness. Perhaps it was that the transformation of a rural to an urban economy had been too abrupt and the artist, whose roots in the past were intellectual as well as personal, had failed to make the readjustment. Perhaps it was that the novelists were, almost by nature, protestants: those who were content rarely bothered to write novels to advertise their felicity. Perhaps it was that the novelists, after all, were idealists, that they took seriously the promise of American life, expected to realize the American dream. They were not put off by the shibboleth of free entreprise, for they knew that the great tradition was the tradition of free men. "We must strike once more for freedom," wrote the [275/276] youthful Dos Passos, "for the sake of the dignity of man." And that was what concerned most of those who addressed themselves to social and economic issues—not, perhaps, Faulkner or Caldwell or Lardner but the major figures from Howells to Steinbeck—freedom and the dignity of man. Thomas Wolfe spoke for them all in almost the last thing that he wrote:

> I believe that we are lost here in America, but I believe we shall be found. . . . I think the true discovery of America is before us. I think the true fulfillment of our spirit, of our people, of our mighty and immortal land, is yet to come. I think the true discovery of our own democracy is still before us. And I think that all these things are certain as the morning, as inevitable as noon. I think I speak for most men living when I say that our America is Here, is Now, and beckons on before us, and that this glorious assurance is not only our living hope, but our dream to be accomplished. (*You Can't Go Home Again*) [276]

RANDOLPH S. BOURNE

For Radicals

THE GREAT social movement of yesterday and to-day and to-morrow has hit us of the younger generation hard. Many of us were early converted to a belief in the possibilities of a regenerated social order, and to a passionate desire to do something in aid of that regeneration. The appeal is not only to our sympathy for the weak and exploited, but also to our delight in a healthy, free, social life, to an artistic longing for a society where the treasures of civilization may be open to all, and to our desire for an environment where we ourselves will be able to exercise our capacities, and exert the untrammeled influences which we believe might be ours and our fellows'. All these good things the social movement seems to demand and seems to offer, and its appeal is irresistible. Before the age of machinery was developed, or before the structure of our social system and the relations between classes and individuals was revealed, the appeal might have been merely sentimental. But it is no longer so. The aims of [291/292] the social movement to-day seem to have all the tremendous power of a practicable ideal. To the satisfactions which its separate ideals give to all the finer instincts of men is added the overwhelming conviction that those satisfactions are most of them realizable here and now by concerted methods which are already partly in operation and partially successful. It is this union of the idealistic and the efficient that gives the movement its hold on the disinterested and serious youth of to-day.

With that conversion has necessarily come the transvaluation of many of our social values. No longer can we pay the conventional respect to success or join in the common opinions of men and causes. The mighty have been pulled down from their seats, and those of low degree exalted. We feel only contempt for college presidents, editors, and statesmen who stultify their talents and pervert

From Randolph S. Bourne, "For Radicals," in *Youth and Life* (Boston and New York: Houghton Mifflin Company, 1913), pp. 291–305.

their logical and historical knowledge in defending outworn political philosophies and economic codes. We can no longer wholly believe in the usefulness or significance of those teachers and writers
who show themselves serenely oblivious to the social problems. We
become keen analysts of the society around us; we put uncomfortable [292/293] questions to our sleek and successful elders. We criticize the activities in which they engage, the hitherto sacred professions and businesses, and learn to distinguish carefully between actually productive work for society, work which makes for the material and spiritual well-being of the people for whom it is done, and
parasitic or wasteful work, which simply extends the friction of
competition, or lives on the labor or profits of others. We distinguish, too, between the instruction and writing that consists in hand-
ing down unexamined and uncriticized moral and political ideas,
and ideas that let in the fresh air and sunlight to the thick prejudices of men. We come to test the papers we read, the teachers we
learn from, the professional men we come into contact with, by
these new standards. Various and surprising are the new interweav-
ings we discover, and the contrasts and ironies of the modern intellectual life. The childlike innocence in which so many seem still to
slumber is almost incredible to those whose vision is so clear. The
mechanical way in which educated men tend to absorb and repeat
whole systems of formulas is a constant surprise to those whose
ideas hum and clash and react against each other. But the minds of
so [293/294] many of these men of position seem to run in automatic
channels, such that, given one set of opinions, one could predict
with accuracy their whole philosophy of life. Our distrust of their
whole spiritual fabric thus becomes fundamental. We can no longer
take most of them seriously. It is true that they are doing the serious
work of the world, while we do nothing as yet except criticize, and
perhaps are doomed to fail altogether when we try. To be sure, it is
exactly their way of doing that serious work that we object to, but
still we are the dreamers, they the doers; we are the theorists, they
the practical achievers. Yet the precision of our view will not down;
we can see in their boasted activity little but a resolute sitting on
the lid, a sort of glorified routine of keeping the desk clear. And we
would rather remain dreamers, we feel, than do much of their work.
Other values we find are changed. We become hopelessly perverted
by democracy. We no longer make the careful distinctions between
the fit and the unfit, the successful and the unsuccessful, the effective and the ineffective, the presentable and the unpresentable. We
are more interested in the influences that have produced these seeming differences than in the fact of the [294/295] differences themselves. We classify people by new categories. We look for personal-

ity, for sincerity, for social sympathy, for democratic feeling, for social productiveness, and we interpret success in terms of these attainments.

The young radical, then, in such a situation and in possession of
these new social values, stands on the verge of his career in a mood
of great perplexity. Two questions he must answer,—"What is to be
done?" and "What must I do?" If he has had an education and is
given a real opportunity for the choice of a vocation, his position is
crucial. For his education, if it has been in one of the advanced universities, will have only tended to confirm his radicalism and render
more vivid the contrast between the new philosophy which is being
crystallized there out of modern science and philosophy and the
new interpretations of history and ethics, and the obscurantist attitude of so many of our intellectual guardians. The youth, ambitious
and aggressive, desires an effective and serviceable career, yet every
career open to him seems a compromise with the old order. If he has
come to see the law as an attempt to fit immutable principles of social action on a dynamic and evergrowing society; if he has come to
see the church [295/296] as an organization working along the lines
of greatest spiritual resistance, preaching a personal where the
world is crying for a social gospel; if he has come to see higher education as an esoteric institution of savants, only casually reaching
down to touch the mass of people with their knowledge and ideas; if
he has come to see business as a clever way of distributing unearned
wealth, and the levying of a refined tribute on the propertyless
workers; if he has come to see the press as devoted to bolstering up
all these institutions in their inefficiency and inertia;—if he has
caught this radical vision of the social institutions about him, he will
find it hard to fit neatly into any of them and let it set its brand
upon him. It would seem to be a treason not only to society but to
his own best self. He would seem to have become one of the vast
conspiracy to keep things as they are. He has spent his youth, perhaps, in studying things as they are in order to help in changing
them into things as they ought to be, but he is now confronted with
the question how the change can be accomplished, and how he can
help in that accomplishment.

The attempt to answer these questions seems at first to bring him
to a deadlock and to inhibit [296/297] all his powers. He desires self-
development and self-expression, and the only opportunities offered
him seem to be ways of life and training that will only mock the
best social ideals that he has. This is the dilemma of latter-day
youth, and it is a dilemma which is new and original to our own
age. Earnest men and women have always had before them the task
of adjusting themselves to this world, of "overcoming the world,"

but the proper method has always been found in withdrawing from it altogether, or in passing through it with as little spot and blemish as possible, not in plunging into its activity and attempting to subjugate it to one's ideals. Yet this is the task that the young radical sets for himself. Subjugation without compromise! But so many young men and women feel that this is impossible. Confident of their sincerity, yet distrustful of their strength, eager yet timorous, they stand on the brink, longing to serve, but not knowing how, and too likely, through their distrust and fears, to make a wreck of their whole lives. They feel somehow that they have no right to seek their own welfare or the training of their own talents until they have paid that service to society which they have learned is its due. [297/298]

It does not do to tell them that one of their best services will be that training. They demand some more direct way of influencing their fellows, some short road to radical activity. It would be good for them to know that they cannot hope to accomplish very much in radiating their ideals without the skill and personality which gives impetus to that radiation. Good-will alone has little efficacy. For centuries well-wishers of men have shown a touching faith in the power of pure ideals to propagate themselves. The tragic failures of the beginnings of the social movement itself were largely due to this belief. Great efforts ended only in sentimentality. But we have no intention now that the fund of intellectual and spiritual energy liberated by radical thought in the younger generation shall die away in such ineffective efforts. To radiate influence, one's light must shine before men, and it must glow, moreover, with a steady and resolute flame, or men will neither see nor believe the good works that are being done.

It would be an easy way out of the dilemma if we could all adopt the solution of Kropotkin, the Russian radical writer, and engage in radical journalism. This seems to be the most direct [298/299] means of bringing one's ideals to the people, to be a real fighting on the firing line. It is well to remember, however, that a weak propagandist is a hindrance rather than an assistance, and that the social movement needs the best of talent, and the skill. This is a challenge to genius, but it is also a reminder that those who fight in other ranks than the front may do as valiant and worthy service. One of the first lessons the young radical has to learn is that influence can be indirect as well as direct, and will be strongest when backed by the most glowing personality. So that self-cultivation becomes almost a duty, if one wants to be effective towards the great end. And not only personality by prestige; for the prestige of the person from whom ideals come is one of the strongest factors in driving home those ideas to the mind of the hearer and making them a motive force in his life. Vested interests do not hesitate to make use of the services of college presidents and other men of intellectual prestige to give their practices a philosophic support; neither should radicals disdain, as many seem to disdain, the use of prestige as a vantage-ground from which to hurl their dogmas. Even though Kropotkin himself deprecated his useless learning, his scientific [299/300] reputation has been a great factor in spreading his radical ideas.

It is the fashion among some radicals to despise the applause of the conventional, unthinking mass, and scorn any success which has that appreciation as an ingredient. But this is not the way to influence that same crass, unthinking mass or convert it to one's doctrines. It is to alienate at the beginning the heathen to whom the gospel is being brought. And even the radical has the right to be wise as a serpent and harmless as a dove. He must see merely that his distinctiveness is based on real merit and not, as many reputations are, on conformity to an established code. Scientific research, engineering, medicine, and any honest craft, are vocations where it is hard to win prestige without being socially productive; their only disadvantage lies in the fact that their activity does not give opportunity for the influence of the kind the radical wishes to exert. Art, literature, and teaching are perilous; the pressures to conform are deadly, but the triumphs of individuality splendid. For one's daily work lies there directly in the line of impressing other minds. The genius can almost swing the lash over men's spirits, and form their ideas for them; he combines [300/301] enormous prestige with enormous direct influence. Law, the ministry, and business seem to be peculiarly deadly; it is hard to see how eminence can be attained in those professions except at the cost of many of one's social ideals.

The radical can thus choose his career with full knowledge of the social possibilities. Where he is forced by economic necessity to engage in distasteful and unsocial work, he may still leave no doubt, in the small realm he does illuminate, as to his attitude and his purpose, his enthusiasm and his hope. For all his powers and talents can be found to contribute something; fusing together they form his personality and create his prestige, and it is these that give the real impetus and the vital impulse that drive one's beliefs and ideals into the hearts of other men. If he speaks, he will be listened to, for it is faith and not doubt that men strain their ears to hear. It is the believing word that they are eager to hear. Let the social faith be in a youth, and it will leak out in every activity of his life, it will permeate his words and color his deeds. The belief and the vision are the essentials; these given, there is little need for him to worry how he may count in society. He will count in spite of himself. He may never know [301/302] just how he is counting, he may never hear the reverberations of his own personality in others, but reverberate it will, and the timbre and resonance will be in proportion to the quality and power of that vision.

The first concrete duty of every youth to whom social idealism is more than a phrase is to see that he is giving back to society as much as or more than he receives, and, moreover, that he is a nourisher of the common life and not a drain upon its resources. This was Tolstoy's problem, and his solution to the question—"What is to be done?"—was—"Get off the other fellow's back!" His duty, he found, was to arrange his life so that the satisfaction of his needs did not involve the servitude or the servility of any of his fellow men; to do away with personal servants, and with the articles of useless luxury whose production meant the labor of thousands who might otherwise have been engaged in some productive and life-bringing work; to make his own living either directly from the soil, or by the coöperative exchange of services, in professional, intellectual, artistic, or handicraft labor. Splendidly sound as this solution is, both ethically and economically, the tragic fact remains that so inextricably are [302/303] we woven into the social web that we cannot live except in some degree at the expense of somebody else, and that somebody is too often a man, woman, or even little child who gives grudgingly, painfully, a stint of labor that we may enjoy. We do not see the labor and the pain, and with easy hearts and quiet consciences we enjoy what we can of the good things of life; or, if we see the truth, as Tolstoy saw it, we still fancy, like him, that we have it in our power to escape the curse by simple living and our own labor. But the very food we eat, the clothes we wear, the simplest necessities of life with which we provide ourselves, have their roots somewhere, somehow, in exploitation and injustice. It is a cardinal necessity of the social system under which we live that this should be so, where the bulk of the work of the world is done, not for human use and happiness, but primarily and directly for the profits of masters and owners. We are all tainted with the original sin; we cannot escape our guilt. And we can be saved out of it only by the skill and enthusiasm which we show in our efforts to change things. We cannot help the poisonous soil from which our sustenance springs, but we can be laboring mightily at agitating that soil, ploughing it, turning it, [303/304] and sweetening it, against the day when new seed will be planted and a fairer fruitage be produced.

The solution of these dilemmas of radical youth will, therefore, not come from a renunciation of the personality or a refusal to participate actively in life. Granted the indignation at our world as it is, and the vision of the world as it might and ought to be, both the heightening of all the powers of the personality and a firm grappling with some definite work-activity of life are necessary to make that indignation powerful and purging, and to transmute that vision into actual satisfaction for our own souls and those of our fellows. It is a fallacy of radical youth to demand all or nothing, and to view every partial activity as compromise. Either engage in something that will bring revolution and transformation all at one blow, or do nothing, it seems to say. But compromise is really only a desperate attempt to reconcile the irreconcilable. It is not compromise to study to understand the world in which one lives, to seek expression for one's inner life, to work to harmonize it and make it an integer, nor is it compromise to work in some small sphere for the harmonization of social life and the relations between men who work together, a harmonization that will bring [304/305] democracy into every sphere of life, industrial and social. . . . [305]

DANIEL AARON

Writers on the Left

THE FIRST MOVEMENT of literary insurgency in the twentieth century began between 1910 and 1912 and ended in 1919, one of the grimmest years in American history. Historians have called it the "joyous season," the "confident years," the "little renaissance." Such phrases suggest its gaiety and rebelliousness, if not its complexities and contradictions, but they perpetuate a misconception: that this interlude of creativeness had nothing or little to do with what preceded or followed it.

Actually, the young rebels who heaved and struggled and effervesced during the early years of Wilson's administration were at once the inheritors, practitioners, and enemies of a traditional culture and the forerunners of new fashions in thought and literature. To understand the "lost generation" of the twenties and the "depression generation" of the thirties, to measure the distance that the American intellectual traveled between 1912 and 1929, we must look hard at the still-inhibited but happy anarchists who flourished just before the outbreak of World War I and the Russian revolution.

Like the hopeful young contemporaries of Emerson, they made their appearance at a time of general economic and social stability when no war seemed imminent and the country was receptive to change. As in Emerson's day, too, the young rebels challenged the hostile guardians of traditional culture without differing from them [5/6] so widely as to make all communication impossible. The "League of Youth" appeared to be tough and irreverent; at bottom it was religious and idealistic. One suspects that even the most ardent pleasure-seekers among them did not advocate an irresponsible hedonism, but made the pursuit of pleasure an almost holy cause, another way of yielding to divine impulses. They also resembled their

From Daniel Aaron, *Writers on the Left: Episodes in American Literary Communism* (New York: Harcourt, Brace & World, 1961), pp. 5–10, 390–96. [Footnotes 14–21 have been renumbered for this volume.]

nineteenth-century transcendental counterparts in their extreme individualism—an individualism that in no way contradicted a vaguely socialist or utopian aspiration.

Floyd Dell, one of the principal spokesmen for the artist-rebels, acknowledged somewhat belatedly the kinship between his group and the Emersonians. Perhaps they were cranks, he wrote in 1921,

> but certainly not the cautious modern reformers. They were engaged in trying to see the world anew—to see in imagination, and with the help of reason, what it might become. Their views represented a fairly undifferentiated mass of anarchism, communism, feminism, and republicanism—but all of an extreme kind, and hence entitled to our respect.[1]

Another young rebel observed many years later that "fifty years after the first publication of *Leaves of Grass*, the words of Whitman—and of Emerson—were the neutral air we breathed, whether we had read them or not. . . . It is really hard to overestimate how much we depended upon transcendental optimism, how much we were under the spell, politically, of Lincoln, Thoreau, Emerson, Jefferson, Rousseau, and the German sentimental poets of a century earlier, and correspondingly in for disillusionment."[2] And Art Young, the genial cartoonist of *The Masses*, testified in his autobiography that he found "enough of revelation to satisfy me" in any page of Emerson. "This pioneer against Puritanism told us young men of forty years ago to 'stun and astonish the intruding rabble of men and books and institutions by a simpler declaration of the divine fact.' Emerson knew that everybody had something divine in him. But, alas, how many of us succumb to the 'intruding rabble' of books and men and institutions? Taken page by page, Emerson reads like serene lightning."[3]

Of all their literary forebears, Whitman alone spoke most directly to them, not only because of his idealism and his contagious democratic gospel, but "because," as Louis Untermeyer surmised in 1917, "of his words": [6/7]

> . . . it was this love and sublimation of the colloquial and racy that made him so great an artistic influence—an influence that was not only liberal but liberating. It was Whitman, more than any single element, unless one includes the indirect force of a wider social feeling, that broke the fetters of the poet and opened the doors of America to him.

[1] *The Liberator*, IV (March 1921), p. 8.
[2] Orrick Johns, *Time of Our Lives: The Story of My Father and Myself* (N.Y., 1937), pp. 128–29.
[3] Art Young, *On My Way* (N.Y., 1928), p. 178.

Ezra Pound agreed, and so did Max Eastman, who confessed that "we have drunk of the universe in Walt Whitman's poetry." James Oppenheim, editor of *The Seven Arts*, saw Whitman as an ally "of those of us who are in revolt against the New England tradition."[4] Van Wyck Brooks proclaimed him the first major American writer to challenge "the abnormal dignity of American letters" and the precipitator of the American character who blended action and theory, idealism and business. Although he regretted the older Whitman's fondness for pompous pronouncements, no better ancestor, he believed, could be found for the League of Youth than this pagan democrat-radical who possessed "rude feeling and a faculty of gathering humane experience," who "retrieved our civilization" and "released personality."[5]

Whitman's friend and secretary, Horace Traubel, was a familiar figure in the offices of *The Masses* and contributed to its successor, *The Liberator*, as late as 1922—a direct link with the Camden poet. Young radicals must have read with approval a remark of Whitman's that Traubel recorded for *The Seven Arts* in 1917:

> The trouble is that writers are too literary—too damned literary. There has grown up—Swinburne I think an apostle of it—the doctrine (you have heard of it? it is dinned everywhere), art for art's sake: think of it—art for art's sake. Let a man really accept that—let that really be his ruling—and he is lost. . . . Instead of regarding literature as only a weapon, an instrument, in the service of something larger than itself, it looks upon itself as an end—as a fact to be finally worshipped, adored. To me that's all a horrible blasphemy—a bad smelling apostasy.[6]

---

[4] The quotations from Untermeyer, Eastman, and Oppenheim are all taken from *The Young Idea* (N.Y., 1917), compiled and edited by Lloyd R. Morris, pp. 75, 17, 68.

[5] Van Wyck Brooks, *America's Coming of Age* (N.Y., 1915), p. 80. Socialists and Communists claimed Whitman without being precisely sure what he really though of capitalism and trade unions. It was enough that he believed in the future and "affirmed." Leslie Fiedler points out that one of Whitman's most characteristic masks was the revolutionist and that Whitman was among the first of the American writers to be translated by the Soviet Government. *Leaves of Grass One Hundred Years After*, ed. by Milton Hindus (Stanford, Calif., 1955). Coincidentally with the decline of the revolutionary spirit in the 1920's, Whitman's reputation sank. For Paul Elmer More, T. S. Eliot, Ezra Pound, Yvor Winters, and others, he was or became the poet of disorder. Revived as a socialist master in the thirties (see Newton Arvin's *Whitman*, N.Y., 1938), he tumbled again after 1946 and is once more being rehabilitated by the formalist critics.

[6] *The Seven Arts*, II (Sept. 1917), p. 633.

"Released personality," "expression of self," "emotion," "intuition," "liberation," "experiment," "freedom," "rebellion"—these phrases and words connote the prevailing spirit of the "new" magazines,[7/8] books, and plays as well as the manifestoes, art exhibitions, and political rallies between 1912 and 1917. The Young Intellectuals were not indiscriminately rebellious. Although the more extreme made disagreement with any vested opinion a point of honor, they did not reject completely the entire battery of cultural, political, and economic assumptions that had sustained an older America. But they irritably brushed aside the "frigidly academic," the sweetened, mollified, but still-restraining "Puritanism" of the genteel custodians of the old culture, who were frightened by the uncontrolled veerings and yawings of the new.

By Puritanism, they meant "repression," "bigotry," "prudishness," "Comstockery," attitudes which they attributed to a dry and arid New England, and they detected its confining influence in politics, economics, religion, education, and art. Mencken was only the most violent and articulate of a whole host of Puritan-baiters. In fact, the indiscriminate and uninformed attack by the rebels against Puritans and Puritan culture prompted a *New Republic* reviewer to observe in 1918: "the whole younger set, including Mr. Dreiser, never see the word 'puritan' without getting out their axes, refreshing their memories of Freud and Forel, remembering bitterly the small towns they were brought up in, thanking God they can find the way to Greenwich Village, even if they do not live there—and taking another whirl at the long-suffering men whose manners and customs, distorted and unillumined by that unearthly light in which they lived, have yet been the mold in which our country's laws, literature, education, religions, economics, morals, and points of view have become petrified."[7]

The Young Intellectuals felt no piety toward these formulators of the American mold and even less for the genteel men of letters, with their white, Protestant, Anglo-Saxon, "schoolmarm" culture, who applied their absolute moral values as rigorously to poetry as they did to politics. In contrast, the Young Intellectuals intended to be "freely experimental, skeptical of inherited values, ready to examine old dogmas, and to submit afresh its sanctions to the test of experience."[8]

[7] *The New Republic*, XVI (Aug. 17, 1918), pp. 84–86. The Puritan remained a symbol of reaction and oppression for the next thirty years, a target for the intellectual Bolsheviks and the foes of Stuart P. Sherman, Paul Elmer More, and other humanists.

[8] Quoted in H. M. Jones, *The Bright Medusa* (Urbana, Ill., 1952), p. 83.

This was the program of a generation trained in the pragmatism of William James, with its sympathetic receptivity to emotion and [8/9] innovation, and in the instrumentalism of John Dewey, which provided a basis for "social and intellectual reconstruction."[9] The Young Intellectual loved "change" for its own sake, because it dissolved rigidities, and agreed with the Dreiser of 1916 who wrote: "Not to cling too pathetically to a religion or a system of government, or a theory of morals or a method of living but to be ready to abandon at a moment's notice the apparent teachings of the ages, and to step out free and willing to accept new and radically different conditions is the ideal state of the human mind."[10]

After a diet of Ibsen, Nietzsche, Bergson, Wells, Shaw, Dostoevsky, and Freud, how could one accept bourgeois moralities uncritically? Intuition, as Bergson demonstrated, was a more reliable guide than the Puritan conscience, and the American undergraduates of 1913 no longer shilly-shallied, but spoke "with manly and womanly directness, even when the most delicate, or indelicate subjects are broached." Boldly they declared, "We will spare no man and no institution, we will revere nothing, but look the facts in the eye and speak out what we think." They took seriously the credo of Louis Dubedat in Shaw's *The Doctor's Dilemma:* "I believe in Michelangelo, Velasquez and Rembrandt, in the might of design, the mystery of color, the redemption of all things by beauty everlasting, and the message of Art that has made these hands blessed, amen."[11]

Young America had welcomed the "liberating gods" from abroad, and by 1918, thanks to enthusiastic popularizers like James Gibbons Huneker, had become familiar with such un-Anglo-Saxon names as Stirner, Schnitzler, Wedekind, Nexö, Sudermann, Hauptman, Maeterlinck, D'Annunzio, Strindberg, Gorky, Baudelaire, Huysman, Laforgue, writers never studied in American universities. Whether or not the Americans quite took in the violent import of their message was another matter. Van Wyck Brooks felt at the time that their ideas and subject matter were still too remote from the American experience to be properly savored, and that, transplanted, they had "at once the pleasing remoteness of literature and the stir of an only half-apprehended actuality." Huneker's indiscriminate enthusiasm for everything European was itself, Brooks thought, a product of Puritan repression, an outpouring of senses too long restrained. He in-

[9] H. F. May, *The End of American Innocence: The First Years of Our Own Time, 1912–1917* (N.Y., 1959), p. 303.

[10] "Change," *The Pagan,* I (Sept. 1916), pp. 27–28.

[11] The first quotation is from Norman Foerster, *The Dial,* LIV (Jan. 1, 1913), p. 4. The quotation from Shaw is in Johns, *op. cit.,* pp. 177–78.

carnated "the banked-up appetite of all America for the color [9/10] and flavor, the gaiety and romance, the sound and smell of continental Europe."[12]

It was, of course, Brooks himself who made the most celebrated attack against the sterile theorist and the vulgar Philistine. He blamed the failure of American culture on the absence of a "collective spiritual life" and on the materialistic social pressures that transformed talented artists into vulgarians or cranks. Because American writers had to serve "ulterior and impersonal ends," Brooks concluded, they fell into the abstract, the nonhuman, the impersonal, or they became social reformers, thus enabling themselves "to do so much good by writing badly that they often came to think of artistic truth itself as an enemy of progress."[13] Brooks's observation, as will be shown, applied even more aptly to the thirties, when "social consciousness" became for some revolutionary enthusiasts a legitimate reason to abnegate literary responsibilities, than it did to Wilsonian America. The contentions of Brooks were seconded and amplified by Waldo Frank, James Oppenheim, and others. In the 1920's, the charges against the inhospitable American milieu became even more common. [10/390]

The Communists longingly looked back to the thirties as the time when Left literature counted for something, when writers and artists willingly collaborated with the party and the working class. They predicted with more vehemence than conviction another proletarian renaissance after the conclusion of the war. Most of their former allies, however, had renounced the old dreams of revolution and by 1940 were already beginning to take stock of themselves and the revolutionary cause they had resolutely or tentatively supported. What happened to American intellectual life in the thirties, Granville Hicks wrote in 1943, "already seems mysterious, even to many who were party members."[14]

Between "Black Thursday," 1929, and the Russian-German pact almost ten years later, the mood of the literary Left had passed from angry elation to disillusionment. Writers who once had marched in May Day parades, picketed department stores, and bled inwardly (and sometimes outwardly) for Spain now wondered why they had given themselves so impetuously to an idea. How could they have been so certain of capitalism's doom? Why had they rapturously

---

[12] Brooks's first quotation is in *America's Coming of Age*, pp. 98–99, his second in *The Freeman*, II (Jan. 12, 1921), p. 431.

[13] Van Wyck Brooks, *Letters and Leadership* (N.Y., 1918), pp. 44–45.

[14] *The New Republic*, CVIII (May 10, 1943), p. 614.

identified themselves with the "toiling masses" and thrilled when [390/391] they met real "workers"? What had led them to expect a dazzling explosion of proletarian culture? Why had Russia become for so many of them the holy land?

Some of those who disparaged their recent enthusiasm or who publicly lamented their gullibility at being "taken in" by the Communists or led astray by ideological chimeras either forgot or chose to ignore the by no means reprehensible motives which first attracted most of them to the party. They did not come into the movement because they were broke or because publishing houses were failing. They became radicals because they thought the economic system had gone kaput, because they saw too many hungry and desperate people, and because men and ideas they detested seemed in the ascendant. Marxism offered a convincing explanation why these conditions obtained as well as a program for changing the world; the party satisfied their latent religiosity and made them feel useful.

The writer who joined the Communist Party, who believed in its doctrines, or who associated in some manner with Communist-controlled organizations was not necessarily simple-minded, easily beguiled, or unworldly. Not every radical writer was neurotic or hungering for a secular religion or on the make. Obviously, many of the intellectuals who went left did so out of some deep-seated personal need; happy, "adjusted" people usually don't join political parties whose acknowledged purpose is the destruction of the old social system and the formation of a new one. But not all literary Communists or fellow travelers were maladjusted by any means, nor did they regard the support of the Left as a violent or a desperate act.

To see the Communist movement "simply as the sum total of the pathologies of its members," or to call the intellectuals' "real revulsion from real lacks in our life a flight from reality," Leslie Fiedler has rightly observed, "is utterly misleading."[15]

The Depression *and* the Communist Party, it has been argued, gave focus to the unformulated radicalism of the 1930's and influenced, directly or indirectly, almost every American writer of any importance. And according to Lionel Trilling, the Left literary movement gave "a large and important part of the intellectual middle class . . . 'something to live for,' a point of view, an object for contempt, [391/392] a direction for anger, a code of excited humanitarianism" which could not be "wholly reprobated." Influence of this kind is hard to measure, but even if the literary impress of Commu-

[15] *Commentary*, XX (Sept. 1955), p. 285.

nism was not so extensive or so labyrinthine as some former Communists would have it, it was certainly considerable.[16]

The Communist Party cannot take sole credit for the W.P.A. writers' projects, although Communists undoubtedly had a great deal to do with the tone and content of some of the writing published under W.P.A. auspices.[17] If it was not alone responsible for the vigorous Left Wing theater which stirred New York audiences in the thirties, it is hard to imagine this theater apart from such names as Clifford Odets, Alfred Hayes, Albert Maltz, George Sklar, Irwin Shaw, Paul Peters, John Howard Lawson, Harold Clurman, Herbert Biberman, Michael Blankfort, Mark Blitzstein, Sidney Howard, and others, all friends or members of the party at one time or another. By no means all of the realistic novels published during the thirties were inspired by Communism, yet its doctrines contributed to the prevailing radical spirit which lifted many writers out of their small and mean preoccupations and lent some dignity to even the most amateurish of literary productions.

But if politics and social questions agitated the literary mind in a wholesome sense and "drew the literary imagination closer to social reality," they tended under party influence to become ends in themselves and to distract the younger writers in particular from equally important aesthetic considerations. What started out as a liberating doctrine developed into a constricting one as dream hardened into dogma and the new and idiosyncratic into ritual. Politics in itself, as Philip Rahv wrote in 1939, is neither good nor bad for the writer. "The real question is more specific: what is the artist actually doing in politics? What is he *doing with it* and what is it *doing to him?* How does his political faith affect him as a craftsman, what influence does it exercise on the moral qualities and on the sensibility of his work?"[18]

The strongest writers of the thirties used politics and were not used by it. The party could not have dictated to a Dos Passos, a Hemingway, a Lewis, a Dreiser, a Steinbeck, a Wolfe even if it had tried to do so. But the Left writer, in and out of the party, faced [392/393] something more insidious than party pressure: his own compulsion to subordinate the problems of his craft and deeply felt intellectual concerns to political policy. He willingly enrolled or inadvertently found himself in the corps of literary shock troops. He

[16] See Hicks, "The Fighting Decade," *The Saturday Review of Literature,* XXII (July 6, 1940), p. 17. Trilling's comments are in *Partisan Review,* VI (Fall 1939), p. 109.

[17] For a fictional account of Communists in the writers' projects, see Norman MacLeod's *You Get What You Ask For* (N.Y., 1939).

[18] Rahv, *Partisan Review,* VI (Summer 1939), pp. 7–8.

attended conventions and wrote resounding manifestoes and signed petitions and protests. He became a spokesman or a partisan in the literary wars, and he accommodated himself too easily to the Philistinism of the party.

The Communist writer under party discipline was expected to take on the literary assignments that would be most immediately beneficial to the revolutionary cause. The primary needs of the party were not poems or novels or critical essays; first and foremost, the party needed journalists for its press. And so, inadvertently, it became a devourer of talent (as militant parties or churches often become), transforming would-be poets and historians and novelists into producers of journalistic ephemera. Those who had acquired a stock of intellectual capital before enlisting as literary shock troops survived the ordeal better than did those who entered the movement without ever having undergone the apprenticeship of study and reflection, but even they did not escape unscathed. Party work, however inspiring it may have been in many respects, was hardly conducive to literary creation or careful scholarship. But because the party inspired selfless devotion and because the Communist vision made personal ambition seem mean and inconsequential, dedicated revolutionaries quite willingly sacrificed their artistic ambitions for the good of humanity. It is surely no accident that, with a few important exceptions, most of the enduring "proletarian" or radical literature was written by fellow travelers not involved in party journalism or by former party members, who, rid of their multitudinous duties, could at last give themselves to literature.

This is not to say that writers ought to have remained politically autonomous, although some of them might have done better work if they had. Nor was the sin of the Left writer, if you can call it such, to think politically. They impoverished themselves not because they were disgusted with capitalism or because they damned social iniquity, but because they were unable or forbidden to enter into the world of their adversaries and retain what F. Scott Fitzgerald called [393/394] the "double vision," the "ability to hold two opposed ideas in the mind, at the same time, and still retain the ability to function."

The literary "giants" glorified by the party after it decided officially to graft the twig of Marxian revolution on the Washington Elm and the Charter Oak—Whitman, Emerson, Thoreau, and Mark Twain, among others—retained this "double vision." Political and social issues touched them deeply, but they were seldom beguiled into making foolish public statements, and, what is more important, they did not stoop to attacking their fellow writers who disagreed with them.

One of the saddest aspects of the thirties was the willingness of so many writers not only to submit to the chastisements or admonishings of their political mentors but to assist them in whipping other writers. The writers who condoned Stalin's "liquidations" or who conducted their own trials and heresy hunts were shortly to be tried and symbolically murdered by American inquisitors.

That was the prediction of the friend and mentor of Jack Reed, the wise old Indian fighter, poet, lawyer, and satirist Colonel Charles Erskine Scott Wood, who rebuked by Earl Browder and the *Daily Worker* for allowing his name to appear on the Trotsky Defense Committee,[19] read them a lecture on the imprudence of American Communists brushing aside constitutional safeguards. "You may need them sometime," he warned them. Trotsky might be guilty, but as yet he had not been proved so; he had not yet received "his day in court."

> "*Shall be confronted with the witnesses against him.*" Is that plain? Can you really comprehend its meaning? It is not schoolboy oratory. It is not

---

[19] The original proposal to investigate the Soviet charges of Trotsky's alleged dealings with fascist terrorists came from the Socialist Party in August 1936. Three months later, a letter signed by Norman Thomas, Deven Allen, John Dewey, Horace Kallen, Freda Kirchwey, and Joseph Wood Krutch, the "Provisional American Committee for the Defense of Leon Trotsky," appealed to liberals to investigate these charges. *The New Masses* denounced the committee, as did *Soviet Russia Today,* a monthly published by the American Friends of the Soviet Union. In March 1937 the latter carried an open letter warning liberals not to permit themselves to be dupes of the Trotskyists or to lend support "to Fascist forces which are attacking democracy in Spain and throughout the world." One need not approve of "all the means" employed by the Soviet Government to improve the conditions of its people, the letter went on to say, but it should be allowed to protect itself from its internal and external foes. The party kept up its barrage against the committee, headed by John Dewey, which conducted an inquiry into Trotsky's case in Coyoacán, Mexico, where Trotsky was then residing. Corliss Lamont unpersuasively attempted to refute the findings of the Dewey commission, and other party spokesman sought to discredit the commission's report (*Not Guilty,* 1938) as well as the manifesto of the Committee for Cultural Freedom, which drew uncomfortable analogies between Soviet, German, Italian, and Japaness totalitarianism. See Peggy E. Gilder, "American Intellectuals and the Moscow Trials," honors thesis, Smith College, 1960. The anti-Trotsky argument is presented in *The New Masses,* XXI (Nov. 10, 1936), p. 20; *Soviet Russia Today,* VI (March 1937), p. 14, VI (Jan. 1938), p. 14; *The New Republic,* XCIII (Dec. 22, 1937), p. 181; *Daily Worker,* Aug. 14, 1939. Eugene Lyons describes the episode, replete with names of fellow-traveling and party letter signers in his *The Red Decade,* pp. 251–52. See also the New York *Times,* Dec. 14, 1937, p. 10, and *The Nation,* CXLVIII (May 27, 1939), p. 626.

only our own "Supreme Law." It is the crystallization of the thought of centuries, crystallized in revolutionary combat with tyrants and autocratic governments, and not to be lightly erased to suit the convenience of Moscow and the emotions of the young American acolytes. Please use your brains.

Wood could write these words in 1936 when he was still the warm supporter of Russia and what he called "the Russian idea of economic equality," but he did not regard "the Stalin government as *Russia*, nor as the sole repository of the Russian idea." That, he said, would "live long after Stalin and Trotsky are gone. I do not regard the [394/395] Russian government as infallible and not to be questioned. . . ." He would have approved the remark Proudhon made to Marx in 1846: "Because we stand in the van of a new movement, let us not act like apostles of a new religion, even if it be a religion of logic, a religion of reason."[20]

The party of Marx disregarded this suggestion as completely as the master himself, and although the overwhelming majority of its priesthood and laity did not commit acts of treason in the McCarthy sense of the word, they did in Julien Benda's sense: that is to say, they "divinized politics," organized "political hatreds," put party ahead of art, and yielded themselves to historical tendency.[21]

During and after the war years, the thirties came to be looked upon by many men and women who had lived through them as a time of "smelly orthodoxies" when the intellectuals took refuge in closed systems of belief. The "irresponsible" twenties looked much better after ten years of intense social consciousness, and, as Granville Hicks predicted, the abandoned ivory towers began to be reclaimed. With the cold war and the crusade of Senator McCarthy, the books and issues of the thirties were considered dangerous as well as dated. The official exhumations of the Red Decade and the memoirs of former Communists (some of them as doctrinaire in their anti-Communism as they had been when they ferreted out class enemies for the party)bathed the decade in a lurid light.

In their excavations of the radical past, the historians have dug up little but fragments and ruins. Yet surely a movement which involved so many intelligent and generous men and women cannot be

---

[20] The quotations from Wood are taken from a typescript copy of an unpublished letter to the *Daily Worker* in reply to an attack against him in the Dec. 17, 1936 issue of that paper. I am indebted to Mr. Herbert Solow for showing me this letter. The quotation from Proudhon is from Martin Buber, *Paths to Utopia* (London, 1949), pp. 11–12.

[21] Julien Benda, *The Betrayal of the Intellectuals* (Boston, paperback edition, 1955), pp. 86, 21.

barren of significance. Communism, it has been said, contributed nothing of permanent value to American literature; but even if the poems, plays, novels, criticism, and reportage composed under party sponsorship or written by writers whose social sympathies had been quickened by party agitation were worthless (which is simply not true), no writer who lived through the revolutionary interlude either as advocate or critic remained unaffected. If his agonizing over the working class, his debates over the nature of art and politics, his temptations, his doubts, despairs, ecstasies, meant little to Browder or Foster (one influential trade-union leader was worth more to [395/396] them than five dozen writers), they were of immense importance to the writer himself. The strong impact of Communism's program upon even those writers who opposed it must be reckoned with. So must the vitalizing influence of the Left Wing intellectuals who stirred up controversies, discovered new novelists and playwrights, opened up hitherto neglected areas of American life, and broke down the barriers that had isolated many writers from the great issues of their times.

We who precariously survive in the sixties can regret their inadequacies and failures, their romanticism, their capacity for self-deception, their shrillness, their self-righteousness. It is less easy to scorn their efforts, however blundering and ineffective, to change the world. [396]

JOSEPH FREEMAN

The Tradition of American
Revolutionary Literature

THE BOURGEOIS revolution at the end of the eighteenth century transformed the life of the Western world under the abstract slogan of
liberty, equality, fraternity. These social goods became the monop-
oly of the bourgeoisie along with the factories, the machines, the
banks, and the state. Literature reflected this profound change in society. The Christian myth was replaced by the myth of sacred ego as
the central theme of nineteenth-century bourgeois literature. We
now know what the sacred ego really was. The freedom of the individual—from the Declaration of the Rights of Man and the Declaration of Independence down to recent plaints that Europe has really
been a success and the promise of American life still a promise—has
meant in reality the freedom of the propertied classes to exploit
those who have nothing to sell but their labor. This freedom for the
privileged has been achieved through the enslavement of the millions. In ignoring those millions, in confining itself to the upper and
middle-class individual, bourgeois literature has been a class literature.

At first it was frankly that. The class concept of literature ante-
dates the organized movement of the proletariat. The ideologues of
the bourgeois revolution demanded a new art and did not hesitate to
name it by its right name. Diderot and Lessing called frankly for the
bourgeois drama. Madame de Staël defended bourgeois against feudal literature, urged a complete break with the ideas of the old
order, and called for a literature animated by specifically bourgeois
values. Prosper de Barante argued that there was a necessary connection between literature and society, and concluded that society

Joseph Freeman, "The Tradition of American Revolutionary Literature," in
American Writers' Congress, ed. Henry Hart (New York: International Publishers, 1935), pp. 52–58.

43

conditions literature. We know to what an extent American literature of the nineteenth century voiced the national-democratic aspirations of the then progressive bourgeoisie of our own country.

This has been called the great tradition. But there are really two
great traditions in the modern literature of the West. Disappointment in the results of the French Revolution ushered in the romantic [52/53] movement of the last century. From the cult of the ego the
romantics developed the myth of the primacy of art which led, until
very recently, to the Ivory Tower. When art failed to satisfy the un-
bounded longings of the poet, overstimulated by the sublime
phrases which concealed the bourgeois pursuit of profit, the poet fell
back for solace into the arms of the church. But by this time, the
church and the bourgeoisie, foes for centuries, had struck up an alliance against the proletariat, which took over rational materialistic
thought where the bourgeoisie had left it. With a background of
classical German philosophy, English political economy, French socialism and revolutionary doctrine, Marx and Engels developed dialectic materialism, the ideology of the working class, which became
the revolutionary class of modern society. The new doctrine revealed more clearly than anything before it not merely the *social*
but the *class* basis of ideas. The thinkers of the proletariat were able
to perceive this profound truth because the proletariat is the first social class in history which fights for the abolition not only of class
privileges, but of social classes altogether.

For the past century we have had a conscious, organized, pur-
poseful struggle between the bourgeoisie and the proletariat. This
has meant two conflicting traditions in economic life, in philosophy,
in literature, in art—bourgeois and proletarian. In the 'forties the
great German poet Ferdinand Freiligrath spoke of himself as a *poet
of the revolution and the proletariat.* Subsequently Communist critics like Franz Mehring analyzed literary classics from the proletarian viewpoint. In Russia a great school of critics developed—including men like Pisarev, Byelinsky and Tchernishevsky—who were not
only able æstheticians, but leaders of thought, teachers of the people,
revolutionaries who linked poetry with politics. From Marx and Engels to our own day, the organized movement of the working class
has been vitally interested in art and literature, past and present; it
has always been interested also in developing that art and literature
which reflects the struggles and aspirations of the proletariat. Wherever the Socialist movement developed, there grew up around it
groups of Socialist writers and artists. Where the class struggle was
latent, the Socialist movement was weak; where the movement was
weak, the art it inspired was weak. Where the class struggle was

sharp, the movement was strong; where the movement was strong, the art it inspired was rich and vital.

America has been no exception to this general law of development. For example: in 1901, when the American Socialist movement [53/54] began to grow, a group of New York Socialists founded *The Comrade*, whose contributors included Edward Carpenter, Walter Crane, Richard Le Gallienne, Maxim Gorky, Jack London, Upton Sinclair, Edwin Markham, and Ryan Walker. This publication—precursor of *The Masses*—announced that its aim was to give its readers *"such literary and artistic productions as reflect the soundness of the socialist philosophy. . . . To mirror socialist thought as it finds expression in art and literature . . . and to develop the æsthetic impulse in the Socialist movement."*

You will be convinced that this was no "Stalinist" plot to put American artists in uniform, when I remind you that this was in 1901 —and that the editors of the magazine included John Spargo and Algernon Lee—at that time more or less Marxians.

The magazine, which ran for four years, employed the phrase *proletarian poet* to describe working-class writers of verse. No one considered the phrase odd. It was a logical corollary to the working-class outlook on life, the obvious poetic by-product of proletarian politics. For all its utopian, sentimental fantasies, brought into the Socialist movement of that period by middle-class intellectuals who were still bound to the class of their origin, *The Comrade* represented a literary movement in America out of which grew Upton Sinclair and Jack London. It brought more or less socialist standards to literary criticism. In its pages Edwin Markham predicted "a great revival of literature" in America and throughout the world, which, he said, would grow out of the movement to emancipate labor.

In America, as in Europe, every decade saw intellectuals join the Socialist movement only to drop out later; yet each decade brought new contingents from the educated classes. Each contingent of writers started afresh. No continuity was maintained in Socialist literary circles. *The Masses* group started directly from the Socialist movement, yet, at the same time, burdened with the middle-class notions which had their roots in the romantic tradition. As persons, the writers and artists of the magazine were Socialists or syndicalists or anarchists. The publication as such was a private venture, unaffiliated with any party, formally owing allegiance to no cause. As individual writers and artists, the *Masses* group championed two causes: socialism and a free art. Sometimes these two ideas were fused; at other times they clashed. When Floyd Dell in 1913 urged Dreiser to write the American novel of rebellion, he was employing the socialist standards of *The Comrade;* when he wondered at the [54/55] *Masses* trial in 1918 what he was doing in court when he should be at home writing fiction, he was reverting to the romantic tradition of the free, unfettered artist above the battle. At odds with bourgeois America, the *Masses-Liberator* writers fought now as journalistic allies of the proletariat, now through the *tour-de-force* of creative art, which ranged, in letters, from the most saccharine sonnets to stirring revolutionary poetry. The best writing of this period was done by men actively engaged in Socialist or I.W.W. organizations—men like Joe Hill, Ralph Chaplin, Arturo Giovanitti, Jack London, the early Upton Sinclair, and John Reed.

The October Revolution in Russia was a turning-point for the proletariat the world over, consequently for its literature. By 1919 Floyd Dell was talking of the proletarian novel in America, and applauding Soviet plans for the development of what was then called "proletarian socialist art." What appealed to our American critic was not only the successful attempt to make literature old and new available to the millions, but the equally important attempt to stir the worker himself to create art. Dell at that time grasped the active element in proletarian art. The new stories, he said, should, above all, teach the worker courage and confidence in his destiny, teach him with their satire to scorn the ideals of capitalist society, deepen his sense of community with his fellow-workers in their world-wide struggle for freedom, and make him face the future with a clear and unshakable resolution, an indomitable will to victory and freedom. Later he urged that the literature of America was above everything else at literature of protest and rebellion. It is only a question of time, he said, which shall rule the world—which will be required by force of circumstances to suppress its enemies by force—the capitalist class or the working class; and for a brief period he demanded that writers take sides in this conflict not only as men but as writers.

For Floyd Dell proletarian literature was one kind of literature; for Michael Gold it was the only kind of literature worth creating. In an essay published in 1921 he called definitely for a proletarian art. The old ideals must die, he said. But let us not fear. Let us fling all we are into the cauldron of the Revolution; for out of our death shall arise new glories. His faith in proletarian culture came from his faith in the proletarian revolution. He was the American exponent of that literary tradition which the organized working class had initiated in every country—and which had already given our own country Hill, Chaplin, London, Sinclair, Giovanitti, Dell [55/56] and Reed. But Gold was more alert about the issues and problems involved: he was molded by the World War and the Bolshevik Revolution.

Everywhere the best writers felt the impact of these two events.

The old order was visibly changing and a number of intellectuals in various countries wanted to orient themselves in the chaos. In 1919 Romain Rolland organized a group of writers around a "declaration of intellectual independence," signed, among others, by Jane Addams, Benedetto Croce, Stefan Zweig, Henri Barbusse, Bertrand Russell and Israel Zangwill. Thought was to be emancipated from serving the selfish interests of state, nation or class. The *Masses-Liberator* group refused to join because the document was not an open declaration for the proletariat. As was to be expected, Rolland's international of thought collapsed. The left intellectuals learned their lesson. In 1919 Barbusse organized *Clarté* under Communist influence. The new group was outspoken in its support of the revolutionary working class. Its first pamphlet was an appeal to the proletariat of all countries to affiliate with the Third International; it called for a radical destruction of the capitalist system. At the same time it founded a publishing house and a magazine which printed revolutionary fiction, poetry, criticism and journalism. *The Liberator* was invited to join *Clarté* as its American branch. Max Eastman, then editor, declined. He argued that the Communist Party must be the *only* revolutionary organization guiding the revolutionary artist. Subsequently he changed his mind a little about this. But those of us who entered the revolutionary movement in the twenties came into a literary heritage based on these ideas:

1. Every social class has its own ideology and its own literature. The proletariat has its own ideology and its own literature.

2. The revolutionary writer not only creates novels, plays and poems which voice the aspirations and struggles of the workers, but himself participates actively in those struggles—directly—in the organizations of the workers.

3. Capitalism retards the development of culture to-day. The proletariat is heir to the best of the old culture, and the initiator of the new. For the purpose of combating capitalism and aiding the proletariat, for the purpose of developing the new culture, intellectuals organize their own organizations.

4. It is not necessary for a writer to subscribe completely to the political program of the proletarian party in order to aid the workers; it is unnecessary for him to abandon poetry for organizational [56/57] activity. If he is against capitalism and for the proletariat on fundamental questions, he can participate in a literary organization like *Clarté* and function in his own specific craft as an ally of the workers.

These ideas were prevalent in left-wing literary circles in this country in the early twenties. During the boom period, many intellectuals who had allied themselves with the workers under the impact of the War and the October Revolution, were absorbed into the then prosperous middle classes. A small group of left-wing writers, influenced by the Communist movement as their predecessors had been influenced by the socialist and syndicalist movements, agitated for a revolutionary art and literature in America. Conditions imposed upon them a task which was primarily propagandistic, educational, organizational. They wrote, lectured and organized with a view to circulating basic Marxian ideas in literature. They founded *The New Masses*, the Theater Union, the *New Theater, Partisan Review*, the John Reed Clubs, the Film and Foto League; they taught literature in the Workers School and wrote about it in *The Daily Worker*, partly to acquaint the workers with contemporary literature, partly to acquaint writers with the viewpoint of the workers and its significance for culture in general and literature in particular. They developed young poets, critics, journalists and novelists who subsequently did creative work of distinction. They published and encouraged revolutionary writers not only in New York, but also in the Middle West, the Coast, the South, among them talented Negro writers like Langston Hughes and Eugene Gordon. In doing so, they were not—as their enemies said—importing a Russian idea imposed upon them by the Kremlin. They were developing in their own country an international idea as old as the proletarian party—an idea that had its own specific American traditions.

They worked for a decade close to the labor movement, to its mass organizations, to the Communist Party—but they were more or less isolated, for various historical reasons, from the majority of American writers. The economic crisis, the spread of fascism, the menace of a new war—the agony and travail of capitalist culture in decay—the barbarization of culture in the capitalist countries—and the colossal triumph of the Soviet workers not only in industry and agriculture—but in science, art, literature, and the cinema opened the eyes of the best of America's writers to the meaning of the class struggle. In the choice which we must all make in this epoch they have [57/58] chosen to side with the working class. Actually, there is no choice. In its final stages of decomposition, capitalism means the doom of everything fine in human thought. The working class alone, in emancipating itself, can emancipate the whole of mankind, and with it release undreamed-of forces for the conquest of knowledge, the creation of art.

You who represent all that is most promising in American literature have taken over the heritage of progressive and revolutionary thought. You have enriched it with your craftsmanship as it has enriched you with its insight. For the first time in the history of our country, the literary allies of the proletariat may be counted not by the dozen but by the hundreds. Moreover, you are the American contingent of that army of writers all over the world which is militantly fighting for the preservation of culture through the triumph of the working class. In that class lies our strength. A brief, inadequate note on the past has no value except as it teaches us something about the present. We ought to know that we have a revolutionary literary heritage behind us in order that we may transcend it. We also ought to know that we are at our best as writers when we are an integral part of the working-class movement, when our writing emerges out of active identification with it. I have mentioned the names of some who, physically alive, have been dead as creative writers since they broke with the proletariat. Consider what a poet like Arturo Giovanitti, silent to-day, could write about the October Revolution when he was an active proletarian fighter in 1920—

Victory, lightning-faced, flame-winged has come,
Just on the day it was told us by your prophets and seers,
The harbingers of your great day, the builders of your highway,
The blazers of your world-trails.

Your teachers enlighten the people without any rest or stint,
And they give them one good rifle with every good book they print;
And the workers now own everything, even their right to be born;
And the peasants have taken in the full flax and the wheat and the corn;
And in Moscow it is high noon, and in Europe it is the morn
And the Soviets are everywhere. [58]

C. WRIGHT MILLS

On the New Left

IT IS NO exaggeration to say that since the end of World War II, smug conservatives, tired liberals and disillusioned radicals in Britain and the United States have carried on a weary discourse in which issues are blurred and potential debate muted; the sickness of complacency has prevailed, the bi-partisan banality flourished. There is no need to explain again why all this has come about among "people in general" in the NATO countries;* but it may be worthwhile to examine one style of cultural work that is in effect an intellectual celebration of apathy.

Many intellectual fashions, of course, do just that; they stand in the way of a release of the imagination—about the cold war, the Soviet bloc, the politics of peace, about any new beginnings at home and abroad. But the fashion I have in mind is the weariness of many NATO intellectuals with what they call "ideology," and their proclamation of "the end of ideology." So far as I know, this fashion began in the mid-fifties, mainly in intellectual circles more or less associated with the Congress for Cultural Freedom and the magazine *Encounter*. Reports on the Milan Conference of 1955 heralded it; since then, many cultural gossips have taken it up as a posture and an unexamined slogan. Does it amount to anything? [63/64]

$-$ I $-$

Its common denominator is not liberalism as a political philosophy, but the liberal rhetoric, become formal and sophisticated and used as an uncriticized weapon with which to attack Marxism. In the approved style, various elements of this rhetoric appear simply

C. Wright Mills, "On the New Left," *Studies on the Left*, II, No. 1 (1961), 63–72. [This essay originally appeared, in a slightly different version, as "Letter to the New Left" in the British *New Left Review*, No. 5 (September–October 1960), pp. 18–23.]

* See, for example, E. P. Thompson, ed., *Out of Apathy* (London: Stevens and Son, 1960).

as snobbish assumptions. Its sophistication is one of tone rather than of ideas: in it, the *New Yorker* style of reportage has become politically triumphant. The disclosure of fact—set forth in a bright-faced or in a dead-pan manner—is the rule. The facts are duly weighed, carefully balanced, always hedged. Their power to outrage, their power truly to enlighten in a political way, their power to aid decision, even their power to clarify some situation—all that is blunted or destroyed.

So reasoning collapses into reasonableness. By the more naive and snobbish celebrants of complacency, arguments and facts of a displeasing kind are simply ignored; by the more knowing, they are duly recognized, but they are neither connected with one another nor related to any general view. Acknowledged in a scattered way, they are never put together: to do so is to risk being called, curiously enough, "one-sided."

This refusal to relate isolated facts and fragmentary comment to the changing institutions of society makes it impossible to understand the structural realities which these facts might reveal or the longer-run trends of which they might be tokens. In brief, fact and idea are isolated, so the real questions are not even raised, analysis of the meanings of facts not even begun.

Practitioners of the no-more-ideology school do, of course, smuggle in general ideas under the guise of reportage, by intellectual gossip, and by their selection of the notions they handle. Ultimately, the-end-of-ideology is based upon a disillusionment with any real commitment to socialism in any recognizable form. *That* is the only "ideology" that has really ended for these writers. But with its ending, *all* ideology, they think, has ended. *That* ideology they talk about; their own ideological assumptions, they do not. Yet these assumptions, which they snobbishly take for granted, provide the terms of their rejection of "all ideology;" and upon these assumptions they themselves stand.

Underneath this style of observation and comment there is the assumption that in the West there are no more real issues or even problems of great seriousness. The mixed economy plus the welfare state plus prosperity—that is the formula. U. S. capitalism will continue to be workable; the welfare state will continue along the road to ever greater justice. In the meantime, things everywhere are very complex; let us not be careless; there are great risks.

This posture—one of the "false consciousness" if there ever was one —stands in the way, I think, of considering with any chances of success what may be happening in the world.

First and above all, this posture rests upon a simple provincialism. If the phrase "the end of ideology" has any meaning at all, it pertains to self-selected circles of intellectuals in the richer countries. It is in fact merely their own self-image. The total population of these countries is a fraction [64/65] of mankind; the period during which such a posture has been assumed is very short indeed. To speak in such terms of much of Latin-America, Africa, Asia, the Soviet bloc is merely ludicrous. Anyone who stands in front of audiences—intellectual or mass—in any of these places and talks in such terms will merely be shrugged off (if the audience is polite) or laughed at out loud (if the audience is more candid and knowledgeable). The end-of-ideology is a slogan of complacency, circulating among the prematurely middle-aged, centered in the present, and in the rich Western societies. In the final analysis, it also rests upon a disbelief in the shaping by men of their own futures—as history and as biography. It is a consensus of a few provincials about their own immediate and provincial position.

Second, the end-of-ideology is of course itself an ideology—a fragmentary one, to be sure, and perhaps more a mood. The end-of-ideology is in reality the ideology of an ending: the ending of political reflection itself as a public fact. It is a weary know-it-all justification, by tone of voice rather than by explicit argument, of the cultural and political default of the NATO intellectuals.

– II –

All this is just the sort of thing that I at least have always objected to, and do object to, in the "socialist realism" of the Soviet Union.

There too, criticism of milieux are of course permitted, but they are not to be connected with criticism of the structure itself: one may not question "the system." There are no "antagonistic contradictions."

There too, in novels and plays, criticisms of characters, even of party members, are permitted, but they must be displayed as "shocking exceptions;" they must be seen as survivals from the old order, not as systematic products of the new.

There too, pessimism is permitted, but only episodically and only within the context of the big optimism; the tendency is to confuse any systematic or structural criticism with pessimism itself. So they admit criticisms, first of this and then of that, but engulf them all by the long-run historical optimism about the system as a whole and the goals proclaimed by its leaders.

I neither want nor need to overstress the parallel, yet in a recent series of interviews in the Soviet Union concerning socialist realism I was very much struck by it. In Uzbekistan and Georgia, as well as in Russia, I kept writing notes to myself at the end of recorded interviews: "This man talks in a style just like Arthur Schlesinger Jr."

"Surely this fellow is the counterpart of Daniel Bell, except not so—what shall I say?—so gossipy; and certainly neither so petty nor so vulgar as the more envious status-climbers. Perhaps this is because here they are not thrown into such a competitive status-panic about the ancient and obfuscating British models of prestige." "The would-be enders of ideology," I kept thinking, "are they not the self-coordinated or, better, the fashion-coordinated, socialist realists of the NATO world?" And: "Check this carefully with the files of *Encounter* and *The Reporter*." I have now done so; it is the same kind of thing.

Certainly there are many differences: above all, the fact that socialist [65/66] realism is part of an official line, while the end of ideology is self-managed. But the differences one knows. It is more useful to stress the parallels, and the generic fact that both of these postures stand opposed to radical criticisms of their respective societies.

In the Soviet Union, only political authorities at the top, or securely on their way up there, can seriously tamper with structural questions and ideological lines. These authorities, of course, are much more likely to be intellectuals (in one or another sense of the word—say a man who actually writes his own speeches) than are American politicians. Moreover, since the death of Stalin, such Soviet authorities *have* begun to tamper quite seriously with structural questions and basic ideology, although for reasons peculiar to the tight and official joining of culture and politics in their set-up, they must try to disguise this fact.

The end-of-ideology is very largely a mechanical reaction, not a creative response, to the ideology of Stalinism. As such it takes from its opponent something of its inner quality. What it all means is that these people have become aware of the uselessness of vulgar marxism, but are not yet aware of the uselessness of the liberal rhetoric.

– III –

But the most immediately important thing about the "end of ideology" is that it *is* merely a fashion, and fashions change. Already this one is on its way out. Even a few diehard anti-Stalinists are showing signs of a reappraisal of their own past views; some are even beginning to recognize publicly that Stalin himself no longer runs the Soviet party and state. They begin to see the poverty of their comfortable ideas as they come to confront Khrushchev's Russia.

We who have been, in moral terms, consistently radical in our work throughout the postwar period are often amused nowadays that various writers, sensing another shift in fashion, are beginning to call upon intellectuals to work once more in ways that are politically explicit. But we should not be merely amused; we ought to try to make their shift more than a fashion change.

The end-of-ideology is on the decline because it stands for the refusal to work out an explicit political philosophy. And alert men everywhere today do feel the need for such a philosophy. What we should do is to continue directly to confront this need. In doing so, it may be useful to keep in mind that to have a working political philosophy means to have a philosophy that enables you to work, and that at least four kinds of work are needed, each of them at once intellectual and political.

In these terms, think for a moment longer of the end-of-ideology:

(1) It is a kindergarten fact that any political reflection that is of possible public significance is *ideological;* in its terms policies, institutions, and men of power are criticized or approved. In this respect, the end-of-ideology stands, negatively, for the attempt to withdraw oneself and one's work from political relevance; positively, it is an ideology of political complacency which seems the only way now open for many writers to acquiesce in or to justify the status quo. [66/67]

(2) So far as orienting *theories* of society and of history are concerned, the end-of-ideology stands for, and presumably stands upon, a fetishism of empiricism: more academically, upon a pretentious methodology used to state trivialities about unimportant social areas; more essayistically, upon a naive journalistic empiricism—which I have already characterized above—and upon a cultural gossip in which "answers" to the vital and pivotal issues are merely assumed. This political bias masquerades as epistomological excellence, and there are no orienting theories.

(3) So far as the *historic agency of change* is concerned, the end-of-ideology rests upon the identification of such agencies with going institutions, perhaps upon their piecemeal reform, but never upon the search for agencies that might be used for, or that might themselves operate toward, a structural change of society. The problem of agency is never posed as a problem to solve, as "our problem." Instead there is endless talk of the need to be pragmatic, flexible, open. Surely all this has already been adequately dealt with: such a view makes sense politically only if the blind drift of human affairs is in general beneficent.

(4) So far as political and human *ideals* are concerned, the end-of-ideology stands for a denial of their relevance, except as abstract ikons. Merely to hold such ideals seriously is in this view "utopian."

– IV –

But enough. Where do *we* stand on each of these four aspects of political philosophy? Various of us are of course at work on each of them, and all of us are generally aware of our needs in regard to each. As for the articulation of ideals, there I think your magazines have done their best work so far.* That is *your* meaning—is it not?—of the emphasis upon cultural affairs. As for ideological analysis and the rhetoric with which to carry it out, I do not think any of us is nearly good enough. But that will come with further advance on the two fronts where we are weakest: theories of society, history, and human nature, and—the major problem—ideas about the historical agencies of structural change.

We have frequently been told by an assorted variety of dead-end people that the meanings of left and of right are now liquidated, by history and by reason. I think we should answer them in some such way as this:

The *Right*, among other things, means what you are doing: celebrating society as it is, a going concern. *Left* means, or ought to mean, just the opposite. It means structural criticism and reportage and theories of society, which at some point or another are focussed politically as demands and programs. These criticisms, demands, theories, programs are guided morally by the humanist and secular ideals of Western civilization—above all, the ideals of reason, freedom and justice. To be "left" means to connect up cultural with political criticism, and both with demands and programs. And it means all this inside *every* country of the world.

Only one more point of definition: absence of public issues there may [67/68] well be, but this is not due to any absence of problems or of contradictions, antagonistic and otherwise. Impersonal and structural changes have not eliminated problems or issues. Their absence from many discussions is an ideological condition, regulated in the first place by whether or not intellectuals detect and state problems as potential *issues* for probable publics, and as *troubles* for a variety of individuals. One indispensable means of such work on these central tasks is what can only be described as ideological analysis. To be actively left, among other things, is to carry on just such analysis.

To take seriously the problem of the need for a political orientation is not, of course, to seek for A Fanatical and Apocalyptic Vision, for An Infallible and Monolithic Lever of Change, for Dogmatic Ideology, for A Startling New Rhetoric, for Treacherous Abstractions, and all the other bogeymen of the dead-enders. These are, of course, "the extremes," the straw men, the red herrings used by our political enemies to characterize the polar opposite of where they think they stand.

* This refers to *The New Left Review, The New Reasoner,* and *Universities & Left Review,* all of Great Britain. [Note by editors of *Studies on the Left.*]

They tell us, for example, that ordinary men cannot always be political "heroes." Who said they could? But keep looking around you;
and why not search out the conditions of such heroism as men do
and might display? They tell us that we are too "impatient," that our
"pretentious" theories are not well enough grounded. That is true,
but neither are our theories trivial. Why don't they get to work to
refute or ground them? They tell us we "do not really understand"
Russia and China today. That is true; we don't; neither do they. We
at least are studying the question. They tell us we are "ominous" in
our formulations. That is true: we do have enough imagination to be
frightened, and we don't have to hide it. We are not afraid we'll
panic. They tell us we are "grinding axes." Of course we are: we do
have, among other points of view, morally grounded ones, and we
are aware of them. They tell us, in their wisdom, that we do not understand that The Struggle is Without End. True: we want to
change its form, its focus, its object.

We are frequently accused of being "utopian" in our criticisms
and in our proposals and, along with this, of basing our hopes for a
new left *politics* "merely on reason," or more concretely, upon the
intelligentsia in its broadest sense.

There is truth in these charges. But must we not ask: What now is
really meant by *utopian?* And is not our utopianism a major source
of our strength? *Utopian* nowadays, I think, refers to any criticism
or proposal that transcends the up-close milieux of a scatter of individuals, the milieux which men and women can understand directly
and which they can reasonably hope directly to change. In this exact
sense, our theoretical work is indeed utopian—in my own case, at
least, deliberately so. What needs to be understood, and what needs
to be changed, is not merely first this and then that detail of some
institution or policy. If there is to be a politics of a new left, what
needs to be analyzed is the *structure* of institutions, the *foundation*
of policies. In this sense, both in its criticisms and in its proposals,
our work is necessarily structural, and so—*for us,* just now—utopian.

This brings us face to face with the most important issue of political reflection and of political action in our time: the problem of the
historical [68/69] agency of change, of the social and institutional
means of structural change. There are several points about this
problem I would like to put to you.

— v —

First, the historic agencies of change for liberals of the capitalist
societies have been an array of voluntary associations, coming to a
political climax in a parliamentary or congressional system. For socialists of almost all varieties, the historic agency has been the work-

ing class—and later the peasantry, or parties and unions composed of members of the working class, or (to blur, for now, a great problem) of political parties acting in its name, "representing its interests."

I cannot avoid the view that both these forms of historic agency have either collapsed or become most ambiguous. So far as structural change is concerned, neither seems to be at once available and effective as *our* agency any more. I know this is a debatable point among us, and among many others as well; I am by no means certain about it. But surely, if it is true, it ought not to be taken as an excuse for moaning and withdrawal (as it is by some of those who have become involved with the end-of-ideology); and it ought not to be bypassed (as it is by many Soviet scholars and publicists, who in their reflections upon the course of advanced capitalist societies simply refuse to admit the political condition and attitudes of the working class).

Is anything more certain than that in 1970—indeed, at this time next year—our situation will be quite different, and—the chances are high—decisively so? But of course, that isn't saying much. The seeming collapse of our historic agencies of change ought to be taken as a problem, an issue, a trouble—in fact, as *the* political problem which *we* must turn into issue and trouble.

Second, it is obvious that when we talk about the collapse of agencies of change, we cannot seriously mean that such agencies do not exist. On the contrary, the means of history-making—of decision and of the enforcement of decision—have never in world history been so enlarged and so available to such small circles of men on both sides of The Curtains as they now are. My own conception of the shape of power, the theory of the power elite, I feel no need to argue here. This theory has been fortunate in its critics, from the most diverse political viewpoints, and I have learned from several of these critics. But I have not seen, as of this date, an analysis of the idea that causes me to modify any of its essential features.

The point that is immediately relevant does seem obvious: what is utopian for us, is not at all utopian for the presidium of the Central Committee in Moscow, or the higher circles of the Presidency in Washington, or, recent events make evident, for the men of SAC and CIA. The historic agencies of change that have collapsed are those which were at least thought to be open to *the left* inside the advanced Western nations, to those who have wished for structural changes of these socieities. Many things follow from this obvious fact; of many of them, I am sure, we are not yet adequately aware.

Third, what I do not quite understand about some new-left writers is [69/70] why they cling so mightily to "the working class" of the advanced capitalist societies as *the* historic agency, or even as the most important agency, in the face of the really impressive historical evidence that now stands against this expectation.

Such a labor metaphysic, I think, is a legacy from Victorian Marxism that is now quite unrealistic.

It is an historically specific idea that has been turned into an a-historical and unspecific hope.

The social and historical conditions under which industrial workers tend to become a-class-for-themselves, and a decisive political force, must be fully and precisely elaborated. There have been, there are, there will be such conditions. These conditions vary according to national social structure and the exact phase of their economic and political development. Of course we cannot "write off the working class." But we must *study* all that, and freshly. Where labor exists as an agency, of course we must work with it, but we must not treat it as The Necessary Lever, as nice old Labour Gentlemen in Britain and elsewhere tend to do.

Although I have not yet completed my own comparative studies of working classes, generally it would seem that only at certain (earlier) stages of industrialization, and in a political context of autocracy, *etc.*, do wage-workers tend to become a class-for-themselves, *etc.* The *etceteras* mean that I can here merely raise the question.

– VI –

It is with this problem of agency in mind that I have been studying, for several years now, the cultural apparatus, the intellectuals, as a possible, immediate, radical agency of change. For a long time, I was not much happier with this idea than were many of you; but it turns out now, at the beginning of the 1960's, that it may be a very relevant idea indeed.

In the first place, is it not clear that if we try to be realistic in our utopianism—and that is no fruitless contradiction—a writer in our countries on the left today *must* begin with the intellectuals? For that is what we are, that is where we stand.

In the second place, the problem of the intelligentsia is an extremely complicated set of problems on which rather little factual work has been done. In doing this work, we must, above all, not confuse the problems of the intellectuals of West Europe and North America with those of the Soviet Bloc or with those of the underdeveloped worlds. In each of the three major components of the world's social structure today, the character and the role of the intelligentsia is distinct and historically specific. Only by detailed comparative studies of them in all their human variety can we hope to understand any one of them.

In the third place, who is it that is getting fed up? Who is it that is getting disgusted with what Marx called "all the old crap?" Who is it that is thinking and acting in radical ways? All over the world—in the bloc, outside the bloc and in between—the answer is the same: it is the young intelligentsia. [70/71]

I cannot resist copying out for you, with a few changes, some materials I recently prepared for a 1960 paperback edition of a book of mine on war:

"In the spring and early summer of 1960, more of the returns from the American decision and default are coming in. In Turkey, after student riots, a military junta takes over the state, of late run by Communist Container Menderes. In South Korea, too, students and others knock over the corrupt American-puppet regime of Syngman Rhee. In Cuba, a genuinely left-wing revolution begins full-scale economic reorganization, without the domination of U. S. corporations. Average age of its leaders: about 30—and certainly a revolution without Labor As Agency. On Taiwan, the eight million Taiwanese under the American-imposed dictatorship of Chiang Kai-shek, with his two million Chinese, grow increasingly restive. On Okinawa, a U. S. military base, the people get their first chance since World War II ended to demonstrate against U. S. seizure of their island; and some students take that chance, snake-dancing and chanting angrily to the visiting President: 'Go home, go home—take away your missiles.' (Don't worry, 12,000 U. S. troops easily handle the generally grateful crowds; also the President is 'spirited out the rear end of the United States compound'—and so by helicopter to the airport.) In Japan, weeks of student rioting succeed in rejecting the President's visit, jeopardizing a new treaty with the U.S.A., and displacing the big-business, pro-American Prime Minister, Kishi. And even in our own pleasant Southland, Negro and white students are—but let us keep that quiet: it really *is* disgraceful.

"That is by no means the complete list; that was yesterday; see today's newspaper. Tomorrow, in varying degree, the returns will be more evident. Will they be evident enough? They will have to be very obvious to attract real American attention: sweet complaints and the voice of reason—these are not enough. In the slum countries of the world today, what are they saying? The rich Americans, they pay attention only to violence—and to money. You don't care what they say, American? Good for you. Still, they may insist; things are no longer under the old control; you're not getting it straight, American: your country—it would seem—may well become the target of a world hatred the like of which the easy-going Americans have never dreamed. Neutralists and Pacifists and Unilateralists and that confusing variety of Leftists around the world—all those tens of millions of people, of course they are misguided, absolutely controlled by small conspiratorial groups of trouble-makers, under direct orders from Moscow and Peking. Diabolically omnipotent, it is *they* who create all this messy unrest. It is *they* who have given the tens of millions the absurd idea that they shouldn't want to remain, or to become, the seat of American nuclear bases—those gay little outposts of American civilization. So now they don't want U-2's on their territory; so now they want to contract out of the American military machine; they want to be neutral among the crazy big antagonists. And they don't want their own societies to be militarized.

"But take heart, American: you won't have time to get really bored with your friends abroad: they won't be your friends much longer. You don't need *them;* it will all go away; don't let them confuse you."

Add to that: In the Soviet bloc, who is it that has been breaking out of apathy? It has been students and young professors and writers; it has [71/72] been the young intelligentsia of Poland and Hungary, and of Russia, too. Never mind that they have not won; never mind that there are other social and moral types among them. First of all, it has been these types. But the point is clear, isn't it?

That is why we have got to study these new generations of intellectuals around the world as real live agencies of historic change. Forget Victorian Marxism, except when you need it; and read Lenin again (be careful)—Rosa Luxemburg, too.

"But it is just some kind of moral upsurge, isn't it?" Correct. But under it: no apathy. Much of it is direct non-violent action, and it seems to be working, here and there. Now we must learn from the practice of these young intellectuals and with them work out new forms of action.

"But it's all so ambiguous—Cuba, for instance." Of course it is; history-making is always ambiguous. Wait a bit; in the meantime, help them to focus their moral upsurge in less ambiguous political ways. Work out with them the ideologies, the strategies, the theories that will help them consolidate their efforts: new theories of structural changes of and by human societies in our epoch.

"But it is utopian, after all, isn't it?" No, not in the sense you mean. Whatever else it may be, it's not that. Tell it to the students of Japan. Tell it to the Negro sit-ins. Tell it to the Cuban Revolutionaries. Tell it to the people of the Hungry-nation bloc. [72]

MARTIN LUTHER KING, JR.

Love, Law and Civil Disobedience

I HAVE been asked to talk about the philosophy behind the student movement. There can be no gain-saying of the fact that we confront a crisis in race relations in the United States. This crisis has been precipitated on the one hand by the determined resistance of reactionary forces in the South to the Supreme Court's decision in 1954 outlawing segregation in the public schools. And we know that at times this resistance has risen to ominous proportions. At times we find the legislative halls of the South ringing loud with such words as interposition and nullification. And all of these forces have developed into massive resistance. But we must also say that the crisis has been precipitated on the other hand by the determination of hundreds and thousands and millions of Negro people to achieve freedom and human dignity. If the Negro stayed in his place and accepted discrimination and segregation, there would be no crisis. [345/346] But the Negro has a new sense of dignity, a new self respect, and new determination. He has re-evaluated his own intrinsic worth. Now this new sense of dignity on the part of the Negro grows out of the same longing for freedom and human dignity on the part of the oppressed people all over the world; for we see it in Africa, we see it in Asia, and we see it all over the world. Now we must say that this struggle for freedom will not come to an automatic halt, for history reveals to us that once oppressed people rise up against that oppression, there is no stopping point short of full freedom. On the other hand, history reveals to us that those who oppose the movement for freedom are those who are in privileged positions who very seldom give up their privileges without strong resistance. And they very seldom do it voluntarily. So the sense of struggle will continue. The question is how will the struggle be waged.

Martin Luther King, Jr., "Love, Law and Civil Disobedience," in *Rhetoric of Racial Revolt*, [ed.] by Roy L. Hill (Denver, Colorado: Golden Bell Press, 1964), pp. 345–56. [A transcript of Dr. King's address to the annual meeting of the Fellowship of the Concerned, November 16, 1961.]

Now there are three ways that oppressed people have generally dealt with their oppression. One way is the method of acquiescence, the method of surrender; that is, the individuals will somehow adjust themselves to oppression, they adjust themselves to discrimination or to segregation or colonialism or what have you. The other method that has been used in history is that of rising up against the oppressor with corroding hatred and physical violence. Now of course we know about this method in western civilization, because in a sense it has been the hallmark of its grandeur, and the inseparable twin of western materialism. But there is a weakness in this method because it ends up creating many more social problems than it solves. And I am convinced that if the Negro succumbs to the temptation of using violence in his struggle for freedom and justice, unborn generations will be the recipients of a long and desolate night of bitterness. And our chief legacy to the future will be an endless reign of meaningless chaos.

But there is another way, namely the way of non-violent resistance. This method was popularized in our generation by a little man from India, whose name was Mohandas K. Gandhi. He used this method in a magnificent way to free his people from the economic exploitation and the political domination inflicted upon them by a foreign power.

This has been the method used by the student movement in the South and all over the United States. And naturally whenever I talk about the student movement I cannot be totally objective. I have to be somewhat subjective [346/347] because of my great admiration for what the students have done. For in a real sense they have taken our deep groans and passionate yearnings for freedom, and filtered them in their own tender souls, and fashioned them into a creative protest which is an epic known all over our nation. As a result of their disciplined, non-violent, yet courageous struggle, they have been able to do wonders in the South, and in our nation. But this movement does have an underlying philosophy, it has certain ideas that are attached to it, it has certain philosophical precepts. These are the things that I would like to discuss for the few moments left.

I would say that the first point or the first principle in the movement is the idea that means must be as pure as the end. This movement is based on the philosophy that ends and means must cohere. Now this has been one of the long struggles in history, the whole idea of means and ends. Great philosophers have grappled with it, and sometimes they have emerged with the idea, from Machiavelli on down, that the end justifies the means. There is a great system of thought in our world today, known as Communism. And I think that with all of the weakness and tragedies of Communism, we find its greatest tragedy right here, that it goes under the philosophy that the end justifies the means that are used in the process. So we can read or we can hear the Lenins say that lying, deceit, or violence, that many of these things justify the ends of the classless society.

This is where the student movement and the non-violent movement that is taking place in our nation would break with Communism and any other system that would argue that the end justifies the means. For in the long run, we must see that the end represents the means in process and the ideal in the making. In other words, we cannot believe, or we cannot go with the idea that the end justifies the means because the end is pre-existent in the means. So the idea of non-violent resistance, the philosophy of non-violent resistance, is the philosophy which says that the means must be as pure as the end, that in the long run of history, immoral destructive means cannot bring about moral and constructive ends.

There is another thing about this philosophy, this method of non-violence which is followed by the student movement. It says that those who adhere to or follow this philosophy must follow a consistent principle of non-injury. They must consistently refuse to inflict injury upon another. [347/348] Sometimes you will read the literature of the student movement and see that, as they are getting ready for the sit-in or stand-in, they will read something like this, "if you are hit do not hit back, if you are cursed do not curse back." This is the whole idea, that the individual who is engaged in a non-violent struggle must never inflict injury upon another. Now this has an external aspect and it has an internal one. From the external point of view it means that the individuals involved must avoid external physical violence. So they don't have guns, they don't retaliate with physical violence. If they are hit in the process, they avoid external physical violence at every point. But it also means that they avoid internal violence of spirit. This is why the love ethic stands so high in the student movement. We have a great deal of talk about love and non-violence in this whole thrust.

Now when the students talk about love, certainly they are not talking about emotional bosh, they are not talking about merely a sentimental outpouring; they're talking something much deeper, and I always have to stop and try to define the meaning of love in this context. The Greek language comes to our aid in trying to deal with this. There are three words in the Greek language for love, one is the word Eros. This is a beautiful type of love, it is an aesthetic love. Plato talks about it a great deal in his *Dialogue,* the yearning of the soul for the realm of the divine. It has come to us to be a sort of romantic love, and so in a sense we have read about it and experienced it. We've read about it in all the beauties of literature. I guess in a sense Edgar Allan Poe was talking about Eros when he talked about his beautiful Annabelle Lee, with the love surrounded by the halo of eternity. In a sense Shakespeare was talking about Eros when he said "Love is not love which alters when it alteration finds, or bends with the remover to remove; O' no! it is an ever fixed mark that looks on tempests and is never shaken, it is the star to every wandering bark." . . . The Greek language talks about Philia which was another level of love. It is an intimate affection between personal friends, it is a reciprocal love. On this level you love because you are loved. It is friendship.

Then the Greek language comes out with another word which is called the Agape. Agape is more than romantic [348/349] love, agape is more than friendship. Agape is understanding, creative, redemptive, good will to all men. It is an overflowing love which seeks nothing in return. Theologians would say that it is the love of God operating in the human heart. So that when one rises to love on this level, he loves men not because he likes them, not because their ways appeal to him, but he loves every man because God loves him. And he rises to the point of loving the person who does an evil deed while hating the deed that the person does. I think this is what Jesus meant when he said "love your enemies." I'm very happy that he didn't say like your enemies, because it is pretty difficult to like some people. Like is sentimental, and it is pretty difficult to like someone bombing your home; it is pretty difficult to like somebody threatening your children; it is difficult to like congressmen who spend all of their time trying to defeat civil rights. But Jesus says love them, and love is greater than like. Love is understanding, redemptive, creative, good will for all men. And it is this idea, it is this whole ethic of love which is the idea standing at the basis of the student movement.

There is something else: that one seeks to defeat the unjust system, rather than individuals who are caught in that system. And that one goes on believing that somehow this is the important thing, to get rid of the evil system and not the individual who happens to be misguided, who happens to be misled, who was taught wrong. The thing to do is to get rid of the system and thereby create a moral balance within society.

Another thing that stands at the center of this movement is another idea: that suffering can be a most creative and powerful social force. Suffering has certain moral attributes involved, but it can be a powerful and creative social force. Now, it is very interesting at this point to notice that both violence and non-violence agree that suffering can be a very powerful social force. But there is this difference: violence says that suffering can be a powerful social force by

KING: Love, Law and Civil Disobedience — p.65

inflicting the suffering on somebody else; so this is what we do in war, this is what we do in the whole violent thrust of the violent movement. It believes that you achieve some end by inflicting suffering on another. The non-violent say that suffering becomes a powerful social force when you willingly accept that violence on yourself, so that self-suffering stands at the center of the non-violent movement and the individuals involved are able to suffer in a creative [349/350] manner, feeling that unearned suffering is redemptive, and that suffering may serve to transform the social situation.

Another thing in this movement is the idea that there is within human nature an amazing potential for goodness. There is within human nature something that can respond to goodness. I know somebody's liable to say that this is an unrealistic movement if it goes on believing that all people are good. Well, I didn't say that. I think the students are realistic enough to believe that there is a strange dichotomy of disturbing dualism within human nature. Many of the great philosophers and thinkers through the ages have seen this. It caused Ovid the Latin poet to say, "I see and approve the better things of life, but the evil things I do." It caused even St. Augustine to say "Lord, make me pure, but not yet." So that that is in human nature. Plato, centuries ago said that the human personality is like a charioteer with two headstrong horses, each wanting to go in different directions, so that within our own individual lives we see this conflict and certainly when we come to the collective life of man, we see a strange badness. But in spite of this there is something in human nature that can respond to goodness. So that man is neither innately good nor is he innately bad; he has potentialities for both. So in this sense, Carlyle was right when he said, that "there are depths in man which go down to the lowest hell, and heights which reach the highest heaven, for are not both heaven and hell made out of him, ever-lasting miracle and mystery that he is?" Man has the capacity to be good, man has the capacity to be evil.

And so the non-violent resister never lets this idea go, that there is something within human nature that can respond to goodness. So that a Jesus of Nazareth or a Mohandas Gandhi, can appeal to human beings and appeal to that element of goodness within them, and a Hitler can appeal to the element of evil within them. But we must never forget that there is something within human nature that can respond to goodness, that man is not totally depraved, to put it in theological terms, the image of God is never totally gone. And so the individuals who believe in this movement and who believe in non-violence and our struggle in the South, somehow believe that even the worst segregationist can become an integrationist. Now sometimes it is hard to believe that this is what this movement says, and it believes it firmly, that there is something within human nature that can be changed, and this stands at the top of the whole [350/351] philosophy of the student movement and the philosophy of non-violence.

It says something else. It says that it is as much a moral obligation to refuse to cooperate with evil as it is to cooperate with good. Non-cooperation with evil is as much a moral obligation as the cooperation with good. So that the student movement is willing to stand up courageously on the idea of civil disobedience. Now I think this is the part of the student movement that is probably misunderstood more than anything else. And it is a difficult aspect, because on the one hand the students would say, and I would say, and all the people who believe in civil rights would say, obey the Supreme Court's decision of 1954 and at the same time, we would disobey certain laws that exist on the statutes of the South today.

This brings in the whole question of how can you be logically consistent when you advocate obeying some laws and disobeying other laws. Well, I think one would have to see the whole meaning of this movement at this point by seeing that the students recognize that there are two types of laws. There are just laws and there are unjust laws. And they would be the first to say obey the just laws, they would be the first to say that men and women have a moral obligation to obey just and right laws. And they would go on to say that we must see that there are unjust laws. Now the question comes into being, what is the difference, and who determines the difference, what is the difference between a just and an unjust law?

Well, a just law is a low that squares with a moral law. It is a law that squares with that which is right, so that any law that uplifts human personality is a just law. Whereas that law which is out of harmony with the moral is a law which does not square with the moral law of the universe. It does not square with the law of God, so for that reason it is unjust and any law that degrades the human personality is an unjust law.

Well, somebody says that that does not mean anything to me; first, I don't believe in these abstract things called moral laws and I'm not too religious, so I don't believe in the law of God; you have to get a little more concrete, and more practical. What do the mean when you say that a law is unjust, and a law is just? Well, I would go on to say in more concrete terms that an unjust law is a code that the majority inflicts on the minority that is not binding on itself. [351/352] So that this becomes difference made legal. Another thing that we can say is that an unjust law is a code which the majority inflicts upon the minority, which that minority had no part in enacting or creating, because that minority had no right to vote in many instances, so that the legislative bodies that made these laws were not democratically elected. Who could ever say that the legislative body of Mississippi was democratically elected, or the legislative body of Alabama was democratically elected, or the legislative body even of Georgia has been democratically elected, when there are people in Terrell County and in other counties because of the color of their skin who cannot vote? They confront reprisals and threats and all of that; so that an unjust law is a law that individuals did not have a part in creating or enacting because they were denied the right to vote.

Now the same token of just law would be just the opposite. A just law becomes saneness made legal. It is a code that the majority, who happen to believe in that code, compel the minority, who don't believe in it, to follow, because they are willing to follow it themselves, so it is saneness made legal. Therefore the individuals who stand up on the basis of civil disobedience realize that they are following something that says that there are just laws and there are unjust laws. Now, they are not anarchists. They believe that there are laws which must be followed; they do not seek to defy the law, they do not seek to evade the law. For many individuals who would call themselves segregationists and who would hold on to segregation at any cost seek to defy the law, they seek to evade the law, and their process can lead on into anarchy. They seek in the final analysis to follow a way of uncivil disobedience, not civil disobedience. And I submit that the individual who disobeys the law, whose conscience tells him it is unjust and who is willing to accept the penalty by staying in jail until that law is altered, is expressing at the moment the very highest respect for law.

This is what the students have followed in their movement. Of course there is nothing new about this, they feel that they are in good company and rightly so. We go back and read the *Apology* and the *Crito*, and you see Socrates practicing civil disobedience. And to a degree academic freedom is a reality today because Socrates practiced civil disobedience. The early Christians practiced civil disobedience [352/353] in a superb manner, to a point where they were willing to be thrown to the lions. They were willing to face all kinds of suffering in order to stand up for what they knew was right even though they knew it was against the laws of the Roman Empire.

We could come up to our own day and we see it in many instances. We must never forget that everything that Hitler did in

Germany was "legal." It was illegal to aid and comfort a Jew, in the days of Hitler's Germany. But I believe that if I had the same attitude then as I have now I would publicly aid and comfort my Jewish brothers in Germany if Hitler were alive today calling this an illegal process. If I lived in South Africa today in the midst of the white supremacy law in South Africa, I would join Chief Luthuli and others in saying break these unjust laws. And even let us come up to America. Our nation in a sense came into being through a massive act of civil disobedience, for the Boston Tea Party was nothing but a massive act of civil disobedience. Those who stood up against the slave laws, the abolitionists, by and large practiced civil disobedience. So I think these students are in good company, and they feel that by practicing civil obedience [*sic*] they are in line with men and women through the ages who have stood up for something that is morally right.

Now there are one or two other things that I want to say about this student movement, moving out of the philosophy of non-violence, something about what it is a revolt against. On the one hand it is a revolt against the negative peace that has encompassed the South for many years. I remember when I was in Montgomery, Ala., one of the white citizens came to me one day and said—and I think he was very sincere about this—that in Montgomery for all of these years we have been such a peaceful community, we have had so much harmony in race relations and then you people have started this movement and boycott, and it has done so much to disturb race relations, and we just don't love the Negro like we used to love them, because you have destroyed the harmony and the peace that we once had in race relations. And I said to him, in the best way I could say and I tried to say it in non-violent terms, we have never had peace in Montgomery, Ala., we have never had peace in the South. We have had a negative peace, which is merely the absence of tension; we've had a negative peace in which the Negro patiently accepted his situation and his [353/354] plight, but we've never had true peace, we've never had positive peace, and what we're seeking now is to develop this positive peace. For we must come to see that peace is not merely the absence of some negative force, it is the presence of a positive force. True peace is not merely the absence of tension, but it is the presence of justice and brotherhood. I think this is what Jesus meant when he said, I come not to bring peace but a sword. Now Jesus didn't mean he came to start war, to bring a physical sword, and he didn't mean, I come not to bring positive peace. But I think what Jesus was saying in substance was this, that I come not to bring an old negative peace, which makes for stagnant passivity and deadening complacency, I come to bring something different, and whenever I come, a conflict is precipitated, between the old and the new, whenever I come a struggle takes place between justice and injustice, between the forces of light and the forces of darkness. I come not to bring a negative peace, but a positive peace, which is brotherhood, which is justice, which is the Kingdom of God.

And I think this what we are seeking to do today, and this movement is a revolt against a negative peace and a struggle to bring into being a positive peace, which makes for true brotherhood, true integration, true person-to-person relationships. This movement is also revolt against what is often called tokenism. Here again many people do not understand this, they feel that in this struggle the Negro will be satisfied with tokens of integration, just a few students and a few schools here and there and a few doors open here and there. But this isn't the meaning of the movement and I think that honesty impels me to admit it everywhere I have an opportunity, that the Negro's aim is to bring about complete integration in American life. And he has come to see that token integration is little more than token democracy, which ends up with many new evasive schemes and it ends up with new discrimination, covered up with such niceties of complexity. It is very interesting to discover that the movement has thrived in many communities that had token integration. So this reveals that the movement is based on a principle that integration must become real and complete, not just token integration.

It is also a revolt against what I often call the myth of time. We hear this quite often, that only time can solve this problem. That if we will only be patient, and only pray—[354/355] which we must do, we must be patient and we must pray—but there are those who say just do these things and wait for time, and time will solve this problem. Well the people who argue this do not themselves realize that time is neutral, that it can be used constructively or destructively. At points the people of ill will, the segregationists, have used time much more effectively than the people of good will. So individuals in the struggle must come to realize that it is necessary to aid time, that without this kind of aid, time itself will become an ally of the insurgent and primitive forces of social stagnation. Therefore, this movement is a revolt against the myth of time.

There is a final thing that I would like to say to you, this movement is a movement based on faith in the future. It is a movement based on a philosophy, the possibility of the future bringing into being something real and meaningful. It is a movement based on hope. I think this is very important. The students have developed a

theme song for their movement, maybe you've heard it. It goes
something like this "we shall overcome, deep in my heart, I do believe, we shall overcome," and then they go on to say another verse,
"we are not afraid, we are not afraid today, deep in my heart I do
believe, we shall overcome." So it is out of this deep faith in the future that they are able to move out and adjourn the councils of despair, and to bring new light in the dark chambers of pessimism. I
can remember the times that we've been together, I remember that
night in Montgomery, Ala., when we had stayed up all night, discussing the Freedom Rides, and that morning came to see that it
was necessary to go on with the Freedom Rides, that we would not
in all good conscience call an end to the Freedom Rides at that
point. And I remember the first group got ready to leave, to take a
bus for Jackson, Miss., we all joined hands and started singing together. "We shall overcome, we shall overcome." And something
within me said, now how is it that these students can sing this, they
are going down to Mississippi, they are going to face hostile and
jeering mobs, and yet they could sing, "We shall overcome." They
may even face physical death, and yet they could sing, "We shall
overcome." Most of them realized that they would be thrown into
jail, and yet they could sing, "We shall overcome, we are not afraid."
Then something caused me to see at that moment the real meaning
of the movement. That students had faith in the future. That the
movement was [355/356] based on hope, that this movement had
something within it that says somehow even though the arc of the
moral universe is long, it bends toward justice. And I think this
should be a challenge to all others who are struggling to transform
the dangling discords of our Southland into a beautiful symphony of
brotherhood. There is something in this student movement which
says to us, that we shall overcome. Before the victory is won some
may have to get scarred up, but we shall overcome. Before the victory of brotherhood is achieved, some will maybe face physical
death, but we shall overcome. Before the victory is won, some will
lose jobs, some will be called Communists, and reds, merely because
they believe in brotherhood, some will be dismissed as dangerous
rabblerousers and agitators merely because they're standing up for
what is right, but we shall overcome. That is the basis of this movement, and as I like to say, there is something in this universe that
justifies Carlyle in saying no lie can live forever. We shall overcome
because there is something in this universe which justifies William
Cullen Bryant in saying truth crushed to earth shall rise again. We
shall overcome because there is something in this universe that justifies James Russell Lowell in saying, truth forever on the scaffold,

wrong forever on the throne. Yet that scaffold sways the future, and behind the dim unknown standeth God within the shadows, keeping watch above His own. With this faith in the future, with this determined struggle, we will be able to emerge from the bleak and desolate midnight of man's inhumanity to man, into the bright and glittering daybreak of freedom and justice. . . . [356]

KENNETH REXROTH

The Students Take Over

WHEN the newspapers have got nothing else to talk about, they cut
loose on the young. The young are always news. If they are up to
something, that's news. If they aren't, that's news, too. Things we
did as kids and thought nothing of, the standard capers of all young
animals, now make headlines, shake up police departments and rend
the frail hearts of social workers. Partly this is due to the mytholo-
gies of modern civilization. Chesterton once pointed out that baby
worship is to be expected of a society where the only immortality
anybody really believes in is childhood. Partly it is due to the personal reactions of reporters, a class of men by and large prevented,
occupationally, from ever growing up. Partly it is hope: "We have
failed, they may do better." Partly it is guilt: "We have failed them.
Are they planning vengeance?"

In talking about the Revolt of Youth we should never forget that
we are dealing with a new concept. For thousands of years nobody
cared what youth were doing. They weren't news. They were minding.

They aren't minding now. That isn't news. They haven't been
minding since the days of John Held, Jr., *College Humor* and F.
Scott Fitzgerald. In those days, they were cutting loose. In the thirties, they were joining up, giving one last try to the noble prescrip-
tions of their elders. During the McCarthy Epoch and the Korean
War, they were turning their backs and walking away. Today they
are striking back. That is news. Nobody else is striking back. Hardly
a person over thirty in our mass societies believes it is possible to
strike back, or would know how to go about it if he did. During the
past couple of years, without caring about the consequences, making
up their techniques as they went along, organizing spontaneously in
the midst of action, young people all over the world have intervened
in history.

Kenneth Rexroth, "The Students Take Over," *The Nation*, CLIXI (2 July
1960), 4–9.

As the University of California student said at the recent Un-American Activities Committee riot in San Francisco, "Chessman was the last straw. I'm fed up." It's about time somebody got fed up, because, to mix the metaphor, all the chickens are coming home to roost. It has become only too apparent that we can no longer afford the old catch-as-catch-can morality with which civilization has muddled through to 1960. Sloth, rascality, predatory dishonesty, evasion, bluster, no longer work. The machinery has become too delicate, too complicated, too world-encompassing. Maybe it was once true, a hundred and fifty years ago, that the sum total of the immoral actions of selfish men produced a social good. It is no longer true. Maybe once, societally speaking, if wolf ate wolf long enough and hard enough, you produced a race of intelligent dogs. Not now. Pretty soon we are just going to have a world populated by dead wolves.

Towards the end of his life, H. G. Wells remarked that "something very queer was creeping over human affairs." He saw a kind of foolish dishonesty, a perverse lust for physical and moral violence, and a total lack of respect for the integrity of the personality invading every walk of life, all the relationships of men, individual and global. He seemed to be not only troubled, but puzzled. In his own *In the Days of the Comet,* the earth passes through the tail of a comet and a beneficent gas fills the atmosphere and makes all men good overnight. You feel that he suspected something very similar might have come upon us unawares out of outer space, but that in actuality, the gas had turned out to be subtly and pervasively malignant. It is easy to see what he was getting at. Nobody sees it better today than the young student, his head filled with "the heritage of the ages," taught in school all the noblest aspirations of mankind, and brought face to face with the chaos of the world beyond the college gates. He's got to enter it, college will be over in a few months or years. He is entering it already fed up.

Think of the great disasters of our time. They have all been the result of a steadily growing immoralism. You could start indefinitely back—with Bismarck's telegram or the Opium War—but think of what those men alive have experienced: the First World War itself; a vast "counter-revolutionary" offensive; the Versailles Treaty; Fascism and Nazism with their institutionalization of every shoddy and crooked paranoia; the Moscow Trials; the betrayal of Spain; Munich; the Second World War, with its noble utterances and its crooked deals; the horrible tale of fifteen years of peace and cold war; the Rosenbergs; the Hungarian Revolution; and, in the last few months, the rascality that has burst around our heads like exploding shrapnel—U-2, phony Summits, an orgy of irresponsibility and lies.

This is the world outside the college gates. Millions of people are asked to enter it cheerfully each June, equipped with draft cards, social security cards, ballots, job-application blanks countersigned by David Sarnoff, J. Edgar Hoover, Allen W. Dulles, the family physician and the pastor of the neighborhood church. Is it surprising that a lot of them should turn away at the door of this banquet hall, turn in their tickets and say, "Sorry, I'm already fed up"?

Marx believed that our civilization was born in the arms of its own executioner, twins who were enemies in the womb. Certainly ours is the only great culture which, throughout its life, has been accompanied by a creative minority which rejected all its values and claims. Almost all others have had a huge majority who shared in few, if any, of the benefits of civilization. Slaves [4/5] and proletarians are nothing new; the words themselves are derived from another civilization. But a society which advances by means of an elite in permanent revolt and alienation is something new. In the last fifty years, this elite itself has slowly gone under; it, too, has been overwhelmed by the society it both led and subverted. *L'Homme Révolté* has come to the end of his tether. One by one he has compromised and been compromised by all his thousand programs. Nobody believes him any more, so he has become a commercial stereotype, along with the cowboy and the Indian, the private detective, the war hero, and the bison and all other extinct animals. As the agent at M.C.A. said to me three years back, "Revolt is the hottest commodity along The Street." The programs are used up and their promulgators are embarrassed. Youth is fed up with them, too. And why not? Hitler fulfilled the entire emergency program of the Communist Manifesto, and in addition made May Day a legal holiday.

For the Bolsheviks, the good society would come automatically if the right power were applied to the right program. But power and program are not the question: what matters is the immediate realization of humane content, here, there, everywhere, in every fact and relationship of society. Today the brutal fact is that society cannot endure without this realization of humane content. The only way to realize it is directly, personally, in the immediate context. Anything else is not just too expensive; it is wrecking the machinery. Modern society is too complex and too delicate to afford social and political Darwinism any more. This means personal moral action. I suppose, if you wish to call it that, it means a spiritual revolution. Prophets and seers have been preaching the necessity for spiritual revolution for at least three thousand years and mankind has yet to come up with a bona fide one. But it is that kind of action and that kind of change that young people are demanding today.

Myself, past fifty, I cannot speak for the young. I am inclined to

think they will fail. But that isn't the point. You might as well be a
hero if society is going to destroy you anyway. There comes a time
when courage and honesty become cheaper than anything else. And,
who knows, you might win. The nuclear explosion that you could
not prevent doesn't care whether you were brave or not. Virtue, they
say, in itself is intrinsically enjoyable. You can lose nothing, then, by
striking back.

Furthermore, just because the machine is so vast, so complex, it is
far more sensitive than ever before. Individual action does tell. Give
a tiny poke at one of the insignificant gears down in its bowels and
slowly it begins to shudder all over and suddenly belches out hot
rivets. It is a question of qualitative change. Thousands of men built
the Pyramids. One punched card fed into a mechanical brain de-
cides the gravest questions. A few punched cards operate whole factories. Modern society has passed the stage when it was a blind, mechanical monster. It is on the verge of becoming an infinitely responsive instrument.

So the first blows struck back were tiny, insignificant things. Not
long after the last war, Bayard Rustin got on a bus in Chicago and
headed south. When they crossed the Mason-Dixon Line, he stayed
where he was. The cops took him off. He "went limp." They beat
him into unconsciousness. They took him to jail and finally to a hospital. When he got out, he got on another bus and continued south.
So it went, for months—sometimes jail, sometimes the hospital, sometimes they just kicked him into the ditch. Eventually he got to New
Orleans. Eventually Jim Crow was abolished on interstate carriers.
Individual non-violent direct action had invaded the South and won.
The Southern Negro had been shown the only technique that had
any possibility of winning.

Things simmered for a while and then, spontaneously, out of nowhere, the Montgomery bus boycott materialized. Every moment of
the birth and growth of this historic action has been elaborately
documented. Hour by hour we can study "the masses" acting by
themselves. It is my modest, well considered opinion that Martin
Luther King, Jr., is the most remarkable man the South has produced since Thomas Jefferson—since, in other words, it became "the
South." Now the most remarkable thing about Martin Luther King
is that he is not remarkable at all. He is just an ordinary minister of
a middle-class Negro church (or what Negroes call "middle class,"
which is pretty poor by white standards). There are thousands of
men like him all over Negro America. When the voice called, he was
ready. He was ready because he was himself part of that voice.
Professional, white-baiting Negroes who thrill millionairesses in
night clubs in the North would call him a square. He was a brave

square. He is the best possible demonstration of the tremendous untapped potential of humanity that the white South has thrown away all these years. He helped to focus that potential and exert it. It won.

No outside organizers formed the [5/6] Montgomery Improvement Association. They came around later, but they could never quite catch up with it. It is pretty hard to "catch up with," to institutionalize, a movement which is simply the form that a whole community has assumed in action. Although the force of such action is shaped by group loyalty, in the final analysis it must always be individual and direct. You can't delegate either boycott or non-violence. A committee can't act for you, you have to act yourself.

The Montgomery bus boycott not only won where Negro Zealotism, as well as Uncle Tomism, had always failed, but it demonstrated something that had always sounded like sheer sentimentality. It is better, braver, far more effective and far more pleasurable, to act with love than with hate. When you have won, you have gained an unimpeachable victory. The material ends pass or are passed beyond. "Desegregated" buses seem natural in many Southern cities today. The guiltless moral victory remains, always as powerful as the day it was gained. Furthermore, each moral victory converts or neutralizes another block of the opponents' forces.

Before the Montgomery episode was over, Bayard Rustin and Martin Luther King had joined forces. Today they are world statesmen in a "'shadow cabinet" that is slowly forming behind the wielders of power, and the advisers and auxiliary leaders in the councils of Negro Africa. At home in America, the Montgomery achievement has become the source from which has flowed the moral awakening, first, of Negro, and following them, of white youth.

Everything seemed to be going along nicely. According to the papers and most of their professors, 99 44/100 per cent of the nation's youth were cautiously preparing for the day when they could offer their young split-level brains to G.M., I.B.M., Oak Ridge or the Voice of America. Madison Avenue had discovered its own pet minority of revolt and tamed it into an obedient mascot. According to *Time, Life,* M.G.M. and the editors and publishers of a new, pseudo *avant-garde,* all the dear little rebels wanted to do was grow beards, dig jazz, take heroin and wreck other people's Cadillacs. While the exurbanite children sat with the baby sitter and thrilled to Wyatt Earp, their parents swooned in the aisles at *The Connection* or sat up past bedtime reading switch-blade novelists. The psychological mechanisms were the same in both cases—sure-fire, time-tested and shopworn.

But as a matter of fact, anyone with any sense traveling about the country lecturing on college campuses during the past five years, could tell that something very, very different was cooking. Time and again, hundreds of times, I have been asked by some well-dressed, unassuming, beardless student, "I agree with you completely, but what shall we, my generation, *do?*" To this question, I have never been able to give but one answer: "I am fifty. You are twenty. It is for you to tell me what to do. The only thing I can say is, don't do the things my generation did. They didn't work." A head of steam was building up, the waters were rising behind the dam; the dam itself, the block to action, was the patent exhaustion of the old forms. What was accumulating was not any kind of programmatic "radicalization," it was a moral demand.

Parenthetically, I might say that a legend of the Red Thirties was growing up, too. Let me say (and I was there): As far as practically every campus except C.C.N.Y. and N.Y.U. was concerned, the Red Thirties are pure myth. At the height of the great upsurge in California labor, led in its own imagination by the Communist Party, neither the Young Communist League nor the Young Peoples Socialist League was able to keep a functioning student cadre in continuous operation on the University of California campus. At least every four years they had to start all over again. And the leadership, the real bosses, were middle-aged party functionaries sent in from "The Center." One of them, bellowing with early senility, was to show up at the recent Un-American Activities Committee riot in San Francisco and scandalize the students.

The plain fact is that today students are incomparably better educated and more concerned than their elders. As the young do, they still tend to believe things written on paper. For the past five years, bull sessions have been discussing Kropotkin, Daniel De Leon, Trotsky, Gandhi, St. Simon, Plato—an incongruous mixture of the world's cat-bellers, looking for the answer. The gap between the generations has been closing up. Teaching them is a new group of young professors, too young to have been compromised by their actual role in the splendid thirties, themselves realistic-minded products of the G.I. Bill; and neither ex-dupes nor ex-fellow travelers, but serious scholars of the radical past. It is only just recently that the creative minority of students has stopped assuming that just because a man stood at a podium he was *ipso facto* a fraud. So the head of steam built up, the waters mounted behind the dike.

And then one day four children walked into a dime store in a small Southern city and pulled out the plug. Four children picked up the massive chain of the Social Lie and snapped it at its weakest link. Everything broke loose.

Children had won at Little Rock, but they had not initiated the action, they had been caught in the middle in a conflict of equally dishonest political forces, and they had won only a token victory. All the world had marveled at those brave young faces, beautiful under the taunts and spittle. If they had not stood fast, the battle would have been lost; it was their bravery alone that won it. But it was a battle officered by their elders, and like all the quarrels amongst their elders nowadays, it ended in a morally meaningless compromise.

From the first sit-ins, the young have kept the command in their own hands. No "regularly constituted outside authority" has been able to catch up with them. The sit-ins swept the South so rapidly that it [6/7] was impossible to catch up with them physically, but it was even harder for routinized bureaucrats with vested interests in race relations and civil liberties to catch up with them ideologically. The whole spring went by before the professional leaders began to get even a glimmering of what was happening. In the meantime, the old leadership was being pushed aside. Young ministers just out of the seminary, maverick young teachers in Jim Crow colleges, choir mistresses and school marms and Sunday school teachers in all the small cities of the South, pitched in and helped—and let the students lead *them*, without bothering to "clear it with Roy." In a couple of months, the NAACP found itself with a whole new cadre sprung up from the grass roots.

The only organization which understood what was going on was CORE, the Committee On Racial Equality, organized years ago in an evacuated Japanese flat, "Sakai House," in San Francisco, by Bayard Rustin, Caleb Foote and a few others, as a direct-action, race-relations off-shoot of the Fellowship of Reconciliation (the FOR) and the Friends Service Committee. CORE was still a small group of intellectual enthusiasts and there simply weren't enough people to go around. To this day, most Negroes know little more of CORE than its name, which they have seen in the Negro press, and the bare fact that its program is direct, non-violent action. This didn't deter the high school and college students in the Jim Crow high schools and colleges in Raleigh and Durham. They set up their own direct non-violent action organization and in imitation of CORE gave it a name whose initials spelled a word, COST. Soon there were COST "cells" in remote hill-country high schools, complete with codes, hand signals, couriers, all the apparatus of youthful enthusiasm. Needless to say, the very words frightened the older Negro leadership out of its wits.

The police hosed and clubbed the sit-inners, the Uncle Tom presidents of the captive Jim Crow colleges expelled them in droves,

white students came South and insisted on being arrested along with
the Negroes, sympathy picket lines were thrown in front of almost
every chain variety store in almost every college town in the North.
Even some stores with no branches in the South, and no lunch
counters anywhere, found themselves picketed until they cleared
themselves of any implication of Jim Crow.

The effect on the civilized white minority in the South was extraordinary. All but a few had gone on accepting the old stereotypes. There were good Negroes, to be sure, but they didn't want to
mix. The majority were ignorant, violent, bitter, half-civilized, incapable of planned, organized action, happy in Jim Crow. "It would
take another two hundred years." In a matter of weeks, in thousands
of white brains, the old stereotypes exploded. Here were the Negro
children of servants, sharecroppers and garbagemen—"their" servants and sharecroppers and garbagemen who had always been content with their place, directly engaged in the greatest controlled
moral action the South had ever seen. They were quiet, courteous,
full of good will to those who abused them; and they sang, softly, all
together, under the clubs and firehoses, "We will not be moved."
Long protest walks of silent Negroes, two abreast, filed through the
provincial capitals. A major historical moral issue looked into the
eyes of thousands of white spectators in Southern towns which were
so locked in "our way of life" that they were unaware they lived in a
great world. The end of Jim Crow suddenly seemed both near and
inevitable. It is a profoundly disturbing thing to find yourself suddenly thrust upon the stage of history.

I was at the first Louisiana sit-in with a girl from the local paper
who had interviewed me that morning. She was typical, full of
dying prejudices, misinformation and superstitious fears. But she
knew it. She was trying to change. Well, the sit-in did a good job of
changing her. It was terrific. A group of well-bred, sweet-faced kids
from Southern University filed into the dime store, hand in hand,
fellows and girls in couples, and sat down quietly. Their faces were
transfused with quiet, innocent dedication. They looked like the
choir coming into a fine Negro church. They weren't served. They
sat quietly, talking together. Nobody, spectators or participants,
raised his voice. In fact, most of the bystanders didn't even stare
rudely. When the police came, the youngsters spoke softly and po-
litely, and once again, fellows and girls hand in hand, they filed out,
singing a hymn, and got in the paddy wagon.

The newspaper girl was shaken to her shoes. Possibly it was the
first time in her life she had ever faced what it meant to be a human
being. She came to the faculty party for me at Louisiana State that

night. Her flesh was still shaking and she couldn't stop talking. She had come up against one of the big things of life and she was going to be always a little different afterwards.

The response on the campuses of the white colleges of the South was immediate. There had always been inter-racial committees and clubs around, but they had been limited to a handful of eccentrics. These increased tremendously, and involved large numbers of quite normal students. Manifestations of sympathy with the sit-ins and joint activities with nearby Negro schools even came to involve student government and student union bodies. Editorials in college papers, with almost no exceptions, gave enthusiastic support. Believe me, it is quite an experience to eat dinner with a fraternity at a fashionable [7/8] Southern school and see a can to collect money for CORE at the end of the table.

More important than sympathy actions for and with the Negroes, the sit-ins stimulated a similar burst, a run-away brush fire, of activity for all sorts of other aims. They not only stimulated the activity, they provided the form and in a sense the ideology. Non-violent direct action popped up everywhere—so fast that even the press wire services could no longer keep track of it, although they certainly played it up as the hottest domestic news of the day. The actions dealt with a few things: compulsory ROTC, peace, race relations, civil liberties, capital punishment—all, in the final analysis, moral issues. In no case were they concerned with politics in the ordinary sense of the word.

Here the ROTC marched out to troop the colors and found a line of students sitting down across the parade ground. In another school, a protest march paraded around and through and between the ranks of the marching ROTC, apparently to everybody's amusement. In other schools, the faculty and even the administration and, in one place, the governor joined in protest rallies against ROTC. There were so many peace and disarmament meetings and marches it is impossible to form a clear picture—they seem to have taken place everywhere and, for the first time, to have brought out large numbers. Off-campus, as it were, the lonely pacifists who had been sitting out the civil-defense propaganda stunt in New York, called their annual "sit out" and were dumbfounded at the turn-out. For the first time, too, the court and even the police weakened. Few were arrested.

The Chessman execution provoked demonstrations, meetings, telegrams, on campuses all over the country. In Northern California, the "mass base" of all forms of protest was among the students and the younger teachers. They provided the cadre, circulated petitions, sent wires, interviewed the Governor, and kept up a continuous vigil at the gates of San Quentin. All this activity was unquestionably spontaneous. At no time did the ACLU or the regular anti-capital-punishment organizations initiate, or even take part in, any mass action, whatever else they may have done. Chessman, of course, had a tremendous appeal to youth; he was young, he was an intellectual, even an artist of sorts; before his arrest he had been the kind of person they could recognize, if not approve of, among themselves. He was not very different from the hero of *On the Road*, who happened to be locked up in San Quentin along with him. As his life drew to a close, he showed a beautiful magnanimity in all he did or said. On all the campuses of the country—of the world, for that matter—he seemed an almost typical example of the alienated and outraged youthful "delinquent" of the post-World War II era—the product of a delinquent society. To the young who refused to be demoralized by society, it appeared that that society was killing him only to sweep its own guilt under the rug. I think almost everyone (Chessman's supporters included) over thirty-five, seriously underestimates the psychological effect of the Chessman case on the young.

At all points, the brutal reactionary tendencies in American life were being challenged, not on a political basis, Left versus Right, but because of their patent dishonesty and moral violence. The most spectacular challenge was the riot at the hearing of the Un-American Activities Committee in San Francisco. There is no question but that this was a completely spontaneous demonstration. The idea that Communist agitators provoked it is ludicrous. True, all that were left of the local Bolsheviks turned out, some thirty of them—Stalinists and the two groups of Trotskyites. Even the "youth leader" who, twenty-eight years before, at the age of thirty, had been assigned to lead the Y.C.L., showed up and roared and stomped incoherently, and provided comic relief. Certainly no one took him seriously. There was one aspect about the whole thing that was not spontaneous. That was the work of the committee. They planned it that way. Over the protests and warnings of the city administration, they deliberately framed up a riot. When the riot came, it was the cops who lost their nerve and rioted, if rioting means uncontrolled mob violence. The kids sat on the floor with their hands in their pockets and sang, "We shall not be moved."

Spectacular as it was, there are actions more important than the San Francisco riot. Here and there about the country, lonely, single individuals have popped up out of nowhere and struck their blows. It is almost impossible to get information about draft resisters, nonregistrants, conscientious objectors, but here and there one pops up in the local press or, more likely, in the student press.

Even more important are the individual actions of high school students whom only a hopeless paranoiac could believe anybody had organized. A sixteen-year-old boy, in Queens, and then three in the Bronx, refused to sign loyalty oaths to get their diplomas. As kudos are distributed in a New York suburban high school, a boy gets up and rejects an award from the American Legion. Everybody is horrified at his bad manners. A couple of days later two of his prizes are offered to the two runners-up, who reject them in turn. This is spontaneous direct action if ever there was. And the important thing about it is that in all these cases, these high school kids have made it clear that they do not object to either loyalty oaths or the American Legion because they are "reactionary," but because they are morally contemptible.

The Negro faculties and presidents of the Jim Crow colleges who not only opposed the sit-ins, but expelled dozens of the sit-inners, now found themselves faced with deserted campuses. They were overtaken by a tremendous groundswell of approval of their youngsters' actions from Negro parents, and were dumbfounded by the sympathy shown by a broad strata of the [8/9] white South. One by one they swung around, until Uncle Toms who had expelled students taking part in sit-ins during their Easter vacations in other states, went on public record as saying, "If your son or daughter telephones you and says he or she has been arrested in a sit-in, get down on your knees and thank God."

Not only did the New Revolt of Youth become the hottest domestic copy in years, but it reached the ears of all the retired and semi-retired and comfortably fixed piecard artists of every lost and every long-since-won cause of the labor and radical movements. Everybody shouted, "Myself when young!" and pitched in with application blanks. The AFL-CIO sent out a well-known leader of the Esperanto movement who reported that the kids were muddled and confused and little interested in the trade-union movement which they, mistakenly in his opinion, thought of as morally compromised. YPSL chapters of the Thomasite Socialists rose from the graves of twenty years. Youth experts with theories about what their grandchildren were talking about went on cross-country tours. "Dissent" had a subscription drive. The Trotskyites came up with programs. Everybody got in the act—except, curiously, the Communists. As a matter of fact, back in a dusty office in New York, they were grimly deadlocked in their fast factional fight. Although the movement was a spontaneous outburst of direct non-violent action, it didn't quite please the libertarians and pacifists. They went about straightening everybody out, and *Liberation* came out with an article defining the correct Line and pointing out the errors of the ideologically immature.

As the kids go back to school this fall, this is going to be the greatest danger they will face—all these eager helpers from the other side of the age barrier, all these cooks, each with a time-tested recipe for the broth. All over the world this kind of ferment is stewing on college campuses. In Korea and Japan and Turkey the students have marched and brought down governments and humbled the President of the greatest power in history. So far the movement is still formless, a world-wide upheaval of disgust. Even in Japan, the Zengakuren, which does have a sort of ideology—the Left communism against which Lenin wrote his famous pamphlet—has only been able to act as a cheer leader. It has failed to impose its leadership, its organization, or its principles on the still chaotic upsurge. In France, the official Neo-Gandhian Movement, in alliance with certain sections of the Catholic Left, does seem to have given some sort of shape and leadership. I am inclined to think that this is due to the almost total ignorance of French youth of this generation—they had to go to the official sources for information and guidance, they just didn't have enough, themselves, to get started.

Is this in fact a "political" upsurge? It isn't now—it is a great moral rejection, a kind of mass vomit. Everybody in the world knows that we are on the verge of extinction and nobody does anything about it. The kids are fed up. The great problems of the world today are immediate world-wide peace, immediate race equality, and immediate massive assistance to the former colonial peoples. All of them could be started toward solution by a few decisive acts of moral courage amongst the boys at the top of the heap. Instead, the leaders of the two ruling nations abuse each other like little boys caught out behind the barn. Their apologists stage elaborate military and ideological defenses of Marxian socialism and laissez-faire capitalism, neither of which has ever existed on the earth or ever will exist. While the Zengakuren howls in the streets, Khrushchev delivers a speech on the anniversary of Lenin's "Leftism, on Infantile Disorder" and uses it to attack—Mao! Meanwhile a boy gets up in a New York surburban school and contemptuously hands back his "patriotic" prize. He is fed up. [9]

KINGSLEY WIDMER

—•—•—

The Diogenes Style

LET US START with a literary gesture that marks the perennial attitude of revolt: "I know thy works, that thou are neither cold nor hot; I would thou wert cold or hot. So then because thou are lukewarm, and neither cold nor hot, I will spew thee out of my mouth."[1] This fragment out of Revelation sets the tone of demand and scorn. While much of life and literature necessarily moves in the realms of the tepid, not the rebellious. If one were to do a systematic history of literary rebels, I suppose some time should be spent on pieces from that old anthology, including those of the first identified literary rebels in the Western traditions—Jeremiah and a few of the other prophets. For our purposes, the most modern of the lot, Jonah, might be to the point because he foreshadows the cosmopolitan wanderers in his comic self-consciousness about being a rebel. More generally, it would be hard to over-value for the rebel tradition the significance of the Judaic prophetic mode, including its condemnation of the ways of power, its exaltation of love and compassion as struggle, its expansive metaphoric forms, and its violent manners of lamentation. (Certainly the voices from the wilderness have had their rebellious place in America, not least because the Protestant evangelical movements transmitted rather more of the prophetic fervor than their parochial values could contain.) Modern literary rebels still refract some of the Old Testament rage and repetition—often the first signs of the rebel posture.[2] But much of the Old Testa-

Kingsley Widmer, "The Diogenes Style," *The Literary Rebel* (Carbondale and Edwardsville, Ill.: Southern Illinois University Press, 1965), pp. 3–12.

[1] My most immediate source for the passage is Dostoevsky; it was a favorite of his (it appears twice in *The Possessed*).

[2] For example, see the traditional stridencies of Allen Ginsberg (*Howl* and *Kaddish*). While I am indebted to some of the literature on the Old Testament prophets, the summary, and probably impertinent, nature of my comments suggests not citing any scholar.

ment prophetic mode of revolt does lack modern relevance. Few moderns, rebels included, have the prophets' faith in an ultimately just cosmos, in the sense of [3/4] personal dialogue with the Divine, or in the engagement to a special historical mission with a peculiar people. There may, of course, come a day when we will find a unique pertinence to the apocalyptic, rather than the moral, passion of the Judeo-Christian prophecies.

The relevance of the Biblical rebel, even in a post-Christian culture, might simply be assumed. Not so, I suspect, with another important and ancient tradition of the rebel voice. The Cynics of the Greco-Roman world, represented by Diogenes of Sinope and his successors, show major parallels with modern literary rebels which may illuminate some of the peculiarities and purposes of even the most recent literature.[3] Though the Cynic does not reveal certain of the self-conscious and syncretistic modern gestures, he does suggest the archetypal pattern of our literary rebels. One obvious reason for his relevance to these times is that, in contrast to many of the Jewish and Christian prophets, the Cynic was the cosmopolitan individualist in a mixed and sophisticated culture and in urbanized and imperial societies. The followers of Diogenes, then and now, may be the sour fruit in an over-ripe time, announcing that rottenness is all. The Cynic program announced most notably a philosophy of failure which also provided a devastating commentary on the fatuous successes of ages of counterfeit. Such rebels are not only disaffiliated from their society and culture but also unaffiliated with any overwhelming religious or revolutionary vision which would create a new society and culture. Thus, the most essential rebel style and attitude, I shall maintain, is just that which reveals rebellion as its central and sustained commitment. Beyond rebellion lies something else, not least the conditions which necessarily produce a new call to rebellion.

While there is considerable variation, historical and individual, in the commitment to rebellion, nonetheless, some generic patterns remain. When, for example, we read the commentaries on Diogenes of Sinope and his followers in Greek and Roman writings, and then read

[3] After previously writing a lengthy discussion of the Beats as analogous to the Cynics—"The Literary Rebel," *Centennial Rev.*, VI (Spring, 1962)—I searched through many books and articles for what then seemed the obvious comparison. The only one I found was by Lewis S. Feur, "Youth in the '60's," *New Leader*, XLIV (March 6, 1961), 18–22. While he notes the basic similarity, he also follows the stock contempt of the liberal ideologue and the usual charges of lack of productivity, political program, normal ambitions, etc.—points I try to answer below.

commentaries on contemporary American literary rebels, the arguments seem almost paraphrases of each other.[4] Take the basic image of the literary rebel that was somewhat misleadingly popularized in the 1950's under the rubrics of an American coterie, the Beat Generation or Beat [4/5] Movement—now the almost world-wide figure of the Beatnik. It shows a rather aging youth, usually with long hair and a beard, in the uniform of the disinherited, obviously contemptuous of cleanliness and decorum. While the beggar's cloak and wallet of the Cynic have been replaced, as signs of office, by jeans and paperback book, the rest of the lineaments, and the essential gestures, remain much the same. In prodigal appearance, in casual domesticity, and in outraging taste, both Cynic and Beat seem similar in the ways in which they rebelliously affront the pretensions of the society at large to "gracious living." So, too, with the language of Cynic and Beat which, in and out of literature, fuses the vulgar and the intellectual in a striking mélange of vivid colloquialisms and highbrow abstractions that persistently violates formality and geniality. Certainly such speech has intrinsic functions, beyond modishness and group identification. For instance, the yoking of terms of obscenity with those of salvation—a Beat stylization which is also one of the most ancient forms of blasphemy—seems part of a demand that we perceive the incongruities in our ordering of the world. "Forbidden" language, used more or less seriously, serves not

[4] The general characteristics of the Beat style seem to be public information. For examples, bibliographies and selected commentaries see the various anthologies: *The Beat Generation and the Angry Young Men,* ed. G. Feldman and M. Gartenberg (New York, 1959); *The Beats,* ed. Seymour Krim (New York, 1960); *A Casebook on the Beat,* ed. Thomas Parkinson (New York, 1961); *Marginal Manners,* ed. F. J. Hoffman (Evanston, 1962). In later sections, but not here, I discuss several writers labeled Beat. For the material on Diogenes and the Cynics I have drawn on the standard sources in translation: *Diogenes Laertius,* trans. R. D. Hicks (2 vols.; London, 1925); *Dio Chrysostom,* trans. J. W. Cahoon (5 vols.; London, 1932); *The Works of the Emperor Julian,* Vol. II, trans. W. C. Wright; *Epictetus,* trans. W. A. Oldfather (2 vols.; London, 1932). See also Farrand Sayre, *The Greek Cynics* (Baltimore, 1948—a considerable improvement over the earlier edition). The half-dozen histories of philosophy that I have consulted have not been very helpful on the aspects of Cynicism that concern us here. See, for example W. Windelband, *A History of Philosophy,* Vol. I (New York, 1958), 86 ff. Neither are the standard reference works helpful; see, for example, Robert Eisler, "Cynics," in the *Encyclopedia of the Social Sciences* who provides a quasi-Marxist polemic. By far the most useful scholarly study for our purposes is Donald R. Dudley, *A History of Cynicism* (London, 1937), who astutely gives much of the essential information. My interpretations, of course, go beyond his suggestions.

only to shock but to re-emphasize natural functions and exalt "common" awareness. Done with skill, curses can provide defiant prayers, obscenity a poetry of outrage. Indeed, a literary rebel whose language does not achieve some such sort of violation in itself is neither very poetic nor very rebellious.

Let us characterize further the archetypal rebel—the shape common to many Cynics, Beats, and others—with particular attention to the Cynics not as an historical phenomena but as a style of defiance. Many of the Diogenes anecdotes, such as that of his carrying a lamp in the daylight because he was looking for a real or honest man, achieved near universal recognition. In being a tragic comment on mankind, yet given a witty twist and presented with burlesque dramatization, it has the distinctive rebel quality. The same style of didactic verve appeared in Diogenes' dramatic emphasis upon perversely free choice in which he matched his metaphors with direct actions. The reader of "existentialist" literature will be struck by the pertinence of the Cynic's insistence that he was a criminal, a debaser of the official coinage (including the [5/6] currency of conventional standards), a defender of moral violations such as incest (which were never examined), and an exalter of his role as both actual and internal exile. In his quest for authenticity, Diogenes made what a cultivated society considered both buffoonish and felonious gestures, being intentionally crude and outspoken. The Cynics were noted for their obscenity, in act as well as word, and they reportedly were willing to "be natural" about fornicating and defecating, anywhere. Their notorious "shamelessness" was both part of their lesson and part of a way of life. Many of their self-conscious violations of commercial, bureaucratic and upperclass morals and manners suggest the Cynics as the first to intentionally *épater le bourgeois*. Put in this perspective, we may see such favorite rebel defiance as neither bohemian high-spirits nor part of nineteenth-century class conflict but as a more universal effort to dramatically mock complacent and restricted awareness.

Diogenes had a radical dialectic for every part of his personal life. He went about unkempt, dressed in the uniform of a beggar, slept almost anywhere, scornfully took what food came to hand, refused to work, condemned anxious luxuries but not direct pleasures, and was committed to the simplest sort of life. Even his famed bad manners were as much principle as temperament. "Other dogs bite their enemies, I bite my friends—for their salvation." He was an anarchist when it came to political authorities, a libertarian when it came to social customs, and a cosmopolitan when it came to loyalties ("The only true country is that which is as wide as the universe"). His

dog's life, physically mean and rough, intellectually tough and biting, was an outrageous dramatization of radical awareness. Plato reportedly called Diogenes a "Socrates gone mad." But Plato was an
authoritarian who refused to recognize tragic absurdity, either by allowing the poets in his republic or in understanding the witty buf-
foonery of a Diogenes. The Cynic, a better judge than the rational
idealist of some parts of human nature, said, "Most men are so
nearly mad that a finger's breadth would make the difference."

Diogenes would seem plausibly credited with certain literary traditions—mordant satire of things as they are and a popular dialectic
of moral discontent. But the [6/7] dialectical extremity that he
lived may be more important, for he was one of the first to drama-
tize some rather important values: equality, even with rulers and
women; freedom, even from the gods and the economic system;
self-sufficiency, even to living a dog's life and masturbating freely;
and directness, even in public speech and philosophy. Rather
more than Thoreau—one of his descendants—and in the city, he attempted to embody individualistic autarchy and immediacy. His
"simplicity" took the form of witty denials of superstitutions, conventions, authorities and ideologies. Naturally, part of Diogenes' significance is confined to the peculiar conditions of his time. As a rebel
against Athenian education (a usual dissident focus), he battled
over the Greek definitions in the various schools of "virtue," "nature," "reason," and so on.[5] The antiquarian interest in Cynicism's
role as "hard primitivism" or as a sort of left-wing Stoicism need not
concern us here. The historical Cynics also display a naïveté about
"rational" argument and "virtue" which can be related to the Soph-
ists and Socrates but which strikes us as quaint and would certainly be antipathetic to most modern rebels who find their "reasons"
in the irrational in an over-rationalized world. Similarly, Diogenes'
literal insistence on doing all "according to nature" hardly appears
so clear anymore since various romanticisms and sciences have inevitably complicated our responses, and faith, in the natural orders.

Of more permanent importance are other curious qualities of the
Cynics. For instance, they were harsh realists, yet also some of the
earliest "utopians" with an exotic dream vision of a world where simplicity and directness reigned: the Island of Para—perhaps the secu-
larization of sacred myths, later desecularized by less rigorous
prophets. Then, too, the Cynics have a special claim on our attention

[5] See A. O. Lovejoy and George Boas, *Primitivism and Related Ideas in
Antiquity* (Baltimore, 1935). My comments throughout intentionally de-
emphasize historical sources and significances of the literary rebels, which is
not to deny them but to focus on the permanent qualities of rebellion.

in being one of the few groups of teachers (really *un*teaching in the Socratic manner) not subsidized by state, church, commerce or their own hierarchy, and also one of the few groups of teachers not submissive to those powers.

But more important to the modern view is the clear extremity of the Cynics' rebel role. For Diogenes, civilization was to be corrected solely by the individual (that ruled out organizations and politics), in active and iconoclastic [7/8] confrontation (that ruled out snobs and mystics), in the streets and going institutions (that ruled out esoterics and revolutionaries), and with intense scorn (that ruled out the stupid and bland). We may suppose that the only reason Diogenes was not against bureaucratic authority, mass genteel education-entertainment, the Bomb, etc., was that our technological nihilisms had not yet been invented. Since Diogenes' literary works, apparently outrageous dialogues and burlesque tragedies, have not survived we can see that his greatest creation was a nullifidian style. This philosophical tramp (he usually went south in the winter) and wise buffoon (there must have been some natural appropriateness for all the wise-cracks fathered on him), set standards for the perennial rebel's defiance of how most men believe and live.

The many anecdotes told of Diogenes and Alexander—no doubt apocryphal but quite in accord with the Cynic role—insist on independence and equality. When the King of Kings reputedly stood in front of Diogenes and asked what favor he could grant, and was told to quit blocking the sunlight, or when the ruler of the world flatteringly compared himself to Diogenes, and Diogenes sardonically confirmed the comparison, we see the power of negative thinking. Another series of anecdotes linked to Diogenes provide a mordant last will and testament—a form of tragic wit drawn upon by many later rebels, such as Villon and Corbière, who also used death as the harsh test of conventional values. Diogenes' reputed last wishes have his usual wayward wisdom. One report is that he asked, in a world deeply responsive to Antigone's funereal scrupulousness, to be cast in a ditch and thus do the beasts some good. So much for death, and your pieties, foolish Athenians! Another report has it that he perversely asked to be buried face down. Dialectical to the end, he explained that the world of his time would soon be turned upside-down, putting him the right way up. While few historians will disagree with his prophecy, we should also note a more basic point: the true rebel may be recognized by his commitment to a sardonically apocalyptic vision. The end of a world—and it is always the end of a world for mortal man—justifies the scorn and negation, and the resulting strategies of simplification and intense living.

Most of the direct history of the Cynics, extending from [8/9] Diogenes, which appears to continue for at least half a dozen centuries, mocks the conventional successes and anxieties of a period marked by fatuous imperial styles and the pervasive sense of meaninglessness. The Cynics' answer was to demonstrate that life could be based on very little, or on a lively nothingness. Thus worldly failure was shown as a choice and a victory—the greatest blasphemy to those in power—and an alternative to the dubious "necessities" and compulsions. But there is more to this style of rebellion. The admirably humane Crates, Diogenes' follower, appears to have been a secular saint—the first of the modern saints without a god that we know of. He gave up his wealth and lived as a simple and compassionate wiseman and teacher. He also mocked the official pedagogy, wrote parodies of accepted morality, and maintained the tradition of contempt for inequality and conventional restrictions. Most delightful of all, Crates made one of the few passionate and equal marriages we hear of in antiquity. Hipparchia, an attractive girl from a "good family," pursued outcast Crates. He honorably tried to dissuade her, finally presenting himself stripped naked in warning that he would provide nothing but a life of honest beggary. Miraculous woman, she accepted, and thus became the first lady philosopher. Their daughter, as a logical result, is one of the first reported sexually emancipated women. Saintly Cynics father pleasure as well as freedom. And much else, for even with the sketchy known history of the Cynics there is a provocative roll-call: Bion, the preaching tramp with a flair for metaphor and arrogance; Menippus, apparently the creator of a major form of satire; Dio Chrysostom, one of the many examples of the wandering Cynic critics of the Roman emperors; Oenomaus, the polemical atheist; and many others.[6] They testify to the greatest creation of Diogenes: the secular prophet. Not Plato in his coterie, not Aristotle in his academy, not the poets at the games and courts, certainly not the priests and magicians, but the Cynic wandering and arguing in the streets is the true forerunner and antitype of the individualistic "outsider" literary intellectual.

In the similar denunciations applied to such rebels in both classical and contemporary writings they are attacked for being outside civilization. Actually, they are right at the [9/10] heart of it, not only in creating styles of life and intellectual confrontations but literally. Though unpatriotic, except perhaps to the purlieus of the cultural capitals where most often found, they take ideas with both passion and wit. Loafers, culture-bums, hangers-on, parasites, immoralists?

---

[6] The main source here is Dudley, *op. cit.* Prof. Marvin Singleton brought to my attention the importance of Crates' wife and daughter.

Though more or less cultured, rebels do not primarily function as performers or merchants of the arts, institutional intellectuals, or even in most ordinary senses as producers of art and edification. The rebel refuses subordination to social function in assertion of the freely human. He remains "unemployed"—even when working—or as close to it as he can manage for both defiance and self-definition. As a member of the discontented or true leisure class he spends time around about the arts, but many rebels avow that their interest in the arts is secondary to ways of life and states of feeling. That only few rebels are artistic should have nothing of accusation about it, unless one is a pietist to a petty psuedo-religion of art. Why should the rebel produce much art or edification? His vocation is denial and defiance.

The rebel, of course, busies himself with the *mystique* of rebellion, rather more than with the muses. Outside organizational conventions and the usual rationalized self-interests, he justifies himself with his nagging and arrogant "why not?" Main principles, from Cynics to Beats, seem to be claims for individuality, voluntary poverty, simplicity, spontaneous feeling, ingenuous communication, intense sense experience, and a general heightening of immediate life. These qualities the rebel supports with considerable invective against official society. The mark-of-the-kind may be that when asked for his identity, the rebel most often defines himself by attacking the nonidentity of the prevailing others.

The official society, in turn, often displays an irritated fascination with the rebel, taking much righteous delight in what it calls his barbarism, crudity, immaturity, sickness, immorality and perversity. Most of our knowledge of the Cynics (as with Christian heretics and later rebels, through the Beats) comes from the perplexed or denouncing reports by the unrebellious. These public apologists insistently attack—perhaps with the morality of envy—the rebel's economic and sexual libertarianism. It is curious also that while official teachers scorn the rebels for their lack of significant productivity and for their corrupting [10/11] effects, the accusers as a group are most open to those very charges. If there were no rebels, public apologists would have to invent them.

At a common-sense level, the attacks on rebels for economic parasitism and lack of social productivity seem the most irrelevant. Even a meager economy could tolerate the simple needs of a rather considerable number of bearded malcontents. Our ornate modern Western societies could, and do, comfortably support vast numbers of people who fit no simple rational needs for goods and services. The hostility of official rhetoricians (and police, employers, welfare services, etc.) to rebels, of course, has little to do with economics or social utility. Similarly, in societies with varied or changing erotic ways, the rebel's views—usually uncoercive demands for sexual directness—do not require more than modest tolerance. Since rebels, in obvious fact as well as almost by definition, are small in number, why the insistent fuss about their ways in such things as work and sex? Could it be that which hardly any of the contemners of rebels grant: much of the society despises its meaningless labors and burns against its arbitrary restrictions?

Many of the other charges against rebels, from Cynics to Beats, seem equally curious. For example, the recurrent disgust with the rebel making an exhibition of his failure and maladjustment must be based on the requirement that one be miserable only in standard ways. The argument that the rebel denies "civilized life" often rests on some weird definitions of "civilized" which give primacy to impersonal powers, social anxiety, individual repression, warfare, and similar sorts of "progress." The awesome fear that rebels, unless put down, will encourage vast numbers to throw off work and orderly life is more a condemnation of the society than of the rebels. For real defiance of conventions and their conveniences is usually too arduous for all but a few strong souls, and if vast numbers really seem ready to imitate the rebel mode the social order is about to flip-flop anyway. Surely a surplus of bearded bad poets is more desirable than a surplus of clean-shaven bad policemen, even to pietists of the conventional authorities. The "universalist fallacy"—the argument that goes by way of "What if everyone were a rebel?"—is usually sheer anxiety or fraud.

Some anti-rebel arguments have considerable merit. [11/12] When rhetoricians of things-as-they-are, for example, attack rebels for being tediously noisy little failures who are not really very rebellious, the contemners are using, and thus justifying, real standards of rebelliousness—and the more candid will learn from them. And the quite true charge that the rebel style attracts a number of the pathetic, the incompetent, the pathological and the fraudulent, provides an admirable discriminatory emphasis even more applicable to the commercial and political and academic styles of life. Equally useful is the persistent anti-rebel contention that the latest manifestation of defiance repeats the same old stuff, not really new or original. Perhaps so, for the first modern literary rebels, the Cynics, may have been an essential part of the first full civilization in our Western traditions, and such rebellion thus remains a positive continuity of civilized tradition. Literary wildmen and arch-bohemians hold as permanent a part in our heritage of response and understanding as the supposedly more honorific roles of humanistic and scientific and political hero types. Though often discussed as mere bellwethers of artistic faddishness, the gropings of the young, and moral and political discontent, the significance of the rebels seems rather greater than the topical issues they raise in the public minded. The rebel's style and distinctive identity remains, and becomes its own justification, an existential choice for meeting the comic incongruities and tragic absurdities.... [12]

JOHN P. SISK

Beatniks and Tradition

The beat generation writers have had a very good press if one uses as a standard the extent to which public curiosity has been focused on them, but they have had an indifferent to poor press if the function of a good press is to clarify. The bulk of what has been written about them has taken their delinquent conduct and assertions of disengagement at face value, with the result that they are condemned as lacking any serious connection with American culture and as being as much outside society as they themselves contend they are.

This is a convenient position to take but not a very useful one, even if the whole truth about them were their adolescent alienation from society. Beat literature may turn out to be an ephemeral oddity that fifty years from now exists only for desperate Ph.D. candidates, or it may prove to have been the nighttown madness out of which one or two authentic writers were born, but that is another matter. In the meantime, the important and easily-overlooked fact is that it is in the American grain, and that however we react to it we are reacting to part of ourselves.

The Beat generation writers are in what may be called the subversive tradition in American literature—"subversive" because writers in this tradition so often appear as destructive forces to the middle class from which they come. To the writers of the subversive tradition organized society tends to be the Enemy. The Enemy is corrupt; hamstrung, by convention; hypocritical, smug, selfish, superficial; ruled by fear, cliché and sentimentality; suspicious of the individual and creative originality; afraid to let itself go, to trust what Keats calls the holiness of the heart's affections; passionately addicted to that great American document, the dollar bill. Obviously, the Enemy does not always recognize itself in this description.

The seeds of this tradition arrived with the first settlers and

John P. Sisk, "Beatniks and Tradition," *Commonweal*, LXX (17 April 1959), 74–77.

quickly flowered in such people as Thomas Morton, Roger Williams and Anne Hutchinson, that antinomian daughter of the inner light who today might be quite at home in a San Francisco pad. But the shape of this tradition is clearer for us if we begin [74/75] with Emerson and Thoreau and the reformist turmoil of the 1840's, when, as Emerson reported to Carlyle, "Not a reading man but has a draft of a new community in his pocket." If the Beats are "way out" the transcendentalists were there ahead of them, less licentiously but not less flamboyantly.

Thoreau (an important figure for the Beats) is the ideal subversive. He not only writes but acts out in hyperbolic terms his criticism of the Enemy's corruption; he both states and is civil disobedience. Then there is Hawthorne, a disputed figure, admittedly, but even by D. H. Lawrence's reading a subversive in disguise; Melville, ambiguous but more certainly a subversive; Whitman, the spiritual father who all but overwhelms Allen Ginsberg, and the Twain of *The Adventures of Huckleberry Finn*, the fatherhood of Kerouac's *On the Road*. The Enemy's reaction to Twain's masterpiece, long ago expressed in the *Boston Transcript*, has a familiar ring today: the Public Library committee decided to exclude the book because it was "rough, coarse and inelegant, dealing with a series of experiences not elevating . . . being more suited to the slums than to intelligent, respectable people."

But it is in our own century that the subversive tradition has proliferated. For nearly two generations now the American writer has been distinguished by his dissatisfaction with the shape and aims of society. This is apparent enough in London, Dreiser, Anderson, O'Neill, Odets, Eliot, Wolfe, Dos Passos, Fitzgerald, Nathan and Mencken, many of whom society has already admitted into the family library. The dissatisfaction—or subversiveness—is even more marked, because in contexts more immediate to us, in writers like Hemingway, Steinbeck, Miller, West, Mailer, Salinger, Wright, Algren, Vidal, Bowles and Saroyan. At present, all writers of value, says Kenneth Rexroth in an apologia for the Beat generation writers, agree on the "diagnosis of an absolute corruption." The statement is defensible only if we allow Mr. Rexroth to pick the valued writers, but at least it puts the emphasis where it belongs.

The fact is that the writer is by nature the critic of the society of "intelligent and respectable people." He [75/76] and that society are locked in a dialectic. The dialectic sometimes proceeds on moderate terms, particularly when there is no question of the writer's important position within society or when he speaks for a socially valued elite. But in America, and especially in the twentieth century, this dialectic has been carried on in hyperbolic terms: the extreme positions that society takes have been countered by the writer's extreme positions.

Thus Dreiser's remorseless realism counters the daydream of an acquisitive paradise; Mencken's irreverent mockery counters the stultification that comes from worshipping false gods; Wolfe's restless, romantic search for the meaning of America counters the naive and dangerous clarity with which a business society tries to define America; Hemingway's tight-lipped heroics counter the attempt to end heroism by organization; Salinger's and Capote's sentimental sympathy for the misfit and the outcast counters the callousness that goes with conformity and respectability; e. e. cummings' anarchism counters the growing conviction (to reverse Emerson's phrase) of the insufficiency of the private man; and Miller's and Kerouac's irrationalism counters the positivism of a society huddled desperately around its nuclear experts.

To recognize this is not necessarily to accept as infallible the diagnosis of society's evils expressed or implied in these writers. Nor is it to demand of them, as a criterion of value, a workable social program, which, if you could find it at all, might only reflect a political, economic and social virginity. The point is that such direction and order as society has depends upon all the dialectic tensions within it, and so far as this argument between the writer and society is concerned the important thing is neither position taken separately but the two together. Each is with respect to the other a control (though by no means a Hegelian guarantee) against potentially destructive excesses.

Thus, for instance, the corruption of society drove Twain to attack it, but his awareness of society's opposition (which was also a demand) freed him from the fear of a nihilistic strain in his own personality which could have been destructive to his artistic effort. One can even say (*contra* Van Wyck Brooks) that the pressure of society forced Twain to measure it by its own professed Christian standards more severely than he would otherwise have been inclined to, which was exactly what his book and society needed. Completely liberated from the tension of this conflict between Twain and society, *Huck Finn* would have little value, morally, socially or artistically.

The trouble is that in proportion as the terms of this dialectic have become extreme, the word "society" in literary circles has come to mean that part of society that is insensitive or hostile to the values of the writer; and the writer, taking his synecdoche literally, has often imagined himself as a thorough-going outsider. This throws an emphasis on the heroic adventure of writing and makes it possible for beginners and second-stringers, who do not pay enough attention to their proper business, to do a good deal of swaggering and posing as they equate literature with opposition to orthodoxy. It also makes it possible to forget the point Twain's great story drama- tizes: that the important moral and social function of writers in the subversive tradition has been to counter the corruption of the whole of which they are articulate parts. That, like Twain and Fitzgerald, they have so often found the corruption to be within themselves only gives their statement of it authenticity and drama.

All of this is true of the Beat generation writers. No matter how completely they try to cut themselves off, they remain a critically engaged part of society, though the directness and value of their en- gagement may be less than that of many of their subversive prede- cessors. One cannot read Holmes, Kerouac, Corso, Ferlinghetti or Ginsberg without realizing that their interest, even to themselves, is always in relation to the society that contains them. They depend upon the city, the physical symbol of society, to exacerbate in them the pearl of beatness.

The inarticulate hipster who feels that a violent attachment to the values of society is square dramatizes by the attitudes he assumes a rebuke of society. But the articulate hipster with his fundamental as- sumption of society's corruption is even more plainly engaged. Even stylistically he depends upon the literature of the square world, the rhythms and patterns of which he cannot get out of his head. Ker- ouac's spontaneous prose depends for its effect upon traditional prose, just as Wordsworth's "language really used by men" de- pended for its effect upon the poetic diction he was trying hard not to write. To recognize this is not necessarily to invalidate Kerouac's prose or Wordsworth's verse, but simply to recognize that in matters of style, as in all other matters, no man is an island.

The Beat writers have an at least functional awareness that they are a part of society that is countered and to an extent controlled by another part. Like Twain they have a kind of subconscious expecta- tion that the rest of society will ultimately keep them from [76/77] destructive excess, even though they may as individuals destroy themselves. On the other hand, society has a similar expectation: that critics of this sort—ideally, granted, more responsible critics than these—will protect it from its excesses. For all the indignation the Beat writers have aroused, I think it must be admitted that the general reading public is remarkably permissive towards them, as it has learned to be towards all writers in the subversive tradition—as if it is a part of a developing national awareness of that tradition's function as the hyper-sensitive, if often quite fantastic, conscience of America. This is indicated in the number of twentieth century writ-

ers now generally accepted as part of the mainstream of American
literature, who when they first appeared seemed shockingly outside
it.

In a pluralist society such as ours there are, of course, all sorts of
tensions: regional, racial, economic, political and religious. The potential for turmoil is tremendous. What stands against it is whatever
we hold in common as Americans, and much of this we are not
aware of, since it is expressed in patterns of conduct that have become habitual. We are very little aware, for instance, of the extent
to which we have protected ourselves by a general, if mainly implicit, agreement not to court turmoil by divisive action. The result
is that the very considerable degree of harmony we live in has as its
base a dangerously negative and apprehensive element, and that a
great deal of the dialectical interchange that is necessary for the
health of society is suppressed.

This fear of dissension helps to explain the dearth of popular satire (why, for instance, T.V. loads up on horse opera and retires Sid
Caesar to the guest-star pool), but it also helps to explain the extreme attitudes of subversive writers like the Beatniks, who are in a
sense forced to bear more than their fair share of the dialectic burden. Society, possibly because of its uneasy conscience, fails to engage itself effectively with such opposition; perhaps it is best to say
that it dares not for fear of coming face to face with its deviation
from the American Dream.

It would follow, I think, that until society releases its normal interplay of criticism the subversive tradition in literature will continue to take up (will be even forced by society to take up) the extreme positions of such works as Miller's *The Air Conditioned
Nightmare*, West's *Miss Lonelyhearts*, Algren's *A Walk on the Wild
Side* or Salinger's *The Catcher in the Rye*. The solution for society is
not to take subversive writers to its bosom, hoping that they will settle down to contented sequels of *Executive Suite*. The solution is to
engage seriously with them in the act of criticism.

Such an engagement would assume that the Beat writers merit no
preferred treatment simply because of their tradition-sanctioned
subversiveness; and it would assume that they must prove themselves as writers and not expect to get by on novelty, shock-effect or
sublime intentions. As a matter of fact, Beat writing suffers as literature because of its unhappy conviction that it is impossible to
"make," in the traditional artist's sense, without corrupting. Hence
the Beat writers' violent and surrealist dislike of the New Critics and
the university poets. The poet is defined as prophet or visionary; he
is a seer more than a maker; the sign of his authentic vision is the

quality of unchecked outpour, of rhapsodic, jazz-inspired improvisation in his utterance. He is the poet as inspired madman. Hence the importance of Kerouac's hero, Dean Moriarty, whose chaotic, rhapsodic life is itself a Beat poem.

The appeal of the Beat writers is, however, bound up with their visionary, rhapsodic concept of the poet. In their enthusiastic acceptance of the visionary and spiritual element in life, in their indiscriminate assertion that all is holy—that we are all, as Kerouac says, angels even if we do not know it, in their passionate concern with the individual and their rejection of all that inhibits his free development, in their unqualified commitment to experience, they underline traditionally sacred American patterns of thought and action.

But at the same time, by isolating and dramatizing to the hilt these patterns, they can force us to reexamine some familiar subversive themes at a moment in our history when we most need to. We are at a point when we can least afford to be uncertain about the role of intellect, about the right relation of the individual to society, about the nature of man, about the extent of our involvement with all men everywhere. Ginsberg's "Howl" is a very American poem and Kerouac's *On the Road* is a very American novel. By this I do not mean that they are for that reason either good or bad as literature, but simply that they give us back as in a distorting mirror the anarchism and antinomianism, the dream of utopian freedom and innocence to be found in a commitment to instinct and feeling, that have always been elements in American culture; and which, if they are not consciously confronted and controlled, will, as they have often in the past, muddle our efforts to live effectively as a society in a complex world.

Dean Moriarty may strike one as the silliest holy fool in all literature. Nevertheless, he is a recognizable caricature of an image in the American heart as he rushes madly about the country, shirking all social obligations, trying passionately to dig everyone and everything, convinced that if he goes fast enough and has enough violent experiences the great ultimate secret will be laid bare to him. Kerouac's subversive service is to hold up that image while we measure ourselves against it. [77]

STOKELY CARMICHAEL and CHARLES V. HAMILTON

———•◆•———

The Concept of Black Power

THE ADOPTION of the concept of Black Power is one of the most legitimate and healthy developments in American politics and race relations in our time. . . . It is a call for black people in this country to unite, to recognize their heritage, to build a sense of community. It is a call for black people to begin to define their own goals, to lead their own organizations and to support those organizations. It is a call to reject the racist institutions and values of this society.

The concept of Black Power rests on a fundamental premise: *Before a group can enter the open society, it must first close ranks.* By this we mean that group solidarity is necessary before a group can operate effectively from a bargaining position of strength in a pluralistic society. Traditionally, each new ethnic group in this society has found the route to social and political viability through the organization of its own institutions with which to represent its needs within the larger society. Studies in voting behavior specifically, [44/45] and political behavior generally, have made it clear that politically the American pot has not melted. Italians vote for Rubino over O'Brien; Irish for Murphy over Goldberg, etc. This phenomenon may seem distasteful to some, but it has been and remains today a central fact of the American political system. . . . The extent to which black Americans can and do "trace their roots" to Africa, to that extent will they be able to be more effective on the political scene. . . . [45/46]

The point is obvious: black people must lead and run their own organizations. Only black people can convey the revolutionary idea— and it is a revolutionary idea—that black people are able to do things

From Stokely Carmichael and Charles V. Hamilton, *Black Power: The Politics of Liberation in America* (New York: Random House, 1967), pp. 44–45, 46, 47–48, 49–53, 55–56.

themselves. Only they can help create in the community an aroused and continuing black consciousness that will provide the basis for political strength. In the past, white allies have often furthered white supremacy without the whites involved realizing it, or even wanting to do so. Black people must come together and do things for themselves. They must achieve self-identity and self-determination in order to have their daily needs met.... [46/47]

Black Power recognizes—it must recognize—the ethnic basis of American politics as well as the power-oriented nature of American politics. Black Power therefore calls for black people to consolidate behind their own, so that they can bargain from a position of strength. But while we endorse the *procedure* of group solidarity and identity for the purpose of attaining certain goals in the body politic, this does not mean that black people should strive for the same kind of rewards (i.e., end results) obtained by the white society. The ultimate values and goals are not domination or exploitation of other groups, but rather an effective share in the total power of the society.

Nevertheless, some observers have labeled those who advocate Black Power as racists; they have said that the call for self-identification and self-determination is "racism in reverse" or "black supremacy." This is a deliberate and absurd lie. There is no analogy—by any stretch of definition or imagination—between the advocates of Black Power and white racists. Racism is not merely exclusion on the basis of race but exclusion for the purpose of subjugating or maintaining subjugation. The goal of the racists is to keep black people on the bottom, arbitrarily and dictatorially, as they have done in this country for over three hundred years. The goal of black self-determination and black self-identity—Black Power—is full participation in the decision-making processes affecting the lives of black people, and recognition of the virtues in themselves as black people. The black people of this country have not lynched whites, bombed their churches, murdered their children and manipulated laws and institutions to maintain oppression. White racists have. Congressional laws, one after the other, have not been necessary to stop black people from oppressing others and denying others the full enjoyment of their rights. White racists have made such laws necessary. The [47/48] goal of Black Power is positive and functional to a free and viable society. No white racist can make this claim.... [48/50]

We have outlined the meaning and goals of Black Power; we have also discussed one major thing which it is not. There are others of greater importance. The advocates of Black Power reject the old slogans and meaningless rhetoric of previous years in the civil rights struggle. The language of yesterday is indeed irrelevant: progress, non-violence, integration, fear of "white backlash," coalition. Let us look at the rhetoric and see why these terms must be set aside or redefined.

One of the tragedies of the struggle against racism is that up to this point there has been no national organization which could speak to the growing militancy of young black people in the urban ghettos and the black-belt South. There has been only a "civil rights" movement, whose tone of voice was adapted to an audience of middle-class whites. It served as a sort of buffer zone between that audience and angry young blacks. It claimed to speak for the needs of a community, but it did not speak in the tone of that community. None of its so-called leaders could go into a rioting community and be listened to. In a sense, the blame must be shared—along with the mass media—by those leaders for what happened in Watts, Harlem, Chicago, Cleveland and other places. Each time the black people in those cities saw Dr. Martin Luther King get slapped they became angry. When they saw little black girls bombed to death *in a church* and civil rights workers ambushed and murdered, they were angrier; and when nothing happened, they were steaming mad. We had nothing to offer that they could see, except to go out and be beaten again. We helped to build their frustration.

We had only the old language of love and suffering. And in most places—that is, from the liberals and middle class—we got back the old language of patience and progress. The civil rights leaders were saying to the country: "Look, you guys are supposed to be nice guys, and we are only going to do what we are supposed to do. Why do you [50/51] beat us up? Why don't you give us what we ask? Why don't you straighten yourselves out?" For the masses of black people, this language resulted in virtually nothing. In fact, their objective day-to-day condition worsened. The unemployment rate among black people increased while that among whites declined. Housing conditions in the black communities deteriorated. Schools in the black ghettos continued to plod along on outmoded techniques, inadequate curricula, and with all too many tired and indifferent teachers. Meanwhile, the President picked up the refrain of "We Shall Overcome" while the Congress passed civil rights law after civil rights law, only to have them effectively nullified by deliberately weak enforcement. "Progress is being made," we were told.

Such language, along with admonitions to remain nonviolent and fear the white backlash, convinced some that that course was the *only* course to follow. It misled some into believing that a black minority could bow its head and get whipped into a meaningful position of power. The very notion is absurd. The white society devised the language, adopted the rules and had the black community narcotized into believing that that language and those rules were, in fact, relevant. The black community was told time and again how *other* immigrants finally won *acceptance:* that is, by following the Protestant Ethic of Work and Achievement. They worked hard; therefore, they achieved. We were not told that it was by building Irish Power, Italian Power, Polish Power or Jewish Power that these groups got themselves togther and operated from positions of strength. We were not told that "the American dream" wasn't designed for black people. That while today, to whites, the dream may *seem* to include black people, it cannot do so by the very nature of this nation's political and economic system, which imposes institutional racism on the black masses if not upon every individual black. A notable comment on that "dream" was made by [51/52] Dr. Percy Julian, the black scientist and director of the Julian Research Institute in Chicago, a man for whom the dream seems to have come true. While not subscribing to "black power" as he understood it, Dr. Julian clearly understood the basis for it: "The false concept of basic Negro inferiority is one of the curses that still lingers. It is a problem created by the white man. Our children just no longer are going to accept the patience we were taught by our generation. We were taught a pretty little lie—excel and the whole world lies open before you. *I obeyed the injunction and found it to be wishful thinking.*" (Authors' italics)*

A key phrase in our buffer-zone days was non-violence. For years it has been thought that black people would not literally fight for their lives. Why this has been so is not entirely clear; neither the larger society nor black people are noted for passivity. The notion apparently stems from the years of marches and demonstration and sit-ins where black people did not strike back and violence always came from white mobs. There are many who still sincerely believe in that approach. From our viewpoint, rampaging white mobs and white night-riders must be made to understand that their days of free head-whipping are over. Black people should and must fight back. Nothing more quickly repels someone bent on destroying you than the unequivocal message: "O.K., fool, make your move, and run the same risk I run—of dying."

When the concept of Black Power is set forth, many people immediately conjure up notions of violence. The country's reaction to the Deacons for Defense of Justice, which originated in Louisiana, is instructive. Here is a group which realized that the "law" and law enforcement agencies would not protect people, so they had to do it themselves. If a nation fails to protect its citizens, then that nation cannot condemn those who take up the task themselves. [52/53] The Deacons and all other blacks who resort to self-defense represent

* *The New York Times* (April 30, 1967), p. 30.

a simple answer to a simple question: what man would not defend his family and home from attack?

But this frightened some white people, because they knew that black people would now fight back. They knew that this was precisely what *they* would have long since done if *they* were subjected to the injustices and oppression heaped on blacks. Those of us who advocate Black Power are quite clear in our own minds that a "nonviolent" approach to civil rights is an approach black people cannot afford and a luxury white people do not deserve. It is crystal clear to us—and it must become so with the white society—*that there can be no social order without social justice.* White people must be made to understand that they must stop messing with black people, or the blacks *will* fight back!

Next, we must deal with the term "integration." According to its advocates, social justice will be accomplished by "integrating the Negro into the mainstream institutions of the society from which he has been traditionally excluded." This concept is based on the assumption that there is nothing of value in the black community and that little of value could be created among black people. The thing to do is siphon off the "acceptable" black people into the surrounding middle-class white community. . . . [53/55]

"Integration" also means that black people must give up their identity, deny their heritage. We recall the conclusion of Killian and Grigg: "At the present time, integration as a solution to the race problem demands that the Negro foreswear his identity as a Negro." The fact is that integration, as traditionally articulated, would abolish the black community. The fact is that what must be abolished is not the black community, but the dependent colonial status that has been inflicted upon it.

The racial and cultural personality of the black community must be preserved and that community must win its freedom while preserving its cultural integrity. Integrity includes a pride—in the sense of self-acceptance, not chauvinism—in being black, in the historical attainments and contributions of black people. No person can be healthy, complete and mature if he must deny a part of himself; this is what "integration" has required thus far. This is the essential difference between integration as it is currently practiced and the concept of Black Power.

The idea of cultural integrity is so obvious that it seems almost simple-minded to spell things out at this length. Yet millions of Americans resist such truths when they are applied to black people. Again, that resistance is a comment on the fundamental racism in the society. Irish Catholics took care of their own first without a lot of apology for doing so, without any dubious language from timid leadership about guarding against "backlash." Everyone [55/56] understood it to be a perfectly legitimate procedure. Of course, there would be "backlash." Organization begets counterorganization, but this was no reason to defer.

The so-called white backlash against black people is something else: the embedded traditions of institutional racism being brought into the open and calling forth overt manifestations of individual racism. In the summer of 1966, when the protest marches into Cicero, Illinois, began, the black people knew they were not allowed to live in Cicero and the white people knew it. When blacks began to demand the right to live in homes in that town, the whites simply reminded them of the status quo. Some people called this "backlash." It was, in fact, racism defending itself. In the black community, this is called "White folks showing their color." It is ludicrous to blame black people for what is simply an overt manifestation of white racism. Dr. Martin Luther King stated clearly that the protest marches were not the cause of the racism but merely exposed a long-term cancerous condition in the society. . . . [56]

2

The Subversive Tradition

ALTHOUGH BENJAMIN FRANKLIN and Allen Ginsberg, the first and last of the writers represented in this section, stand two centuries apart in time and an immeasurable distance apart in their aesthetic, philosophic, and social attitudes, they are both representatives of what John P. Sisk has referred to as "the subversive tradition in American literature." Born and reared in a culture constrained by puritanical conventions stemming from the conviction that morality could indeed be legislated, Franklin was fond of turning his pragmatic eye upon the inconsistencies between the creature that man actually is and the creature that conventions assumed him to be. His anonymously published "Speech of Polly Baker" is clearly subversive in the sense employed by Sisk, since it makes an incisive indictment of a society that "is corrupt; hamstrung by convention; hypocritical, smug, selfish, superficial; ruled by fear, cliché and sentimentality; suspicious of the individual and creative originality; afraid to let itself go, to trust what Keats calls the holiness of the heart's affections. . . ." And the fictional Polly Baker, in her defense before a New England bench, represents the social rebel in the attitude of defiance of the society that has made a pariah of her.

In his own time, and in his other works, Franklin was also a subversive: his attention to the earthly life of man, rather than to his eternal life, challenged the Puritan emphasis that had tenuously prevailed in American life for the century before Franklin emerged as the epitome of the eighteenth century American. Franklin's materialism was in itself a rebellious development marking the rise of a middle class culture and the destruction of the economic and social aristocracy, as well as the theological aristocracy, that had prevailed in America during the seventeenth century. This materialism has long since been viewed as the hallmark of American society, which, again in Sisk's words, is "passionately addicted to that great American document, the dollar bill."

In his left-handed salute to America, Ginsberg indicts the Franklinian heritage of materialism. He notes his economic resources ("two dollars and twentyseven cents"), is repelled by America's technological materialism ("Your machinery is too much for me"), and ironically offers for sale his poems ("I will sell you strophes $2500 apiece $500 down on your old strophe") in the language and terms of American commerce. Thus the rebel of one age may be the one rebelled against in the next; and the particular object or attitude for which a rebel strives may, after it has been accepted as a standard feature of society, be the object of attack by a succeeding generation of rebels.

Despite the changing currents in the stream of American social rebellion, however, the onward drift of the subversive tradition has remained continuous. It has been observed of serious literature in general that one of its principal functions is to jar the complacency of the reader, to challenge him to reconsider his values and those of his society. This is the function that Widmer labels "the Diogenes style." In American literature this feature of literature has been particularly pronounced. The American writer is frequently a writer in revolt, and though the particular attitudes or conventions against which he has revolted have changed through the course of American history, some of them have remained constant: social and political injustice, the hypocrisy stemming from puritanical assumptions about the nature of man, the excesses of materialism, an awesome respect for the past. In more general terms, the rebellion expressed in the principal pages of American literature strikes a blow at the presiding *status quo,* or what has now become labeled the "Establishment." In a society that places a high premium on the tradition of freedom of expression and that is founded on the right of individual and collective dissent, such a rebellion attests to the essential vitality of both the society and the literature which reflects it. For a literature which merely applauds "things-as-they-are" (in Widmer's phrase) necessarily reflects a social paradise or, more likely, a stagnant society or one in which the freedom of dissent has been withdrawn.

The writers in this section, from Benjamin Franklin to Allen Ginsberg, represent the diverse manifestations of the rebellious or subversive tradition reflected in American literature. Each of the selections subverts a particular social or moral attitude or convention. Some of the writers, like Franklin and Nathaniel Hawthorne, are not remembered primarily as rebels themselves, but their sympathetic portrayals of rebels as heroes or heroines suggest their essential allegiances. Others, like Ralph Waldo Emerson, Walt Whitman, and Mark Twain, have achieved through the passing of years reputations that place them in the company of America's most celebrated, and consequently respectable, citizens. But each of them was an outspoken proponent of the subversive tradition.

Emerson, attuned to a law higher than man's, refused to conform to a society dedicated to materialism ("Things are in the saddle, / And ride mankind.") and tolerant of the subjugation of one's fellowman in any form. In his ode to the humanitarian William Henry Channing, he advocated a humanistic individual philosophy ("Live for friendship, live for love") that would develop better human beings and hence a better society. His comments follow by three-quarters of a century the statement of the Quaker John Woolman, who forsook financial success for "a plain way of living" whereby he could be a better Christian, and anticipate by another three-quarters of a century the dramatic gesture of Sherwood Anderson in abruptly walking out of his Ohio paint factory to devote his life to art. In three different centuries and in widely separated social and geographical areas, Woolman, Emerson, and Anderson indict American materialism for its capacity to lure man to prostitute his manhood for money and to forsake his inner or artistic life.

Their indictments are, however, farther reaching. Implicit in the statements of Emerson and Anderson is the idea that the conformity to conventions demanded by society alienates the man whose vision is not that of his society. Emerson suggests that he would be less a man—not merely less his own man—if he answered the call to use his pen for propaganda. Anderson holds America to its original promise for the self-determination of its citizens; he demands a private hearing and is willing to place himself outside society to have it. Sinclair Lewis's small-town rebel, a type of American institution, similarly removes himself from respectable society in order to reap the harvest of the promised "life, liberty, and the pursuit of happiness." In like vein, but with society dramatically emblemized as the regime of military authority, Dos Passos' young artist deserts—outlaws and condemns himself—in his quest to attain the rights of man. The rebellions of these writers or their protagonists underscore what the writers regard as hypocrisy in a society that is founded on the concept of individual rights but is suspicious and fearful of the private or artistic expression.

The most conspicuously persistent object of attack in the literature of the present century has been the heritage of Puritanism, which has left its mark on almost all areas of American life. Theodore Dreiser was one of the first novelists to examine Puritan concepts of morality in the glaring light of actuality; in his character Sister Carrie he illustrates his thesis that men are motivated not by evil, but are impelled rather by vaguely felt (and often biological) desires. Carrie's longing for comfort leads her down a path rigorously avoided by respectable women, but she suffers no retributive punishment. If she is unhappy in her success at the end, it is not because she has outraged the moral conventions. Mark Twain's rebel in "The War Prayer" is adjudged a lunatic for applying logic to the deeper meanings of prayer, in this case one justified by patriotism. By juxtaposing the sentiments of religion, the fervor of patriotism, and the horrors of war, Twain achieves a bitingly ironic commentary on a conventionally moral society. In "Duty" and "The Iconoclast," H. L. Mencken—an arch-foe of Puritanism and all bourgeois conventionality, in fact—succinctly expresses the tenor of the rebellious spirit that enlivened the 1920's.

James Baldwin's ironic title "Notes of a Native Son" points up the role of the minority race member of American society who is frequently forced into a rebellious stance—born of feelings of bitterness and frustration—by the circumstances that deny him not only his birthright but his freedom to live what Baldwin calls his "*real* life." In this sense Baldwin's essay can be placed in the tradition of the subversives. It is an eloquent statement for civil rights, but it is also an indictment of the social pressures that impose such conformity on the members of society that they must choose between its values and their own. The expression of that choice in American literature reflects the restless democratic individuality that is the principal feature of the American character.

BENJAMIN FRANKLIN

The Speech of Polly Baker

THE SPEECH of Miss Polly Baker before a Court of Judicatory, in New England, where she was prosecuted [129/130] for a fifth time, for having a Bastard Child; which influenced the Court to dispense with her punishment, and which induced one of her judges to marry her the next day—by whom she had fifteen children.

"May it please the honourable bench to indulge me in a few words: I am a poor, unhappy woman, who have no money to fee lawyers to plead for me, being hard put to it to get a living. I shall not trouble your honours with long speeches; for I have not the presumption to expect that you may, by any means, be prevailed on to deviate in your sentence from the law, in my favour. All I humbly hope is, that your honours would charitably move the governor's goodness on my behalf, that my fine may be remitted. This is the fifth time, gentlemen, that I have been dragged before your court on the same account; twice I have paid heavy fines, and twice I have been brought to public punishment, for want of money to pay those fines. This may have been agreeable to the laws, and I don't dispute it; but since the laws are sometimes unreasonable in themselves, and therefore repealed; and others bear too hard on the subject in particular instances, and therefore there is left a power somewhere to dispense with the execution of them, I take the liberty to say, that I think this law, by which I am punished, both unreasonable in itself, and particularly severe with regard to me, who have always lived an inoffensive life in the neighbourhood where I was born, and defy my enemies (if I have any) to say that I have wronged any man, woman, or child. Abstracted from the [130/131] law, I cannot conceive (may it please your honours) what the nature of my offence is.

Benjamin Franklin, "The Speech of Polly Baker," in *The Works of Benjamin Franklin*, ed. John Bigelow (New York and London: G. P. Putnam's Sons, 1904), II, 129–33. [The original facts of publication of this piece are obscure. Bigelow attributes it to the year 1745.]

I have brought five children into the world, at the risque of my life; I have maintained them well by my own industry, without burthening the township, and would have done it better, if it had not been for the heavy charges and fines I have paid. Can it be a crime (in the nature of things, I mean) to add to the King's subjects, in a new country that really wants people? I own it, I should think it rather a praiseworthy than a punishable action. I have debauched no other woman's husband, nor enticed any youth; these things I never was charged with; nor has any one the least cause of complaint against me, unless, perhaps, the ministers of justice, because I have had children without being married, by which they have missed a wedding fee. But can this be a fault of mine? I appeal to your honours. You are pleased to allow I don't want sense; but I must be stupefied to the last degree, not to prefer the honourable state of wedlock to the condition I have lived in. I always was, and still am willing to enter into it; and doubt not my behaving well in it, having all the industry, frugality, fertility, and skill in economy appertaining to a good wife's character. I defy any one to say I ever refused an offer of that sort; on the contrary, I readily consented to the only proposal of marriage that ever was made me, which was when I was a virgin, but too easily confiding in the person's sincerity that made it, I unhappily lost my honour by trusting to his; for he got me with child, and then forsook me. [131/132]

"That very person, you all know, he is now become a magistrate of this country; and I had hopes he would have appeared this day on the bench, and have endeavoured to moderate the Court in my favour; then I should have scorned to have mentioned it; but I must now complain of it, as unjust and unequal, that my betrayer, and undoer, the first cause of all my faults and miscarriages (if they must be deemed such), should be advanced to honor and power in the government that punishes my misfortunes with stripes and infamy. I should be told, 't is like, that were there no act of Assembly in the case, the precepts of religion are violated by my transgressions. If mine is a religious transgression, leave it to religious punishment. You have already excluded me from the comforts of your church communion. Is not that sufficient? What need is there then of your additional fines and whipping? You believe I have offended heaven, and must suffer eternal fire; will not that be sufficient? I own I do not think as you do, for, if I thought what you call a sin was really such, I could not presumptuously commit it. But how can it be believed that Heaven is angry at my having children, when to the little done by me towards it, God has been pleased to add his divine skill and admirable workmanship in the formation of their bodies, and crowned the whole by furnishing them with rational and

immortal souls? Forgive me, gentlemen, if I talk a little extrava-
gantly on these matters: I am no divine, but if you, gentlemen, must
be making laws, do not turn natural and useful actions into crimes
by your prohibitions. But [132/133] take into your wise consideration
the great and growing number of bachelors in the country, many of
whom, from the mean fear of the expense of a family, have never
sincerely and honestly courted a woman in their lives; and by their
manner of living leave unproduced (which is little better than murder) hundreds of their posterity to the thousandth generation. Is not
this a greater offence against the public good than mine? Compel
them, then, by law, either to marriage, or to pay double the fine of
fornication every year. What must poor young women do, whom
customs and nature forbid to solicit the men, and who cannot force
themselves upon husbands, when the laws take no care to provide
them any, and yet severely punish them if they do their duty without them; the duty of the first and great command of nature and nature's God, increase and multiply; a duty, from the steady performance of which nothing has been able to deter me, but for its sake I
have hazarded the loss of the public esteem, and have frequently
endured public disgrace and punishment; and therefore ought, in
my humble opinion, instead of a whipping, to have a statue erected
to my memory." [133]

JOHN WOOLMAN

A Plain Way of Living

THROUGH THE humbling dispensations of Divine Providence, men are sometimes fitted for his service. The messages of the prophet Jeremiah were so disagreeable to the people, and so adverse to the spirit they lived in, that he became the object of their reproach, and in the weakness of nature he thought of desisting from his prophetic office; but saith he, "His word was in my heart as a burning fire shut up in my bones; and I was weary with forbearing, and could not stay." I saw at this time that if I was honest in declaring that which truth opened in me, I could not please all men; and I labored to be content in the way of my duty, however disagreeable to my own inclination. After this I went homeward, taking Woodbridge and Plainfield in my way, in both which meetings the pure influence of Divine love was manifested, in an humbling sense whereof I went home. I had been out about twenty-four days, and rode about three hundred and sixteen miles.

While I was out on this journey my heart was much affected with a sense of the state of the churches in our southern provinces; and believing the Lord was calling me to some further labor amongst them, I was bowed in reverence before him, with fervent desires that I might find strength to resign myself to his heavenly will.

Until this year, 1756, I continued to retail goods, besides following my trade as a tailor; about which time I grew uneasy on account of my business growing too cumbersome. I had begun with selling trimmings for garments, and from thence proceeded to sell cloths and linens; and at length, having got a considerable shop of goods, my trade increased every year, and the way to large business appeared open, but I felt a stop in my mind.

Through the mercies of the Almighty, I had, in a good degree, learned to be content with a plain way of living. I had but a small

From John Woolman, *The Journal of John Woolman,* in *The Harvard Classics,* ed. Charles W. Eliot (New York: P. F. Collier & Son, 1909), I, 203–06. [Originally published in 1774.]

family; and, on serious consideration, believed [203/204] truth did
not require me to engage much in cumbering affairs. It had been my
general practice to buy and sell things really useful. Things that
served chiefly to please the vain mind in people, I was not easy to
trade in; seldom did it; and whenever I did I found it weaken me
as a Christian.

The increase of business became my burden; for though my natural inclination was toward merchandise, yet I believed truth required me to live more free from outward cumbers; and there was
now a strife in my mind between the two. In this exercise my prayers were put up to the Lord, who graciously heard me, and gave me
a heart resigned to his holy will. Then I lessened my outward business, and, as I had opportunity, told my customers of my intentions,
that they might consider what shop to turn to; and in a while I
wholly laid down merchandise, and followed my trade as a tailor by
myself, having no apprentice. I also had a nursery of apple-trees, in
which I employed some of my time in hoeing, grafting, trimming,
and inoculating. In merchandise it is the custom where I lived to sell
chiefly on credit, and poor people often get in debt; when payment
is expected, not having wherewith to pay, their creditors often sue
for it at law. Having frequently observed occurrences of this kind, I
found it good for me to advise poor people to take such goods as
were most useful, and not costly.

In the time of trading I had an opportunity of seeing that the too
liberal use of spirituous liquors and the custom of wearing too costly
apparel led some people into great inconveniences; and that these
two things appear to be often [204/205] connected with each other.
By not attending to that use of things which is consistent with universal righteousness, there is an increase of labor which extends beyond what our Heavenly Father intends for us. And by great labor,
and often of much sweating, there is even among such as are not
drunkards a craving of liquors to revive the spirits; that partly by
the luxurious drinking of some, and partly by the drinking of others
(led to it through immoderate labor), very great quantities of rum
are every year expended in our colonies; the greater part of which
we should have no need of, did we steadily attend to pure wisdom.

When men take pleasure in feeling their minds elevated with
strong drink, and so indulge their appetite as to disorder their un-
derstandings, neglect their duty as members of a family or civil society, and cast off all regard to religion, their case is much to be
pitied. And where those whose lives are for the most part regular,
and whose examples have a strong influence on the minds of others,
adhere to some customs which powerfully draw to the use of more
strong liquor than pure wisdom allows, it hinders the spreading of

the spirit of meekness, and strengthens the hands of the more excessive drinkers. This is a case to be lamented.

Every degree of luxury hath some connection with evil; and if those who profess to be disciples of Christ, and are looked upon as leaders of the people, have that mind in them which was also in Christ, and so stand separate from every wrong way, it is a means of help to the weaker. As I have sometimes been much spent in the heat and have taken spirits to revive me, I have found by experience, that in such circumstances the mind is not so calm, nor so fitly disposed for Divine meditation, as when all such extremes are avoided. I have felt an increasing care to attend to that Holy Spirit which sets right bounds to our desires, and leads those who faithfully follow it to apply all the gifts of Divine Providence to the purposes for which they were intended. Did those who have the care of great estates attend with singleness of heart to this heavenly Instructor, which so opens and enlarges the mind as to cause men to love their neighbors as themselves, they would have wisdom given them to manage their concerns, without employing some people in providing [205/206] luxuries of life, or others in laboring too hard; but for want of steadily regarding this principle of Divine love, a selfish spirit takes place in the minds of people, which is attended with darkness and manifold confusions in the world.

Though trading in things useful is an honest employ, yet through the great number of superfluities which are bought and sold, and through the corruption of the times, they who apply to merchandise for a living have great need to be well experienced in that precept which the Prophet Jeremiah laid down for his scribe: "Seekest thou great things for thyself? seek them not." [206]

NATHANIEL HAWTHORNE

The Maypole of Merry Mount

There is an admirable foundation for a philosophic romance in the curious history of the early settlement of Mount Wollaston, or Merry Mount. In the slight sketch here attempted, the facts, recorded on the grave pages of our New England annalists, have wrought themselves, almost spontaneously, into a sort of allegory. The masques, mummeries, and festive customs, described in the text, are in accordance with the manners of the age. Authority on these points may be found in Strutt's Book of English Sports and Pastimes.

BRIGHT WERE the days at Merry Mount, when the Maypole was the banner staff of that gay colony! They who reared it, should their banner be triumphant, were to pour sunshine over New England's rugged hills, and scatter flower seeds throughout the soil. Jollity and gloom were contending for an empire. Midsummer eve had come, bringing deep verdure to the forest, and roses in her lap, of a more vivid hue than the tender buds of Spring. But May, of her mirthful spirit, dwelt all the year round at Merry Mount, sporting with the Summer months, and revelling with Autumn, and basking in the glow of Winter's fireside. Through a world of toil and care she flitted with a dreamlike smile, and came hither to find a home among the lightsome hearts of Merry Mount.

Never had the Maypole been so gayly decked as at sunset on midsummer eve. This venerated emblem was a pine-tree, which had preserved the slender grace of youth, while it equalled the loftiest height of the old wood monarchs. From its top streamed a silken banner, colored like the rainbow. Down nearly to the [70/71] ground the pole was dressed with birchen boughs, and others of the liveliest green, and some with silvery leaves, fastened by ribbons that fluttered in fantastic knots of twenty different colors, but no sad ones.

Nathaniel Hawthorne, "The Maypole of Merry Mount," in *The Works of Nathaniel Hawthorne,* ed. George Parsons Lathrop (Boston and New York: Houghton, Mifflin and Company [1882]), I, 70–84. [Included in *Twice-Told Tales* (1837).]

Garden flowers, and blossoms of the wilderness, laughed gladly forth amid the verdure, so fresh and dewy that they must have grown by magic on that happy pine-tree. Where this green and flowery splendor terminated, the shaft of the Maypole was stained with the seven brilliant hues of the banner at its top. On the lowest green bough hung an abundant wreath of roses, some that had been gathered in the sunniest spots of the forest, and others, of still richer blush, which the colonists had reared from English seed. O, people of the Golden Age, the chief of your husbandry was to raise flowers!

But what was the wild throng that stood hand in hand about the Maypole? It could not be that the fauns and nymphs, when driven from their classic groves and homes of ancient fable, had sought refuge, as all the persecuted did, in the fresh woods of the West. These were Gothic monsters, though perhaps of Grecian ancestry. On the shoulders of a comely youth uprose the head and branching antlers of a stag; a second, human in all other points, had the grim visage of a wolf; a third, still with the trunk and limbs of a mortal man, showed the beard and horns of a venerable he-goat. There was the likeness of a bear erect, brute in all but his hind legs, which were adorned with pink silk stockings. And here again, almost as wondrous, stood a real bear of the dark forest, lending each of his fore paws to the grasp of a human hand, and as ready for the dance as any in that circle. His inferior nature rose half way, to [71/72] meet his companions as they stooped. Other faces wore the similitude of man or woman, but distorted or extravagant, with red noses pendulous before their mouths, which seemed of awful depth, and stretched from ear to ear in an eternal fit of laughter. Here might be seen the Savage Man, well known in heraldry, hairy as a baboon, and girdled with green leaves. By his side, a noble figure, but still a counterfeit, appeared an Indian hunter, with feathery crest and wampum belt. Many of this strange company wore foolscaps, and had little bells appended to their garments, tinkling with a silvery sound, responsive to the inaudible music of their gleesome spirits. Some youths and maidens were of soberer garb, yet well maintained their places in the irregular throng by the expression of wild revelry upon their features. Such were the colonists of Merry Mount, as they stood in the broad smile of sunset round their venerated Maypole.

Had a wanderer, bewildered in the melancholy forest, heard their mirth, and stolen a half-affrighted glance, he might have fancied them the crew of Comus, some already transformed to brutes, some midway between man and beast, and the others rioting in the flow of tipsy jollity that foreran the change. But a band of Puritans, who watched the scene, invisible themselves, compared the masques to those devils and ruined souls with whom their superstition peopled the black wilderness.

Within the ring of monsters appeared the two airiest forms that had ever trodden on any more solid footing than a purple and golden cloud. One was a youth in glistening apparel, with a scarf of the rainbow pattern crosswise on his breast. His right hand held a gilded staff, the ensign of high dignity among [72/73] the revellers, and his left grasped the slender fingers of a fair maiden, not less gayly decorated than himself. Bright roses glowed in contrast with the dark and glossy curls of each, and were scattered round their feet, or had sprung up spontaneously there. Behind this lightsome couple, so close to the Maypole that its boughs shaded his jovial face, stood the figure of an English priest, canonically dressed, yet decked with flowers, in heathen fashion, and wearing a chaplet of the native vine leaves. By the riot of his rolling eye, and the pagan decorations of his holy garb, he seemed the wildest monster there, and the very Comus of the crew.

"Votaries of the Maypole," cried the flower-decked priest, "merrily, all day long, have the woods echoed to your mirth. But be this your merriest hour, my hearts! Lo, here stand the Lord and Lady of the May, whom I, a clerk of Oxford, and high priest of Merry Mount, am presently to join in holy matrimony. Up with your nimble spirits, ye morris-dancers, green men, and glee maidens, bears and wolves, and horned gentlemen! Come; a chorus now, rich with the old mirth of Merry England, and the wilder glee of this fresh forest; and then a dance, to show the youthful pair what life is made of, and how airily they should go through it! All ye that love the Maypole, lend your voices to the nuptial song of the Lord and Lady of the May!"

This wedlock was more serious than most affairs of Merry Mount, where jest and delusion, trick and fantasy, kept up a continual carnival. The Lord and Lady of the May, though their titles must be laid down at sunset, were really and truly to be partners for the dance of life, beginning the measure that same [73/74] bright eve. The wreath of roses, that hung from the lowest green bough of the Maypole, had been twined for them, and would be thrown over both their heads, in symbol of their flowery union. When the priest had spoken, therefore, a riotous uproar burst from the rout of monstrous figures.

"Begin you the stave, reverend Sir," cried they all; "and never did the woods ring to such a merry peal as we of the Maypole shall send up!"

Immediately a prelude of pipe, cithern, and viol, touched with practised minstrelsy, began to play from a neighboring thicket, in

such a mirthful cadence that the boughs of the Maypole quivered to
the sound. But the May Lord, he of the gilded staff, chancing to
look into his Lady's eyes, was wonder struck at the almost pensive
glance that met his own.

"Edith, sweet Lady of the May," whispered he reproachfully, "is
yon wreath of roses a garland to hang above our graves, that you
look so sad? O, Edith, this is our golden time! Tarnish it not by any
pensive shadow of the mind; for it may be that nothing of futurity
will be brighter than the mere remembrance of what is now passing."

"That was the very thought that saddened me! How came it in
your mind too?" said Edith, in a still lower tone than he, for it was
high treason to be sad at Merry Mount. "Therefore do I sigh amid
the festive music. And besides, dear Edgar, I struggle as with a
dream, and fancy that these shapes of our jovial friends are visionary, and their mirth unreal, and that we are no true Lord and Lady
of the May. What is the mystery in my heart?"

Just then, as if a spell had loosened them, down came a little
shower of withering rose leaves from the [74/75] Maypole. Alas, for
the young lovers! No sooner had their hearts glowed with real passion than they were sensible of something vague and unsubstantial
in their former pleasures, and felt a dreary presentiment of inevitable change. From the moment that they truly loved, they had subjected themselves to earth's doom of care and sorrow, and troubled
joy, and had no more a home at Merry Mount. That was Edith's
mystery. Now leave we the priest to marry them, and the masquers
to sport round the Maypole, till the last sunbeam be withdrawn
from its summit, and the shadows of the forest mingle gloomily in
the dance. Meanwhile, we may discover who these gay people were.

Two hundred years ago, and more, the old world and its inhabitants became mutually weary of each other. Men voyaged by thousands to the West: some to barter glass beads, and such like jewels,
for the furs of the Indian hunter; some to conquer virgin empires;
and one stern band to pray. But none of these motives had much
weight with the colonists of Merry Mount. Their leaders were men
who had sported so long with life, that when Thought and Wisdom
came, even these unwelcome guests were led astray by the crowd of
vanities which they should have put to flight. Erring Thought and
perverted Wisdom were made to put on masques, and play the fool.
The men of whom we speak, after losing the heart's fresh gayety,
imagined a wild philosophy of pleasure, and came hither to act out
their latest day-dream. They gathered followers from all that giddy
tribe whose whole life is like the festal days of soberer men. In their
train were minstrels, not unknown in London streets; wandering

players, whose theatres had been the halls [75/76] of noblemen; mummers, rope-dancers, and mountebanks, who would long be missed at wakes, church ales, and fairs; in a word, mirth makers of every sort, such as abounded in that age, but now began to be discountenanced by the rapid growth of Puritanism. Light had their footsteps been on land, and as lightly they came across the sea. Many had been maddened by their previous troubles into a gay despair; others were as madly gay in the flush of youth, like the May Lord and his Lady; but whatever might be the quality of their mirth, old and young were gay at Merry Mount. The young deemed themselves happy. The elder spirits, if they knew that mirth was but the counterfeit of happiness, yet followed the false shadow wilfully, because at least her garments glittered brightest. Sworn triflers of a lifetime, they would not venture among the sober truths of life not even to be truly blest.

All the hereditary pastimes of Old England were transplanted hither. The King of Christmas was duly crowned, and the Lord of Misrule bore potent sway. On the Eve of St. John, they felled whole acres of the forest to make bonfires, and danced by the blaze all night, crowned with garlands, and throwing flowers into the flame. At harvest time, though their crop was of the smallest, they made an image with the sheaves of Indian corn, and wreathed it with autumnal garlands, and bore it home triumphantly. But what chiefly characterized the colonists of Merry Mount was their veneration for the Maypole. It has made their true history a poet's tale. Spring decked the hallowed emblem with young blossoms and fresh green boughs; Summer brought roses of the deepest blush, and the perfected foliage of the forest; Autumn enriched [76/77] it with that red and yellow gorgeousness which converts each wildwood leaf into a painted flower; and Winter silvered it with sleet, and hung it round with icicles, till it flashed in the cold sunshine, itself a frozen sunbeam. Thus each alternate season did homage to the Maypole, and paid it a tribute of its own richest splendor. Its votaries danced round it, once, at least, in every month; sometimes they called it their religion, or their altar; but always, it was the banner staff of Merry Mount.

Unfortunately, there were men in the new world of a sterner faith than those Maypole worshippers. Not far from Merry Mount was a settlement of Puritans, most dismal wretches, who said their prayers before daylight, and then wrought in the forest or the cornfield till evening made it prayer time again. Their weapons were always at hand to shoot down the straggling savage. When they met in conclave, it was never to keep up the old English mirth, but to hear sermons three hours long, or to proclaim bounties on the heads of wolves and the scalps of Indians. Their festivals were fast days, and their chief pastime the singing of psalms. Woe to the youth or maiden who did but dream of a dance! The selectman nodded to the constable; and there sat the light-heeled reprobate in the stocks; or if he danced, it was round the whipping-post, which might be termed the Puritan Maypole.

A party of these grim Puritans, toiling through the difficult woods, each with a horseload of iron armor to burden his footsteps, would sometimes draw near the sunny precincts of Merry Mount. There were the silken colonists, sporting round their Maypole; perhaps teaching a bear to dance, or striving to communicate [77/78] their mirth to the grave Indian; or masquerading in the skins of deer and wolves, which they had hunted for that especial purpose. Often, the whole colony were playing at blindman's buff, magistrates and all, with their eyes bandaged, except a single scape-goat, whom the blinded sinners pursued by the tinkling of the bells at his garments. Once, it is said, they were seen following a flower-decked corpse, with merriment and festive music, to his grave. But did the dead man laugh? In their quietest times, they sang ballads and told tales, for the edification of their pious visitors; or perplexed them with juggling tricks; or grinned at them through horse collars; and when sport itself grew wearisome, they made game of their own stupidity, and began a yawning match. At the very least of these enormities, the men of iron shook their heads and frowned so darkly that the revellers looked up imagining that a momentary cloud had overcast the sunshine, which was to be perpetual there. On the other hand, the Puritans affirmed that, when a psalm was pealing from their place of worship, the echo which the forest sent them back seemed often like the chorus of a jolly catch, closing with a roar of laughter. Who but the fiend, and his bond slaves, the crew of Merry Mount, had thus disturbed them? In due time, a feud arose, stern and bitter on one side, and as serious on the other as anything could be among such light spirits as had sworn allegiance to the Maypole. The future complexion of New England was involved in this important quarrel. Should the grizzly saints establish their jurisdiction over the gay sinners, then would their spirits darken all the clime, and make it a land of clouded visages, of hard toil, of sermon and psalm forever. But should the banner [78/79] staff of Merry Mount be fortunate, sunshine would break upon the hills, and flowers would beautify the forest, and late posterity do homage to the Maypole.

After these authentic passages from history, we return to the nuptials of the Lord and Lady of the May. Alas! we have delayed too long, and must darken our tale too suddenly. As we glance again at the Maypole, a solitary sunbeam is fading from the summit, and leaves only a faint, golden tinge blended with the hues of the rainbow banner. Even that dim light is now withdrawn, relinquishing the whole domain of Merry Mount to the evening gloom, which has rushed so instantaneously from the black surrounding woods. But some of these black shadows have rushed forth in human shape.

Yes, with the setting sun, the last day of mirth had passed from Merry Mount. The ring of gay masquers was disordered and broken; the stag lowered his antlers in dismay; the wolf grew weaker than a lamb; the bells of the morris-dancers tinkled with tremulous affright. The Puritans had played a characteristic part in the Maypole mummeries. Their darksome figures were intermixed with the wild shapes of their foes, and made the scene a picture of the moment, when waking thoughts start up amid the scattered fantasies of a dream. The leader of the hostile party stood in the centre of the circle, while the route of monsters cowered around him, like evil spirits in the presence of a dread magician. No fantastic foolery could look him in the face. So stern was the energy of his aspect, that the whole man, visage, frame, and soul, seemed wrought of iron, gifted with life and thought, yet all of one substance with his headpiece and breastplate. It was the Puritan of Puritans; it was Endicott himself! [79/80]

"Stand off, priest of Baal!" said he, with a grim frown, and laying no reverent hand upon the surplice. "I know thee, Blackstone![1] Thou art the man who couldst not abide the rule even of thine own corrupted church, and hast come hither to preach iniquity, and to give example of it in thy life. But now shall it be seen that the Lord hath sanctified this wilderness for his peculiar people. Woe unto them that would defile it! And first, for this flower-decked abomination, the altar of thy worship!"

And with his keen sword Endicott assaulted the hallowed Maypole. Nor long did it resist his arm. It groaned with a dismal sound; it showered leaves and rosebuds upon the remorseless enthusiast; and finally, with all its green boughs and ribbons and flowers, symbolic of departed pleasures, down fell the banner staff of Merry Mount. As it sank, tradition says, the evening sky grew darker, and the woods threw forth a more sombre shadow.

"There," cried Endicott, looking triumphantly on his work, "there lies the only Maypole in New England! The thought is strong within me that, by its fall, is shadowed forth the fate of light and idle mirth makers, amongst us and our posterity. Amen, said John Endicott."

"Amen!" echoed his followers.

[1] Did Governor Endicott speak less positively, we should suspect a mistake here. The Rev. Mr. Blackstone, though an eccentric, is not known to have been an immoral man. We rather doubt his identity with the priest of Merry Mount. [Hawthorne's note.]

But the votaries of the Maypole gave one groan for their idol. At the sound, the Puritan leader glanced at the crew of Comus, each a figure of broad mirth, yet, at this moment, strangely expressive of sorrow and dismay. [80/81]

"Valiant captain," quoth Peter Palfrey, the Ancient of the band, "what order shall be taken with the prisoners?"

"I thought not to repent me of cutting down a Maypole," replied Endicott, "yet now I could find in my heart to plant it again, and give each of these bestial pagans one other dance round their idol. It would have served rarely for a whipping-post!"

"But there are pine-trees enow," suggested the lieutenant.

"True, good Ancient," said the leader. "Wherefore, bind the heathen crew, and bestow on them a small matter of stripes apiece, as earnest of our future justice. Set some of the rogues in the stocks to rest themselves, so soon as Providence shall bring us to one of our own well-ordered settlements where such accommodations may be found. Further penalties, such as branding and cropping of ears, shall be thought of hereafter."

"How many stripes for the priest?" inquired Ancient Palfrey.

"None as yet," answered Endicott, bending his iron frown upon the culprit. "It must be for the Great and General Court to determine, whether stripes and long imprisonment, and other grievous penalty, may atone for his transgressions. Let him look to himself! For such as violate our civil order, it may be permitted us to show mercy. But woe to the wretch that troubleth our religion."

"And this dancing bear," resumed the officer. "Must he share the stripes of his fellows?"

"Shoot him through the head!" said the energetic Puritan. "I suspect witchcraft in the beast."

"Here be a couple of shining ones," continued [81/82] Peter Palfrey, pointing his weapon at the Lord and Lady of the May. "They seem to be of high station among these misdoers. Methinks their dignity will not be fitted with less than a double share of stripes."

Endicott rested on his sword, and closely surveyed the dress and aspect of the hapless pair. There they stood, pale, downcast, and apprehensive. Yet there was an air of mutual support and of pure affection, seeking aid and giving it, that showed them to be man and wife, with the sanction of a priest upon their love. The youth, in the peril of the moment, had dropped his gilded staff, and thrown his arm about the Lady of the May, who leaned against his breast, too lightly to burden him, but with weight enough to express that their destinies were linked together, for good or evil. They looked first at each other, and then into the grim captain's face. There they stood, in the first hour of wedlock, while the idle pleasures, of which their companions were the emblems, had given place to the sternest cares of life, personified by the dark Puritans. But never had their youthful beauty seemed so pure and high as when its glow was chastened by adversity.

"Youth," said Endicott, "ye stand in an evil case, thou and thy maiden wife. Make ready presently, for I am minded that ye shall both have a token to remember your wedding day!"

"Stern man," cried the May Lord, "how can I move thee? Were the means at hand, I would resist to the death. Being powerless, I entreat! Do with me as thou wilt, but let Edith go untouched!"

"Not so," replied the immitigable zealot. "We are not wont to show an idle courtesy to that sex, which requireth the stricter discipline. What sayest [82/83] thou, maid? Shall thy silken bridegroom suffer thy share of the penalty, besides his own?"

"Be it death," said Edith, "and lay it all on me!"

Truly, as Endicott had said, the poor lovers stood in a woful case. Their foes were triumphant, their friends captive and abased, their home desolate, the benighted wilderness around them, and a rigorous destiny, in the shape of the Puritan leader, their only guide. Yet the deepening twilight could not altogether conceal that the iron man was softened; he smiled at the fair spectacle of early love; he almost sighed for the inevitable blight of early hopes.

"The troubles of life have come hastily on this young couple," observed Endicott. "We will see how they comport themselves under their present trials ere we burden them with greater. If, among the spoil, there be any garments of a more decent fashion, let them be put upon this May Lord and his Lady, instead of their glistening vanities. Look to it, some of you."

"And shall not the youth's hair be cut?" asked Peter Palfrey, looking with abhorrence at the lovelock and long glossy curls of the young man.

"Crop it forthwith, and that in the true pumpkin-shell fashion," answered the captain. "Then bring them along with us, but more gently than their fellows. There be qualities in the youth, which may make him valiant to fight, and sober to toil, and pious to pray; and in the maiden, that may fit her to become a mother in our Israel, bringing up babes in better nurture than her own hath been. Nor think ye, young ones, that they are the happiest, even in our lifetime of a moment, who misspend it in dancing round a Maypole!" [83/84]

And Endicott, the severest Puritan of all who laid the rock foundation of New England, lifted the wreath of roses from the ruin of the Maypole, and threw it, with his own gauntleted hand, over the heads of the Lord and Lady of the May. It was a deed of prophecy.

As the moral gloom of the world overpowers all systematic gayety, even so was their home of wild mirth made desolate amid the sad forest. They returned to it no more. But as their flowery garland was wreathed of the brightest roses that had grown there, so, in the tie that united them, were intertwined all the purest and best of their early joys. They went heavenward, supporting each other along the difficult path which it was their lot to tread, and never wasted one regretful thought on the vanities of Merry Mount. [84]

RALPH WALDO EMERSON

Ode

INSCRIBED TO W. H. CHANNING

Though loath to grieve
The evil time's sole patriot,
I cannot leave
My honied thought
For the priest's cant,
Or statesman's rant.

If I refuse
My study for their politique,
Which at the best is trick,
The angry Muse
Puts confusion in my brain.

But who is he that prates
Of the culture of mankind,
Of better arts and life?
Go, blindworm, go,
Behold the famous States
Harrying Mexico
With rifle and with knife!

Or who, with accent bolder,
Dare praise the freedom-loving mountaineer? [76/77]
I found by thee, O rushing Contoocook!

Ralph Waldo Emerson, "Ode Inscribed to W. H. Channing," in *The Complete Works of Ralph Waldo Emerson*, ed. Edward Waldo Emerson (Boston and New York: Houghton Mifflin Company, 1903–1904), IX, 76–79. [First published in 1846.]

And in thy valleys, Agiochook!
The jackals of the negro-holder.

The God who made New Hampshire
Taunted the lofty land
With little men;—
Small bat and wren
House in the oak:—
If earth-fire cleave
The upheaved land, and bury the folk,
The southern crocodile would grieve.
Virtue palters; Right is hence;
Freedom praised, but hid;
Funeral eloquence
Rattles the coffin-lid.

What boots thy zeal,
O glowing friend,
That would indignant rend
The northland from the south?
Wherefore? to what good end?
Boston Bay and Bunker Hill
Would serve things still;—
Things are of the snake.

The horseman serves the horse,
The neatherd serves the neat, [77/78]
The merchant serves the purse,
The eater serves his meat;
'T is the day of the chattel,
Web to weave, and corn to grind;
Things are in the saddle,
And ride mankind.

There are two laws discrete,
Not reconciled,—
Law for man, and law for thing;
The last builds town and fleet,
But it runs wild,
And doth the man unking.

'T is fit the forest fall,
The steep be graded,
The mountain tunnelled,

The sand shaded,
The orchard planted,
The glebe tilled,
The prairie granted,
The steamer built.

Let man serve law for man;
Live for friendship, live for love,
For truth's and harmony's behoof;
The state may follow how it can,
As Olympus follows Jove. [78/79]

Yet do not I implore
The wrinkled shopman to my sounding woods,
Nor bid the unwilling senator
Ask votes of thrushes in the solitudes.
Every one to his chosen work;—
Foolish hands may mix and mar;
Wise and sure the issues are.
Round they roll till dark is light,
Sex to sex, and even to odd;—
The over-god
Who marries Right to Might,
Who peoples, unpeoples,—
He who exterminates
Races by stronger races,
Black by white faces,—
Knows to bring honey
Out of the lion;
Grafts gentlest scion
On pirate and Turk.

The Cossack eats Poland,
Like stolen fruit;
Her last noble is ruined,
Her last poet mute:
Straight, into double band
The victors divide;
Half for freedom strike and stand;—
The astonished Muse finds thousands at her side. [79]

WALT WHITMAN

From Song of Myself

– 1 –

I celebrate myself, and sing myself,
And what I assume you shall assume,
For every atom belonging to me as good belongs to you.

I loafe and invite my soul,
I lean and loafe at my ease observing a spear of summer grass.

My tongue, every atom of my blood form'd from this soil, this air,
Born here of parents born here from parents the same, and their
    parents the same,
I, now thirty-seven years old in perfect health begin,
Hoping to cease not till death.

Creeds and schools in abeyance.
Retiring back a while sufficed at what they are, but never forgotten,
I harbor for good or bad, I permit to speak at every hazard,
Nature without check with original energy.

– 2 –

Houses and rooms are full of perfumes, the shelves are crowded
    with perfumes, [33/34]
I breathe the fragrance myself and know it and like it,
The distillation would intoxicate me also, but I shall not let it.

The atmosphere is not a perfume, it has no taste of the distillation, it
    is odorless,
It is for my mouth forever, I am in love with it,

From Walt Whitman, "Song of Myself," in *The Complete Writings of Walt
Whitman*, ed. Richard Maurice Bucke, Thomas B. Harned, and Horace L.
Traubel (New York and London: G. P. Putnam's Sons, 1902), I, 33–35, 56–65.
[Originally published in 1855.]

I will go to the bank by the wood and become undisguised and
naked,
I am mad for it to be in contact with me.
The smoke of my own breath,
Echoes, ripples, buzz'd whispers, love-root, silk-thread, crotch and
vine,
My respiration and inspiration, the beating of my heart, the passing
of blood and air through my lungs.
The sniff of green leaves and dry leaves, and of the shore and dark-
color'd sea-rocks, and of hay in the barn.
The sound of the belch'd words of my voice loos'd to the eddies of
the wind,
A few light kisses, a few embraces, a reaching around of arms,
The play of shine and shade on the trees as the supple boughs wag,
The delight alone or in the rush of the streets, or along the fields
and hill-sides,
The feeling of health, the full-noon trill, the song of me rising from
bed and meeting the sun.

Have you reckon'd a thousand acres much? have you reckon'd the
earth much?
Have you practis'd so long to learn to read?
Have you felt so proud to get at the meaning of poems? [34/35]

Stop this day and night with me and you shall possess the origin of
all poems,
You shall possess the good of the earth and sun, (there are millions
of suns left,)
You shall no longer take things at second or third hand, nor look
through the eyes of the dead, nor feed on the spectres in books,
You shall not look through my eyes either, nor take things from me,
You shall listen to all sides and filter them from your self. [35/56]

– 20 –

Who goes there? hankering, gross, mystical, nude;
How is it I extract strength from the beef I eat?

What is a man anyhow? what am I? what are you?

All I mark as my own you shall offset it with your own,
Else it were time lost listening to me.

I do not snivel that snivel the world over,
That months are vacuums and the ground but wallow and filth.

Whimpering and truckling fold with powders for invalids, conformity goes to the fourth-remov'd,

I wear my hat as I please indoors or out.

Why should I pray? why should I venerate and be ceremonious?

Having pried through the strata, analyzed to a hair, counsel'd with
   doctors and calculated close,
I find no sweeter fat than sticks to my own bones.

In all people I see myself, none more and not only a barley-corn
   less,
And the good or bad I say of myself I say of them. [56/57]

I know I am solid and sound,
To me the converging objects of the universe perpetually flow,
All are written to me, and I must get what the writing means.

I know I am deathless,
I know this orbit of mine cannot be swept by a carpenter's compass,
I know I shall not pass like a child's carlacue cut with a burnt stick
   at night.

I know I am august,
I do not trouble my spirit to vindicate itself or be understood,
I see that the elementary laws never apologize,
(I reckon I behave no prouder than the level I plant my house by,
   after all.)

I exist as I am, that is enough,
If no other in the world be aware I sit content,
And if each and all be aware I sit content.

One world is aware and by far the largest to me, and that is myself,
And whether I come to my own to-day or in ten thousand or ten
   million years,
I can cheerfully take it now, or with equal cheerfulness I can wait.

My foothold is tenon'd and mortis'd in granite,
I laugh at what you call dissolution,
And I know the amplitude of time. [57/58]

– 21 –

I am the poet of the Body and I am the poet of the Soul,
The pleasures of heaven are with me and the pains of hell are with
   me,
The first I graft and increase upon myself, the latter I translate into
   a new tongue.

I am the poet of the woman the same as the man,
And I say it is as great to be a woman as to be a man,

And I say there is nothing greater than the mother of men.

I chant the chant of dilation or pride,
We have had ducking and deprecating about enough,
I show that size is only development.

Have you outstript the rest? are you the President?
It is a trifle, they will more than arrive there every one, and still pass
    on.

I am he that walks with the tender and growing night,
I call to the earth and sea half-held by the night.

Press close bare-bosom'd night—press close magnetic nourishing
    night!
Night of south winds—night of the large few stars!
Still nodding night—mad naked summer night.

Smile O voluptuous cool-breath'd earth!
Earth of the slumbering and liquid trees!
Earth of departed sunset—earth of the mountains misty-topt! [58/59]
Earth of the vitreous pour of the full moon just tinged with blue!
Earth of shine and dark mottling the tide of the river!
Earth of the limpid gray of clouds brighter and clearer for my sake!
Far-swooping elbow'd earth—rich apple-blossom'd earth!
Smile, for your lover comes.

Prodigal, you have given me love—therefore I to you give love!
O unspeakable passionate love.

– 22 –

You sea! I resign myself to you also—I guess you mean,
I behold from the beach your crooked inviting fingers,
I believe you refuse to go back without feeling of me,
We must have a turn together, I undress, hurry me out of sight of
    the land,
Cushion me soft, rock me in billowy drowse,
Dash me with amorous wet, I can repay you.

Sea of stretch'd ground-swells,
Sea breathing broad and convulsive breaths,
Sea of the brine of life and of unshovell'd yet always-ready graves,
Howler and scooper of storms, capricious and dainty sea,
I am integral with you, I too am of one phase and of all phases.

Partaker of influx and efflux I, extoller of hate and conciliation,
Extoller of amies and those that sleep in each others' arms. [59/60]

I am he attesting sympathy,
(Shall I make my list of things in the house and skip the house that
    supports them?)

I am not the poet of goodness only, I do not decline to be the poet
    of wickedness also.

What blurt is this about virtue and about vice?
Evil propels me and reform of evil propels me, I stand indifferent,
My gait is no fault-finder's or rejecter's gait,
I moisten the roots of all that has grown.

Did you fear some scrofula out of the unflagging pregnancy?
Did you guess the celestial laws are yet to be work'd over and recti-
    fied?

I find one side a balance and the antipodal side a balance,
Soft doctrine as steady help as stable doctrine,
Thoughts and deeds of the present our rouse and early start.

This minute that comes to me over the past decillions,
There is no better than it and now.

What behaved well in the past or behaves well to-day is not such a
    wonder,
The wonder is always and always how there can be a mean man or
    an infidel.

– 23 –

Endless unfolding of words of ages!
And mine a word of the modern, the word En-Masse. [60/61]
A word of the faith that never balks,
Here or henceforward it is all the same to me, I accept Time abso-
    lutely.

It alone is without flaw, it alone rounds and completes all,
That mystic baffling wonder alone completes all.

I accept Reality and dare not question it,
Materialism first and last imbuing.

Hurrah for positive science! long live exact demonstration!
Fetch stonecrop mixt with cedar and branches of lilac,
This is the lexicographer, this the chemist, this made a grammar of
    the old cartouches,
These mariners put the ship through dangerous unknown seas,
This is the geologist, this works with the scalpel, and this is a mathe-
    matician.

Gentlemen, to you the first honors always!
Your facts are useful, and yet they are not my dwelling,
I but enter by them to an area of my dwelling.

Less the reminders of properties told my words,
And more the reminders they of life untold, and of freedom and ex-
    trication,
And make short account of neuters and geldings, and favor men and
    women fully equipt,
And beat the gong of revolt, and stop with fugitives and them that
    plot and conspire. [61/62]

– 24 –

Walt Whitman, a kosmos, of Manhattan the son,
Turbulent, fleshly, sensual, eating, drinking and breeding,
No sentimentalist, no stander above men and women or apart from
    them,
No more modest than immodest.

Unscrew the locks from the doors!
Unscrew the doors themselves from their jambs!

Whoever degrades another degrades me,
And whatever is done or said returns at last to me.

Through me the afflatus surging and surging, through me the cur-
    rent and index.

I speak the pass-word primeval, I give the sign of democracy,
By God! I will accept nothing which all cannot have their counter-
    part of on the same terms.

Through me many long dumb voices,
Voices of the interminable generations of prisoners and slaves,
Voices of the diseas'd and despairing and of thieves and dwarfs,
Voices of cycles of preparation and accretion,
And of the threads that connect the stars, and of wombs and of the
    father-stuff,

And of the rights of them the others are down upon,
Of the deform'd, trivial, flat, foolish, despised,
Fog in the air, beetles rolling balls of dung. [62/63]

Through me forbidden voices,
Voices of sexes and lusts, voices veil'd and I remove the veil,
Voices indecent by me clarified and transfigur'd.

I do not press my fingers across my mouth,

I keep as delicate around the bowels as around the head and heart,
Copulation is no more rank to me than death is.

I believe in the flesh and the appetites,
Seeing, hearing, feeling, are miracles, and each part and tag of me is
   a miracle.

Divine am I inside and out, and I make holy whatever I touch or am
   touch'd from,
The scent of these arm-pits aroma finer than prayer,
This head more than churches, bibles, and all the creeds.

If I worship one thing more than another it shall be the spread of
   my own body, or any part of it,
Translucent mould of me it shall be you!
Shaded ledges and rests it shall be you!
Firm masculine colter it shall be you!
Whatever goes to the tilth of me it shall be you!
You my rich blood! your milky stream pale strippings of my life!
Breast that presses against other breasts it shall be you!
My brain it shall be your occult convolutions!
Root of wash'd sweet-flag! timorous pond-snipe! nest of guarded du-
   plicate eggs! it shall be you! [63/64]
Mix'd tussled hay of head, beard, brawn, it shall be you!
Trickling sap of maple, fibre of manly wheat, it shall be you!
Sun so generous it shall be you!
Vapors lighting and shading my face it shall be you!
You sweaty brooks and dews it shall be you!
Winds whose soft-tickling genitals rub against me it shall be you!
Broad muscular fields, branches of live oak, loving lounger in my
   winding paths, it shall be you!
Hands I have taken, face I have kiss'd, mortal I have ever touch'd, it
   shall be you.

I dote on myself, there is that lot of me and all so luscious,
Each moment and whatever happens thrills me with joy,
I cannot tell how my ankles bend, nor whence the cause of my fain-
   test wish,
Nor the cause of the friendship I emit, nor the cause of the friend-
   ship I take again.

That I walk up my stoop, I pause to consider if it really be,
A morning-glory at my window satisfies me more than the metaphysics of books.

To behold the day-break!
The little light fades the immense and diaphanous shadows,

The air tastes good to my palate.

Hefts of the moving world at innocent gambols silently rising, freshly
    exuding,
Scooting obliquely high and low. [64/65]

Something I cannot see puts upward libidinous prongs,
Seas of bright juice suffuse heaven.

The earth by the sky staid with, the daily close of their junction,
The heav'd challenge from the east that moment over my head,
The mocking taunt, See then whether you shall be master! [65]

THEODORE DREISER

Sister Carrie:

The Pursuit of Dreams

IN THE LIGHT of the world's attitude toward woman and her duties, the nature of Carrie's mental state deserves consideration. Actions such as hers are measured by an arbitrary scale. Society possesses a conventional standard whereby it judges all things. All men should be good, all women virtuous. Wherefore, villain, hast thou failed?

For all the liberal analysis of Spencer and our modern naturalistic philosophers, we have but an infantile perception of morals. There is more in the subject than mere conformity to a law of evolution. It is yet deeper than conformity to things of earth alone. It is more involved than we, as yet, perceive. Answer, first, why the heart thrills; explain wherefore some plaintive note goes wandering about the world, undying; make clear the rose's subtle alchemy evolving its ruddy lamp in light and rain. In the essence of these facts lie the first principles of morals.

"Oh," thought Drouet, "how delicious is my conquest."

"Ah," thought Carrie, with mournful misgivings, "what is it I have lost?"

Before this world-old proposition we stand, serious, interested, confused; endeavouring to evolve the true theory of morals—the true answer to what is right.

In the view of a certain stratum of society, Carrie was [101/102] comfortably established—in the eyes of the starveling, beaten by every wind and gusty sheet of rain, she was safe in a halcyon harbour. Drouet had taken three rooms, furnished, in Ogden Place, facing Union Park, on the West Side. That was a little, green-carpeted breathing spot, than which, to-day, there is nothing more beautiful in Chicago. It afforded a vista pleasant to contemplate. The best

From Theodore Dreiser, *Sister Carrie* (New York: The Modern Library, n.d.), pp. 101–05, 554–57. [Originally published in 1900.]

room looked out upon the lawn of the park, now sear and brown, where a little lake lay sheltered. Over the bare limbs of the trees, which now swayed in the wintry wind, rose the steeple of the Union Park Congregational Church, and far off the towers of several others.

The rooms were comfortably enough furnished. There was a good Brussels carpet on the floor, rich in dull red and lemon shades, and representing large jardinières filled with gorgeous, impossible flowers. There was a large pier-glass mirror between the two windows. A large, soft, green, plush-covered couch occupied one corner, and several rocking-chairs were set about. Some pictures, several rugs, a few small pieces of bric-à-brac, and the tale of contents is told.

In the bedroom, off the front room, was Carrie's trunk, bought by Drouet, and in the wardrobe built into the wall quite an array of clothing—more than she had ever possessed before, and of very becoming designs. There was a third room for possible use as a kitchen, where Drouet had Carrie establish a little portable gas stove for the preparation of small lunches, oysters, Welsh rarebits, and the like, of which he was exceedingly fond; and, lastly, a bath. The whole place was cosey, in that it was lighted by gas and heated by furnace registers, possessing also a small grate, set with an asbestos back, a method of cheerful warming which was then first coming into use. By her industry and natural love of order, which now developed, the place maintained an air pleasing in the extreme. [102/103]

Here, then, was Carrie, established in a pleasant fashion, free of certain difficulties which most ominously confronted her, laden with many new ones which were of a mental order, and altogether so turned about in all of her earthly relationships that she might well have been a new and different individual. She looked into her glass and saw a prettier Carrie than she had seen before; she looked into her mind, a mirror prepared of her own and the world's opinions, and saw a worse. Between these two images she wavered, hesitating which to believe.

"My, but you're a little beauty," Drouet was wont to exclaim to her. She would look at him with large, pleased eyes.

"You know it, don't you?" he would continue.

"Oh, I don't know," she would reply, feeling delight in the fact that one should think so, hesitating to believe, though she really did, that she was vain enough to think so much of herself.

Her conscience, however, was not a Drouet, interested to praise. There she heard a different voice, with which she argued, pleaded, excused. It was no just and sapient counsellor, in its last analysis. It was only an average little conscience, a thing which represented the world, her past environment, habit, convention, in a confused way. With it, the voice of the people was truly the voice of God.

"Oh, thou failure!" said the voice.

"Why?" she questioned.

"Look at those about," came the whispered answer. "Look at those who are good. How would they scorn to do what you have done. Look at the good girls; how will they draw away from such as you when they know you have been weak. You had not tried before you failed."

It was when Carrie was alone, looking out across the park, that she would be listening to this. It would come [103/104] infrequently —when something else did not interfere, when the pleasant side was not too apparent, when Drouet was not there. It was somewhat clear in utterance at first, but never wholly convincing. There was always an answer, always the December days threatened. She was alone; she was desireful; she was fearful of the whistling wind. The voice of want made answer for her.

Once the bright days of summer pass by, a city takes on that sombre garb of grey, wrapt in which it goes about its labours during the long winter. Its endless buildings look grey, its sky and its streets assume a sombre hue; the scattered, leafless trees and wind-blown dust and paper but add to the general solemnity of colour. There seems to be something in the chill breezes which scurry through the long, narrow thoroughfares productive of rueful thoughts. Not poets alone, nor artists, nor that superior order of mind which arrogates to itself all refinement, feel this, but dogs and all men. These feel as much as the poet, though they have not the same power of expression. The sparrow upon the wire, the cat in the doorway, the dray horse tugging his weary load, feel the long, keen breaths of winter. It strikes to the heart of all life, animate and inanimate. If it were not for the artificial fires of merriment, the rush of profit-seeking trade, and pleasure-selling amusements; if the various merchants failed to make the customary display within and without their establishments; if our streets were not strung with signs of gorgeous hues and thronged with hurrying purchasers, we would quickly discover how firmly the chill hand of winter lays upon the heart; how dispiriting are the days during which the sun withholds a portion of our allowance of light and warmth. We are more dependent upon these things than is often thought. We are insects produced by heat, and pass without it. [104/105]

In the drag of such a grey day the secret voice would reassert itself, feebly and more feebly.... [105/554]

And now Carrie had attained that which in the beginning seemed

life's object, or, at least, such fraction of it as human beings ever attain of their original desires. She could look about on her gowns and
carriage, her furniture and bank account. Friends there were, as the
world takes it—those who would bow and smile in acknowledgment
of her success. For these she had [554/555] once craved. Applause
there was, and publicity—once far off, essential things, but now
grown trivial and indifferent. Beauty also—her type of loveliness—
and yet she was lonely. In her rocking-chair she sat, when not otherwise engaged—singing and dreaming.

Thus in life there is ever the intellectual and the emotional nature—
the mind that reasons, and the mind that feels. Of one come the
men of action—generals and statesmen; of the other, the poets and
dreamers—artists all.

As harps in the wind, the latter respond to every breath of fancy,
voicing in their moods all the ebb and flow of the ideal.

Man has not yet comprehended the dreamer any more than he
has the ideal. For him the laws and morals of the world are unduly
severe. Ever hearkening to the sound of beauty, straining for the
flash of its distant wings, he watches to follow, wearying his feet in
travelling. So watched Carrie, so followed, rocking and singing.

And it must be remembered that reason had little part in this.
Chicago dawning, she saw the city offering more of loveliness than
she had ever known, and instinctively, by force of her moods alone,
clung to it. In fine raiment and elegant surroundings, men seemed to
be contented. Hence, she drew near these things. Chicago, New
York; Drouet, Hurstwood; the world of fashion and the world of
stage—these were but incidents. Not them, but that which they represented, she longed for. Time proved the representation false.

Oh, the tangle of human life! How dimly as yet we see. Here was
Carrie, in the beginning poor, unsophisticated, emotional; responding with desire to everything most lovely in life, yet finding herself
turned as by a wall. Laws to say: "Be allured, if you [555/556] will,
be everything lovely, but draw not nigh unless by righteousness."
Convention to say: "You shall not better your situation save by honest labour." If honest labour be unremunerative and difficult to endure; if it be the long, long road which never reaches beauty, but
wearies the feet and the heart; if the drag to follow beauty be such
that one abandons the admired way, taking rather the despised path
leading to her dreams quickly, who shall cast the first stone? Not
evil, but longing for that which is better, more often directs the
steps of the erring. Not evil, but goodness more often allures the
feeling mind unused to reason.

Amid the tinsel and shine of her state walked Carrie, unhappy. As
when Drouet took her, she had thought: "Now I am lifted into that

which is best"; as when Hurstwood seemingly offered her the better way: "Now am I happy." But since the world goes its way past all who will not partake of its folly, she now found herself alone. Her purse was open to him whose need was greatest. In her walks on Broadway, she no longer thought of the elegance of the creatures who passed her. Had they more of that peace and beauty which glimmered afar off, then were they to be envied.

Drouet abandoned his claim and was seen no more. Of Hurstwood's death she was not even aware. A slow, black boat setting out from the pier at Twenty-seventh Street upon its weekly errand bore, with many others, his nameless body to the Potter's Field.

Thus passed all that was of interest concerning these twain in their relation to her. Their influence upon her life is explicable alone by the nature of her longings. Time was when both represented for her all that was most potent in early success. They were the personal representatives of a state most blessed to attain—the titled ambassadors of comfort and peace, [556/557] aglow with their credentials. It is but natural that when the world which they represented no longer allured her, its ambassadors should be discredited. Even had Hurstwood returned in his original beauty and glory, he could not now have allured her. She had learned that in his world, as in her own present state, was not happiness.

Sitting alone, she was now an illustration of the devious ways by which one who feels, rather than reasons, may be led in the pursuit of beauty. Though often disillusioned, she was still waiting for that halcyon day when she would be led forth among dreams become real. Ames had pointed out a farther step, but on and on beyond that, if accomplished, would lie others for her. It was forever to be the pursuit of that radiance of delight which tints the distant hilltops of the world.

Oh, Carrie, Carrie! Oh, blind strivings of the human heart! Onward onward, it saith, and where beauty leads, there it follows. Whether it be the tinkle of a lone sheep bell o'er some quiet landscape, or the glimmer of beauty in sylvan places, or the show of soul in some passing eye, the heart knows and makes answer, following. It is when the feet weary and hope seems vain that the heartaches and the longings arise. Know, then, that for you is neither surfeit nor content. In your rocking-chair, by your window dreaming, shall you long, alone. In your rocking-chair, by your window, shall you dream such happiness as you may never feel. [557]

MARK TWAIN

The War Prayer

It was a time of great and exalting excitement. The country was up in arms, the war was on, in every breast burned the holy fire of patriotism; the drums were beating, the bands playing, the toy pistols popping, the bunched firecrackers hissing and spluttering; on every hand and far down the receding and fading spread of roofs and balconies a fluttering wilderness of flags flashed in the sun; daily the young volunteers marched down the wide avenue gay and fine in their new uniforms, the proud fathers and mothers and sisters and sweethearts cheering them with voices choked with happy emotion as they swung by; nightly the packed mass meetings listened, panting, to patriot oratory which stirred the deepest deeps of their hearts, and which they interrupted at briefest intervals with cyclones of applause, the tears running down their cheeks the while; in the churches the pastors preached devotion to flag and country, and invoked the God of Battles, beseeching His aid in our good cause in outpouring of fervid eloquence which moved every listener. It was indeed a glad and gracious time, and the half dozen rash spirits that ventured to disapprove of the war and cast a doubt upon its righteousness straightway got such a stern and angry [394–395] warning that for their personal safety's sake they quickly shrank out of sight and offended no more in that way.

Sunday morning came—next day the battalions would leave for the front; the church was filled; the volunteers were there, their young faces alight with martial dreams—visions of the stern advance, the gathering momentum, the rushing charge, the flashing sabers, the flight of the foe, the tumult, the enveloping smoke, the fierce pursuit, the surrender!—them [sic] home from the war, bronzed heroes, welcomed, adored, submerged in golden seas of glory! With the volunteers sat their dear ones, proud, happy, and

Mark Twain, "The War Prayer," in Europe and Elsewhere, The Writings of Mark Twain, Stormfield Edition (New York and London: Harper & Brothers, 1929), XXIX, 394–98. [Dictated in 1904–1905 and first published in 1923.]

envied by the neighbors and friends who had no sons and brothers to send forth to the field of honor, there to win for the flag, or, failing, die the noblest of noble deaths. The service proceeded; a war chapter from the Old Testament was read; the first prayer was said; it was followed by an organ burst that shook the building, and with one impulse the house rose, with glowing eyes and beating hearts, and poured out that tremendous invocation—

> "God the all-terrible! Thou who ordainest,
> Thunder thy clarion and lightning thy sword!"

Then came the "long" prayer. None could remember the like of it for passionate pleading and moving and beautiful language. The burden of its supplication was, that an ever-merciful and benignant Father of us all would watch over our noble young soldiers, and aid, comfort, and encourage them in their patriotic work; bless them, shield them in the day of battle [395/396] and the hour of peril, bear them in His mighty hand, make them strong and confident, invincible in the bloody onset; help them to crush the foe, grant to them and to their flag and country imperishable honor and glory—

An aged stranger entered and moved with slow and noiseless step up the main aisle, his eyes fixed upon the minister, his long body clothed in a robe that reached to his feet, his head bare, his white hair descending in a frothy cataract to his shoulders, his seamy face unnaturally pale, pale even to ghastliness. With all eyes following him and wondering, he made his silent way; without pausing, he ascended to the preacher's side and stood there, waiting. With shut lids the preacher, unconscious of his presence, continued his moving prayer, and at last finished it with the words, uttered in fervent appeal, "Bless our arms, grant us the victory, O Lord our God, Father and Protector of our land and flag!"

The stranger touched his arm, motioned him to step aside—which the startled minister did—and took his place. During some moments he surveyed the spellbound audience with solemn eyes, in which burned an uncanny light; then in a deep voice he said:

"I come from the Throne—bearing a message from Almighty God!" The words smote the house with a shock; if the stranger perceived it he gave no attention. "He has heard the prayer of His servant your shepherd, and will grant it if such shall be your desire after I, His messenger, shall have explained to you its import—that is to say, its full import. [396/397] For it is like unto many of the prayers of men, in that it asks for more than he who utters it is aware of —except he pause and think.

"God's servant and yours has prayed his prayer. Has he paused and taken thought? Is it one prayer? No, it is two—one uttered, the other not. Both have reached the ear of Him Who heareth all supplications, the spoken and the unspoken. Ponder this—keep it in mind. If you would beseech a blessing upon yourself, beware! lest without intent you invoke a curse upon a neighbor at the same time. If you pray for the blessing of rain upon your crop which needs it, by that act you are possibly praying for a curse upon some neighbor's crop which may not need rain and can be injured by it.

"You have heard your servant's prayer—the uttered part of it. I am commissioned of God to put into words the other part of it—that part which the pastor—and also you in your hearts—fervently prayed silently. And ignorantly and unthinkingly? God grant that it was so! You heard these words: 'Grant us the victory, O Lord our God!' That is sufficient. The *whole* of the uttered prayer is compact into those pregnant words. Elaborations were not necessary. When you have prayed for victory you have prayed for many unmentioned results which follow victory—*must* follow it, cannot help but follow it. Upon the listening spirit of God the Father fell also the unspoken part of the prayer. He commandeth me to put it into words. Listen!

"O Lord our Father, our young patriots, idols of [397/398] our hearts, go forth to battle—be Thou near them! With them—in spirit —we also go forth from the sweet peace of our beloved firesides to smite the foe. O Lord our God, help us to tear their soldiers to bloody shreds with our shells; help us to cover their smiling fields with the pale forms of their patriot dead; help us to drown the thunder of the guns with the shrieks of their wounded, writhing in pain; help us to lay waste their humble homes with a hurricane of fire; help us to wring the hearts of their unoffending widows with unavailing grief; help us to turn them out roofless with their little children to wander unfriended the wastes of their desolated land in rags and hunger and thirst, sports of the sun flames of summer and the icy winds of winter, broken in spirit, worn with travail, imploring Thee for the refuge of the grave and denied it—for our sakes who adore Thee, Lord, blast their hopes, blight their lives, protract their bitter pilgrimage, make heavy their steps, water their way with their tears, stain the white snow with the blood of their wounded feet! We ask it, in the spirit of love, of Him Who is the Source of Love, and Who is the ever-faithful refuge and friend of all that are sore beset and seek His aid with humble and contrite hearts. Amen."

(*After a pause.*) "Ye have prayed it; if ye still desire it, speak! The messenger of the Most High waits."

It was believed afterward that the man was a lunatic, because there was no sense in what he said. [398]

SINCLAIR LEWIS

—•—•—

The Red Swede

[CAROL KENNICOTT] started for home, through the small slum. Before a tar-paper shack, at a gateless gate, a man in rough brown dogskin coat and black plush cap with lappets was watching her. His square face was confident, his foxy mustache was picaresque. He stood erect, his hands in his side-pockets, his pipe puffing slowly. He was forty-five or -six, perhaps.

"How do, Mrs. Kennicott," he drawled.

She recalled him—the town handyman, who had repaired their furnace at the beginning of winter.

"Oh, how do you do," she fluttered.

"My name 's Bjornstam. 'The Red Swede' they call me. Remember? Always thought I'd kind of like to say howdy to you again."

"Ye—yes—— I've been exploring the outskirts of town."

"Yump. Fine mess. No sewage, no street cleaning, and the Lutheran minister and the priest represent the arts and sciences. Well, thunder, we submerged tenth down here in Swede Hollow are no worse off than you folks. Thank God, we don't have to go and purr at Juanity Haydock at the Jolly Old Seventeen."

The Carol who regarded herself as completely adaptable was uncomfortable at being chosen as comrade by a pipe-reeking odd-job man. Probably he was one of her husband's patients. But she must keep her dignity.

"Yes, even the Jolly Seventeen isn't always so exciting. It's very cold again today, isn't it. Well——"

Bjornstam was not respectfully valedictory. He showed no signs of pulling a forelock. His eyebrows moved as though they had a life of their own. With a subgrin he went on:

"Maybe I hadn't ought to talk about Mrs. Haydock and [114/115] her Solemcholy Seventeen in that fresh way. I suppose I'd be tickled to death if I was invited to sit in with that gang. I'm what they call

From Sinclair Lewis, *Main Street* (New York: Harcourt, Brace and Company, 1920), pp. 114–18.

a pariah, I guess. I'm the town badman, Mrs. Kennicott: town atheist, and I suppose I must be an anarchist, too. Everybody who
doesn't love the bankers and the Grand Old Republican Party is an
anarchist."

Carol had unconsciously slipped from her attitude of departure
into an attitude of listening, her face full toward him, her muff lowered. She fumbled:

"Yes, I suppose so." Her own grudges came in a flood. "I don't see
why you shouldn't criticize the Jolly Seventeen if you want to. They
aren't sacred."

"Oh yes, they are! The dollar-sign chased the crucifix clean off
the map. But then, I've got no kick. I do what I please, and I suppose I ought to let them do the same."

"What do you mean by saying you're a pariah?"

"I'm poor, and yet I don't decently envy the rich. I'm an old bach.
I make enough money for a stake, and then I sit around by myself,
and shake hands with myself, and have a smoke, and read history,
and I don't contribute to the wealth of Brother Elder or Daddy
Cass."

"You— I fancy you read a good deal."

"Yep. In a hit-or-a-miss way. I'll tell you: I'm a lone wolf. I trade
horses, and saw wood, and work in lumber-camps—I'm a first-rate
swamper. Always wished I could go to college. Though I s'pose I'd
find it pretty slow, and they'd probably kick me out."

"You really are a curious person, Mr.——"

"Bjornstam. Miles Bjornstam. Half Yank and half Swede. Usually
known as 'that damn lazy big-mouth calamity-howler that ain't satisfied with the way we run things.' No, I ain't curious—whatever you
mean by that! I'm just a bookworm. Probably too much reading for
the amount of digestion I've got. Probably half-baked. I'm going to
get in 'half-baked' first, and beat you to it, because it's dead sure to
be handed to a radical that wears jeans!"

They grinned together. She demanded:

"You say that the Jolly Seventeen is stupid. What makes you think
so?"

"Oh, trust us borers into the foundation to know about your leisure class. Fact, Mrs. Kennicott, I'll say that far as I can make out,
the only people in this man's town that do [115/116] have any brains
—I don't mean ledger-keeping brains or duck-hunting brains or
baby-spanking brains, but real imaginative brains—are you and me
and Guy Pollock and the foreman at the flour-mill. He's a socialist,
the foreman. (Don't tell Lym Cass that! Lym would fire a socialist
quicker than he would a horse-thief!)"

"Indeed no, I sha'n't tell him."

"This foreman and I have some great set-to's. He's a regular old-line party-member. Too dogmatic. Expects to reform everything from deforestration to nosebleed by saying phrases like 'surplus value.' Like reading the prayer-book. But same time, he's a Plato J. Aristotle compared with people like Ezry Stowbody or Professor Mott or Julius Flickerbaugh."

"It's interesting to hear about him."

He dug his toe into a drift, like a schoolboy. "Rats. You mean I talk too much. Well, I do, when I get hold of somebody like you. You probably want to run along and keep your nose from freezing."

"Yes, I must go, I suppose. But tell me: Why did you leave Miss Sherwin, of the high school, out of your list of the town intelligentsia?"

"I guess maybe she does belong in it. From all I can hear she's in everything and behind everything that looks like a reform—lot more than most folks realize. She lets Mrs. Reverend Warren, the president of this-here Thanatopsis Club, think she's running the works, but Miss Sherwin is the secret boss, and nags all the easy-going dames into doing something. But way I figure it out—— You see, I'm not interested in these dinky reforms. Miss Sherwin's trying to repair the holes in this barnacle-covered ship of a town by keeping busy bailing out the water. And Pollock tries to repair it by reading poetry to the crew! Me, I want to yank it up on the ways, and fire the poor bum of a shoemaker that built it so it sails crooked, and have it rebuilt right, from the keel up."

"Yes—that—that would be better. But I must run home. My poor nose is nearly frozen."

"Say, you better come in and get warm, and see what an old bach's shack is like."

She looked doubtfully at him, at the low shanty, the yard that was littered with cord-wood, moldy planks, a hoopless wash-tub. She was disquieted, but Bjornstam did not give her the opportunity to be delicate. He flung out his hand in a [116/117] welcoming gesture which assumed that she was her own counselor, that she was not a Respectable Married Woman but fully a human being. With a shaky, "Well, just a moment, to warm my nose," she glanced down the street to make sure that she was not spied on, and bolted toward the shanty.

She remained for one hour, and never had she known a more considerate host than the Red Swede.

He had but one room: bare pine floor, small work-bench, wall bunk with amazingly neat bed, frying-pan and ash-stippled coffee-pot on the shelf behind the pot-bellied cannonball stove, backwoods chairs—one constructed from half a barrel, one from a tilted plank—

and a row of books incredibly assorted; Byron and Tennyson and Stevenson, a manual of gas-engines, a book by Thorstein Veblen, and a spotty treatise on "The Care, Feeding, Diseases, and Breeding of Poultry and Cattle."

There was but one picture—a magazine color-plate of a steep-roofed village in the Harz Mountains which suggested kobolds and maidens with golden hair.

Bjornstam did not fuss over her. He suggested, "Might throw open your coat and put your feet up on the box in front of the stove." He tossed his dogskin coat into the bunk, lowered himself into the barrel chair, and droned on:

"Yeh, I'm probably a yahoo, but by gum I do keep my independence by doing odd jobs, and that's more 'n these polite cusses like the clerks in the banks do. When I'm rude to some slob, it may be partly because I don't know better (and God knows I'm not no authority on trick forks and what pants you wear with a Prince Albert), but mostly it's because I mean something. I'm about the only man in Johnson County that remembers the joker in the Declaration of Independence about Americans being supposed to have the right to 'life, liberty, and the pursuit of happiness.'

"I meet old Ezra Stowbody on the street. He looks at me like he wants me to remember he's a highmuckamuck and worth two hundred thousand dollars, and he says, 'Uh, Bjornquist——'

" 'Bjornstam's my name, Ezra,' I says. *He* knows my name, all righ-tee.

" 'Well, whatever your name is,' he says, 'I understand you have a gasoline saw. I want you to come around and saw up four cords of maple for me,' he says. [117/118]

" 'So you like my looks, eh?' I says, kind of innocent.

" 'What difference does that make? Want you to saw that wood before Saturday,' he says, real sharp. Common workman going and getting fresh with a fifth of a million dollars all walking around in a hand-me-down fur coat!

" 'Here's the difference it makes,' I says, just to devil him. 'How do you know I like *your* looks?' Maybe he didn't look sore! 'Nope,' I says, 'thinking it all over, I don't like your application for a loan. Take it to another bank, only there ain't any,' I says, and I walks off on him.

"Sure. Probably I was surly—and foolish. But I figured there had to be *one* man in town independent enough to sass the banker!"

He hitched out of his chair, made coffee, gave Carol a cup, and talked on, half defiant and half apologetic, half wistful for friendliness and half amused by her surprise at the discovery that there was a proletarian philosophy.

At the door, she hinted:

"Mr. Bjornstam, if you were I, would you worry when people thought you were affected?"

"Huh? Kick 'em in the face! Say, if I were a sea-gull and all over silver, think I'd care what a pack of dirty seals thought about my flying?"

It was not the wind at her back, it was the thrust of Bjornstam's scorn which carried her through town. She faced Juanita Haydock, cocked her head at Maud Dyer's brief nod, and came home to Bea radiant. She telephoned Vida Sherwin to "run over this evening." She lustily played Tschaikowsky—the virile chords an echo of the red laughing philosopher of the tar-paper shack.

(When she hinted to Vida, "Isn't there a man here who amuses himself by being irreverent to the village gods—Bjornstam, some such a name?" the reform-leader said "Bjornstam? Oh yes. Fixes things. He's awfully impertinent.") [118]

JOHN DOS PASSOS

In the Treadmill

THE NEXT MORNING [Andrews] walked out early along the river, trying to occupy himself until it should be time to go to see Geneviève. The memory of his first days in the army, spent washing windows at the training camp, was very vivid in his mind. He saw himself again standing naked in the middle of a wide, bare room, while the recruiting sergeant measured and prodded him. And now he was a deserter. Was there any sense to it all? Had his life led in any particular direction, since he had been caught haphazard in the treadmill, or was it all chance? A toad hopping across a road in front of a steam roller.

He stood still, and looked about him. Beyond a clover field was the river with its sand banks and its broad silver reaches. A boy was wading far out in the river catching minnows with a net. Andrews watched his quick movements as he jerked the net through the water. And that boy, too, would be a soldier; the lithe body would be thrown into a mould to be made the same as other bodies, the quick movements would be standardized into the manual at arms, the inquisitive, petulant mind would be battered into servility. The stockade was built; not one of the sheep would [415/416] escape. And those that were not sheep? They were deserters; every rifle muzzle held death for them; they would not live long. And yet other nightmares had been thrown off the shoulders of men. Every man who stood up courageously to die loosened the grip of the nightmare.

Andrews walked slowly along the road, kicking his feet into the dust like a schoolboy. At a turning he threw himself down on the grass under some locust trees. The heavy fragrance of their flowers and the grumbling of the bees that hung drunkenly on the white racemes made him feel very drowsy. A cart passed, pulled by heavy white horses; an old man with his back curbed like the top of a sunflower stalk hobbled after, using the whip as a walking stick. An-

From John Dos Passos, *Three Soldiers* (New York: George H. Doran Company, 1921), pp. 415–33.

drews saw the old man's eyes turned on him suspiciously. A faint pang of fright went through him; did the old man know he was a deserter? The cart and the old man had already disappeared round the bend in the road. Andrews lay a long while listening to the jingle of the harness thin into the distance, leaving him again to the sound of the drowsy bees among the locust blossoms.

When he sat up, he noticed that through a break in the hedge beyond the slender black trunks of the locusts, he could see rising above the trees the extinguisher-shaped roof of the tower of Geneviève Rod's house. He remembered the day he had first seen Geneviève, and the boyish awkwardness with which she poured tea. Would he and Geneviève ever find a moment of real contact? All at once a bitter thought came to him. "Or is it that she wants a tame pianist as an ornament to a clever young woman's drawing room?" He jumped to his feet and started walking fast towards the town again. He would go to see her at once and settle all that forever. The village clock had begun to strike; the clear notes vibrated crisply across the fields: ten.

Walking back to the village he began to think of money. His room was twenty francs a week. He had in his purse a hundred and twenty-four francs. After fishing in all his pockets for silver, he found three francs and a half more. A hundred and twenty-seven francs fifty. If he could live on forty francs a week, he would have three weeks in which to work on the "Body and Soul of John Brown." Only [416/417] three weeks; and then he must find work. In any case he would write Henslowe to send him money if he had any; this was no time for delicacy; everything depended on his having money. And he swore to himself that he would work for three weeks, that he would throw the idea that flamed within him into shape on paper, whatever happened. He racked his brains to think of someone in America he could write to for money. A ghastly sense of solitude possessed him. And would Geneviève fail him too?

Geneviève was coming out by the front door of the house when he reached the carriage gate beside the road.

She ran to meet him.

"Good morning. I was on my way to fetch you."

She seized his hand and pressed it hard.

"How sweet of you!"

"But, Jean, you're not coming from the village."

"I've been walking."

"How early you must get up!"

"You see, the sun rises just opposite my window, and shines in on my bed. That makes me get up early."

She pushed him in the door ahead of her. They went through the hall to a long high room that had a grand piano and many old high-backed chairs, and in front of the French windows that opened on the garden, a round table of black mahogany littered with books. Two tall girls in muslin dresses stood beside the piano.

"These are my cousins. . . . Here he is at last. Monsieur Andrews, ma cousine Berthe et ma cousine Jeanne. Now you've got to play to us; we are bored to death with everything we know."

"All right. . . . But I have a great deal to talk to you about later," said Andrews in a low voice.

Geneviève nodded understandingly.

"Why don't you play us *La Reine de Saba,* Jean?"

"Oh, do play that," twittered the cousins.

"If you don't mind, I'd rather play some Bach."

"There's a lot of Bach in that chest in the corner," cried Geneviève. "It's ridiculous; everything in the house is jammed with music."

They leaned over the chest together, so that Andrews [417/418] felt her hair brush against his cheek, and the smell of her hair in his nostrils. The cousins remained by the piano.

"I must talk to you alone soon," whispered Andrews.

"All right," she said, her face reddening as she leaned over the chest.

On top of the music was a revolver.

"Look out, it's loaded," she said, when he picked it up.

He looked at her inquiringly. "I have another in my room. You see Mother and I are often alone here, and then, I like firearms. Don't you?"

"I hate them," muttered Andrews.

"Here's tons of Bach."

"Fine. . . . Look, Geneviève," he said suddenly, "lend me that revolver for a few days. I'll tell you why I want it later."

"Certainly. Be careful, because it's loaded," she said in an offhand manner, walking over to the piano with two volumes under each arm. Andrews closed the chest and followed her, suddenly bubbling with gaiety. He opened a volume haphazard.

"To a friend to dissuade him from starting on a journey," he read. "Oh, I used to know that."

He began to play, putting boisterous vigor into the tunes. In a pianissimo passage he heard one cousin whisper to the other:

"Qu'il a l'air intéressant."

"Farouche, n'est-ce pas? Genre révolutionnaire," answered the other cousin, tittering. Then he noticed that Mme. Rod was smiling at him. He got to his feet.

"Mais ne vous dérangez pas," she said.

A man with white flannel trousers and tennis shoes and a man in black with a pointed grey beard and amused grey eyes had come into the room, followed by a stout woman in hat and veil, with long white cotton gloves on her arms. Introductions were made. Andrews's spirits began to ebb. All these people were making strong the barrier between him and Geneviève. Whenever he looked at her, some well-dressed person stepped in front of her with a gesture of politeness. He felt caught in a ring of well-dressed conventions that danced about him with grotesque gestures of politeness. All [418/419] through lunch he had a crazy desire to jump to his feet and shout: "Look at me; I'm a deserter. I'm under the wheels of your system. If your system doesn't succeed in killing me, it will be that much weaker, it will have less strength to kill others." There was talk about his demobilization, and his music, and the Schola Cantorum. He felt he was being exhibited. "But they don't know what they're exhibiting," he said to himself with a certain bitter joy.

After lunch they went out into the grape arbor, where coffee was brought. Andrews sat silent, not listening to the talk, which was about Empire furniture and the new taxes, staring up into the broad sun-splotched leaves of the grape vines, remembering how the sun and shade had danced about Geneviève's hair when they had been in the arbor alone the day before, turning it all to red flame. Today she sat in shadow, and her hair was rusty and dull. Time dragged by very slowly.

At last Geneviève got to her feet.

"You haven't seen my boat," she said to Andrews. "Let's go for a row. I'll row you about."

Andrews jumped up eagerly.

"Make her be careful, Monsieur Andrews, she's dreadfully imprudent," said Madame Rod.

"You were bored to death," said Geneviève, as they walked out on the road.

"No, but those people all seemed to be building new walls between you and me. God knows there are enough already."

She looked him sharply in the eyes a second, but said nothing.

They walked slowly through the sand of the river edge, till they came to an old flat-bottomed boat painted green with an orange stripe, drawn up among the reeds.

"It will probably sink; can you swim?" she asked, laughing.

Andrews smiled, and said in a stiff voice:

"I can swim. It was by swimming that I got out of the army."

"What do you mean?"

"When I deserted."

"When you deserted?" [419/420]

Geneviève leaned over to pull on the boat. Their heads almost touching, they pulled the boat down to the water's edge, then pushed it half out on to the river.

"And if you are caught?"

"They might shoot me; I don't know. Still, as the war is over, it would probably be life imprisonment, or at least twenty years."

"You can speak of it as coolly as that?"

"It is no new idea to my mind."

"What induced you to do such a thing?"

"I was not willing to submit any longer to the treadmill."

"Come, let's go out on the river."

Geneviève stepped into the boat and caught up the oars.

"Now push her off, and don't fall in," she cried.

The boat glided out into the water. Geneviève began pulling on the oars slowly and regularly. Andrews looked at her without speaking.

"When you're tired, I'll row," he said after a while.

Behind them the village, patched white and buff-color and russet and pale red with stucco walls and steep, tiled roofs, rose in an irregular pyramid to the church. Through the wide pointed arches of the belfry they could see the bells hanging against the sky. Below in the river the town was reflected complete, with a great rift of steely blue across it where the wind ruffled the water.

The oars creaked rhythmically as Geneviève pulled on them.

"Remember, when you are tired," said Andrews again after a long pause.

Geneviève spoke through clenched teeth:

"Of course, you have no patriotism."

"As you mean it, none."

They rounded the edge of a sand bank where the current ran hard. Andrews put his hands beside her hands on the oars and pushed with her. The bow of the boat grounded in some reeds under willows.

"We'll stay here," she said, pulling in the oars that flashed in the sun as she jerked them, dripping silver, out of the water. [420/421]

She clasped her hands round her knees and leaned over towards him.

"So that is why you want my revolver. . . . Tell me all about it, from Chartres," she said, in a choked voice.

"You see, I was arrested at Chartres and sent to a labor battalion, the equivalent for your army prison, without being able to get word to my commanding officer in the School Detachment. . . ." He paused.

A bird was singing in the willow tree. The sun was under a cloud; beyond the long pale green leaves that fluttered ever so slightly in the wind, the sky was full of silvery and cream-colored clouds, with here and there a patch the color of a robin's egg. Andrews began laughing softly.

"But, Geneviève, how silly those words are, those pompous, efficient words: detachment, battalion, commanding officer. It would have all happened anyway. Things reached the breaking point; that was all. I could not submit any longer to the discipline. . . . Oh, those long Roman words, what millstones they are about men's necks! That was silly, too; I was quite willing to help in the killing of Germans, I had no quarrel with, out of curiosity or cowardice. . . . You see, it has taken me so long to find out how the world is. There was no one to show me the way."

He paused as if expecting her to speak. The bird in the willow tree was still singing.

Suddenly a dangling twig blew aside a little so that Andrews could see him—a small grey bird, his throat all puffed out with song.

"It seems to me," he said very softly, "that human society has been always that, and perhaps will be always that: organizations growing and stifling individuals, and individuals revolting hopelessly against them, and at last forming new societies to crush the old societies and becoming slaves again in their turn. . . ."

"I thought you were a socialist," broke in Geneviève sharply, in a voice that hurt him to the quick, he did not know why.

"A man told me at the labor battalion," began Andrews again, "that they'd tortured a friend of his there once by making him swallow lighted cigarettes; well, every order [421/422] shouted at me, every new humiliation before the authorities, was as great an agony to me. Can't you understand?" His voice rose suddenly to a tone of entreaty.

She nodded her head. They were silent. The willow leaves shivered in a little wind. The bird had gone.

"But tell me about the swimming part of it. That sounds exciting."

"We were working unloading cement at Passy—cement to build the stadium the army is presenting to the French, built by slave labor, like the pyramids."

"Passy's where Balzac lived. Have you ever seen his house there?"

"There was a boy working with me, the Kid, 'le gosse,' it'd be in French. Without him, I should never have done it. I was completely crushed. . . . I suppose that he was drowned. . . . Anyway, we swam under water as far as we could, and, as it was nearly dark, I managed to get on a barge, where a funny anarchist family took care of me. I've never heard of the Kid since. Then I bought these clothes that amuse you so, Geneviève, and came back to Paris to find you, mainly."

"I mean as much to you as that?" whispered Geneviève.

"In Paris, too. I tried to find a boy named Marcel, who worked on a farm near St. Germain. I met him out there one day. I found he'd gone to sea. . . . If it had not been that I had to see you, I should have gone straight to Bordeaux or Marseilles. They aren't too particular who they take as a seaman now."

"But in the army didn't you have enough of that dreadful life, always thrown among uneducated people, always in dirty, foul-smelling surroundings, you, a sensitive person, an artist? No wonder you are almost crazy after years of that." Geneviève spoke passionately, with her eyes fixed on his face.

"Oh, it wasn't that," said Andrews with despair in his voice. "I rather like the people you call low. Anyway, the differences between people are so slight. . . ." His sentence trailed away. He stopped speaking, sat stirring uneasily on the seat, afraid he would cry out. He noticed the hard shape of the revolver against his leg. [422/423]

"But isn't there something you can do about it? You must have friends," burst out Geneviève. "You were treated with horrible injustice. You can get yourself reinstated and properly demobilised. They'll see you are a person of intelligence. They can't treat you as they would anybody."

"I must be, as you say, a little mad, Geneviève," said Andrews. "But now that I, by pure accident, have made a gesture, feeble as it is, towards human freedom, I can't feel that . . . Oh, I suppose I'm a fool. . . . But there you have me, just as I am, Geneviève."

He sat with his head drooping over his chest, his two hands clasping the gunwales of the boat. After a long while Geneviève said in a dry little voice:

"Well, we must go back now; it's time for tea."

Andrews looked up. There was a dragon fly poised on the top of a reed, with silver wings and a long crimson body.

"Look just behind you, Geneviève."

"Oh, a dragon fly! What people was it that made them the symbol of life? It wasn't the Egyptians. O, I've forgotten."

"I'll row, " said Andrews.

The boat was hurried along by the current. In a very few minutes they had pulled it up on the bank in front of the Rods' house.

"Come and have some tea," said Geneviève.

"No, I must work."

"You are doing something new, aren't you?"

Andrews nodded.

"What's its name?"

"The Soul and Body of John Brown."

"Who's John Brown?"

"He was a madman who wanted to free people. There's a song about him."

"It is based on popular themes?"

"Not that I know of. . . . I only thought of the name yesterday. It came to me by a very curious accident."

"You'll come tomorrow?"

"If you're not too busy." [423/424]

"Let's see, the Boileaus are coming to lunch. There won't be anybody at tea time. We can have tea together alone."

He took her hand and held it, awkward as a child with a new playmate.

"All right, at about four. If there's nobody there, we'll play music," he said.

She pulled her hand from him hurriedly, made a curious formal gesture of farewell, and crossed the road to the gate without looking back. There was one idea in his head, to get to his room and lock the door and throw himself face down on the bed. The idea amused some distant part of his mind. That had been what he had always done when, as a child, the world had seemed too much for him. He would run upstairs and lock the door and throw himself face downward on the bed. "I wonder if I shall cry?" he thought.

Madame Boncour was coming down the stairs as he went up. He backed down and waited. When she got to the bottom, pouting a little, she said:

"So you are a friend of Mme. Rod, Monsieur?"

"How did you know that?"

A dimple appeared near her mouth in either cheek.

"You know, in the country, one knows everything," she said.

"Au revoir," he said, starting up the stairs.

"Mais, Monsieur. You should have told me. If I had known I should not have asked you to pay in advance. Oh, never. You must pardon me, Monsieur."

"All right."

"Monsieur est Américain? You see I know a lot." Her puffy cheeks shook when she giggled. "And Monsieur has known Mme. Rod et Mlle. Rod a long time. An old friend. Monsieur is a musician."

"Yes. Bon soir." Andrews ran up the stairs.

"Au revoir, Monsieur." Her canting voice followed him up the stairs.

He slammed the door behind him and threw himself on the bed. [424/425]

When Andrews awoke next morning, his first thought was how long he had to wait that day to see Geneviève. Then he remembered their talk of the day before. Was it worth while going to see her at all, he asked himself. And very gradually he felt cold despair taking hold of him. He felt for a moment that he was the only living thing in a world of dead machines; the toad hopping across the road in front of a steam roller. Suddenly he thought of Jeanne. He remembered her grimy, overworked fingers lying in her lap. He pictured her walking up and down in front of the Café de Rohan one Wednesday night, waiting for him. In the place of Geneviève, what would Jeanne have done? Yet people were always alone, really; however much they loved each other, there could be no real union. Those who rode in the great car could never feel as the others felt; the toads hopping across the road. He felt no rancour against Geneviève.

These thoughts slipped from him while he was drinking the coffee and eating the dry bread that made his breakfast; and afterwards, walking back and forth along the river bank, he felt his mind and body becoming as if fluid, and supple, trembling, bent in the rush of his music like a poplar tree bent in a wind. He sharpened a pencil and went up to his room again.

The sky was cloudless that day. As he sat at his table the square of blue through the window and the hills topped by their windmill and the silver-blue of the river, were constantly in his eyes. Sometimes he wrote notes down fast, thinking nothing, feeling nothing, seeing nothing; other times he sat for long periods staring at the sky and at the windmill vaguely happy, playing with unexpected thoughts that came and vanished, as now and then a moth fluttered in the window to blunder about the ceiling beams, and, at last, to disappear without his knowing how.

When the clock struck twelve, he found he was very hungry. For two days he had eaten nothing but bread, sausage and cheese. Finding Madame Boncour behind the bar downstairs, polishing glasses, he ordered dinner of her. She brought him a stew and a bottle of wine at once, and [425/426] stood over him watching him eat it, her arms akimbo and the dimples showing in her huge red cheeks.

"Monsieur eats less than any young man I ever saw," she said.

"I'm working hard," said Andrews, flushing.

"But when you work you have to eat a great deal, a great deal."

"And if the money is short?" asked Andrews with a smile. Something in the steely searching look that passed over her eyes for a minute startled him.

"There are not many people here now, Monsieur, but you should see it on a market day. . . . Monsieur will take some dessert?"

"Cheese and coffee."

"Nothing more? It's the season of strawberries."

"Nothing more, thank you."

When Madame Boncour came back with the cheese, she said:

"I had Americans here once, Monsieur. A pretty time I had with them, too. They were deserters. They went away without paying, with the gendarmes after them. I hope they were caught and sent to the front, those good-for-nothings."

"There are all sorts of Americans," said Andrews in a low voice. He was angry with himself because his heart beat so.

"Well, I'm going for a little walk. Au revoir, Madame."

"Monsieur is going for a little walk. Amusez-vous bien, Monsieur. Au revoir, Monsieur," Madame Boncour's sing-song tones followed him out.

A little before four Andrews knocked at the front door of the Rods' house. He could hear Santo, the little black and tan, barking inside. Madame Rod opened the door for him herself.

"Oh, here you are," she said. "Come and have some tea. Did the work go well to-day?"

"And Geneviève?" stammered Andrews.

"She went out motoring with some friends. She left a note for you. It's on the tea-table."

He found himself talking, making questions and answers, [426/427] drinking tea, putting cakes into his mouth, all through a white dead mist.

Geneviève's note said:

"Jean:—I'm thinking of ways and means. You must get away to a neutral country. Why couldn't you have talked it over with me first, before cutting off every chance of going back. I'll be in tomorrow at the same time.

"Bien à vous.   G. R."

"Would it disturb you if I played the piano a few minutes, Madame Rod?" Andrews found himself asking all at once.

"No, go ahead. We'll come in later and listen to you."

It was only as he left the room that he realized he had been talking to the two cousins as well as to Madame Rod.

At the piano he forgot everything and regained his mood of vague joyousness. He found paper and a pencil in his pocket, and played the theme that had come to him while he had been washing windows at the top of a stepladder at training camp arranging it, modelling it, forgetting everything, absorbed in his rhythms and cadences. When he stopped work it was nearly dark. Geneviève Rod, a veil round her head, stood in the French window that led to the garden.

"I heard you," she said, "Go on."

"I'm through. How was your motor ride?"

"I loved it. It's not often I get a chance to go motoring."

"Nor is it often I get a chance to talk to you alone," cried Andrews bitterly.

"You seem to feel you have rights of ownership over me. I resent it. No one has rights over me." She spoke as if it were not the first time she had thought of the phrase.

He walked over and leaned against the window beside her.

"Has it made such a difference to you, Geneviève, finding out that I am a deserter?"

"No, of course not," she said hastily.

"I think it has, Geneviève. . . . What do you want me to do? Do you think I should give myself up? A man I knew in Paris has given himself up, but he hadn't taken his uniform off. It seems that makes a difference. He was a nice fellow. His name was Al, he was from San Francisco. [427/428] He had nerve, for he amputated his own little finger when his hand was crushed by a freight car."

"Oh, no, no. Oh, this is so frightful. And you would have been a great composer. I feel sure of it."

"Why, would have been? The stuff I'm doing now's better than any of the dribbling things I've done before, I know that."

"Oh, yes, but you'll need to study, to get yourself known."

"If I can pull through six months, I'm safe. The army will have gone. I don't believe they extradite deserters."

"Yes, but the shame of it, the danger of being found out all the time."

"I am ashamed of many things in my life, Geneviève. I'm rather proud of this."

"But can't you understand that other people haven't your notions of individual liberty?"

"I must go, Geneviève."

"You must come in again soon."

"One of these days."

And he was out in the road in the windy twilight, with his music papers crumpled in his hand. The sky was full of tempestuous purple clouds; between them were spaces of clear claret-colored light, and here and there a gleam of opal. There were a few drops of rain in the wind that rustled the broad leaves of the lindens and filled the wheat fields with waves like the sea, and made the river very dark between rosy sand banks. It began to rain. Andrews hurried home so as not to drench his only suit. Once in his room he lit four candles and placed them at the corners of his table. A little cold crimson light still filtered in through the rain from the afterglow, giving the candles a ghostly glimmer. Then he lay on his bed, and staring up at the flickering light on the ceiling, tried to think.

"Well, you're alone now, John Andrews," he said aloud, after a half-hour, and jumped jauntily to his feet. He stretched himself and yawned. Outside the rain pattered loudly and steadily. "Let's have a general accounting," he said to himself. "It'll be easily a month before I hear from old Howe in America, and longer before I hear from Henslowe, [428/429] and already I've spent twenty francs on food. Can't make it this way. Then, in real possessions, I have one volume of Villon, a green book on counterpoint, a map of France torn in two, and a moderately well-stocked mind."

He put the two books on the middle of the table before him, on top of his disorderly bundle of music papers and notebooks. Then he went on, piling his possessions there as he thought of them. Three pencils, a fountain pen. Automatically he reached for his watch, but he remembered he'd given it to Al to pawn in case he didn't decide to give himself up, and needed money. A toothbrush. A shaving set. A piece of soap. A hairbrush and a broken comb. Anything else? He groped in the musette that hung on the foot of the bed. A box of matches. A knife with one blade missing, and a mashed cigarette. Amusement growing on him every minute, he contemplated the pile. Then, in the drawer, he remembered, was a clean shirt and two pairs of soiled socks. And that was all, absolutely all. Nothing saleable there. Except Geneviève's revolver. He pulled it out of his pocket. The candlelight flashed on the bright nickel. No, he might need that; it was too valuable to sell. He pointed it towards himself. Under the chin was said to be the best place. He wondered if he would pull the trigger when the barrel was pressed against his chin. No, when his money gave out he'd sell the revolver. An expensive death for a starving man. He sat on the edge of the bed and laughed.

Then he discovered he was very hungry. Two meals in one day; shocking! He said to himself. Whistling joyfully, like a schoolboy, he strode down the crickety stairs to order a meal of Madame Boncour.

It was with a strange start that he noticed that the tune he was whistling was:

> "John Brown's body lies a-mouldering in the grave,
> But his soul goes marching on."

The lindens were in bloom. From a tree beside the house great gusts of fragrance, heavy as incense, came in through the open window. Andrews lay across the table with his eyes closed and his cheek in a mass of ruled papers. He was [429/430] very tired. The first movement of the "Soul and Body of John Brown" was down on paper. The village clock struck two. He got to his feet and stood a moment looking absently out of the window. It was a sultry afternoon of swollen clouds that hung low over the river. The windmill on the hilltop opposite was motionless. He seemed to hear Geneviève's voice the last time he had seen her, so long ago. "You would have been a great composer." He walked over to the table and turned over some sheets without looking at them. "Would have been." He shrugged his shoulders. So you couldn't be a great composer and a deserter too in the year 1919. Probably Geneviève was right. But he must have something to eat.

"But how late it is," expostulated Madame Boncour, when he asked for lunch.

"I know it's very late. I have just finished a third of the work I'm doing."

"And do you get paid a great deal, when that is finished?" asked Madame Boncour, the dimples appearing in her broad cheeks.

"Some day, perhaps."

"You will be lonely now that the Rods have left."

"Have they left?"

"Didn't you know? Didn't you go to say goodby? They've gone to the seashore. . . . But I'll make you a little omelette."

"Thank you."

When Madame Boncour came back with the omelette and fried potatoes, she said to him in a mysterious voice:

"You didn't go to see the Rods as often these last weeks."

"No."

Madame Boncour stood staring at him, with her red arms folded round her breasts, shaking her head.

When he got up to go upstairs again, she suddenly shouted:

"And when are you going to pay me? It's two weeks since you have paid me."

"But, Madame Boncour, I told you I had no money. If you wait a day or two, I'm sure to get some in the mail. It can't be more than a day or two." [430/431]

"I've heard that story before."

"I've even tried to get work at several farms round here."

Madame Boncour threw back her head and laughed showing the blackened teeth of her lower jaw.

"Look here," she said at length, "after this week, it's finished. You either pay me, or . . . And I sleep very lightly, Monsieur." Her voice took on suddenly its usual sleek singsong tone.

Andrews broke away and ran upstairs to his room.

"I must fly the coop tonight," he said to himself. But suppose then letters came with money the next day. He writhed in indecision all the afternoon.

That evening he took a long walk. In passing the Rods' house he

saw that the shutters were closed. It gave him a sort of relief to
know that Geneviève no longer lived near him. His solitude was
complete, now.

And why, instead of writing music that would have been worth
while if he hadn't been a deserter, he kept asking himself, hadn't he
tried long ago to act, to make a gesture, however feeble, however
forlorn, for other people's freedom? Half by accident he had managed to free himself from the treadmill. Couldn't he have helped
others? If he only had his life to live over again. No; he had not
lived up to the name of John Brown.

It was dark when he got back to the village. He had decided to
wait one more day.

The next morning he started working on the second movement.
The lack of a piano made it very difficult to get ahead, yet he said to
himself that he should put down what he could, as it would be long
before he found leisure again.

One night he had blown out his candle and stood at the window
watching the glint of the moon on the river. He heard a soft heavy
step on the landing outside his room. A floorboard creaked, and the
key turned in the lock. The step was heard again on the stairs. John
Andrews laughed aloud. The window was only twenty feet from the
ground, and there was a trellis. He got into bed contentedly. He
must sleep well, for tomorrow night he would slip out of the window and make for Bordeaux.

Another morning. A brisk wind blew, fluttering Andrews's
[431/432] papers as he worked. Outside the river was streaked blue
and silver and slate-colored. The windmill's arms waved fast against
the piled clouds. The scent of the lindens came only intermittently
on the sharp wind. In spite of himself, the tune of "John Brown's
Body" had crept in among his ideas. Andrews sat with a pencil at
his lips, whistling softly, while in the back of his mind a vast chorus
seemed singing:

> "John Brown's body lies a-mouldering in the grave,
> But his soul goes marching on.
> Glory, glory, hallelujah!
> But his soul goes marching on."

If one could only find freedom by marching for it, came the
thought.

All at once he became rigid, his hands clutched the table edge.

There was an American voice under his window:

"D'you think she's kiddin' us, Charley?"

Andrews was blinded, falling from a dizzy height. God, could things repeat themselves like that? Would everything be repeated? And he seemed to hear voices whisper in his ears: "One of you men teach him how to salute."

He jumped to his feet and pulled open the drawer. It was empty. The woman had taken the revolver. "It's all planned, then. She knew," he said aloud in a low voice.

He became suddenly calm.

A man in a boat was passing down the river. The boat was painted bright green; the man wore a curious jacket of a burnt-brown color, and held a fishing pole.

Andrews sat in his chair again. The boat was out of sight now, but there was the windmill turning, turning against the piled white clouds.

There were steps on the stairs.

Two swallows, twittering, curved past the window, very near, so that Andrews could make out the markings on their wings and the way they folded their legs against their pale-grey bellies.

There was a knock.

"Come in," said Andrews firmly. [432/433]

"I beg yer pardon," said a soldier with his hat, that had a band, in his hand. "Are you the American?"

"Yes."

"Well, the woman down there said she thought your papers wasn't in very good order." The man stammered with embarrassment.

Their eyes met.

"No, I'm a deserter," said Andrews.

The M. P. snatched for his whistle and blew it hard. There was an answering whistle from outside the window.

"Get your stuff together."

"I have nothing."

"All right, walk downstairs slowly in front of me."

Outside the windmill was turning, turning, against the piled white clouds of the sky.

Andrews turned his eyes towards the door. The M.P. closed the door after them, and followed on his heels down the steps.

On John Andrews's writing table the brisk wind rustled among the broad sheets of paper. First one sheet, then another, blew off the table, until the floor was littered with them. [433]

H. L. MENCKEN

Duty

SOME OF THE loosest thinking in ethics has duty for its theme. Practically all writers on the subject agree that the individual owes certain unescapable duties to the race—for example, the duty of engaging in productive labor, and that of marrying and begetting offspring. In support of this position it is almost always argued that if *all* men neglected such duties the race would perish. The logic is hollow enough to be worthy of the college professors who are guilty of it. It simply confuses the conventionality, the pusillanimity, the lack of imagination of the majority of men with the duty of *all* men. There is not the slightest ground for assuming, even as a matter of mere argumentation, that *all* men will ever neglect these alleged duties. There will always remain a safe majority that is willing to do whatever is ordained—that accepts docilely the government it is born under, obeys its laws, and supports its theory. But that majority does not comprise the men who render the highest and most intelligent services to the [313/314] race; it comprises those who render nothing save their obedience.

For the man who differs from this inert and well-regimented mass, however slightly, there are no duties *per se*. What he is spontaneously inclined to do is of vastly more value to all of us than what the majority is willing to do. There is, indeed, no such thing as duty-in-itself; it is a mere chimera of ethical theorists. Human progress is furthered, not by conformity, but by aberration. The very concept of duty is thus a function of inferiority; it belongs naturally only to timorous and incompetent men. Even on such levels it remains largely a self-delusion, a soothing apparition, a euphemism for necessity. When a man succumbs to duty he merely succumbs to the habit and inclination of other men. Their collective interests invariably pull against his individual interests. Some of us can resist a pretty strong pull—the pull perhaps of thousands. But it is only the miraculous man who can withstand the pull of a whole nation. [314]

H. L. Mencken, "Duty," in *Prejudices, Third Series* (New York: Alfred A. Knopf, 1922), pp. 313–14.

H. L. MENCKEN

The Iconoclast

OF A PIECE with the absurd pedagogical demand for so-called constructive criticism is the doctrine that an iconoclast is a hollow and evil fellow unless he can prove his case. Why, indeed, should he prove it? Doesn't he prove enough when he proves by his blasphemy that this or that idol is defectively convincing—that at least *one* visitor to the shrine is left full of doubts? The fact is enormously significant; it indicates that instinct has somehow risen superior to the shallowness of logic, the refuge of fools. The pedant and the priest have always been the most expert of logicians—and the most diligent disseminators of nonsense and worse. The liberation of the human mind has never been furthered by such learned dunderheads; it has been furthered by gay fellows who heaved dead cats into sanctuaries and then went roistering down the highways of the world, proving to all men that doubt, after all, was safe—[139/140] that the god in the sanctuary was finite in his power, and hence a fraud. One horse-laugh is worth ten thousand syllogisms. It is not only more effective; it is also vastly more intelligent. [140]

H. L. Mencken, "The Iconoclast," in *Prejudices, Fourth Series* (New York: Alfred A. Knopf, 1924), pp. 139-40.

SHERWOOD ANDERSON

Over the Threshold

ON AN EVENING of the late summer I got off a train at a growing Ohio industrial town where I had once lived. I was rapidly becoming a middle-aged man. Two years before I had left the place in disgrace. There I had tried to be a manufacturer, a money-maker, and had failed, and I had been trying and failing ever since. In the town some thousands of dollars had been lost for others. An effort to conform to the standard dreams of the men of my times had failed and in the midst of my disgrace and generally hopeless outlook, as regards making a living, I had been filled with joy at coming to the end of it all. One morning I had left the place afoot, leaving my poor little factory, like an illegitimate child, on another man's doorstep. I had left, merely taking what money was in my pocket, some eight or ten dollars.

What a moment that leaving had been! To one of the European artists I afterward came to know the situation would have been unbelievably grotesque. Such a man could not have believed in my earnestness about it all and would have thought my feelings of the moment a worked-up thing. I can in fancy hear one of the Frenchmen, Italians or Russians I later knew laughing at me. "Well, but why get so worked up? A factory is a factory, is it not? Why may not one [298/299] break it like an empty bottle? You have lost some money for others? See the light on that field over there. These others, for whom you lost money, were they compelled to beg in the streets, were their children torn by wolves? What is it you Americans get so excited about when a little money is lost?"

A European artist may not understand but an American will understand. The devil! It is not a question of money. No men are so careless and free with money as the Americans. There is another matter involved.

It strikes rather deeply at the roots of our beings. Childish as it all

From Sherwood Anderson, A Story Teller's Story (New York: B. W. Huebsch, Inc., 1924), pp. 298–313.

may have seemed to an older and more sophisticated world, we Americans, from the beginning, have been up to something, or we have wanted to think we were up to something. We came here, or our fathers or grandfathers came here, from a hundred diverse places—and you may be sure it was not the artists who came. Artists do not want to cut down trees, root stumps out of the ground, build towns and railroads. The artist wants to sit with a strip of canvas before him, face an open space on a wall, carve a bit of wood, make combinations of words and sentences, as I am doing now—and try to express to others some thought or feeling of his own. He wants to dream of color, to lay hold of form, free the sensual in himself, live more fully and freely in his contact with the materials before him than he can possibly live in life. He seeks a kind of controlled ecstasy and is a man with a passion, a "nut," as we love to say in America. And very often, when he is not in actual contact with his materials, he is a much more vain and disagreeable ass than any man, not [299/300] an artist, could possibly be. As a living man he is almost always a pest. It is only when dead he begins to have value.

The simple truth is that in a European country the artist is more freely accepted than he is among us, and only because he has been longer about. They know how harmless he really is—or rather do not know how subtly dangerous he can be—and accept him only as one might accept a hybrid cross between a dog and a cat that went growling mewing barking and spitting about the house. One might want to kill the first of such strange beasts one sees but after one has seen a dozen and has realized that, like the mule, they cannot breed their own kind one laughs and lets them live, paying no more attention to them than modern France for example pays to its artists.

But in America things are somewhat different. Here something went wrong in the beginning. We pretended to so much and were going to do such great things here. This vast land was to be a refuge for all the outlawed brave foolish folk of the world. The declaration of the rights of man was to have a new hearing in a new place. The devil! We did get ourselves into a bad hole. We were going to be superhuman and it turned out we were sons of men who were not such devilish fellows after all. You cannot blame us that we are somewhat reluctant about finding out the very human things concerning ourselves. One does so hate to come down off the perch.

We are now losing our former feeling of inherent virtue, are permitting ourselves occasionally to laugh at ourselves for our pretensions, but there was a time [300/301] here when we were sincerely in earnest about all this American business, "the land of the free and the home of the brave." We actually meant it and no one will ever understand present-day America or Americans who does not concede that we meant it and that while we were building all of our big ugly hurriedly thrown-together towns, creating our great industrial system, growing always more huge and prosperous, we were as much in earnest about what we thought we were up to as were the French of the thirteenth century when they built the cathedral of Chartres to the glory of God.

They built the cathedral of Chartres to the glory of God and we really intended building here a land to the glory of Man, and thought we were doing it too. That was our intention and the affair only blew up in the process, or got perverted, because Man, even the brave and the free Man, is somewhat a less worthy object of glorification than God. This we might have found out long ago but that we did not know each other. We came from too many different places to know each other well, had been promised too much, wanted too much. We were afraid to know each other.

Oh, how Americans have wanted heroes, wanted brave simple fine men! And how sincerely and deeply we Americans have been afraid to understand and love one another, fearing to find ourselves at the end no more brave heroic and fine than the people of almost any other part of the world.

I however digress. What I am trying to do is to give the processes of my own mind at two distinct moments of my own life. First, the moment when after [301/302] many years of effort to conform to an unstated but dimly understood American dream by making myself a successful man in the material world I threw all overboard and then at another moment when, having come back to the same spot where I passed through the first moment, I attempted to confront myself with myself with a somewhat changed point of view.

As for the first of these moments, it was melodramatic and even silly enough. The struggle centred itself at the last within the walls of a particular moment and within the walls of a particular room.

I sat in the room with a woman who was my secretary. For several years I had been sitting there, dictating to her regarding the goods I had made in my factory and that I was attempting to sell. The attempt to sell the goods had become a sort of madness in me. There were certain thousands or perhaps hundreds of thousands of men living in towns or on farms in many states of my country who might possibly buy the goods I had made rather than the goods made in another factory by another man. How I had wheedled! How I had schemed! In some years I gave myself quite fully to the matter in hand and the dollars trickled in. Well, I was about to become rich. It was a possibility. After a good day or week, when many dollars had come, I went to walk and when I had got into a quiet place where I was unobserved I threw back my shoulders and strutted. During the year I had made for myself so many dollars. Next year I would make so many more, and the next year so many more. But my thoughts of the matter did not express themselves in the dollars. [302/303] It never does to the American man. Who calls the American a dollar-lover is foolish. My factory was of a certain size—it was really a poor haphazardly enough run place—but after a time I would build a great factory and after that a greater and greater. Like a true American, I thought in size.

My fancy played with the matter of factories as a child would play with a toy. There would be a great factory with walls going up and up and a little open place for a lawn at the front, shower baths for the workers with perhaps a fountain playing on a lawn, and up before the door of this place I would drive in a large automobile.

Oh, how I would be respected by all, how I would be looked up to by all! I walked in a little dark street, throwing back my shoulders. How grand and glorious I felt!

The houses along the street in which I walked were small and ugly and dirty-faced children played in the yards. I wondered. Having walked, dreaming my dream for a long time I returned to the neighborhood of my factory and opening my office went in to sit at my desk smoking a cigarette. The night watchman came in. He was an old man who had once been a school-teacher but, as he said, his eyes had gone back on him.

When I had walked alone I had been able to make myself feel somewhat as I fancied a prince might have felt but when anyone came near me something exploded inside. I was a deflated balloon. Well, in fancy, I had a thousand workmen under me. They were children and I was their father and would look out for them. Perhaps I would build them model [303/304] houses to live in, a town of model houses built about my great factory, eh? The workmen would be my children and I would look out for my children. "Land of the free—home of the brave."

But I was back in my factory now and the night watchman sat smoking with me. Sometimes we talked far into the night. The devil! He was a fellow like myself, having the same problems as myself. How could I be his father? The thought was absurd. Once, when he was a younger man, he had dreamed of being a scholar but his eyes had gone back on him. What had he wanted to do? He spoke of it for a time. He had wanted to be a scholar and I had myself spent those earlier years eagerly reading books. "I would really like to have been a learned monk, one of those fellows such as appeared in the Middle Ages, one of the fellows who went off and lived by himself and gave himself up wholly to learning, one who believed in learning, who spent his life humbly seeking new truths—but I got married and my wife had kids, and then, you see, my eyes went back on me." He spoke of the matter philosophically. One did not

let oneself get too much excited. After a time one got over any feeling of bitterness. The night watchman had a boy, a lad of fifteen,
who also loved books. "He is pretty lucky, can get all the books he
wants at the public library. In the afternoon after school is out and
before I come down here to my job he reads aloud to me." . . .

Men and women, many men and many women! There were men
and women working in my factory, [304/305] men and women walking in streets with me, many men and women scattered far and wide
over the country to whom I wanted to sell my goods. I sent men,
salesmen, to see them— I wrote letters; how many thousands of letters, all to the same purpose! "Will you buy my goods?" And again,
"Will you buy my goods?"

What were the other men thinking about? What was I myself
thinking about? Suppose it were possible to know something of the
men and women, to know something of oneself, too. The devil!
These were not thoughts that would help me to sell my goods to all
the others. What were all the others like? What was I myself like?
Did I want a large factory with a little lawn and a fountain in front
and with a model town built about it?

Days of endlessly writing letters to men, nights of walking in
strange quiet streets. What had happened to me? "I shall go get
drunk," I said to myself and I did go and get drunk. Taking a train
to a near-by city I drank until a kind of joy came to me and with
some man I had found and who had joined in my carousal I walked
in streets, shouting to other men, singing songs, going sometimes into
strange houses to laugh with people, to talk with people I found
there.

Here was something I liked and something the others liked too.
When I had come to people in strange houses, half drunk, released,
they were not afraid of me. "Well, he wants to talk," they seemed to
be saying to themselves. "That's fine!" There was something broken
down between us, a wall broken down. We talked of outlandish
things for Anglo-Saxon [305/306] trained people to speak of, of love
between men and women, of what children's coming meant. Food
was brought forth. Often in a single evening of this sort I got more
from people than I could get from weeks of ordinary intercourse.
The people were a little excited by the strangeness of two unknown
men in their houses. With my companion I went boldly to the door
and knocked. Laughter. "Hello, the house!" It might be the house of
a laborer or that of a well-to-do merchant. I had hold of my new-
found friend's arm and explained our presence as well as I could.
"We are a little drunk and we are travelers. We just want to sit and
visit with you a while."

There was a kind of terror in people's eyes, and a kind of gladness too. An old workman showed us a relic he had brought home with him from the Civil War while his wife ran into a bedroom and changed her dress. Then a child awoke in a near-by room and began to cry and was permitted to come in in her nightgown and lie in my arms or in the arms of the new-found friend who had got drunk with me. The talk swept over strange intimate subjects. What were men up to? What were women up to? There was a kind of deep taking of breath, as though we had all been holding something back from one another and had suddenly decided to let go. Once or twice we stayed all night in the house to which we had gone.

And then back to the writing of letters—to sell my goods. In the city to which I had gone to carouse I had seen many women of the streets, standing at corners, looking furtively about. My thoughts got [306/307] fixed upon prostitution. Was I a prostitute? Was I prostituting my life?

What thoughts in the mind! There was a note due and payable at the bank. "Now here, you man, attend to your affairs. You have induced others to put money into your enterprises. If you are to build a great enterprise here you must be up and at it."

How often in after years I have laughed at myself for the thoughts and emotions of that time. There is a thought I have had that is very delicious. It is this, and I dare say it will be an unwelcome thought to many, "I am the American man. I think there is no doubt of it. I am just the mixture, the cold, moral man of the North into whose body has come the warm pagan blood of the South. I love and am afraid to love. Behold in me the American man striving to become an artist, to become conscious of himself, filled with wonder concerning himself and others, trying to have a good time and not fake a good time. I am not English Italian Jew German Frenchman Russian. What am I? I am tremendously serious about it all but at the same time I laugh constantly at myself for my own seriousness. Like all real American men of our day I wander constantly from place to place striving to put down roots into the American soil and not quite doing it. If you say the real American man is not yet born, you lie. I am the type of the fellow."

This is somewhat of a joke on me but it is a greater joke on the reader. As respectable and conventional a man as Calvin Coolidge has me in him—and I have him in myself? Do not doubt it. [307/308] I have him in me and Eugene Debs in me and the crazy political idealists of the Western States and Mr. Gary of the Steel Trust and the whole crew. I accept them all as part of myself. Would to God they would thus accept me! . . .

And being this thing I tried to describe I return now to myself sitting between the walls of a certain room and between the walls of a certain moment too. Just why was that moment so pregnant? I will never quite know.

It came with a rush, the feeling that I must quit buying and selling, the overwhelming feeling of uncleanliness. I was in my whole nature a tale-teller. My father had been one and his not knowing had destroyed him. The tale-teller cannot bother with buying and selling. To do so will destroy him. No class of men I have ever known are so dull and cheerless as the writers of glad sentimental romances, the painters of glad pretty pictures. The corrupt unspeakable thing that had happened to tale-telling in America was all concerned with this matter of buying and selling. The horse cannot sing like a canary bird nor the canary bird pull a plow like a horse and either of them attempting it becomes something ridiculous. [308/309]

There was a door leading out from my office to the street. How many steps to the door? I counted them, "five, six, seven." "Suppose," I asked myself, "I could take those five, six, seven steps to the door, pass out at the door, go along that railroad track out there, disappear into the far horizon beyond. Where was I to go? In the town where my factory was located I had still the reputation of being a bright young business man. In my first years there I had been filled with shrewd vast schemes. I had been admired, looked up to. Since that time I had gone down and down as a bright young man but no one yet knew how far I had gone. I was still respected in the town, my word was still good at the bank. I was a respectable man.

Did I want to do something not respectable, not decent? I am trying to give you the history of a moment and as a tale-teller I have come to think that the true history of life is but a history of moments. It is only at rare moments we live. I wanted to walk out at a door and go away into the distance. The American is still a wanderer, a migrating bird not yet ready to build a nest. All our cities are built temporarily as are the houses in which we live. We are on the way—toward what? There have been other times in the history of the world when many [309/310] strange peoples came together in a new strange land. To assume that we have made an America, even materially, seems to me now but telling ourselves fairy tales in the night. We have not even made it materially yet and the American man has only gone in for money-making on a large scale to quiet his own restlessness, as the monk of old days was given the Regula of Augustine to quiet him and still the lusts in himself. For the monk, kept occupied with the saying of prayers and the doing of many little sacred offices, there was no time for the lusts of the world to enter in and for the American to be perpetually busy with his affairs, with his automobiles, with his movies, there is no time for unquiet thoughts.

On that day in the office at my factory I looked at myself and laughed. The whole struggle I am trying to describe and that I am confident will be closer to the understanding of most Americans than anything else I have ever written was accompanied by a kind of mocking laughter at myself and my own seriousness about it all.

Very well, then, I wanted to go out of the door and never come back. How many Americans want to go—but where do they want to go? I wanted to accept for myself all the little restless thoughts of which myself and the others had been so afraid and you, who are Americans, will understand the necessity of my continually laughing at myself and at all things dear to me. I must laugh at the thing I love the more intensely because of my love. Any American will understand that.

It was a trying moment for me. There was the woman, my secretary, now looking at me. What did [310/311] she represent? What did she not represent? Would I dare be honest with her? It was quite apparent to me I would not. I had got to my feet and we stood looking at each other. "It is now or never," I said to myself, and I remember that I kept smiling. I had stopped dictating to her in the midst of a sentence. "The goods about which you have inquired are the best of their kind made in the—"

I stood and she sat and we were looking at each other intently. "What's the matter?" she asked. She was an intelligent woman, more intelligent I am sure than myself, just because she was a woman and good, while I have never been good, do not know how to be good. Could I explain all to her? The words of a fancied explanation marched through my mind: "My dear young woman, it is all very silly but I have decided to no longer concern myself with this buying and selling. It may be all right for others but for me it is poison. There is this factory. You may have it if it please you. It is of little value I dare say. Perhaps it is money ahead and then again it may well be it is money behind. I am uncertain about it all and now I am going away. Now, at this moment, with the letter I have been dictating, with the very sentence you have been writing left unfinished, I am going out that door and never come back. What am I going to do? Well now, that I don't know. I am going to wander about. I am going to sit with people, listen to words, tell tales of people, what they are thinking, what they are feeling. The devil! It may even be I am going forth in search of myself."

The woman was looking into my eyes the while I looked into hers.

Perhaps I had grown a little pale [311/312] and now she grew pale. "You're sick," she said and her words gave me an idea. There was wanted a justification of myself, not to myself but to the others. A crafty thought came. Was the thought crafty or was I, at the moment, a little insane, a "nut," as every American so loves to say of every man who does something a little out of the groove.

I had grown pale and it may be I was ill but nevertheless I was laughing—the American laugh. Had I suddenly become a little insane? What a comfort that thought would be, not to myself but to the others. My leaving the place I was then in would tear up roots that had gone down a little into the ground. The ground I did not think would support the tree that was myself and that I thought wanted to grow.

My mind dwelt on the matter of roots and I looked at my feet. The whole question with which I was at the moment concerned became a matter of feet. I had two feet that could take me out of the life I was then in and that, to do so, would need but take three or four steps to a door. When I had reached the door and had stepped out of my little factory office everything would be quite simplified, I was sure. I had to lift myself out. Others would have to tackle the job of getting me back, once I had stepped over that threshold.

Whether at the moment I merely became shrewd and crafty or whether I really became temporarily insane I shall never quite know. What I did was to step very close to the woman and looking directly into her eyes I laughed gayly. Others besides herself would, I knew, hear the words I was now speaking. [312/313] I looked at my feet. "I have been wading in a long river and my feet are wet," I said.

Again I laughed as I walked lightly toward the door and out of a long and tangled phase of my life, out of the door of buying and selling, out of the door of affairs.

"They want me to be a 'nut,' will love to think of me as a 'nut,' and why not? It may just be that's what I am," I thought gayly and at the same time turned and said a final confusing sentence to the woman who now stared at me in speechless amazement. "My feet are cold wet and heavy from long wading in a river. Now I shall go walk on dry land," I said, and as I passed out at the door a delicious thought came. "Oh, you little tricky words, you are my brothers. It is you, not myself, have lifted me over this threshold. It is you who have dared give me a hand. For the rest of my life I will be a servant to you," I whispered to myself as I went along a spur of railroad track, over a bridge, out of a town and out of that phase of my life. [313]

JAMES BALDWIN

Notes of a Native Son

ON THE 29th of July, in 1943, my father died. On the same day, a few hours later, his last child was born. Over a month before this, while all our energies were concentrated in waiting for these events, there had been, in Detroit, one of the bloodiest race riots of the century. A few hours after my father's funeral, while he lay in state in the undertaker's chapel, a race riot broke out in Harlem. On the morning of the 3rd of August, we drove my father to the graveyard through a wilderness of smashed plate glass.

The day of my father's funeral had also been my nineteenth birthday. As we drove him to the graveyard, the spoils of injustice, anarchy, discontent, and hatred were all around us. It seemed to me that God himself had devised, to mark my father's end, the most sustained and brutally dissonant of codas. And it seemed to me, too, that the violence which rose all about us as my father left the world had been devised as a corrective for the pride of his eldest son. I had declined to believe in that apocalypse which had been central to my father's vision; very well, life seemed to be saying, here is something that will certainly pass for an apocalypse until the real thing comes along. I had inclined to be contemptuous of my [85/86] father for the conditions of his life, for the conditions of our lives. When his life had ended I began to wonder about that life and also, in a new way, to be apprehensive about my own.

I had not known my father very well. We had got on badly, partly because we shared, in our different fashions, the vice of stubborn pride. When he was dead I realized that I had hardly ever spoken to him. When he had been dead a long time I began to wish I had. It seems to be typical of life in America, where opportunities, real and fancied, are thicker than anywhere else on the globe, that the second generation has no time to talk to the first. No one, including my father, seems to have known exactly how old he was, but his mother

James Baldwin, "Notes of a Native Son," in *Notes of a Native Son* (Boston: Beacon Press, 1955), pp. 85–98.

had been born during slavery. He was of the first generation of free men. He, along with thousands of other Negroes, came North after 1919 and I was part of that generation which had never seen the landscape of what Negroes sometimes call the Old Country.

He had been born in New Orleans and had been a quite young man there during the time that Louis Armstrong, a boy, was running errands for the dives and honky-tonks of what was always presented to me as one of the most wicked of cities—to this day, whenever I think of New Orleans, I also helplessly think of Sodom and Gomorrah. My father never mentioned Louis Armstrong, except to forbid us to play his records; but there was a picture of him on our wall for a long time. One of my father's strong-willed female relatives had placed it there and forbade my father to take it down. He never did, but he eventually maneuvered her out of the house and when, some [86/87] years later, she was in trouble and near death, he refused to do anything to help her.

He was, I think, very handsome. I gather this from photographs and from my own memories of him, dressed in his Sunday best and on his way to preach a sermon somewhere, when I was little. Handsome, proud, and ingrown, "like a toe-nail," somebody said. But he looked to me, as I grew older, like pictures I had seen of African tribal chieftains: he really should have been naked, with war-paint on and barbaric mementos, standing among spears. He could be chilling in the pulpit and indescribably cruel in his personal life and he was certainly the most bitter man I have ever met; yet it must be said that there was something else in him, buried in him, which lent him his tremendous power and, even, a rather crushing charm. It had something to do with his blackness, I think—he was very black —with his blackness and his beauty, and with the fact that he knew that he was black but did not know that he was beautiful. He claimed to be proud of his blackness but it had also been the cause of much humiliation and it had fixed bleak boundaries to his life. He was not a young man when we were growing up and he had already suffered many kinds of ruin; in his outrageously demanding and protective way he loved his children, who were black like him and menaced, like him; and all these things sometimes showed in his face when he tried, never to my knowledge with any success, to establish contact with any of us. When he took one of his children on his knee to play, the child always became fretful and began to cry; when he tried to help one of us with our homework the absolutely unabating [87/88] tension which emanated from him caused our minds and our tongues to become paralyzed, so that he, scarcely knowing why, flew into a rage and the child, not knowing why, was punished. If it ever entered his head to bring a surprise home for his children, it was, almost unfailingly, the wrong surprise and even the big watermelons he often brought home on his back in the summertime led to the most appalling scenes. I do not remember, in all those years, that one of his children was ever glad to see him come home. From what I was able to gather of his early life, it seemed that this inability to establish contact with other people had always marked him and had been one of the things which had driven him out of New Orleans. There was something in him, therefore, groping and tentative, which was never expressed and which was buried with him. One saw it most clearly when he was facing new people and hoping to impress them. But he never did, not for long. We went from church to smaller and more improbable church, he found himself in less and less demand as a minister, and by the time he died none of his friends had come to see him for a long time. He had lived and died in an intolerable bitterness of spirit and it frightened me, as we drove him to the graveyard through those unquiet, ruined streets, to see how powerful and overflowing this bitterness could be and to realize that this bitterness now was mine.

When he died I had been away from home for a little over a year. In that year I had had time to become aware of the meaning of all my father's bitter warnings, had discovered the secret of his proudly pursed lips and rigid carriage: I had discovered the weight of white people in the world. I saw that this had been for my ancestors and [88/89] now would be for me an awful thing to live with and that the bitterness which had helped to kill my father could also kill me.

He had been ill a long time—in the mind, as we now realized, reliving instances of his fantastic intransigence in the new light of his affliction and endeavoring to feel a sorrow for him which never, quite, came true. We had not known that he was being eaten up by paranoia, and the discovery that his cruelty, to our bodies and our minds, had been one of the symptoms of his illness was not, then, enough to enable us to forgive him. The younger children felt, quite simply, relief that he would not be coming home anymore. My mother's observation that it was he, after all, who had kept them alive all these years meant nothing because the problems of keeping children alive are not real for children. The older children felt, with my father gone, that they could invite their friends to the house without fear that their friends would be insulted or, as had sometimes happened with me, being told that their friends were in league with the devil and intended to rob our family of everything we owned. (I didn't fail to wonder, and it made me hate him, what on earth we owned that anybody else would want.)

His illness was beyond all hope of healing before anyone realized that he was ill. He had always been so strange and had lived, like a prophet, in such unimaginable close communion with the Lord that his long silences which were punctuated by moans and hallelujahs and snatches of old songs while he sat at the living-room window never seemed odd to us. It was not until he refused to eat because, he said, his family was trying to poison him that my mother was forced to accept as a fact what [89/90] had, until then, been only an unwilling suspicion. When he was committed, it was discovered that he had tuberculosis and, as it turned out, the disease of his mind allowed the disease of his body to destroy him. For the doctors could not force him to eat, either, and, though he was fed intravenously, it was clear from the beginning that there was no hope for him.

In my mind's eye I could see him, sitting at the window, locked up in his terrors; hating and fearing every living soul including his children who had betrayed him, too, by reaching towards the world which had despised him. There were nine of us. I began to wonder what it could have felt like for such a man to have had nine children whom he could barely feed. He used to make little jokes about our poverty, which never, of course, seemed very funny to us; they could not have seemed very funny to him, either, or else our all too feeble response to them would never have caused such rages. He spent great energy and achieved, to our chagrin, no small amount of success in keeping us away from the people who surrounded us, people who had all-night rent parties to which we listened when we should have been sleeping, people who cursed and drank and flashed razor blades on Lenox Avenue. He could not understand why, if they had so much energy to spare, they could not use it to make their lives better. He treated almost everybody on our block with a most uncharitable asperity and neither they, nor, of course, their children were slow to reciprocate.

The only white people who came to our house were welfare workers and bill collectors. It was almost always my mother who dealt with them, for my father's temper, which was at the mercy of his pride, was never to be [90/91] trusted. It was clear that he felt their very presence in his home to be a violation: this was conveyed by his carriage, almost ludicrously stiff, and by his voice, harsh and vindictively polite. When I was around nine or ten I wrote a play which was directed by a young, white schoolteacher, a woman, who then took an interest in me, and gave me books to read and, in order to corroborate my theatrical bent, decided to take me to see what she somewhat tactlessly referred to as "real" plays. Theater-going was forbidden in our house, but, with the really cruel intuitiveness of a child, I suspected that the color of this woman's skin would carry the day for me. When, at school, she suggested taking me to the theater, I did not, as I might have done if she had been a Negro, find a way of discouraging her, but agreed that she should pick me up at my house one evening. I then, very cleverly, left all the rest to my mother, who suggested to my father, as I knew she would, that it would not be very nice to let such a kind woman make the trip for nothing. Also, since it was a schoolteacher, I imagine that my mother countered the idea of sin with the idea of "education," which word, even with my father, carried a kind of bitter weight.

Before the teacher came my father took me aside to ask *why* she was coming, what *interest* she could possibly have in our house, in a boy like me. I said I didn't know but I, too, suggested that it had something to do with education. And I understood that my father was waiting for me to say something—I didn't quite know what; perhaps that I wanted his protection against this teacher and her "education." I said none of these things and the teacher came and we went out. It was clear, during the brief interview in our living room, that my father was [91/92] agreeing very much against his will and that he would have refused permission if he had dared. The fact that he did not dare caused me to despise him: I had no way of knowing that he was facing in that living room a wholly unprecedented and frightening situation.

Later, when my father had been laid off from his job, this woman became very important to us. She was really a very sweet and generous woman and went to a great deal of trouble to be of help to us, particularly during one awful winter. My mother called her by the highest name she knew: she said she was a "christian." My father could scarcely disagree but during the four or five years of our relatively close association he never trusted her and was always trying to surprise in her open, Midwestern face the genuine, cunningly hidden, and hideous motivation. In later years, particularly when it began to be clear that this "education" of mine was going to lead me to perdition, he became more explicit and warned me that my white friends in high school were not really my friends and that I would see, when I was older, how white people would do anything to keep a Negro down. Some of them could be nice, he admitted, but none of them were to be trusted and most of them were not even nice. The best thing was to have as little to do with them as possible. I did not feel this way and I was certain, in my innocence, that I never would.

But the year which preceded my father's death had made a great change in my life. I had been living in New Jersey, working in defense plants, working and living among southerners, white and black. I knew about the south, of course, and about how southerners treated Negroes and how they expected them to behave, but it

[92/93] had never entered my mind that anyone would look at me and expect *me* to behave that way. I learned in New Jersey that to be a Negro meant, precisely, that one was never looked at but was simply at the mercy of the reflexes the color of one's skin caused in other people. I acted in New Jersey as I had always acted, that is as though I thought a great deal of myself—I had to *act* that way—with results that were, simply, unbelievable. I scarcely arrived before I had earned the enmity, which was extraordinarily ingenious, of all my superiors and nearly all my co-workers. In the beginning, to make matters worse, I simply did not know what was happening. I did not know what I had done, and I shortly began to wonder what *anyone* could possibly do, to bring about such unanimous, active, and unbearably vocal hostility. I knew about jim-crow but I had never experienced it. I went to the same self-service restaurant three times and stood with all the Princeton boys before the counter, waiting for a hamburger and coffee; it was always an extraordinarily long time before anything was set before me; but it was not until the fourth visit that I learned that, in fact, nothing had ever been set before me: I had simply picked something up. Negroes were not served there, I was told, and they had been waiting for me to realize that I was always the only Negro present. Once I was told this, I determined to go there all the time. But now they were ready for me and, though some dreadful scenes were subsequently enacted in that restaurant, I never ate there again.

It was the same story all over New Jersey, in bars, bowling alleys, diners, places to live. I was always being forced to leave, silently, or with mutual imprecations. I very [93/94] shortly became notorious and children giggled behind me when I passed and their elders whispered or shouted—they really believed that I was mad. And it did begin to work on my mind, of course; I began to be afraid to go anywhere and to compensate for this I went places to which I really should not have gone and where, God knows, I had no desire to be. My reputation in town naturally enhanced my reputation at work and my working day became one long series of acrobatics designed to keep me out of trouble. I cannot say that these acrobatics succeeded. It began to seem that the machinery of the organization I worked for was turning over, day and night with but one aim: to eject me. I was fired once, and contrived, with the aid of a friend from New York, to get back on the payroll; was fired again, and bounced back again. It took a while to fire me for the third time, but the third time it took. There were no loopholes anywhere. There was not even any way of getting back inside the gates.

That year in New Jersey lives in my mind as though it were the year during which, having an unsuspected predilection for it, I first contracted some dread, chronic disease, the unfailing symptom of which is a kind of blind fever, a pounding in the skull and fire in the bowels. Once this disease is contracted, one can never be really carefree again, for the fever, without an instant's warning, can recur at any moment. It can wreck more important things than race relations. There is not a Negro alive who does not have this rage in his blood—one has the choice, merely, of living with it consciously or surrendering to it. As for me, this fever has recurred in me, and does, and will until the day I die. [94/95]

My last night in New Jersey, a white friend from New York took me to the nearest big town, Trenton, to go to the movies and have a few drinks. As it turned out, he also saved me from, at the very least, a violent whipping. Almost every detail of that night stands out very clearly in my memory. I even remember the name of the movie we saw because its title impressed me as being so patly ironical. It was a movie about the German occupation of France, starring Maureen O'Hara and Charles Laughton and called *This Land Is Mine*. I remember the name of the diner we walked into when the movie ended: it was the "American Diner." When we walked in the counterman asked what we wanted and I remember answering with the casual sharpness which had become my habit: "We want a hamburger and a cup of coffee, what do you think we want?" I do not know why, after a year of such rebuffs, I so completely failed to anticipate his answer, which was, of course, "We don't serve Negroes here." This reply failed to discompose me, at least for the moment. I made some sardonic comment about the name of the diner and we walked out into the streets.

This was the time of what was called the "brown-out," when the lights in all American cities were very dim. When we re-entered the streets something happened to me which had the force of an optical illusion, or a nightmare. The streets were very crowded and I was facing north. People were moving in every direction but it seemed to me, in that instant, that all of the people I could see, and many more than that, were moving toward me, against me, and that everyone was white. I remember how their faced gleamed. And I felt, like a physical sensation, a *click* at the nape of my neck as though some [95/96] interior string connecting my head to my body had been cut. I began to walk. I heard my friend call after me, but I ignored him. Heaven only knows what was going on in his mind, but he had the good sense not to touch me—I don't know what would have happened if he had—and to keep me in sight. I don't know what was going on in my mind, either; I certainly had no conscious plan. I wanted to do something to crush these white faces, which were crushing me. I walked for perhaps a block or two until I came to an enormous, glittering, and fashionable restaurant in which I knew not even the intercession of the Virgin would cause me to be served. I pushed through the doors and took the first vacant seat I saw, at a table for two, and waited.

I do not know how long I waited and I rather wonder, until today, what I could possibly have looked like. Whatever I looked like, I frightened the waitress who shortly appeared, and the moment she appeared all of my fury flowed towards her. I hated her for her white face, and for her great, astounded, frightened eyes. I felt that if she found a black man so frightening I would make her fright worth-while.

She did not ask me what I wanted, but repeated, as though she had learned it somewhere, "We don't serve Negroes here." She did not say it with the blunt, derisive hostility to which I had grown so accustomed, but, rather, with a note of apology in her voice, and fear. This made me colder and more murderous than ever. I felt I had to do something with my hands. I wanted her to come close enough for me to get her neck between my hands.

So I pretended not to have understood her, hoping to draw her closer. And she did step a very short step closer, [96/97] with her pencil poised incongruously over her pad, and repeated the formula: ". . . don't serve Negroes here."

Somehow, with the repetition of that phrase, which was already ringing in my head like a thousand bells of a nightmare, I realized that she would never come any closer and that I would have to strike from a distance. There was nothing on the table but an ordinary water-mug half full of water, and I picked this up and hurled it with all my strength at her. She ducked and it missed her and shattered against the mirror behind the bar. And, with that sound, my frozen blood abruptly thawed, I returned from wherever I had been, I *saw*, for the first time, the restaurant, the people with their mouths open, already, as it seemed to me, rising as one man, and I realized what I had done, and where I was, and I was frightened. I rose and began running for the door. A round, potbellied man grabbed me by the nape of the neck just as I reached the doors and began to beat me about the face. I kicked him and got loose and ran into the streets. My friend whispered, "*Run!*" and I ran.

My friend stayed outside the restaurant long enough to misdirect my pursuers and the police, who arrived, he told me, at once. I do not know what I said to him when he came to my room that night. I could not have said much. I felt, in the oddest, most awful way, that I had somehow betrayed him. I lived it over and over and over again, the way one relives an automobile accident after it has happened and one finds oneself alone and safe. I could not get over two facts, both equally difficult for the imagination to grasp, and one was that I could have been murdered. But the other was that I had been ready to commit murder. I saw nothing very clearly but I did [97/98] see this: that my life, my *real* life, was in danger, and not from anything other people might do but from the hatred I carried in my own heart. [98]

ALLEN GINSBERG

America

America I've given you all and now I'm nothing.
America two dollars and twentyseven cents January 17, 1956.
I can't stand my own mind.
America when will we end the human war?
Go fuck yourself with your atom bomb.
I don't feel good don't bother me.
I won't write my poem till I'm in my right mind.
America when will you be angelic?
When will you take off your clothes?
When will you look at yourself through the grave?
When will you be worthy of your million Trotskyites?
America why are your libraries full of tears?
America when will you send your eggs to India?
I'm sick of your insane demands.
When can I go into the supermarket and buy what I need with my
    good looks?
America after all it is you and I who are perfect not the next world.
Your machinery is too much for me.
You made me want to be a saint.
There must be some other way to settle this argument.
Burroughs is in Tangiers I don't think he'll come back it's sinister.
Are you being sinister or is this some form of practical joke?
I'm trying to come to the point.
I refuse to give up my obsession.
America stop pushing I know what I'm doing.
America the plum blossoms are falling.
I haven't read the newspapers for months, everyday somebody goes
    on trial for murder.
American I feel sentimental about the Wobblies.

Allen Ginsberg, "America," in *Howl and Other Poems*, Pocket Poets Series, No. 4 (San Francisco: City Lights Books, 1959), pp. 31–34.

America I used to be a communist when I was a kid I'm not sorry.
    [31/32]
I smoke marijuana every chance I get.
I sit in my house for days on end and stare at the roses in the closet.
When I go to Chinatown I get drunk and never get laid.
My mind is made up there's going to be trouble.
You should have seen me reading Marx.
My psychoanalyst thinks I'm perfectly right.
I won't say the Lord's Prayer.
I have mystical visions and cosmic vibrations.
America I still haven't told you what you did to Uncle Max after he
    came over from Russia.

I'm addressing you.
Are you going to let your emotional life be run by Time Magazine?
I'm obsessed by Time Magazine.
I read it every week.
Its cover stares at me every time I slink past the corner candystore.
I read it in the basement of the Berkeley Public Library.
It's always telling me about responsibility. Businessmen are serious.
    Movie producers are serious. Everybody's serious but me.
It occurs to me that I am America.
I am talking to myself again.

Asia is rising against me.
I haven't got a chinaman's chance.
I'd better consider my national resources.
My national resources consist of two joints of marijuana millions of
    genitals an unpublishable private literature that goes 1400 miles
    an hour and twenty-five thousand mental institutions.
I say nothing about my prisons nor the millions of underprivileged
    who live in my flowerpots under the light of five hundred suns.
    [32/33]
I have abolished the whorehouses of France, Tangiers is the next to
    go.
My ambition is to be President despite the fact that I'm a Catholic.

America how can I write a holy litany in your silly mood?
I will continue like Henry Ford my strophes are as individual as au-
    tomobiles more so they're all different sexes.
America I will sell you strophes $2500 apiece $500 down on your old
    strophe.
America free Tom Mooney
America save the Spanish Loyalists

America Sacco & Vanzetti must not die
America I am the Scottsboro boys.
America when I was seven momma took me to Communist Cell
meetings they sold us garbanzos a handful per ticket a ticket
costs a nickel and the speeches were free everybody was angelic
and sentimental about the workers it was all so sincere you
have no idea what a good thing the party was in 1935 Scott
Nearing was a grand old man a real mensch Mother Bloor
made me cry I once saw Israel Amter plain. Everybody must
have been a spy.
America you don't really want to go to war.
America it's them bad Russians.
Them Russians them Russians and them Chinamen. And them Russians.
The Russia wants to eat us alive. The Russia's power mad. She
wants to take our cars from out our garages.
Her wants to grab Chicago. Her needs a Red Readers' Digest. Her
wants our auto plants in Siberia. Him big bureaucracy running
our filling stations. [33/34]
That no good. Ugh. Him make Indians learn read. Him need big
black niggers. Hah. Her make us all work sixteen hours a day.
Help.
America this is quite serious.
America this is the impression I get from looking in the television
set.
America is this correct?
I'd better get right down to the job.
It's true I don't want to join the Army or turn lathes in precision
parts factories, I'm nearsighted and psychopathic anyway.
America I'm putting my queer shoulder to the wheel. [34]

3

Radicals and Reformers

DEFINITIONS of the words "rebel," "radical," and "reformer" are vague at best and in the context of a changing American society become at times meaningless. Was Jefferson a radical in his statement, "the earth belongs always to the living generation"? Simply arguing that because one generation cannot bind another, Jefferson charged that "Every constitution . . . and every law, naturally expires at the end of 19 years. If it be enforced longer, it is an act of force and not of right." In another letter he wrote: "I hold it, that a little rebellion, now and then, is a good thing, and as necessary in the political world as storms in the physical." May we then interpret these words, as they have been interpreted, as a justification for revolution? What is a "little" rebellion? Was Henry David Thoreau a rebel in his assertion that individual moral laws supersede society-made laws? In "Civil Disobedience" he wrote: "The only obligation which I have a right to assume is to do at any time what I think right." John Brown justified insurrection at Harpers Ferry by arguing the supremacy of the law of humanity, which condemned slavery, over the laws of Virginia, which protected slavery. Among other crimes for which Brown was executed, there was the one of "treason against the Commonwealth," meaning treason against the state of Virginia, which in not very many months was to itself assert the option of rebellion against what it considered the oppression of the federal government. And in more recent times, is Martin Luther King preaching rebellion when he distinguishes between just and unjust laws—a just law "squares with a moral law," and an unjust law is "any law that degrades the human personality"? According to King, an individual has a right, even an obligation, to refuse to obey an unjust law: "the individual who disobeys the [unjust] law . . . is expressing at the moment the very highest respect for law." The implication to note in this statement is that the individual himself is the one to make the critical distinction between the two laws.

In one sense, the sanction for radical reform, or what may be referred to by some as rebellion, was inserted into the Constitution in the Bill of Rights and in the Fourteenth Amendment, in those articles advocating individual liberty of speech and action. Also in the Constitution, however, were articles protecting property, these separate articles thereby laying the groundwork for later conflict between the two interests. The process of rebellion must be seen, therefore, within the traditional dialectic of human versus property rights, political and social theorists later accepting political labels in terms of their commitment to one or the other of these rights. Historically, the more radical stand has been the stand to the left, which traditionally has favored human over property rights. All this is common knowledge, but a reminder is necessary about the process itself, the fact that the dialectic changes in character when the pressures on any one of these rights grow more intense. Jefferson and Thoreau, both on the side of individual rights, lived in predominantly agrarian communities where the citizen could utilize his freedoms with a reasonable assurance of the meaningfulness of his actions. The signs of the change to an industrial culture were present even in Thoreau's time—the railroad was not far from the cabin door at Walden Pond—and the individual–society confrontation that Thoreau was particularly sensitive to was assuming new forms and a new seriousness even at the moment when Thoreau spoke of it. Soon after the Civil War ended the slavery controversy, controversy of another kind entered the social and economic fields. Industrialism, as it may be defined by a predominantly business environment as well as by a corporate business structure, was creating forces which many people began to perceive violated basic moral and humanitarian principles. Writers before Edward Bellamy, Walt Whitman for one, recognized the dangers of capitalism to the individual and to a healthy society, but it was Bellamy's enormously popular *Looking Backward* which crystallized the thinking of many of those who objected to capitalism. Bellamy created an orderly socialist utopia for the year 2000 by which to measure the capitalist community of 1889, judging Boston of his own day not only in moral and humanitarian terms but by using the capitalist's criterion of efficiency to condemn the wastefulness of capitalism. Was Bellamy a rebel? He would be judged one certainly if one were to equate capitalism—including in this conception the principle of the sanctity of property as interpreted under capitalism—with democracy, but Bellamy himself was not making this equation. Jack London in the excerpt from *Iron Heel*, "A Night with the Philomaths," works within a conception of class division that is Marxist, but we can see in this work that London clearly recognizes the danger of totalitarianism, a danger most advocates of democracy today can also recognize. The muckrakers of the first two decades of the twentieth century, including the novelists Upton Sinclair, Robert Herrick, David Graham Phillips, and Winston Churchill, were interested primarily in exposing the moral damage imposed by unrestrained industrialization and therefore were basically reformers; they suggested no alternatives on the scale of Bellamy's, but in criticizing the ethical behavior of the most notable practitioners of the industrial system, they also were attacking the *status quo,* and in some respects could be referred to as rebels.

A more realistic corrective to the economic power of the business interests came in the form of labor unionism. Concessions to labor were not given willingly or easily and a history of unionism is a record of the unions' attempts to gain recognition, or legality, so this history has in it the undertones of subversion and rebellion. Eugene Debs suffered imprisonment. Joe Hill and many others were martyred for the cause of justice for the working man—all of this in preparation for a few laws granting a person the right to unionize and to strike. Many of the laws they sought have been adopted, so yesterday's rebels are today's respectable members of America's middle class, and again the change in society's structure creates a change in our conception of the social rebel.

Edward Bellamy's avowed purpose in writing his book was social reform, but quite obviously the implications to be gained in examining the outline of his socialist utopia make Bellamy's message truly revolutionary. The fictional studies of communism, particularly in the work of the 1930's, represent this more serious revolutionary intent, this time against the background of international power politics. Added to the ugliness of the strike conflict in Steinbeck's *In Dubious Battle* is the complicated, perhaps "dubious" nature of loyalties of the strike leaders, men selflessly giving their work and labor, and even their lives on necessity, to the improvement of the laborer's working conditions, but on necessity again sacrificing even the workers for the cause. The history of the American communistic writer in the Depression thirties reveals the complexities arising from the Communist Party's involvement in the international communistic movement, where even a work favorable to communism, such as Joseph Freeman's *American Testament,* from which the excerpt included in the following section is taken, was refused Moscow approval and was therefore withdrawn from American circulation by the author himself even after the book showed promise of becoming a popular success. The history of communism in American literature, by Daniel Aaron, Walter Rideout, and others, reveals an uneasy, shifting relationship, each side, the writer and the party, suspicious of the other. The record of the thirties is largely a story of the failure of doctrinaire communism to retain the support of the

American writer and intellectual, but the record illustrates also the large and general appeal during these critical days of the Depression in the moral and humanitarian features of a socialist program. In what ways was a writer, in answering this appeal, meeting the definition of revolutionary or rebel? The question was to become crucial years later in the period of McCarthyism.

The prominent areas of rebellion since World War II have been in the field of civil rights or in more private "hippie" worlds on the fringe of the American middle class structure. In other sections of this anthology we have Martin Luther King's arguments for action and James Baldwin's account of the reasons why action seems necessary. The scene for the rebellion has shifted to demands for "equal protection" guarantees. The New Deal, the Fair Deal, the Great Society, all have expressed noble social ideals, and the rebellions of today erupt because of the disparity between these ideals, or others equally worthy in human terms, and social reality. The activist social rebel now is the civil rights leader, or leader of student movements, all working for limited goals perhaps, but all seeking the fulfillment of basic guarantees. The cause creates the rebel—and a society that does not remain static will have these rebels. Our reassurance is that a healthy, flexible society remains healthy and flexible because of them—their justification perhaps until the perfect utopia has been found.

THOMAS JEFFERSON

A Little Rebellion:
Letters to James Madison

PARIS January 30, 1787.

... I AM IMPATIENT to learn your sentiments on the late troubles in the Eastern states. So far as I have yet seen, they do not appear to threaten serious consequences. Those states have suffered by the stoppage of the channels of their commerce, which have not yet found other issues. This must render money scarce, and make the people uneasy. This uneasiness has produced acts absolutely unjustifiable; but [254/255] I hope they will provoke no severities from their governments. A consciousness of those in power that their administration of the public affairs has been honest, may perhaps produce too great a degree of indignation: and those characters wherein fear predominates over hope may apprehend too much from these instances of irregularity. They may conclude too hastily that nature has formed man insusceptible of any other government but that of force, a conclusion not founded in truth, nor experience. Societies exist under three forms sufficiently distinguishable. 1. Without government, as among our Indians. 2. Under governments wherein the will of every one has a just influence, as is the case in England in a slight degree, and in our states, in a great one. 3. Under governments of force: as is the case in all other monarchies and in most of the other republics. To have an idea of the curse of existence under these last, they must be seen. It is a government of wolves over sheep. It is a problem, not clear in my mind, that the first condition is not the best. But I believe it to be inconsistent with any great degree of population. The second state has a great deal of good in it. The mass of mankind under that enjoys a precious degree of liberty & happiness. It has it's evils too: the principal of which is

From *The Works of Thomas Jefferson*, ed. Paul Leicester Ford (New York and London: G. P. Putnam's Sons, 1904), V, 254–56; VI, 3–4, 8–10.

the turbulence to which it is subject. But weigh this against the oppressions of monarchy, and it becomes nothing. *Malo periculosam libertatem quam quietam servitutem.* Even this evil is productive of good. It prevents the degeneracy of government, and nourishes a general attention to the [255/256] public affairs. I hold it that a little rebellion now and then is a good thing, & as necessary in the political world as storms in the physical. Unsuccessful rebellions indeed generally establish the encroachments on the rights of the people which have produced them. An observation of this truth should render honest republican governors so mild in their punishment of rebellions, as not to discourage them too much. It is a medicine necessary for the sound health of government.... [256]

PARIS, September 6, 1789.

Dear Sir,—I sit down to write to you without knowing by what occasion I shall send my letter. I do it because a subject comes into my head which I would wish to develope a little more than is practicable in the hurry of the moment of making up general despatches.

The question Whether one generation of men has a right to bind another, seems never to have been started either on this or our side of the water. Yet it is a question of such consequences as not only to merit decision, but place also, among the fundamental principles of every government. The course of reflection in which we are immersed here on the elementary principles of society has presented this question to my mind; and that no such obligation can be transmitted I think very capable of proof. I set out on this ground which I suppose to be self evident, *"that the earth belongs in usufruct to the* [3/4] *living;"* that the dead have neither powers nor rights over it. ... [4/8] ... [N]o society can make a perpetual constitution or even a [8/9] perpetual law. The earth belongs always to the living generation. They may manage it then, and what proceeds from it, as they please, during their usufruct. They are masters too of their own persons, and consequently may govern them as they please. But persons and property make the sum of the objects of government. The constitution and the laws of their predecessors extinguished them, in their natural course, with those whose will gave them being. This could preserve that being till it ceased to be itself, and no longer. Every constitution, then, and every law, naturally expires at the end of 19 years. If it be enforced longer, it is an act of force and not of right.

It may be said that the succeeding generation exercising in fact the power of repeal, this leaves them as free as if the constitution or law had been expressly limited to 19 years only. In the first place, this objection admits the right, in proposing an equivalent. But the power of repeal is not an equivalent. It might be indeed if every form of government were so perfectly contrived that the will of the majority could always be obtained fairly and without impediment. But this is true of no form. The people cannot assemble themselves; their representation is unequal and vicious. Various checks are opposed to every legislative proposition. Factions get possession of the public councils. Bribery corrupts them. Personal interests lead them astray from the general interests of their constituents; and other impediments arise so as to prove to every practical man that a law of limited duration is much more manageable than one which needs a repeal. [9/10]

This principle that the earth belongs to the living and not to the dead is of very extensive application and consequences in every country, and most especially in France. It enters into the resolution of the questions whether the nation may change the descent of lands holden in tail? Whether they may change the appropriation of lands given antiently to the church, to hospitals, colleges, orders of chivalry, and otherwise in perpetuity? whether they may abolish the charges and privileges attached on lands, including the whole catalogue ecclesiastical and feudal? it goes to hereditary offices, authorities and jurisdictions; to hereditary orders, distinctions and appellations; to perpetual monopolies in commerce, the arts or sciences; with a long train of *et ceteras:* and it renders the question of reimbursement a question of generosity and not of right. In all these cases the legislature of the day could authorize such appropriations and establishments for their own time, but no longer; and the present holders, even where they or their ancestors have purchased, are in the case of *bona fide* purchasers of what the seller had no right to convey. . . . [10]

HENRY DAVID THOREAU

Civil Disobedience

I HEARTILY accept the motto: "That government is best which governs least"; and I should like to see it acted up to more rapidly and systematically. Carried out, it finally amounts to this, which also I believe: "That government is best which governs not at all"; and when men are prepared for it, that will be the kind of government which they will have. Government is at best but an expedient; but most governments are usually, and all governments are sometimes, inexpedient. The objections which have been brought against a standing army, and they are many and weighty and deserve to prevail, may also at last be brought against a standing government. The standing army is only an arm of the standing government. The government itself, which is only the mode which the people have chosen to execute their will, is equally liable to be abused and perverted before the people can act through it. Witness the present Mexican War, the work of comparatively a few individuals using [131/132] the standing government as their tool; for, in the outset, the people would not have consented to this measure.

This American government—what is it but a tradition, though a recent one, endeavoring to transmit itself unimpaired to posterity, but each instant losing some of its integrity? It has not the vitality and force of a single living man, for a single man can bend it to his will. It is a sort of wooden gun to the people themselves. But it is not the less necessary for this; for the people must have some complicated machinery or other, and hear its din, to satisfy that idea of government which they have. Governments show thus how successfully men can be imposed on, even impose on themselves, for their own advantage. It is excellent, we must all allow. Yet this government never of itself furthered any enterprise but by the alacrity with

From Henry David Thoreau, "Civil Disobedience," in *The Writings of Henry David Thoreau* (Boston and New York: Houghton, Mifflin and Company, 1893), X, 131–40, 142–50, 153–56, 159–62, 164–65, 169–70. [Originally published in *Aesthetic Papers,* ed. Elizabeth Peabody, 1849.]

which it got out of its way. *It* does not keep the country free. *It* does not settle the West. *It* does not educate. The character inherent in the American people has done all that has been accomplished; and it would have done somewhat more, if the government had not sometimes got in its way. For government is an expedient by which men would fain succeed in letting one another alone; and, as has been said, when it is most expedient, the governed are [132/133] most let alone by it. Trade and commerce, if they were not made of India rubber, would never manage to bounce over the obstacles which legislators are continually putting in their way; and, if one were to judge these men wholly by the effects of their actions and not partly by their intentions, they would deserve to be classed and punished with those mischievous persons who put obstructions on the railroads.

But, to speak practically and as a citizen, unlike those who call themselves no-government men, I ask for not at once no government, but *at once* a better government. Let every man make known what kind of government would command his respect, and that will be one step toward obtaining it.

After all, the practical reason why, when the power is once in the hands of the people, a majority are permitted, and for a long period continue, to rule is not because they are most likely to be in the right nor because this seems fairest to the minority, but because they are physically the strongest. But a government in which the majority rule in all cases cannot be based on justice, even as far as men understand it. Can there not be a government in which majorities do not virtually decide right and wrong, but conscience?—in which majorities decide only those questions to which the rule [133/134] of expediency is applicable? Must the citizen ever for a moment, or in the least degree, resign his conscience to the legislator? Why has every man a conscience, then? I think that we should be men first and subjects afterward. It is not desirable to cultivate a respect for the law so much as for the right. The only obligation which I have a right to assume is to do at any time what I think right. It is truly enough said that a corporation has no conscience; but a corporation of conscientious men is a corporation *with* a conscience. Law never made men a whit more just; and, by means of their respect for it, even the well-disposed are daily made the agents of injustice. A common and natural result of an undue respect for law is that you may see a file of soldiers: colonel, captain, corporal, privates, powder monkeys, and all, marching in admirable order over hill and dale to the wars, against their wills, aye, against their common sense and consciences, which makes it very steep marching indeed, and produces a palpitation of the heart. They have no doubt that it is a damnable business in which they are concerned; they are all peaceably inclined. Now, what are they? Men at all? or small movable forts and magazines at the service of some unscrupulous man in power? Visit the Navy-Yard, and behold a marine, such a [134/135] man as an American government can make, or such as it can make a man with its black arts—a mere shadow and reminiscence of humanity, a man laid out alive and standing, and already, as one may say, buried under arms with funeral accompaniments, though it may be—

> Not a drum was heard, not a funeral note,
>   As his corse to the rampart we hurried;
> Not a soldier discharged his farewell shot
>   O'er the grave where our hero we buried.

The mass of them serve the State thus: not as men mainly, but as machines, with their bodies. They are the standing army and the militia, jailors, constables, posse comitatus, etc. In most cases there is no free exercise whatever of the judgment or of the moral sense, but they put themselves on a level with wood and earth and stones; and wooden men can perhaps be manufactured that will serve the purpose as well. Such command no more respect than men of straw or a lump of dirt. They have the same sort of worth only as horses and dogs. Yet such as these even are commonly esteemed good citizens. Others—as most legislators, politicians, lawyers, ministers, and officeholders—serve the State chiefly with their heads; and, as they rarely make any moral distinctions, they are as likely to serve the Devil, without *intending* it, as God. A very few—as heroes, patriots, [135/136] martyrs, reformers in the great sense, and *men*—serve the State with their consciences also, and so necessarily resist it for the most part; and they are commonly treated as enemies by it. A wise man will only be useful as a man, and will not submit to be "clay" and "stop a hole to keep the wind away," but leave that office to his dust at least—

> I am too high-born to be propertied,
> To be a secondary at control,
> Or useful serving-man and instrument
> To any sovereign state throughout the world.

He who gives himself entirely to his fellow men appears to them useless and selfish; but he who gives himself partially to them is pronounced a benefactor and philanthropist.

How does it become a man to behave toward this American government today? I answer that he cannot without disgrace be associated with it. I cannot for an instant recognize that political organization as *my* government which is the *slave's* government also.

All men recognize the right of revolution, that is, the right to refuse allegiance to, and to resist, the government when its tyranny or its inefficiency are great and unendurable. But almost all say that such is not the case now. But such was the case, they think, in the Revolution of '75. If one were to tell me that this [136/137] was a bad government because it taxed certain foreign commodities brought to its ports, it is most probable that I should not make an ado about it, for I can do without them. All machines have their friction; and possibly this does enough good to counterbalance the evil. At any rate, it is a great evil to make a stir about it. But when the friction comes to have its machine, and oppression and robbery are organized, I say, let us not have such a machine any longer. In other words, when a sixth of the population of a nation which has undertaken to be the refuge of liberty are slaves, and a whole country is unjustly overrun and conquered by a foreign army and subjected to military law, I think that it is not too soon for honest men to rebel and revolutionize. What makes his duty the more urgent is the fact that the country so overrun is not our own, but ours is the invading army.

Paley, a common authority with many on moral questions, in his chapter on the "Duty of Submission to Civil Government" resolves all civil obligation into expediency; and he proceeds to say "that so long as the interest of the whole society requires it, that is, so long as the established government cannot be resisted or changed without public inconvenience, it is the will of God that the established government [137/138] be obeyed, and no longer. . . . This principle being admitted, the justice of every particular case of resistance is reduced to a computation of the quantity of the danger and grievance on the one side and of the probability and expense of redressing it on the other." Of this, he says, every man shall judge for himself. But Paley appears never to have contemplated those cases to which the rule of expediency does not apply, in which a people, as well as an individual, must do justice, cost what it may. If I have unjustly wrested a plank from a drowning man, I must restore it to him though I drown myself. This, according to Paley, would be inconvenient. But he that would save his life, in such a case, shall lose it. This people must cease to hold slaves and to make war on Mexico, though it cost them their existence as a people.

In their practice, nations agree with Paley; but does anyone think that Massachusetts does exactly what is right at the present crisis?

> A drab of state, a cloth-o'-silver slut,
> To have her train borne up, and her soul trail in the dirt.

Practically speaking, the opponents to a reform in Massachusetts are
not a hundred thousand politicians at the South, but a hundred
thousand merchants and farmers here, who are more interested in
commerce and agriculture [138/139] than they are in humanity and
are not prepared to do justice to the slave and to Mexico *cost what
it may.* I quarrel not with far-off foes, but with those who near at
home cooperate with, and do the bidding of, those far away, and
without whom the latter would be harmless. We are accustomed to
say that the mass of men are unprepared; but improvement is slow,
because the few are not materially wiser or better than the many. It
is not so important that many should be as good as you as that there
be some absolute goodness somewhere; for that will leaven the
whole lump. There are thousands who are *in opinion* opposed to
slavery and to the war, who yet in effect do nothing to put an end to
them; who, esteeming themselves children of Washington and
Franklin, sit down with their hands in their pockets and say that
they know not what to do, and do nothing; who even postpone the
question of freedom to the question of free trade and quietly read
the prices-current along with the latest advices from Mexico, after
dinner, and, it may be, fall asleep over them both. What is the
price-current of an honest man and patriot today? They hesitate,
and they regret, and sometimes they petition; but they do nothing in
earnest and with effect. They will wait, well-disposed, for others to
remedy the evil, that they may no longer [139/140] have it to regret.
At most, they give only a cheap vote and a feeble countenance and
God-speed to the right, as it goes by them. There are nine hundred
and ninety-nine patrons of virtue to one virtuous man. But it is eas-
ier to deal with the real possessor of a thing than with the tempo-
rary guardian of it.

All voting is a sort of gaming, like checkers or backgammon, with
a slight moral tinge to it, a playing with right and wrong, with
moral questions; and betting naturally accompanies it. The character of the voters is not staked. I cast my vote, perchance, as I think
right, but I am not vitally concerned that the right should prevail. I
am willing to leave it to the majority. Its obligation, therefore, never
exceeds that of expediency. Even voting *for the right* is *doing* nothing for it. It is only expressing to men feebly your desire that it
should prevail. A wise man will not leave the right to the mercy of
chance, nor wish it to prevail through the power of the majority.
There is but little virtue in the action of masses of men. When the

majority shall at length vote for the abolition of slavery, it will be because they are indifferent to slavery, or because there is but little slavery left to be abolished by their vote. *They* will then be the only slaves. Only *his* vote can hasten the abolition of slavery who asserts his own freedom by his vote. . . . [140/142]

It is not a man's duty, as a matter of course, to devote himself to the eradication of any, even the most enormous wrong; he may still properly have other concerns to engage him; but it is his duty, at least, to wash his hands of it, and, if he gives it no thought longer, not to give it practically his support. If I devote myself to other pursuits and contemplations, I must first see, at least, that I do not pursue them sitting upon another man's shoulders. I must get off him first, that he may pursue his contemplations too. See what gross inconsistency is tolerated. I have heard some of my townsmen say: "I should like to have them order me out to help put down an insurrection of the slaves, or to march to Mexico—see if I would go"; and yet these very men have each, directly by their allegiance, and so indirectly, [142/143] at least, by their money, furnished a substitute. The soldier is applauded who refuses to serve in an unjust war by those who do not refuse to sustain the unjust government which makes the war, is applauded by those whose own act and authority he disregards and sets at naught, as if the State were penitent to that degree that it hired one to scourge it while it sinned, but not to that degree that it left off sinning for a moment. Thus, under the name of Order and Civil Government, we are all made at last to pay homage to and support our own meanness. After the first blush of sin comes its indifference; and from immoral it becomes, as it were, *un*moral and not quite unnecessary to that life which we have made.

The broadest and most prevalent error requires the most disinterested virtue to sustain it. The slight reproach to which the virtue of patriotism is commonly liable the noble are most likely to incur. Those who, while they disapprove of the character and measures of a government, yield to it their allegiance and support are undoubtedly its most conscientious supporters, and so frequently the most serious obstacles to reform. Some are petitioning the State to dissolve the Union, to disregard the requisitions of the President. Why do they not dissolve it themselves—the union between [143/144] themselves and the State—and refuse to pay their quota into its treasury? Do not they stand in the same relation to the State that the State does to the Union? And have not the same reasons prevented the State from resisting the Union which have prevented them from resisting the State?

How can a man be satisfied to entertain an opinion merely, and enjoy *it?* Is there any enjoyment in it if his opinion is that he is aggrieved? If you are cheated out of a single dollar by your neighbor, you do not rest satisfied with knowing that you are cheated, or with saying that you are cheated, or even with petitioning him to pay you your due, but you take effectual steps at once to obtain the full amount and see that you are never cheated again. Action from principle, the perception and the performance of right, changes things and relations; it is essentially revolutionary, and does not consist wholly with anything which was. It not only divides states and churches, it divides families; aye, it divides the *individual,* separating the diabolical in him from the divine.

Unjust laws exist; shall we be content to obey them, or shall we endeavor to amend them and obey them until we have succeeded, or shall we transgress them at once? Men generally, under such a government as this, think that they [144/145] ought to wait until they have persuaded the majority to alter them. They think that, if they should resist, the remedy would be worse than the evil. But it is the fault of the government itself that the remedy is worse than the evil. *It* makes it worse. Why is it not more apt to anticipate and provide for reform? Why does it not cherish its wise minority? Why does it cry and resist before it is hurt? Why does it not encourage its citizens to be on the alert to point out its faults and *do* better than it would have them? Why does it always crucify Christ and excommunicate Copernicus and Luther and pronounce Washington and Franklin rebels?

One would think that a deliberate and practical denial of its authority was the only offense never contemplated by government; else, why has it not assigned its definite, its suitable and proportionate penalty? If a man who has no property refuses but once to earn nine shillings for the State, he is put in prison for a period unlimited by any law that I know, and determined only by the discretion of those who placed him there; but if he should steal ninety times nine shillings from the State, he is soon permitted to go at large again.

If the injustice is part of the necessary friction of the machine of government, let it go, [145/146] let it go; perchance it will wear smooth—certainly the machine will wear out. If the injustice has a spring, or a pulley, or a rope, or a crank exclusively for itself, then perhaps you may consider whether the remedy will not be worse than the evil; but if it is of such a nature that it requires you to be the agent of injustice to another, then, I say, break the law. Let your life be a counterfriction to stop the machine. What I have to do is to see, at any rate, that I do not lend myself to the wrong which I condemn.

As for adopting the ways which the State has provided for remedying the evil, I know not of such ways. They take too much time, and a man's life will be gone. I have other affairs to attend to. I came into this world not chiefly to make this a good place to live in, but to live in it, be it good or bad. A man has not everything to do, but something; and because he cannot do *everything*, it is not necessary that he should do *something* wrong. It is not my business to be petitioning the Governor or the Legislature any more than it is theirs to petition me; and if they should not hear my petition, what should I do then? But in this case the State has provided no way; its very Constitution is the evil. This may seem to be harsh and stubborn and unconciliatory, but it is to [146/147] treat with the utmost kindness and consideration the only spirit that can appreciate or deserves it. So is all change for the better, like birth and death, which convulse the body.

I do not hesitate to say that those who call themselves Abolitionists should at once effectually withdraw their support, both in person and property, from the government of Massachusetts and not wait till they constitute a majority of one before they suffer the right to prevail through them. I think that it is enough if they have God on their side, without waiting for that other one. Moreover, any man more right than his neighbors constitutes a majority of one already.

I meet this American government, or its representative, the state government, directly and face to face once a year—no more—in the person of its taxgatherer; this is the only mode in which a man situated as I am necessarily meets it; and it then says distinctly, "Recognize me"; and the simplest, most effectual, and, in the present posture of affairs, the indispensablest mode of treating with it on this head, of expressing your little satisfaction with and love for it, is to deny it then. My civil neighbor, the taxgatherer, is the very man I have to deal with—for it is, after all, with men and not with parchment that I quarrel—and he has [147/148] voluntarily chosen to be a agent of the government. How shall he ever know well what he is and does as an officer of the government, or as a man, until he is obliged to consider whether he shall treat me, his neighbor, for whom he has respect, as a neighbor and well-disposed man or as a maniac and disturber of the peace, and see if he can get over this obstruction to his neighborliness without a ruder and more impetuous thought or speech corresponding with his action. I know this well, that if one thousand, if one hundred, if ten men whom I could name —if ten *honest* men only—aye, if *one* HONEST man, in this State of Massachusetts, *ceasing to hold slaves*, were actually to withdraw from this copartnership and be locked up in the county jail therefor, it would be the abolition of slavery in America. For it matters not how small the beginning may seem to be; what is once well done is done forever. But we love better to talk about it; that we say is our mission. Reform keeps many scores of newspapers in its service, but not one man. If my esteemed neighbor, the State's ambassador, who will devote his days to the settlement of the question of human rights in the Council Chamber instead of being threatened with the prisons of Carolina, were to sit down the prisoner of Massachusetts, that State which is so anxious [148/149] to foist the sin of slavery upon her sister—though at present she can discover only an act of inhospitality to be the ground of a quarrel with her—the Legislature would not wholly waive the subject the following winter.

Under a government which imprisons any unjustly the true place for a just man is also a prison. The proper place today, the only place which Massachusetts has provided for her freer and less desponding spirits, is in her prisons, to be put out and locked out of the State by her own act, as they have already put themselves out by their principles. It is there that the fugitive slave and the Mexican prisoner on parole and the Indian come to plead the wrongs of his race should find them, on that separate, but more free and honorable ground, where the State places those who are not *with* her, but *against* her—the only house in a slave state in which a free man can abide with honor. If any think that their influence would be lost there and their voices no longer afflict the ear of the State, that they would not be as an enemy within its walls, they do not know by how much truth is stronger than error, nor how much more eloquently and effectively he can combat injustice who has experienced a little in his own person. Cast your whole vote, not a strip of paper merely, but your whole influence. A [149/150] minority is powerless while it conforms to the majority; it is not even a minority then; but it is irresistible when it clogs by its whole weight. If the alternative is to keep all just men in prison or give up war and slavery, the State will not hesitate which to choose. If a thousand men were not to pay their tax bills this year, that would not be a violent and bloody measure, as it would be to pay them and enable the State to commit violence and shed innocent blood. This is, in fact, the definition of a peaceable revolution, if any such is possible. If the taxgatherer or any other public officer asks me, as one has done, "But what shall I do?" my answer is, "If you really wish to do anything, resign your office." When the subject has refused allegiance and the officer has resigned his office, then the revolution is accomplished. But even suppose blood should flow. Is there not a sort of bloodshed when the conscience is wounded? Through this wound a man's real manhood and immortality flow out, and he bleeds to an everlasting death. I see this blood flowing now. . . . [150/153]

Some years ago, the State met me in behalf of the Church, and commanded me to pay a certain sum toward the support of a clergyman whose preaching my father attended, but never I myself. "Pay," it said, "or be locked up in the jail." I declined to pay, but, unfortunately, another man saw fit to pay it. I did not see why the schoolmaster should be taxed to [153/154] support the priest, and not the priest the schoolmaster; for I was not the State's schoolmaster, but I supported myself by voluntary subscription. I did not see why the lyceum should not present its tax bill and have the State to back its demand, as well as the Church. However, at the request of the selectmen, I condescended to make some such statement as this in writing:—"Know all men by these presents, that I, Henry Thoreau, do not wish to be regarded as a member of any incorporated society which I have not joined." This I gave to the town clerk, and he has it. The State, having thus learned that I did not wish to be regarded as a member of that church, has never made a like demand on me since; though it said that it must adhere to its original presumption that time. If I had known how to name them, I should then have signed off in detail from all the societies which I never signed on to; but I did not know where to find a complete list.

I have paid no poll tax for six years. I was put into a jail once on this account for one night; and, as I stood considering the walls of solid stone, two or three feet thick, the door of wood and iron, a foot thick, and the iron grating which strained the light, I could not help being struck with the foolishness of that institution [154/155] which treated me as if I were mere flesh and blood and bones to be locked up. I wondered that it should have concluded at length that this was the best use it could put me to and had never thought to avail itself of my services in some way. I saw that, if there was a wall of stone between me and my townsmen, there was a still more difficult one to climb or break through before they could get to be as free as I was. I did not for a moment feel confined, and the walls seemed a great waste of stone and mortar. I felt as if I alone of all my townsmen had paid my tax. They plainly did not know how to treat me, but behaved like persons who are underbred. In every threat and in every compliment there was a blunder; for they thought that my chief desire was to stand the other side of that stone wall. I could not but smile to see how industriously they locked the door on my meditations, which followed them out again without let or hindrance, and *they* were really all that was dangerous. As they could not reach me, they had resolved to punish my body; just as boys, if they cannot come at some person against whom they have a spite, will abuse his dog. I saw that the State was half-witted, that it was timid as a lone woman with her silver spoons, and that it did not know its friends from its foes, and I [155/156] lost all my remaining respect for it and pitied it.

Thus the State never intentionally confronts a man's sense, intellectual or moral, but only his body, his senses. It is not armed with superior wit or honesty, but with superior physical strength. I was not born to be forced. I will breathe after my own fashion. Let us see who is the strongest. What force has a multitude? They only can force me who obey a higher law than I. They force me to become like themselves. I do not hear of *men* being *forced* to live this way or that by masses of men. What sort of life were that to live? When I meet a government which says to me: "Your money or your life," why should I be in haste to give it my money? It may be in a great strait and not know what to do; I cannot help that, it must help itself; do as I do. It is not worth the while to snivel about it. I am not responsible for the successful working of the machinery of society. I am not the son of the engineer. I perceive that, when an acorn and a chestnut fall side by side, the one does not remain inert to make way for the other, but both obey their own laws and spring and grow and flourish as best they can, till one, perchance, overshadows and destroys the other. If a plant cannot live according to its nature, it dies; and so a man. . . . [156/159]

When I came out of prison—for some one interfered and paid that tax—I did not perceive [159/160] that great changes had taken place on the common, such as he observed who went in a youth and emerged a tottering and gray-headed man; and yet a change had to my eyes come over the scene—the town and State and country—greater than any that mere time could effect. I saw yet more distinctly the State in which I lived. I saw to what extent the people among whom I lived could be trusted as good neighbors and friends: that their friendship was for summer weather only; that they did not greatly propose to do right; that they were a distinct race from me by their prejudices and superstitions, as the Chinamen and Malays are; that in their sacrifices to humanity they ran no risks, not even to their property; that after all they were not so noble but they treated the thief as he had treated them, and hoped, by a certain outward observance and a few prayers and by walking in a particular straight though useless path from time to time, to save their souls. This may be to judge my neighbors harshly, for I believe that many of them are not aware that they have such an institution as the jail in their village.

It was formerly the custom in our village, when a poor debtor came out of jail, for his acquaintances to salute him, looking through their fingers, which were crossed to represent [160/161] the grating a jail window, "How do ye do?" My neighbors did not thus salute me, but first looked at me, and then at one another, as if I had returned from a long journey. I was put into jail as I was going to the shoemaker's to get a shoe which was mended. When I was let out the next morning, I proceeded to finish my errand and, having put on my mended shoe, joined a huckleberry party, who were impatient to put themselves under my conduct; and in half an hour—for the horse was soon tackled—was in the midst of a huckleberry field on one of our highest hills, two miles off, and then the State was nowhere to be seen.

This is the whole history of "My Prisons."

I have never declined paying the highway tax, because I am as desirous of being a good neighbor as I am of being a bad subject; and as for supporting schools, I am doing my part to educate my fellow countrymen now. It is for no particular item in the tax bill that I refuse to pay it. I simply wish to refuse allegiance to the State, to withdraw and stand aloof from it effectually. I do not care to trace the course of my dollar, if I could, till it buys a man or a musket to shoot with—the dollar is innocent—but I am concerned to trace the effects of my allegiance. In fact, I quietly [161/162] declare war with the State, after my fashion, though I will still make what use and get what advantage of her I can, as is usual in such cases.

If others pay the tax which is demanded of me from a sympathy with the State, they do but what they have already done in their own case, or rather they abet injustice to a greater extent than the State requires. If they pay the tax from a mistaken interest in the individual taxed, to save his property or prevent his going to jail, it is because they have not considered wisely how far they let their private feelings interfere with the public good.

This, then, is my position at present. But one cannot be too much on his guard in such a case, lest his action be biased by obstinacy or an undue regard for the opinions of men. Let him see that he does only what belongs to himself and to the hour. ... [162/164]

I do not wish to quarrel with any man or nation. I do not wish to split hairs, to make fine distinctions, or set myself up as better than my neighbors. I seek rather, I may say, even an excuse for conforming to the laws of the land. I am but too ready to conform to them. Indeed, I have reason to suspect myself on this head; and each year, as the taxgatherer comes round, I find myself disposed to review the acts and position of the general and state governments and the spirit of the people to discover a pretext for conformity.

> We must affect our country as our parents,
> And if at any time we alienate
> Our love or industry from doing it honor,
> We must respect effects and teach the soul

Matter of conscience and religion
And not desire of rule or benefit.

I believe that the State will soon be able to take all my work of this sort out of my hands, and then I shall be no better a patriot than my fellow countrymen. Seen from a lower point of view, the Constitution, with all its faults, is very good; the law and the courts are very respectable; even this State and this American government are, in many respects, very admirable [164/165] and rare things to be thankful for, such as a great many have described them; but seen from a point of view a little higher, they are what I have described them; seen from a higher still, and the highest, who shall say what they are, or that they are worth looking at or thinking of at all?

However, the government does not concern me much, and I shall bestow the fewest possible thoughts on it. It is not many moments that I live under a government, even in this world. If a man is thought-free, fancy-free, imagination-free, that which *is not* never for a long time appearing *to be* to him, unwise rulers or reformers cannot fatally interrupt him. . . . [165/169]

The authority of government, even such as I am willing to submit to—for I will cheerfully obey those who know and can do better than I, and in many things even those who neither know nor can do so well—is still an impure one; to be strictly just, it must have the sanction and consent of the governed. It can have no pure right over my person and property but what I concede to it. The progress from an absolute to a limited monarchy, from a limited monarchy to a democracy is a progress toward a true respect for the individual. Even the Chinese philosopher was wise enough to regard the individual as the basis of the empire. Is a democracy, such as we know it, the last improvement possible in government? Is it not possible to take a step further toward recognizing and organizing the rights of man? There will never be a really free and enlightened state until the state comes to recognize the individual as a higher and independent power, from which all its own power and authority are derived, and treats him accordingly. I please myself with imagining a state at last which [169/170] can afford to be just to all men and to treat the individual with respect as a neighbor; which even would not think it inconsistent with its own repose if a few were to live aloof from it, not meddling with it nor embraced by it, who fulfilled all the duties of neighbors and fellow men. A state which bore this kind of fruit and suffered it to drop off as fast as it ripened would prepare the way for a still more perfect and glorious state, which also I have imagined but not yet anywhere seen. [170]

HENRY DAVID THOREAU

The Martyrdom of John Brown

WHO IS IT whose safety requires that Captain Brown be hung? Is it indispensable to any Northern man? Is there no resource but to cast this man also to the Minotaur? If you do not wish it, say so distinctly. While these things are being done, beauty stands veiled and music is a screeching lie. Think of him,—of his rare qualities!—such a man as it takes ages to make, and ages to understand; no mock hero, nor the representative of any party. A man such as the sun may not rise upon again in this benighted land. To whose making went the costliest material, the finest adamant; sent to be the redeemer of those in captivity; and the only use to which you can put him is to hang him at the end of a rope! You who pretend to care for Christ crucified, consider what you are about to do to him who offered himself to be the saviour of four millions of men.

Any man knows when he is justified, and all the wits in the world cannot enlighten him on that point. The murderer always knows that he is justly punished; but when a government takes the life of a man without the consent of his conscience, it is an audacious government, and is taking a step towards its own dissolution. Is it not possible that an individual may be [232/233] right and a government wrong? Are laws to be enforced simply because they were made? or declared by any number of men to be good, if they are *not* good? Is there any necessity for a man's being a tool to perform a deed of which his better nature disapproves? Is it the intention of lawmakers that *good* men shall be hung ever? Are judges to interpret the law according to the letter, and not the spirit? What right have *you* to enter into a compact with yourself that you *will* do thus or so, against the light within you? Is it for you to *make up* your mind,—to form any resolution whatever,—and not accept the convictions that

From Henry David Thoreau, "A Plea for Captain John Brown," in *The Writings of Henry David Thoreau* (Boston and New York: Houghton, Mifflin and Company, 1893), X, 232–36. [Originally delivered as an address at Concord, Massachusetts, on October 30, 1859.]

are forced upon you, and which ever pass your understanding? I do not believe in lawyers, in that mode of attacking or defending a man, because you descend to meet the judge on his own ground, and, in cases of the highest importance, it is of no consequence whether a man breaks a human law or not. Let lawyers decide trivial cases. Business men may arrange that among themselves. If they were the interpreters of the everlasting laws which rightfully bind man, that would be another thing. A counterfeiting law-factory, standing half in a slave land and half in a free! What kind of laws for free men can you expect from that?

I am here to plead his cause with you. I [233/234] plead not for his life, but for his character,—his immortal life; and so it becomes your cause wholly, and is not his in the least. Some eighteen hundred years ago Christ was crucified; this morning, perchance, Captain Brown was hung. These are the two ends of a chain which is not without its links. He is not Old Brown any longer; he is an angel of light.

I see now that it was necessary that the bravest and humanest man in all the country should be hung. Perhaps he saw it himself. I *almost fear* that I may yet hear of his deliverance, doubting if a prolonged life, if *any* life, can do as much good as his death.

"Misguided!" "Garrulous!" "Insane!" "Vindictive!" So ye write in your easy-chairs, and thus he wounded responds from the floor of the Armory, clear as a cloudless sky, true as the voice of nature is: "No man sent me here; it was my own prompting and that of my Maker. I acknowledge no master in human form."

And in what a sweet and noble strain he proceeds, addressing his captors, who stand over him: "I think, my friends, you are guilty of a great wrong against God and humanity, and it would be perfectly right for any one to interfere with you so far as to free those you willfully and wickedly hold in bondage." [234/235]

And, referring to his movement: "It is, in my opinion, the greatest service a man can render to God."

"I pity the poor in bondage that have none to help them; that is why I am here; not to gratify any personal animosity, revenge, or vindictive spirit. It is my sympathy with the oppressed and the wronged, that are as good as you, and as precious in the sight of God."

You don't know your testament when you see it.

"I want you to understand that I respect the rights of the poorest and weakest of colored people, oppressed by the slave power, just as much as I do those of the most wealthy and powerful."

"I wish to say, furthermore, that you had better, all you people at the South, prepare yourselves for a settlement of that question, that must come up for settlement sooner than you are prepared for it. The sooner you are prepared the better. You may dispose of me very easily. I am nearly disposed of now; but this question is still to be settled,—this negro question, I mean; the end of that is not yet."

I foresee the time when the painter will paint that scene, no longer going to Rome for a subject; the poet will sing it; the historian record it; and, with the Landing of the Pilgrims and [235/236] the Declaration of Independence, it will be the ornament of some future national gallery, when at least the present form of slavery shall be no more here. We shall then be at liberty to weep for Captain Brown. Then, and not till then, we will take our revenge. [236]

EDWARD BELLAMY

— • —

Return to Chaos

"It's a little after the time you told me to wake you, sir. You did not come out of it as quick as common, sir."

The voice was the voice of my man Sawyer. I started bolt upright in bed and stared around. I was in my underground chamber. The mellow light of the lamp which always burned in the room when I occupied it illumined the familiar walls and furnishings. By my bedside, with the glass of sherry in his hand which Dr. Pillsbury prescribed on first rousing from a mesmeric sleep, by way of awakening the torpid physical functions, stood Sawyer.

"Better take this right off, sir," he said, as I stared blankly at him. "You look kind of flushed like, sir, and you need it."

I tossed off the liquor and began to realize what had happened to me. It was, of course, very plain. All that about the twentieth century had been a dream. I had but dreamed of that enlightened and care-free race of men and their ingeniously simple institutions, of the glorious new Boston with its domes and pinnacles, its gardens and fountains, and its universal reign of comfort. [307/308] The amiable family which I had learned to know so well, my genial host and Mentor, Dr. Leete, his wife, and their daugher, the second and more beauteous Edith, my betrothed,—these, too, had been but figments of a vision.

For a considerable time I remained in the attitude in which this conviction had come over me, sitting up in bed gazing at vacancy, absorbed in recalling the scenes and incidents of my fantastic experience. Sawyer, alarmed at my looks, was meanwhile anxiously inquiring what was the matter with me. Roused at length by his importunities to a recognition of my surroundings, I pulled myself together with an effort and assured the faithful fellow that I was all right. "I have had an extraordinary dream, that's all, Sawyer," I said, "most-ex-traor-dinary-dream."

From Edward Bellamy, *Looking Backward 2000–1887* (Boston and New York: Houghton Mifflin Company, n.d.), pp. 307–32. [Originally published in 1888.]

I dressed in a mechanical way, feeling lightheaded and oddly uncertain of myself, and sat down to the coffee and rolls which Sawyer
was in the habit of providing for my refreshment before I left the
house. The morning newspaper lay by the plate. I took it up, and
my eye fell on the date, May 31, 1887. I had known, of course, from
the moment I opened my eyes that my long and detailed experience
in another century had been a dream, and yet it was startling to
have it so conclusively demonstrated that the world was but a few
hours older than when I had lain down to sleep. [308/309]

Glancing at the table of contents at the head of the paper, which
reviewed the news of the morning, I read the following summary:—

"FOREIGN AFFAIRS.—The impending war between France and Germany. The French Chambers asked for new military credits to meet
Germany's increase of her army. Probability that all Europe will be
involved in case of war.—Great suffering among the unemployed in
London. They demand work. Monster demonstration to be made.
The authorities uneasy.—Great strikes in Belgium. The government
preparing to repress outbreaks. Shocking facts in regard to the employment of girls in Belgium coal mines.—Wholesale evictions in Ire-
land.

"HOME AFFAIRS.—The epidemic of fraud unchecked. Embezzlement
of a half a million in New York.—Misappropriation of a trust fund
by executors. Orphans left penniless.—Clever system of thefts by a
bank teller; $50,000 gone.—The coal barons decide to advance the
price of coal and reduce production.—Speculators engineering a
great wheat corner at Chicago.—A clique forcing up the price of
coffee.—Enormous land-grabs of Western syndicates.—Revelations of
shocking corruption among Chicago officials. Systematic bribery.—
The trials of the Boodle aldermen to go on at New York.—Large failures of business houses. Fears of a business crisis.—A large grist
[309/310] of burglaries and larcenies.—A woman murdered in cold
blood for her money at New Haven.—A householder shot by a bur-
glar in this city last night.—A man shoots himself in Worcester because he could not get work. A large family left destitute.—An aged
couple in New Jersey commit suicide rather than go to the poor-
house.—Pitiable destitution among the women wage-workers in the
great cities.—Startling growth of illiteracy in Massachusetts.—More
insane asylums wanted.—Decoration Day addresses. Professor
Brown's oration on the moral grandeur of nineteenth century civilization."

It was indeed the nineteeth century to which I had awaked; there
could be no kind of doubt about that. Its complete microcosm this

summary of the day's news had presented, even to that last unmistakable touch of fatuous self-complacency. Coming after such a damning indictment of the age as that one day's chronicle of worldwide bloodshed, greed, and tyranny, was a bit of cynicism worthy of Mephistopheles, and yet of all whose eyes it had met this morning I was, perhaps, the only one who perceived the cynicism, and but yesterday I should have perceived it no more than the others. That strange dream it was which had made all the difference. For I know not how long, I forgot my surroundings after this, and was again in fancy moving in that vivid [310/311] dream-world, in that glorious city, with its homes of simple comfort and its gorgeous public palaces. Around me were again faces unmarred by arrogance or servility, by envy or greed, by anxious care or feverish ambition, and stately forms of men and women who had never known fear of a fellow man or depended on his favor, but always, in the words of that sermon which still rang in my ears, had "stood up straight before God."

With a profound sigh and a sense of irreparable loss, not the less poignant that it was a loss of what had never really been, I roused at last from my reverie, and soon after left the house.

A dozen times between my door and Washington Street I had to stop and pull myself together, such power had been in that vision of the Boston of the future to make the real Boston strange. The squalor and malodorousness of the town struck me, from the moment I stood upon the street, as facts I had never before observed. But yesterday, moreover, it had seemed quite a matter of course that some of my fellow-citizens should wear silks, and other rags, that some should look well fed, and others hungry. Now on the contrary the glaring disparities in the dress and condition of the men and women who brushed each other on the sidewalks shocked me at every step, and yet more the entire indifference which the prosperous showed to the plight of the unfortunate. Were these human beings, who could behold the wretchedness of [311/312] their fellows without so much as a change of countenance? And yet, all the while, I knew well that it was I who had changed, and not my contemporaries. I had dreamed of a city whose people fared all alike as children of one family and were one another's keepers in all things.

Another feature of the real Boston, which assumed the extraordinary effect of strangeness that marks familiar things seen in a new light, was the prevalence of advertising. There had been no personal advertising in the Boston of the twentieth century, because there was no need of any, but here the walls of the buildings, the windows, the broadsides of the newspapers in every hand, the very pavements, everything in fact in sight, save the sky, were covered with the appeals of individuals who sought, under innumerable pretexts, to attract the contributions of others to their support. However the wording might vary, the tenor of all these appeals was the same:—

"Help John Jones. Never mind the rest. They are frauds. I, John Jones, am the right one. Buy of me. Employ me. Visit me. Hear me, John Jones. Look at me. Make no mistake, John Jones is the man and nobody else. Let the rest starve, but for God's sake remember John Jones!"

Whether the pathos or the moral repulsiveness of the spectacle most impressed me, so suddenly become a stranger in my own city, I know not. [312/313] Wretched men, I was moved to cry, who, because they will not learn to be helpers of one another, are doomed to be beggars of one another from the least to the greatest! This horrible babel of shameless self-assertion and mutual depreciation, this stunning clamor of conflicting boasts, appeals, and adjurations, this stupendous system of brazen beggary, what was it all but the necessity of a society in which the opportunity to serve the world according to his gifts, instead of being secured to every man as the first object of social organization, had to be fought for!

I reached Washington Street at the busiest point, and there I stood and laughed aloud, to the scandal of the passers-by. For my life I could not have helped it, with such a mad humor was I moved at sight of the interminable rows of stores on either side, up and down the street so far as I could see,—scores of them, to make the spectacle more utterly preposterous, within a stone's throw devoted to selling the same sort of goods. Stores! stores! stores! miles of stores! ten thousand stores to distribute the goods needed by this one city, which in my dream had been supplied with all things from a single warehouse, as they were ordered through one great store in every quarter, where the buyer, without waste of time or labor, found under one roof the world's assortment in whatever line he desired. There the labor of distribution had been so slight as to add but a [313/314] scarcely perceptible fraction to the cost of commodities to the user. The cost of production was virtually all he paid. But here the mere distribution of the goods, their handling alone, added a fourth, a third, a half and more, to the cost. All these ten thousand plants must be paid for, their rent, their staffs of superintendence, their platoons of salesmen, their ten thousand sets of accountants, jobbers, and business dependents, with all they spent in advertising themselves and fighting one another, and the consumers must do the paying. What a famous process for beggaring a nation!

Were these serious men I saw about me, or children, who did their business on such a plan? Could they be reasoning beings, who did not see the folly which, when the product is made and ready for use, wastes so much of it in getting it to the user? If people eat with a spoon that leaks half its contents between bowl and lip, are they not likely to go hungry?

I had passed through Washington Street thousands of times before and viewed the ways of those who sold merchandise, but my curiosity concerning them was as if I had never gone by their way before. I took wondering note of the show windows of the stores, filled with goods arranged with a wealth of pains and artistic device to attract the eye. I saw the throngs of ladies looking in, and the proprietors eagerly watching the effect of [314/315] the bait. I went within and noted the hawk-eyed floor-walker watching for business, overlooking the clerks, keeping them up to their task of inducing the customers to buy, buy, buy, for money if they had it, for credit if they had it not, to buy what they wanted not, more than they wanted, what they could not afford. At times I momentarily lost the clue and was confused by the sight. Why this effort to induce people to buy? Surely that had nothing to do with the legitimate business of distributing products to those who needed them. Surely it was the sheerest waste to force upon people what they did not want, but what might be useful to another. The nation was so much the poorer for every such achievement. What were these clerks thinking of? Then I would remember that they were not acting as distributors like those in the store I had visited in the dream Boston. They were not serving the public interest, but their immediate personal interest, and it was nothing to them what the ultimate effect of their course on the general prosperity might be, if but they increased their own hoard, for these goods were their own, and the more they sold and the more they got for them, the greater their gain. The more wasteful the people were, the more articles they did not want which they could be induced to buy, the better for these sellers. To encourage prodigality was the express aim of the ten thousand stores of Boston. [315/316]

Nor were these storekeepers and clerks a whit worse men than any others in Boston. They must earn a living and support their families, and how were they to find a trade to do it by which did not necessitate placing their individual interests before those of others and that of all? They could not be asked to starve while they waited for an order of things such as I had seen in my dream, in which the interest of each and that of all were identical. But, God in heaven! what wonder, under such a system as this about me—what wonder that the city was so shabby, and the people so meanly dressed, and so many of them ragged and hungry!

Some time after this it was that I drifted over into South Boston and found myself among the manufacturing establishments. I had been in this quarter of the city a hundred times before, just as I had been on Washington Street, but here, as well as there, I now first perceived the true significance of what I witnessed. Formerly I had taken pride in the fact that, by actual count, Boston had some four thousand independent manufacturing establishments; but in this very multiplicity and independence I recognized now the secret of the insignificant total product of their industry.

If Washington Street had been like a lane in Bedlam, this was a spectacle as much more melancholy as production is a more vital function than [316/317] distribution. For not only were these four thousand establishments not working in concert, and for that reason alone operating at prodigious disadvantage, but, as if this did not involve a sufficiently disastrous loss of power, they were using their utmost skill to frustrate one another's effort, praying by night and working by day for the destruction of one another's enterprises.

The roar and rattle of wheels and hammers resounding from every side was not the hum of a peaceful industry, but the clangor of swords wielded by foemen. These mills and shops were so many forts, each under its own flag, its guns trained on the mills and shops about it, and its sappers busy below, undermining them.

Within each one of these forts the strictest organization of industry was insisted on; the separate gangs worked under a single central authority. No interference and no duplicating of work were permitted. Each had his allotted task, and none were idle. By what hiatus in the logical faculty, by what lost link of reasoning, account, then, for the failure to recognize the necessity of applying the same principle to the organization of the national industries as a whole, to see that if lack of organization could impair the efficiency of a shop, it must have effects as much more disastrous in disabling the industries of the nation at large as the latter are vaster in volume and more complex in the relationship of their parts. [317/318]

People would be prompt enough to ridicule an army in which there were neither companies, battalions, regiments, brigades, divisions, or army corps,—no unit of organization, in fact, larger than the corporal's squad, with no officer higher than a corporal, and all the corporals equal in authority. And yet just such an army were the manufacturing industries of nineteenth century Boston, an army of four thousand independent squads led by four thousand independent corporals, each with a separate plan of campaign.

Knots of idle men were to be seen here and there on every side, some idle because they could find no work at any price, others because they could not get what they thought a fair price.

I accosted some of the latter, and they told me their grievances. It was very little comfort I could give them. "I am sorry for you," I said. "You get little enough, certainly, and yet the wonder to me is, not that industries conducted as these are do not pay you living wages, but that they are able to pay you any wages at all."

Making my way back again after this to the peninsular city, toward three o'clock I stood on State Street, staring, as if I had never seen them before, at the banks and brokers' offices, and other financial institutions, of which there had been in the State Street of my vision no vestige. Business men, confidential clerks, and errand boys were thronging in and out of the banks, for it wanted [318/319] but a few minutes of the closing hour. Opposite me was the bank where I did business, and presently I crossed the street, and, going in with the crowd, stood in a recess of the wall looking on at the army of clerks handling money, and the cues of depositors at the tellers' windows. An old gentleman whom I knew, a director of the bank, passing me and observing my contemplative attitude, stopped a moment.

"Interesting sight, isn't it, Mr. West," he said. "Wonderful piece of mechanism; I find it so myself. I like sometimes to stand and look on at it just as you are doing. It's a poem, sir, a poem, that's what I call it. Did you ever think, Mr. West, that the bank is the heart of the business system? From it and to it, in endless flux and reflux, the life blood goes. It is flowing in now. It will flow out again in the morning;" and pleased with his little conceit, the old man passed on smiling.

Yesterday I should have considered the simile apt enough, but since then I had visited a world incomparably more affluent than this, in which money was unknown and without conceivable use. I had learned that it had a use in the world around me only because the work of producing the nation's livelihood, instead of being regarded as the most strictly public and common of all concerns, and as such conducted by the nation, was abandoned to the hap-hazard efforts of individuals. This original [319/320] mistake necessitated endless exchanges to bring about any sort of general distribution of products. These exchanges money effected—how equitably, might be seen in a walk from the tenement house districts to the Back Bay—at the cost of an army of men taken from productive labor to manage it, with constant ruinous breakdowns of its machinery, and a generally debauching influence on mankind which had justified its description, from ancient time, as the "root of all evil."

Alas for the poor old bank director with his poem! He had mistaken the throbbing of an abscess for the beating of the heart. What he called "a wonderful piece of mechanism" was an imperfect device to remedy an unnecessary defect, the clumsy crutch of a self-made cripple.

After the banks had closed I wandered aimlessly about the busi-

ness quarter for an hour or two, and later sat a while on one of the
benches of the Common, finding an interest merely in watching the
throngs that passed, such as one has in studying the populace of a
foreign city, so strange since yesterday had my fellow citizens and
their ways become to me. For thirty years I had lived among them,
and yet I seemed to have never noted before how drawn and anxious were their faces, of the rich as of the poor, the refined, acute
faces of the educated as well as the dull masks of the ignorant. And
well it might be so, for I saw now, as never before I had seen so
plainly, that each as [320/321] he walked constantly turned to catch
the whispers of a spectre at his ear, the spectre of Uncertainty. "Do
your work never so well," the spectre was whispering,—"rise early
and toil till late, rob cunningly or serve faithfully, you shall never
know security. Rich you may be now and still come to poverty at
last. Leave never so much wealth to your children, you cannot buy
the assurance that your son may not be the servant of your servant,
or that your daughter will not have to sell herself for bread."

A man passing by thrust an advertising card in my hand, which
set forth the merits of some new scheme of life insurance. The incident reminded me of the only device, pathetic in its admission of
the universal need it so poorly supplied, which offered these tired
and hunted men and women even a partial protection from uncertainty. By this means, those already well-to-do, I remembered, might
purchase a precarious confidence that after their death their loved
ones would not, for a while at least, be trampled under the feet of
men. But this was all, and this was only for those who could pay
well for it. What idea was possible to these wretched dwellers in the
land of Ishmael, where every man's hand was against each and the
hand of each against every other, of true life insurance as I had seen
it among the people of that dream land, each of whom, by virtue
merely of his membership in the national family, was guaranteed
[321/322] against need of any sort, by a policy underwritten by one
hundred million fellow countrymen.

Some time after this it was that I recall a glimpse of myself standing on the steps of a building on Tremont Street, looking at a military parade. A regiment was passing. It was the first sight in that
dreary day which had inspired me with any other emotions than
wondering pity and amazement. Here at last were order and reason,
an exhibition of what intelligent coöperation can accomplish. The
people who stood looking on with kindling faces,—could it be that
the sight had for them no more than but a spectacular interest?
Could they fail to see that it was their perfect concert of action,
their organization under one control, which made these men the tremendous engine they were, able to vanquish a mob ten times as nu-

merous? Seeing this so plainly, could they fail to compare the scientific manner in which the nation went to war with the unscientific manner in which it went to work? Would they not query since what time the killing of men had been a task so much more important than feeding and clothing them, that a trained army should be deemed alone adequate to the former, while the latter was left to a mob?

It was now toward nightfall, and the streets were thronged with the workers from the stores, the shops, and mills. Carried along with the stronger part of the current, I found myself, as it [322/323] began to grow dark, in the midst of a scene of squalor and human degradation such as only the South Cove tenement district could present. I had seen the mad wasting of human labor; here I saw in direst shape the want that waste had bred.

From the black doorways and windows of the rookeries on every side came gusts of fetid air. The streets and alleys reeked with the effluvia of a slave ship's between-decks. As I passed I had glimpses within of pale babies gasping out their lives amid sultry stenches, of hopeless-faced women deformed by hardship, retaining of womanhood no trait save weakness, while from the windows leered girls with brows of brass. Like the starving bands of mongrel curs that infest the streets of Moslem towns, swarms of half-clad brutalized children filled the air with shrieks and curses as they fought and tumbled among the garbage that littered the court-yards.

There was nothing in all this that was new to me. Often had I passed through this part of the city and witnessed its sights with feelings of disgust mingled with a certain philosophical wonder at the extremities mortals will endure and still cling to life. But not alone as regarded the economical follies of this age, but equally as touched its moral abominations, scales had fallen from my eyes since that vision of another century. No more did I look upon the woful dwellers in this Inferno with a callous curiosity as creatures scarcely human. I [323/324] saw in them my brothers and sisters, my parents, my children, flesh of my flesh, blood of my blood. The festering mass of human wretchedness about me offended not now my senses merely, but pierced my heart like a knife, so that I could not repress sighs and groans. I not only saw but felt in my body all that I saw.

Presently, too, as I observed the wretched beings about me more closely, I perceived that they were all quite dead. Their bodies were so many living sepulchres. On each brutal brow was plainly written the *hic jacet* of a soul dead within.

As I looked, horror struck, from one death's head to another, I was affected by a singular hallucination. Like a wavering translucent spirit face superimposed upon each of these brutish masks I saw the ideal, the possible face that would have been the actual if mind and soul had lived. It was not till I was aware of these ghostly faces, and of the reproach that could not be gain-said which was in their eyes, that the full piteousness of the ruin that had been wrought was revealed to me. I was moved with contrition as with a strong agony, for I had been one of those who had endured that these things should be. I had been one of those who, well knowing that they were, had not desired to hear or be compelled to think much of them, but had gone on as if they were not, seeking my own pleasure and profit. Therefore now I found upon my garments the [324/325] blood of this great multitude of strangled souls of my brothers. The voice of their blood cried out against me from the ground. Every stone of the reeking pavements, every brick of the pestilential rookeries, found a tongue and called after me as I fled: What hast thou done with thy brother Abel?

I have no clear recollection of anything after this till I found myself standing on the carved stone steps of the magnificent home of my betrothed in Commonwealth Avenue. Amid the tumult of my thoughts that day, I had scarcely once thought of her, but now obeying some unconscious impulse my feet had found the familiar way to her door. I was told that the family were at dinner, but word was sent out that I should join them at table. Besides the family, I found several guests present, all known to me. The table glittered with plate and costly china. The ladies were sumptuously dressed and wore the jewels of queens. The scene was one of costly elegance and lavish luxury. The company was in excellent spirits, and there was plentiful laughter and a running fire of jests.

To me it was as if, in wandering through the place of doom, my blood turned to tears by its sights, and my spirit attuned to sorrow, pity, and despair, I had happened in some glade upon a merry party of roisterers. I sat in silence until Edith began to rally me upon my sombre looks, [325/326] What ailed me? The others presently joined in the playful assault, and I became a target for quips and jests. Where had I been, and what had I seen to make such a dull fellow of me?

"I have been in Golgotha," at last I answered. "I have seen Humanity hanging on a cross! Do none of you know what sights the sun and stars look down on in this city, that you can think and talk of anything else? Do you not know that close to your doors a great multitude of men and women, flesh of your flesh, live lives that are one agony from birth to death? Listen! their dwellings are so near that if you hush your laughter you will hear their grievous voices, the piteous crying of the little ones that suckle poverty, the hoarse curses of men sodden in misery, turned half-way back to brutes, the chaffering of an army of women selling themselves for bread. With what have you stopped your ears that you do not hear these doleful sounds? For me, I can hear nothing else."

Silence followed my words. A passion of pity had shaken me as I spoke, but when I looked around upon the company, I saw that, far from being stirred as I was, their faces expressed a cold and hard astonishment, mingled in Edith's with extreme mortification, in her father's with anger. The ladies were exchanging scandalized looks, while one of the gentlemen had put up his eyeglass and was study-ing me with an air of scientific [326/327] curiosity. When I saw that things which were to me so intolerable moved them not at all, that words that melted my heart to speak had only offended them with the speaker, I was at first stunned and then overcome with a desper-ate sickness and faintness at the heart. What hope was there for the wretched, for the world, if thoughtful men and tender women were not moved by things like these! Then I bethought myself that it must be because I had not spoken aright. No doubt I had put the case badly. They were angry because they thought I was berating them, when God knew I was merely thinking of the horror of the fact without any attempt to assign the responsibility for it.

I restrained my passion, and tried to speak calmly and logically that I might correct this impression. I told them that I had not meant to accuse them, as if they, or the rich in general, were respon-sible for the misery of the world. True indeed it was, that the super-fluity which they wasted would, otherwise bestowed, relieve much bitter suffering. These costly viands, these rich wines, these gorgeous fabrics and glistening jewels represented the ransom of many lives. They were verily not without the guiltiness of those who waste in a land stricken with famine. Nevertheless, all the waste of all the rich, were it saved, would go but a little way to cure the poverty of the world. There was so little to divide that even if the rich went share and share with [327/328] the poor, there would be but a common fare of crusts, albeit made very sweet then by brotherly love.

The folly of men, not their hard-heartedness, was the great cause of the world's poverty. It was not the crime of man, nor of any class of men, that made the race so miserable, but a hideous, ghastly mis-take, a colossal world-darkening blunder. And then I showed them how four fifths of the labor of men was utterly wasted by the mutual warfare, the lack of organization and concert among the workers. Seeking to make the matter very plain, I instanced the case of arid lands where the soil yielded the means of life only by careful use of the watercourses for irrigation. I showed how in such countries it was counted the most important function of the government to see that the water was not wasted by the selfishness or ignorance of in-dividuals, since otherwise there would be famine. To this end its use was strictly regulated and systematized, and individuals of their mere caprice were not permitted to dam it or divert it, or in any way to tamper with it.

The labor of men, I explained, was the fertilizing stream which alone rendered earth habitable. It was but a scanty stream at best, and its use required to be regulated by a system which expended every drop to the best advantage, if the world were to be supported in abundance. But how far from any system was the actual practice! Every man [328/329] wasted the precious fluid as he wished, animated only by the equal motives of saving his own crop and spoiling his neighbor's, that his might sell the better. What with greed and what with spite some fields were flooded while others were parched, and half the water ran wholly to waste. In such a land, though a few by strength or cunning might win the means of luxury, the lot of the great mass must be poverty, and of the weak and ignorant bitter want and perennial famine.

Let but the famine-stricken nation assume the function it had neglected, and regulate for the common good the course of the life-giving stream, and the earth would bloom like one garden, and none of its children lack any good thing. I described the physical felicity, mental enlightenment, and moral elevation which would then attend the lives of all men. With fervency I spoke of that new world, blessed with plenty, purified by justice and sweetened by brotherly kindness, the world of which I had indeed but dreamed, but which might so easily be made real. But when I had expected now surely the faces around me to light up with emotions akin to mine, they grew ever more dark, angry, and scornful. Instead of enthusiasm, the ladies showed only aversion and dread, while the men interrupted me with shouts of reprobation and contempt. "Madman!" "Pestilent fellow!" "Fanatic!" "Enemy of society!" were some of their cries, and the one who had before taken his [329/330] eyeglass to me exclaimed, "He says we are to have no more poor. Ha! ha!"

"Put the fellow out!" exclaimed the father of my betrothed, and at the signal the men sprang from their chairs and advanced upon me.

It seemed to me that my heart would burst with the anguish of finding that what was to me so plain and so all-important was to them meaningless, and that I was powerless to make it other. So hot had been my heart that I had thought to melt an iceberg with its glow, only to find at last the overmastering chill seizing my own vitals. It was not enmity that I felt toward them as they thronged me, but pity only, for them and for the world.

Although despairing, I could not give over. Still I strove with them. Tears poured from my eyes. In my vehemence I became inarticulate. I panted, I sobbed, I groaned, and immediately afterward found myself sitting upright in bed in my room in Dr. Leete's house, and the morning sun shining through the open window into my eyes. I was gasping. The tears were streaming down my face, and I quivered in every nerve.

As with an escaped convict who dreams that he has been recaptured and brought back to his dark and reeking dungeon, and opens his eyes to see the heaven's vault spread above him, so it was with me, as I realized that my return to the nineteenth [330/331] century had been the dream, and my presence in the twentieth was the reality.

The cruel sights which I had witnessed in my vision, and could so well confirm from the experience of my former life, though they had, alas! once been, and must in the retrospect to the end of time move the compassionate to tears, were, God be thanked, forever gone by. Long ago oppressor and oppressed, prophet and scorner, had been dust. For generations, rich and poor had been forgotten words.

But in that moment, while yet I mused with unspeakable thankfulness upon the greatness of the world's salvation and my privilege in beholding it, there suddenly pierced me like a knife a pang of shame, remorse, and wondering self-reproach, that bowed my head upon my breast and made me wish the grave had hid me with my fellows from the sun. For I had been a man of that former time. What had I done to help on the deliverance whereat I now presumed to rejoice? I who had lived in those cruel, insensate days, what had I done to bring them to an end? I had been every whit as indifferent to the wretchedness of my brothers, as cynically incredulous of better things, as besotted a worshipper of Chaos and Old Night, as any of my fellows. So far as my personal influence went, it had been exerted rather to hinder than to help forward the enfranchisement of the race which was even then preparing. What right [331/332] had I to hail a salvation which reproached me, to rejoice in a day whose dawning I had mocked?

"Better for you, better for you," a voice within me rang, "had this evil dream been the reality, and this fair reality the dream; better your part pleading for crucified humanity with a scoffing generation, than here, drinking of wells you digged not, and eating of trees whose husbandmen you stoned;" and my spirit answered, "Better, truly."

When at length I raised my bowed head and looked forth from the window, Edith, fresh as the morning, had come into the garden and was gathering flowers. I hastened to descend to her. Kneeling before her, with my face in the dust, I confessed with tears how little was my worth to breathe the air of this golden century, and how infinitely less to wear upon my breast its consummate flower. Fortunate is he who, with a case so desperate as mine, finds a judge so merciful. [332]

JACK LONDON

A Night with the Philomaths

. . . It was at the Philomath Club—a wonderful night of battle, wherein Ernest bearded the masters in their lair. Now the Philomath Club was the most select on the Pacific Coast. It was the creation of Miss Brentwood, an enormously wealthy old maid; and it was her husband, and family, and toy. Its members were the wealthiest in the community, and the strongest-minded of the wealthy, with, of course, a sprinkling of scholars to give it intellectual tone.

The Philomath had no club house. It was not that kind of a club. Once a month its members gathered at some one of their private houses to listen to a lecture. The lecturers were usually, though not always, hired. If a chemist in New York made a new discovery in say radium, all his expenses across the continent were paid, and as well he received a princely fee for his time. The same with a returning explorer from the polar regions, or the latest literary or artistic success. No visitors were allowed, while it was the Philomath's policy to permit none of its discussions to get into the papers. Thus great statesmen—and there had been such occasions—were able fully to speak their minds.

I spread before me a wrinkled letter, written to me by Ernest twenty years ago, and from it I copy the following: [73/74]

"Your father is a member of the Philomath, so you are able to come. Therefore come next Tuesday night. I promise you that you will have the time of your life. In your recent encounters, you failed to shake the masters. If you come, I'll shake them for you. I'll make them snarl like wolves. You merely questioned their morality. When their morality is questioned, they grow only the more complacent and superior. But I shall menace their money-bags. That will shake them to the roots of their primitive natures. If you can come, you will see the cave-man, in evening dress, snarling and snapping over a bone. I promise you a great caterwauling and an illuminating in-

From Jack London, *The Iron Heel* (New York: The Macmillan Company, 1907), pp. 73–99.

sight into the nature of the beast.

"They've invited me in order to tear me to pieces. This is the idea of Miss Brentwood. She clumsily hinted as much when she invited me. She's given them that kind of fun before. They delight in getting trustful-souled gentle reformers before them. Miss Brentwood thinks I am as mild as a kitten and as good-natured and stolid as the family cow. I'll not deny that I helped to give her that impression. She was very tentative at first, until she divined my harmlessness. I am to receive a handsome fee—two hundred and fifty dollars—as befits the man who, though a radical, once ran for governor. Also, I am to wear evening dress. This is compulsory. I never was so apparelled in my life. I suppose I'll have to hire one somewhere. [74/75] But I'd do more than that to get a chance at the Philomaths."

Of all places, the Club gathered that night at the Pertonwaithe house. Extra chairs had been brought into the great drawing-room, and in all there must have been two hundred Philomaths that sat down to hear Ernest. They were truly lords of society. I amused myself with running over in my mind the sum of fortunes represented, and it ran well into the hundreds of millions. And the possessors were not of the idle rich. They were men of affairs who took most active parts in industrial and political life.

We were all seated when Miss Brentwood brought Ernest in. They moved at once to the head of the room, from where he was to speak. He was in evening dress, and, what of his broad shoulders and kingly head, he looked magnificent. And then there was that faint and unmistakable touch of awkwardness in his movements. . . .

At the head of the room, Miss Brentwood introduced [75/76] him to Colonel Van Gilbert, and I knew that the latter was to preside. Colonel Van Gilbert was a great corporation lawyer. In addition, he was immensely wealthy. The smallest fee he would deign to notice was a hundred thousand dollars. He was a master of law. The law was a puppet with which he played. He moulded it like clay, twisted and distorted it like a Chinese puzzle into any design he chose. In appearance and rhetoric he was old-fashioned, but in imagination and knowledge and resource he was as young as the latest statute. His first prominence had come when he broke the Shardwell will.[1] His fee for this one act was five hundred thousand dollars. From then on he had risen like a rocket. He was often called the

---

[1] This breaking of wills was a peculiar feature of the period. With the accumulation of vast fortunes, the problem of disposing of these fortunes after death was a vexing one to the accumulators. Will-making and will-breaking became complementary trades, like armor-making and gun-making. The shrewdest will-making lawyers were called in to make wills that could not be

greatest lawyer in the country—corporation lawyer, of course; and no classification of the three greatest lawyers in the United States could have excluded him.

He arose and began, in a few well-chosen phrases that [76/77] carried an undertone of faint irony, to introduce Ernest. Colonel Van Gilbert was subtly facetious in his introduction of the social reformer and member of the working class, and the audience smiled. It made me angry, and I glanced at Ernest. The sight of him made me doubly angry. He did not seem to resent the delicate slurs. Worse than that, he did not seem to be aware of them. There he sat, gentle, and stolid, and somnolent. He really looked stupid. And for a moment the thought arose in my mind, What if he were overawed by this imposing array of power and brains? Then I smiled. He couldn't fool me. But he fooled the others, just as he had fooled Miss Brentwood. She occupied a chair right up to the front, and several times she turned her head toward one or another of her *confrères* and smiled her appreciation of the remarks.

Colonel Van Gilbert done, Ernest arose and began to speak. He began in a low voice, haltingly and modestly, and with an air of evident embarrassment. He spoke of his birth in the working class, and of the sordidness and wretchedness of his environment, where flesh and spirit were alike starved and tormented. He described his ambitions and ideals, and his conception of the paradise wherein lived the people of the upper classes. As he said:

"Up above me, I knew, were unselfishnesses of the spirit, clean and noble thinking, keen intellectual living. [77/78] I knew all this because I read 'Seaside Library'[2] novels, in which, with the exception of the villains and adventuresses, all men and women thought beautiful thoughts, spoke a beautiful tongue, and performed glorious deeds. In short, as I accepted the rising of the sun, I accepted that up above me was all that was fine and noble and gracious, all that gave decency and dignity to life, all that made life worth living and that remunerated one for his travail and misery."

He went on and traced his life in the mills, the learning of the horseshoeing trade, and his meeting with the socialists. Among them, he said, he had found keen intellects and brilliant wits, ministers of the Gospel who had been broken because their Christianity

---

broken. But these wills were always broken, and very often by the very lawyers that had drawn them up. Nevertheless the delusion persisted in the wealthy class that an absolutely unbreakable will could be cast; and so, through the generations, clients and lawyers pursued the illusion. It was a pursuit like unto that of the Universal Solvent of the mediæval alchemists.

[2] A curious and amazing literature that served to make the working class utterly misapprehend the nature of the leisure class.

was too wide for any congregation of mammon-worshippers, and professors who had been broken on the wheel of university subservience to the ruling class. The socialists were revolutionists, he said, struggling to overthrow the irrational society of the present and out of the material to build the rational society of the future. Much more he said that would take too long to write, but I shall never forget how he described the life among the revolutionists. All halting utterance vanished. His voice grew strong and confident, and it glowed as he glowed, and as the thoughts glowed that poured out from him. He said: [78/79]

"Amongst the revolutionists I found, also, warm faith in the human, ardent idealism, sweetnesses of unselfishness, renunciation, and martyrdom—all the splendid, stinging things of the spirit. Here life was clean, noble, and alive. I was in touch with great souls who exalted flesh and spirit over dollars and cents, and to whom the thin wail of the starved slum child meant more than all the pomp and circumstance of commercial expansion and world empire. All about me were nobleness of purpose and heroism of effort, and my days and nights were sunshine and starshine, all fire and dew, with before my eyes, ever burning and blazing, the Holy Grail, Christ's own Grail, the warm human, long-suffering and maltreated but to be rescued and saved at the last."

As before I had seen him transfigured, so now he stood transfigured before me. His brows were bright with the divine that was in him, and brighter yet shone his eyes from the midst of the radiance that seemed to envelop him as a mantle. But the others did not see this radiance, and I assumed that it was due to the tears of joy and love that dimmed my vision. At any rate, Mr. Wickson, who sat behind me, was unaffected, for I heard him sneer aloud, "Utopian."[3] [79/80]

Ernest went on to his rise in society, till at last he came in touch with members of the upper classes, and rubbed shoulders with the men who sat in the high places. Then came his disillusionment, and this disillusionment he described in terms that did not flatter his audience. He was surprised at the commonness of the clay. Life

---

[3] The people of that age were phrase slaves. The abjectness of their servitude is incomprehensible to us. There was a magic in words greater than the conjurer's art. So befuddled and chaotic were their minds that the utterance of a single word could negative the generalizations of a lifetime of serious research and thought. Such a word was the adjective *Utopian*. The mere utterance of it could damn any scheme, no matter how sanely conceived, of economic amelioration or regeneration. Vast populations grew frenzied over such phrases as "an honest dollar" and "a full dinner pail." The coinage of such phrases was considered strokes of genius.

proved not to be fine and gracious. He was appalled by the selfishness he encountered, and what had surprised him even more than that was the absence of intellectual life. Fresh from his revolutionists, he was shocked by the intellectual stupidity of the master class. And then, in spite of their magnificent churches and well-paid preachers, he had found the masters, men and women, grossly material. It was true that they prattled sweet little ideals and dear little moralities, but in spite of their prattle the dominant key of the life they lived was materialistic. And they were without real morality—for instance, that which Christ had preached but which was no longer preached.

"I met men," he said, "who invoked the name of the Prince of Peace in their diatribes against war, and who put rifles in the hands of Pinkertons[4] with which [80/81] to shoot down strikers in their own factories. I met men incoherent with indignation at the brutality of prize-fighting, and who, at the same time, were parties to the adulteration of food that killed each year more babes than even red-handed Herod had killed.

"This delicate, aristocratic-featured gentleman was a dummy director and a tool of corporations that secretly robbed widows and orphans. This gentleman, who collected fine editions and was a patron of literature, paid blackmail to a heavy-jowled, black-browed boss of a municipal machine. This editor, who published patent medicine advertisements, called me a scoundrelly demagogue because I dared him to print in his paper the truth about patent medicines.[5] This man, talking soberly and earnestly about the beauties of idealism and the goodness of God, had just betrayed his comrades in a business deal. This man, a pillar of the church and heavy contributor to foreign missions, worked his shop girls ten hours a day on a starvation wage and thereby directly encouraged prostitution. This man, who endowed chairs in universities and erected magnificent chapels, perjured himself in courts of law over dollars and cents. This railroad magnate broke his word as a citizen, as a gentleman, and as a Christian, when he granted a secret rebate, and he [81/82] granted many secret rebates. This senator was the tool and the slave, the little puppet, of a brutal uneducated machine boss;[6] so was this governor and this supreme court judge; and all

[4] Originally, they were private detectives; but they quickly became hired fighting men of the capitalists, and ultimately developed into the Mercenaries of the Oligarchy.

[5] *Patent medicines* were patent lies, but, like the charms and indulgences of the Middle Ages, they deceived the people. The only difference lay in that the patent medicines were more harmful and more costly.

[6] Even as late as 1912, A.D., the great mass of the people still persisted in

three rode on railroad passes; and, also, this sleek capitalist owned the machine, the machine boss, and the railroads that issued the passes.

"And so it was, instead of in paradise, that I found myself in the arid desert of commercialism. I found nothing but stupidity, except for business. I found none clean, noble, and alive, though I found many who were alive—with rottenness. What I did find was monstrous selfishness and heartlessness, and a gross, gluttonous, practised, and practical materialism."

Much more Ernest told them of themselves and of his disillusionment. Intellectually they had bored him; morally and spiritually they had sickened him; so that he was glad to go back to his revolutionists, who were clean, noble, and alive, and all that the capitalists were not.

"And now," he said, "let me tell you about that revolution."

But first I must say that his terrible diatribe had [82/83] not touched them. I looked about me at their faces and saw that they remained complacently superior to what he had charged. And I remembered what he had told me: that no indictment of their morality could shake them. However, I could see that the boldness of his language had affected Miss Brentwood. She was looking worried and apprehensive.

Ernest began by describing the army of revolution, and as he gave the figures of its strength (the votes cast in the various countries), the assemblage began to grow restless. Concern showed in their faces, and I noticed a tightening of lips. At last the gage of battle had been thrown down. He described the international organization of the socialists that united the million and a half in the United States with the twenty-three millions and a half in the rest of the world.

"Such an army of revolution," he said, "twenty-five millions strong, is a thing to make rulers and ruling classes pause and consider. The cry of this army is: 'No quarter! We want all that you possess. We will be content with nothing less than all that you possess. We want in our hands the reins of power and the destiny of mankind. Here are our hands. They are strong hands. We are going to take your governments, your palaces, and all your purpled ease away from you, and in that day you shall work for your bread even as the peas-

---

the belief that they ruled the country by virtue of their ballots. In reality, the country was ruled by what were called *political machines*. At first the machine bosses charged the master capitalists extortionate tolls for legislation; but in a short time the master capitalists found it cheaper to own the political machines themselves and to hire the machine bosses.

ant in the field or the starved and runty clerk [83/84] in your metrop-
olises. Here are our hands. They are strong hands!'"

And as he spoke he extended from his splendid shoulders his two
great arms, and the horseshoer's hands were clutching the air like
eagle's talons. He was the spirit of regnant labor as he stood there,
his hands outreaching to rend and crush his audience. I was aware
of a faintly perceptible shrinking on the part of the listeners before
this figure of revolution, concrete, potential, and menacing. That is,
the women shrank, and fear was in their faces. Not so with the men.
They were of the active rich, and not the idle, and they were fighters. A low, throaty rumble arose, lingered on the air a moment, and
ceased. It was the forerunner of the snarl, and I was to hear it many
times that night—the token of the brute in man, the earnest of his
primitive passions. And they were unconscious that they had made
this sound. It was the growl of the pack, mouthed by the pack, and
mouthed in all unconsciousness. And in that moment, as I saw the
harshness form in their faces and saw the fight-light flashing in their
eyes, I realized that not easily would they let their lordship of the
world be wrested from them.

Ernest proceeded with his attack. He accounted for the existence
of the million and a half of revolutionists in the United States by
charging the capitalist class with having mismanaged society. He
sketched the economic condition of the cave-man and of the [84/85]
savage peoples of to-day, pointing out that they possessed neither
tools nor machines, and possessed only a natural efficiency of one in
producing power. Then he traced the development of machinery
and social organization so that to-day the producing power of civilized man was a thousand times greater than that of the savage.

"Five men," he said, "can produce bread for a thousand. One man
can produce cotton cloth for two hundred and fifty people, woollens
for three hundred, and boots and shoes for a thousand. One would
conclude from this that under a capable management of society
modern civilized man would be a greater deal better off than the
cave-man. But is he? Let us see. In the United States to-day there
are fifteen million[7] people living in poverty; and by poverty is meant
that condition in life in which, through lack of food and adequate
shelter, the mere standard of working efficiency cannot be maintained. In the United States to-day, in spite of all your so-called
labor legislation, there are three millions of child laborers.[8] In
twelve years their numbers have been doubled. And in passing I will

[7] Robert Hunter, in 1906, in a book entitled "Poverty," pointed out that at
that time there were ten millions in the United States living in poverty.

[8] In the United States Census of 1900 (the last census the figures of which
were made public), the number of child laborers was placed at 1,752,187.

ask you managers of society why you did [85/86] not make public
the census figures of 1910? And I will answer for you, that you were
afraid. The figures of misery would have precipitated the revolution
that even now is gathering.

"But to return to my indictment. If modern man's producing
power is a thousand times greater than that of the cave-man, why
then, in the United States to-day, are there fifteen million people
who are not properly sheltered and properly fed? Why then, in the
United States to-day, are there three million child laborers? It is a
true indictment. The capitalist class has mismanaged. In face of the
facts that modern man lives more wretchedly than the cave-man,
and that his producing power is a thousand times greater than that
of the cave-man, no other conclusion is possible than that the capitalist class has mismanaged, that you have mismanaged, my masters,
that you have criminally and selfishly mismanaged. And on this
count you cannot answer me here to-night, face to face, any more
than can your whole class answer the million and a half of revolutionists in the United States. You cannot answer. I challenge you to
answer. And furthermore, I dare to say to you now that when I have
finished, you will not answer. On that point you will be tongue-tied,
though you will talk wordily enough about other things.

"You have failed in your management. You have made a shambles
of civilization. You have been blind [86/87] and greedy. You have
risen up (as you to-day rise up), shamelessly, in our legislative halls,
and declared that profits were impossible without the toil of children and babes. Don't take my word for it. It is all in the records
against you. You have lulled your conscience to sleep with prattle of
sweet ideals and dear moralities. You are fat with power and possession, drunken with success; and you have no more hope against us
than have the drones, clustered about the honey-vats, when the
worker-bees spring upon them to end their rotund existence. You
have failed in your management of society, and your management is
to be taken away from you. A million and a half of the men of the
working class say that they are going to get the rest of the working
class to join with them and take the management away from you.
This is the revolution, my masters. Stop it if you can."

For an appreciable lapse of time Ernest's voice continued to ring
through the great room. Then arose the throaty rumble I had heard
before, and a dozen men were on their feet clamoring for recognition from Colonel Van Gilbert. I noticed Miss Brentwood's shoulders
moving convulsively, and for the moment I was angry, for I thought
that she was laughing at Ernest. And then I discovered that it was
not laughter, but hysteria. She was appalled by what she had done in
bringing this firebrand before her blessed Philomath Club. [87/88]

Colonel Van Gilbert did not notice the dozen men, with passion-wrought faces, who strove to get permission from him to speak. His own face was passion-wrought. He sprang to his feet, waving his arms, and for a moment could utter only incoherent sounds. Then speech poured from him. But it was not the speech of a one-hundred-thousand-dollar lawyer, nor was the rhetoric old-fashioned.

"Fallacy upon fallacy!" he cried. "Never in all my life have I heard so many fallacies uttered in one short hour. And besides, young man, I must tell you that you have said nothing new. I learned all that at college before you were born. Jean Jacques Rousseau enunciated your socialistic theory nearly two centuries ago. A return to the soil, forsooth! Reversion! Our biology teaches the absurdity of it. It has been truly said that a little learning is a dangerous thing, and you have exemplified it to-night with your madcap theories. Fallacy upon fallacy! I was never so nauseated in my life with overplus of fallacy. That for your immature generalizations and childish reasonings!"

He snapped his fingers contemptuously and proceeded to sit down. There were lip-exclamations of approval on the part of the women, and hoarser notes of confirmation came from the men. As for the dozen men who were clamoring for the floor, half of them began speaking at once. The confusion and babel was indescribable. Never had Mrs. Pertonwaithe's spacious [88/89] walls beheld such a spectacle. These, then, were the cool captains of industry and lords of society, these snarling, growling savages in evening clothes. Truly Ernest had shaken them when he stretched out his hands for their money-bags, his hands that had appeared in the eyes as the hands of the fifteen hundred thousand revolutionists.

But Ernest never lost his head in a situation. Before Colonel Van Gilbert had succeeded in sitting down, Ernest was on his feet and had sprung forward.

"One at a time!" he roared at them.

The sound arose from his great lungs and dominated the human tempest. By sheer compulsion of personality he commanded silence.

"One at a time," he repeated softly. "Let me answer Colonel Van Gilbert. After that the rest of you can come at me—but one at a time, remember. No mass-plays here. This is not a football field.

"As for you," he went on, turning toward Colonel Van Gilbert, "you have replied to nothing I have said. You have merely made a few excited and dogmatic assertions about my mental caliber. That may serve you in your business, but you can't talk to me like that. I am not a workingman, cap in hand, asking you to increase my wages or to protect me from the machine at which I work. You cannot be dogmatic with truth when you deal with me. Save that for dealing with your wage-slaves. They will not dare [89/90] reply to you because you hold their bread and butter, their lives, in your hands.

"As for this return to nature that you say you learned at college before I was born, permit me to point out that on the face of it you cannot have learned anything since. Socialism has no more to do with the state of nature than has differential calculus with a Bible class. I have called your class stupid when outside the realm of business. You, sir, have brilliantly exemplified my statement."

This terrible castigation of her hundred-thousand-dollar lawyer was too much for Miss Brentwood's nerves. Her hysteria became violent, and she was helped, weeping and laughing, out of the room. It was just as well, for there was worse to follow.

"Don't take my word for it," Ernest continued, when the interruption had been led away. "Your own authorities with one unanimous voice will prove you stupid. Your own hired purveyors of knowledge will tell you that you are wrong. Go to your meekest little assistant instructor of sociology and ask him what is the difference between Rousseau's theory of the return to nature and the theory of socialism; ask your greatest orthodox bourgeois political economists and sociologists; question through the pages of every text-book written on the subject and stored on the shelves of your subsidized libraries; and from one and all the answer will be that there is nothing congruous [90/91] between the return to nature and socialism. On the other hand, the unanimous affirmative answer will be that the return to nature and socialism are diametrically opposed to each other. As I say, don't take my word for it. The record of your stupidity is there in the books, your own books that you never read. And so far as your stupidity is concerned, you are but the exemplar of your class.

"You know law and business, Colonel Van Gilbert. You know how to serve corporations and increase dividends by twisting the law. Very good. Stick to it. You are quite a figure. You are a very good lawyer, but you are a poor historian, you know nothing of sociology, and your biology is contemporaneous with Pliny."

Here Colonel Van Gilbert writhed in his chair. There was perfect quiet in the room. Everybody sat fascinated—paralyzed, I may say. Such fearful treatment of the great Colonel Van Gilbert was unheard of, undreamed of, impossible to believe—the great Colonel Van Gilbert before whom judges trembled when he arose in court. But Ernest never gave quarter to an enemy.

"This is, of course, no reflection on you," Ernest said. "Every man to his trade. Only you stick to your trade, and I'll stick to mine. You have specialized. When it comes to a knowledge of the law, of how best to evade the law or make new law for the benefit of [91/92] thieving corporations, I am down in the dirt at your feet. But when it comes to sociology—my trade—you are down in the dirt at my feet. Remember that. Remember, also, that your law is the stuff of a day, and that you are not versatile in the stuff of more than a day. Therefore your dogmatic assertions and rash generalizations on things historical and sociological are not worth the breath you waste on them."

Ernest paused for a moment and regarded him thoughtfully, noting his face dark and twisted with anger, his panting chest, his writhing body, and his slim white hands nervously clenching and unclenching.

"But it seems you have breath to use, and I'll give you a chance to use it. I indicted your class. Show me that my indictment is wrong. I pointed out to you the wretchedness of modern man—three million child slaves in the United States, without whose labor profits would not be possible, and fifteen million under-fed, ill-clothed, and worse-housed people. I pointed out that modern man's producing power through social organization and the use of machinery was a thousand times greater than that of the cave-man. And I stated that from these two facts no other conclusion was possible than that the capitalist class had mismanaged. This was my indictment, and I specifically and at length challenged you to answer it. Nay, I did more. I prophesied that you would not answer. It remains [92/93] for your breath to smash my prophecy. You called my speech fallacy. Show the fallacy, Colonel Van Gilbert. Answer the indictment that I and my fifteen hundred thousand comrades have brought against your class and you."

Colonel Van Gilbert quite forgot that he was presiding, and that in courtesy he should permit the other clamorers to speak. He was on his feet, flinging his arms, his rhetoric, and his control to the winds, alternately abusing Ernest for his youth and demagoguery, and savagely attacking the working class, elaborating its inefficiency and worthlessness.

"For a lawyer, you are the hardest man to keep to a point I ever saw," Ernest began his answer to the tirade. "My youth has nothing to do with what I have enunciated. Nor has the worthlessness of the working class. I charged the capitalist class with having mismanaged society. You have not answered. You have made no attempt to answer. Why? Is it because you have no answer? You are the champion of this whole audience. Every one here, except me, is hanging on your lips for that answer. They are hanging on your lips for that answer because they have no answer themselves. As for me, as I said before, I know that you not only cannot answer, but that you will not attempt an answer."

"This is intolerable!" Colonel Van Gilbert cried out. "This is insult!" [93/94]

"That you should not answer is intolerable," Ernest replied gravely. "No man can be intellectually insulted. Insult, in its very nature, is emotional. Recover yourself. Give me an intellectual answer to my intellectual charge that the capitalist class has mismanaged society."

Colonel Van Gilbert remained silent, a sullen, superior expression on his face, such as will appear on the face of a man who will not bandy words with a ruffian.

"Do not be downcast," Ernest said. "Take consolation in the fact that no member of your class has ever yet answered that charge." He turned to the other men who were anxious to speak. "And now it's your chance. Fire away, and do not forget that I here challenge you to give the answer that Colonel Van Gilbert has failed to give."

It would be impossible for me to write all that was said in the discussion. I never realized before how many words could be spoken in three short hours. At any rate, it was glorious. The more his opponents grew excited, the more Ernest deliberately excited them. He had an encyclopædic command of the field of knowledge, and by a word or a phrase, by delicate rapier thrusts, he punctured them. He named the points of their illogic. This was a false syllogism, that conclusion had no connection with the premise, while that next premise was an impostor because it had cunningly [94/95] hidden in it the conclusion that was being attempted to be proved. This was an error, that was an assumption, and the next was an assertion contrary to ascertained truth as printed in all the text-books.

And so it went. Sometimes he exchanged the rapier for the club and went smashing amongst their thoughts right and left. And always he demanded facts and refused to discuss theories. And his facts made for them a Waterloo. When they attacked the working class, he always retorted, "The pot calling the kettle black; that is no answer to the charge that your own face is dirty." And to one and all he said: "Why have you not answered the charge that your class has mismanaged? You have talked about other things and things concerning other things, but you have not answered. Is it because you have no answer?"

It was at the end of the discussion that Mr. Wickson spoke. He was the only one that was cool, and Ernest treated him with a respect he had not accorded the others.

"No answer is necessary," Mr. Wickson said with slow deliberation. "I have followed the whole discussion with amazement and disgust. I am disgusted with you, gentlemen, members of my class. You have behaved like foolish little schoolboys, what with intruding ethics and the thunder of the common politician into such a discussion. You have been out-generalled and outclassed. You have been very

wordy, [95/96] and all you have done is buzz. You have buzzed like
gnats about a bear. Gentlemen, there stands the bear" (he pointed
at Ernest), "and your buzzing has only tickled his ears.

"Believe me, the situation is serious. That bear reached out his
paws to-night to crush us. He has said there are a million and a half
of revolutionists in the United States. That is a fact. He has said that
it is their intention to take away from us our governments, our palaces, and all our purpled ease. That, also, is a fact. A change, a great
change, is coming in society; but, haply, it may not be the change
the bear anticipates. The bear has said that he will crush us. What if
we crush the bear?"

The throat-rumble arose in the great room, and man nodded to
man with indorsement and certitude. Their faces were set hard.
They were fighters, that was certain.

"But not by buzzing will we crush the bear," Mr. Wickson went
on coldly and dispassionately. "We will hunt the bear. We will not
reply to the bear in words. Our reply shall be couched in terms of
lead. We are in power. Nobody will deny it. By virtue of that power
we shall remain in power."

He turned suddenly upon Ernest. The moment was dramatic.

"This, then, is our answer. We have no words to waste on you.
When you reach out your vaunted [96/97] strong hands for our palaces and purpled ease, we will show you what strength is. In roar of
shell and shrapnel and in whine of machine-guns will our answer be
couched.[9] We will grind you revolutionists down under our heel,
and we shall walk upon your faces. The world is ours, we are its
lords, and ours it shall remain. As for the host of labor, it has been
in the dirt since history began, and I read history aright. And in the
dirt it shall remain so long as I and mine and those that come after
us have the power. There is the word. It is the king of words—
Power. Not God, not Mammon, but Power. Pour it over your tongue
till it tingles with it. Power."

"I am answered," Ernest said quietly. "It is the only answer that
could be given. Power. It is what we of the working class preach.
We know, and well we know by bitter experience, that no appeal
for the right, for justice, for humanity, can ever touch you. Your
hearts are hard as your heels with which you tread upon the faces of
the poor. So we have preached power. By the power of our ballots
on election day will we take your government away from you—"

"What if you do get a majority, a sweeping majority, on election

---

[9] To show the tenor of thought, the following definition is quoted from "The
Cynic's Word Book" (1906 A.D.), written by one Ambrose Bierce, an avowed
and confirmed misanthrope of the period: "Grapeshot, *n. An argument which
the future is preparing in answer to the demands of American Socialism.*"

day?" Mr. Wickson broke in to demand. [97/98] "Suppose we refuse to turn the government over to you after you have captured it at the ballot-box?"

"That, also, have we considered," Ernest replied. "And we shall give you an answer in terms of lead. Power, you have proclaimed the king of words. Very good. Power it shall be. And in the day that we sweep to victory at the ballot-box, and you refuse to turn over to us the government we have constitutionally and peacefully captured, and you demand what we are going to do about it—in that day, I say, we shall answer you; and in roar of shell and shrapnel and in whine of machine-guns shall our answer be couched.

"You cannot escape us. It is true that you have read history aright. It is true that labor has from the beginning of history been in the dirt. And it is equally true that so long as you and yours and those that come after you have power, that labor shall remain in the dirt. I agree with you. I agree with all that you have said. Power will be the arbiter, as it always has been the arbiter. It is a struggle of classes. Just as your class dragged down the old feudal nobility, so shall it be dragged down by my class, the working class. If you will read your biology and your sociology as clearly as you do your history, you will see that this end I have described is inevitable. It does not matter whether it is in one year, ten, or a thousand—your class [98/99] shall be dragged down. And it shall be done by power. We of the labor hosts have conned that word over till our minds are all a-tingle with it. Power. It is a kingly word."

And so ended the night with the Philomaths. [99]

JOHN DOS PASSOS

Lover of Mankind

Debs was a railroad man, born in a weather-boarded shack at Terre Haute.

He was one of ten children.

His father had come to America in a sailingship in '49,

an Alsatian from Colmar; not much of a money-maker, fond of music and reading,

he gave his children a chance to finish public school and that was about all he could do.

At fifteen Gene Debs was already working as a machinist on the Indianapolis and Terre Haute Railway.

He worked as locomotive fireman,

clerked in a store

joined the local of the Brotherhood of Locomotive Firemen, was elected secretary, traveled all over the country as organizer.

He was a tall shamblefooted man, had a sort of gusty rhetoric that set on fire the railroad workers in their pineboarded halls

made them want the world he wanted,

a world brothers might own

where everybody would split even:

I am not a labor leader. I don't want you to follow me or anyone else. If you are looking for a Moses to lead you out of the capitalist wilderness you will stay right where you are. I would not lead you into this promised land if I could, because if I could lead you in, someone else would lead you out.

That was how he talked to freighthandlers and gandywalkers, to firemen and switchmen and engineers, telling them it wasn't enough to organize the railroadmen, that all workers must be organized, that all workers must be organized in the workers' cooperative commonwealth.

Locomotive fireman on many a long night's run,

John Dos Passos, "Lover of Mankind," in *The 42nd Parallel* (Boston: Houghton Mifflin Company, 1946), pp. 29–31. [Originally published in 1930.]

under the smoke a fire burned him up, burned in gusty words
[29/30] that beat in pineboarded halls; he wanted his brothers to be
free men.

That was what he saw in the crowd that met him at the Old
Wells Street Depot when he came out of jail after the Pullman
strike,

those were the men that chalked up nine hundred thousand votes
for him in nineteen twelve and scared the frockcoats and the tophats
and diamonded hostesses at Saratoga Springs, Bar Harbor, Lake Ge-
neva with the bogy of a socialist president.

But where were Gene Debs' brothers in nineteen eighteen when
Woodrow Wilson had him locked up in Atlanta for speaking against
war,

where were the big men fond of whisky and fond of each other,
gentle rambling tellers of stories over bars in small towns in the
Middle West,

quiet men who wanted a house with a porch to putter around and
a fat wife to cook for them, a few drinks and cigars, a garden to dig
in, cronies to chew the rag with

and wanted to work for it

and others to work for it;

where were the locomotive firemen and engineers when they hus-
tled him off to Atlanta Penitentiary?

And they brought him back to die in Terre Haute
to sit on his porch in a rocker with a cigar in his mouth,
beside him American Beauty roses his wife fixed in a bowl;
and the people of Terre Haute and the people in Indiana and the
people of the Middle West were fond of him and afraid of him and
thought of him as an old kindly uncle who loved them, and wanted
to be with him and to have him give them candy,

but they were afraid of him as if he had contracted a social disease, syphilis or leprosy, and thought it was too bad,

but on account of the flag
and prosperity [30/31]
and making the world safe for democracy,
they were afraid to be with him,
or to think much about him for fear they might believe him;
for he said:

*While there is a lower class I am of it, while there is a criminal
class I am of it, while there is a soul in prison I am not free.* [31]

JOHN DOS PASSOS

Joe Hill

A YOUNG SWEDE named Hillstrom went to sea, got himself calloused hands on sailingships and tramps, learned English in the focastle of the steamers that make the run from Stockholm to Hull, dreamed the Swede's dream of the west;

when he got to America they gave him a job polishing cuspidors in a Bowery saloon.

He moved west to Chicago and worked in a machineshop.

He moved west and followed the harvest, hung around employment agencies, paid out many a dollar for a job in a construction camp, walked out many a mile when the grub was too bum, or the boss too tough, or too many bugs in the bunkhouse;

read Marx and the I.W.W. Preamble and dreamed about forming the structure of the new society within the shell of the old.

He was in California for the S.P. strike (*Casey Jones, two locomotives, Casey Jones*), used to play the concertina outside the bunkhouse door, after supper, evenings (*Longhaired preachers come out every night*), had a knack for setting rebel words to tunes (*And the union makes us strong*).

Along the coast in cookshacks flophouses jungles wobblies hoboes bindlestiffs began singing Joe Hill's songs. They sang 'em in the county jails of the State of Washington, Oregon, California, Nevada, Idaho, in the bullpens in Montana and Arizona, sang 'em in Walla Walla, San Quentin and Leavenworth,

forming the structure of the new society within the jails of the old.

At Bingham, Utah, Joe Hill organized the workers of the Utah Construction Company in the One Big Union, won a new wagescale, shorter hours, better grub. (The angel Moroni didn't like laboror-

John Dos Passos, "Joe Hill," in *Nineteen Nineteen* (Boston: Houghton Mifflin Company, 1946), pp. 487–88. [Originally published in 1932.]

ganizers any better than the Southern Pacific did.) [487/488]

The angel Moroni moved the hearts of the Mormons to decide it was Joe Hill shot a grocer named Morrison. The Swedish consul and President Wilson tried to get him a new trial but the angel Moroni moved the hearts of the supreme court of the State of Utah to sustain the verdict of guilty. He was in jail a year, went on making up songs. In November 1915 he was stood up against the wall in the jail yard in Salt Lake City.

"Don't mourn for me organize," was the last word he sent out to the workingstiffs of the I.W.W. Joe Hill stood up against the wall of the jail yard, looked into the muzzles of the guns and gave the word to fire.

They put him in a black suit, put a stiff collar around his neck and a bow tie, shipped him to Chicago for a bangup funeral, and photographed his handsome stony mask staring into the future.

The first of May they scattered his ashes to the wind. [488]

ALBERT HALPER

The Workers Take Over

"FRIENDS," said the president as the house grew hushed, "some information has just reached me which has made it necessary for me to interrupt the show, I regret this, but the news is serious." And here he paused to glance at a small piece of paper hidden in his hand. In the wings the man in oily overalls, cap in hand, stood waiting. "I have just learned," continued the president of Bowman House, "that we've a big spoilage on our rotaries at our North Side plant and, until we can get new plates made, the presses will stand idle."

A stir went through the block of foundrymen. At this point the president took the opportunity to moisten his [480/481] lips and steady himself, and the hand that held the paper shook a little.

"Under any other circumstances the idle presses would not be so important, but as conditions stand it is imperative that we get new plates for them as soon as new plates can be made. I address these words to the employees of the Fort Dearborn Electrotype Foundry who are sitting in this theater with us tonight." There was a brief pause, then the president continued speaking. "Bowman House is under a rigorous contract to the mail-order house which has given us the job of printing their big semi-annual catalogues, and, frankly speaking, any refusal to co-operate with us in this predicament might mean the loss of our next season's printing contract. I can make myself more clearly understood when I say that it is imperative that the catalogues be run off as quickly as possible from the presses to beat, by two days, the catalogue run of a rival mail-order house. Two days' start in the mails to hundreds of thousands of customers means a distinct advantage over the other house when it comes to getting the business. The first batch of catalogues in the hands of these thousands means the first rush of business for the mail-order house whose catalogues we are printing. That, my

From Albert Halper, *The Foundry* (New York: The Viking Press, 1934), pp. 480–93.

friends, is the whole situation in a nutshell. Are any of the owners of the foundry in the house?"

The electrician put the front tier of lights on. The whole show was disrupted, ruined. The president called Max'l's name, then Mr. Cranly's, and finally Duffy's. None of the partners were found to be in the house. Max'l lay home sick in bed and Mr. Cranly, stricken with piles, also lay home in bed, tossing feverishly and shouting something in a half-shriek about the stock market. The president called [481/482] out Jack Duffy's name twice. There was no answer. Mr. Bowman then asked if either of the two foremen were present. He was rewarded by more silence. By this time the whole house, aware of the importance of the situation, took in the drama of the scene: the old man on the stage calling for co-operation and the block of foundrymen sitting stolidly in their seats.

For the second time the president, lifting his voice, inquired if either of the foremen were present in the house. He received no response. The old man's voice began to break. If he had had to deal with his own help he would have sent an underling upon the stage and his employees would dutifully have marched back to the plant, but he was not addressing his own employees now: he was talking to the foundrymen, and he knew that stolid, stubborn breed. He went cautiously. He again said something about co-operation, but again the only response was silence. (To be sure, Nero, who was as soft-hearted as a cow, cleared his throat a few times but, shorn of his authority, he uttered not a single word.)

"If there are neither owners nor foremen among you, to whom can I address my appeal?"

More silence.

In the lower boxes the men and women in full dress sat holding back their fury. One of the men there pushed back his chair. (What he was about to do is not certain.) The eyes of of the women blazed with anger. To make such an aristocratic old man stand up before common workmen, pleading for co-operation!

But finally someone in that stubborn block stood up. Yes, someone stood up from his seat—Karl Heitman.

The president on the stage made his voice ingratiating. "Do you represent the men?" [482/483]

"I'm the shop chairman."

"Then be so good as to pick out enough of your comrades to go back with you to the foundry in order to get out the plates."

"Now?"

"Yes," said the president patiently, while the eyes of the women in the private boxes were fairly shooting sparks. "Yes, now, please."

Please? One of the women felt like screaming with rage. In the end her face grew so red with anger that tears came to her eyes. What beasts!

Karl Heitman, every eye of the house upon him, seemed to be turning something over in his mind.

"Please," repeated the president, urging patiently. "Please go now. Our night shift in the composing rooms will have the type forms up to your shop by the time you arrive, ready for molding, everything has been taken care of. I'll pay your men overtime, I'll pay them time-and-a-half."

"You'll pay us double time," said Karl Heitman. "According to our union contract, we receive time-and-a-half up to eight-thirty, but double time from then on. That's in our contract, we can't break the rules and work for less."

"All right, I'll pay you double time, then," agreed the president, his voice starting to shake with emotion. "Only go now, every minute counts." Ah, he was jittery, the old boy was. Now that the world had cracked under his feet, he was afraid of more losses, was afraid that a delayed delivery of catalogues would jeopardize his biggest printing account. And he had reason to be jittery, for all big printing plants in the country were competing and cut-throating for each other's business.

"Please," he said, for the third time. [483/484]

But Karl didn't answer. He looked at the men. They had something to say, and he looked at them. Some of them began to grumble. They were tired out; they didn't want to go back to the shop. They had come to see the show, hadn't they? But others, even though they were tired, said with their eyes that they would go back to the foundry. The plate-making would take a good five hours, and five hours at double pay (three dollars an hour) was nothing to be sneezed at; they needed the money, winter was coming with its coal bills, taxes, and outlay for heavier clothing for the children. Karl Heitman stood looking at them, not saying a word. But though he said nothing, one thing was certain: whatever he told them to do, they would do. Up in the balconies folks craned their necks to get a look at such a leader.

"What about our women?" Karl asked, breaking the silence. "If we agree to work tonight, who'll see them home?"

"I'll see that they get home in taxis," said the president, still urging patiently. "I'll pay their taxi bills."

The whole house began to buzz. Home in taxicabs? Ah, those foundrymen, those North American Rocky Mountain grizzlies! Here was collective bargaining with a vengeance.

"How many men do you need to get out twenty-two plates to-night?" asked the president from the stage.

"That's not the issue," answered Heitman. "I haven't asked the men yet whether or not they want to go. After all, it's not our fault if, because of faulty make-ready and presswork, the big plate spoilage occurred, is it?"

Now indeed the house was gasping like a fish on dry land. The Bowman employees, sitting with their wives, were thunderstruck. Who was this fellow, who were these stubborn [484/485] workmen anyway? They leaned forward, stretching their necks. The whole house, buzzing, began to get disorderly. The boys sitting behind Karl, however, didn't move a muscle.

On the stage, seeing that the situation was getting out of hand, the old man's mouth began to tremble. The drone of his murmuring employees swam stageward to him. He moistened his lips, held up a hand.

"Please," he said, "if you go back now, I'll pay you triple time."

The house went dead quiet all at once. Tier after tier the employees in the balconies sat hushed. Triple time? They sat with the breath knocked out of them, and in the long, long silence that followed no one said a word. Then Karl Heitman, taking his time, was heard to clear his throat.

"Such being the case," he began quietly, "I think I can get enough volunteers together to assist you in this emergency. All I need is about half a force." And right then and there, still speaking quietly (though he stared once toward the private boxes where the quiet fury raging there almost overflowed), he started calling out the names of the men who were to go with him. "Pojac, Rukevitch, and Kubec for molders."

But Kubec couldn't go; he said his home was out in the country where no taxi could deliver his wife. "Besides, I no trust those cab-drivers." No, Kubec would not go.

Heitman smiled. "Objection sustained," he said. "Bernstadt, will you volunteer, then?"

And Bernstadt, who was dying to get his paws on some of that triple time, volunteered. Karl then called for Brown and Slavony to man the batteries. But here he struck another snag. Slavony would not go. He couldn't explain it, [485/486] right here before the whole audience, but you see, his wife was in no, er, condition to go bumping along in a strange taxi all by herself so late at night, she was, er, expecting something— He refused, rather firmly.

"I can handle it alone," said Brown; "co-operating."

"Good," said Karl, then started to pick out the necessary finishers, routers, and builders. The house, still hushed, heard every word he said. He spoke quietly, clearly, until the plant employees began to sense what a compact unit the little block of men made up. They sat tensely, filled with admiration for the group, "Pete, the caster, of course will be at the furnace," said Karl. And Pete said he would, God knows he was more than willing to escape the glare of his hawk-eyed wife, for during that waggle specialty, when he had his eye glued on the stage, his wife had been staring at him sideways with needle-points in her eyes. Yes, Pete was glad to go back to the foundry. But who would check the plates, make out the receipt? Silence. August volunteered.

At this point, the president, from the stage, promised to have his own drivers call for the plates and take them to the North Side plant, so that Luke and Tom would not have to leave the show. Everything, then, was set, the men stood up.

And a few seconds later, in a shuffling compact group, thirty-two foundrymen headed up the aisles leading toward the doors and made their way outside. August went along, telling his parents he'd be home late.

The moon was shining high above the depot as they crossed Wabash Avenue and plunged into the darkness [486/487] of Polk Street. It was half-past ten and quiet, and the station clock was striking. As they came up to South State Street, they could see, in the distance, the lighted windows of several printeries which had their night shifts working and soon, still walking on, they heard the chug of locomotives and saw white clouds of steam rise hugely from the freight yards. The street ahead stretched dead and empty, with not a soul or even a dog in sight.

They turned into South Dearborn and neared the entrance of the plant, which stood old and gloomy like the gateway to a ruin. Will, the number-one watchman, was not around, so Earl, the number-two man, an automatic rounds-clock hanging from a thin leather strap around his faithful neck, let the men inside. Earl knew all about the spoilage. He got inside the cage, and making three trips, took all of them up to the foundry.

August, going up on the first load, turned on the outer office lights and stood behind his shipping table. The last load of men came up, filing by. They punched in before undressing, to get the benefit of the extra minutes, then changed into their working clothes, not talking much, and soon some of the men, feeling the cold floor against their stockinged feet, began to grumble.

"Well, boys, I know just how you feel," muttered Heitman, bending down and changing clothes with the others. "It's no joke to be jerked out of your seats at this time of night, especially when we had such a hard day today, even if we do get triple time for it."

"Then why did you lead us over here?" growled Buckley, turning darkly around.

Heitman looked up, scowling. "I have my reasons," he retorted, loud enough for the others to hear. [487/488]

By this time all the other men were looking at their chairman.

"Come on up in front, boys, as soon as you change into your work clothes," said Karl. "I've got something to say to you."

"Something tells me he's got a soap-boxer coming on," muttered Buckley.

"You guessed it the first time," said Heitman tartly. "But if you don't want to listen, you can rest your weight in the lavatory a while."

The big finisher's face began to burn.

"You others," said Heitman, "can take it easy, don't break your necks getting down to work, the old guy is paying for our time tonight."

The men came over, grinning.

"All right," said Heitman, when they had all gathered in front of him. "All right," he said, "has any man here any idea why I led you back to the shop? Who knows why I did it?"

None of them knew; they could make neither head nor tail of it. Nero scratched his head, looked puzzled, and stared at Pinky. The little trimmer was perched upon a big machine, and his small sharp face was attentive.

"Why did I do it?" asked Karl, louder.

"Yes, why?" asked Tapioca quietly, and a few men behind him began to smile.

"Keep your shirt on and I'll tell you," answered Heitman, injecting a tinge of sarcasm into his voice. "I don't want to stand up here and make a spiel, but as your shop chairman I feel I've got to say a few things tonight. A lot of things are happening in this country and yet I don't hear a single one of you talking sanely about the situation. Why, only this noon at the sink I heard someone say: 'At [488/489] last the bosses are getting theirs.' As if it's as simple as all that! Suppose the big boys do sustain some heavy losses on the market, what of it? Do you think they're going to take it on the chin with a smile? Do you? Of course not! They'll start to tighten their belts. And you know what that means."

"What does it mean?" asked Tapioca, feeling good because some of the men were behind him.

"Just a second there, I'm talking! What does it mean, eh? It means retrenching. Now that's a good word, you men will have to get acquainted with it."

The men stood stolid, scratching their heads.

"Ah, I see you don't know what that word means," smiled Karl.

"It's just a simple word, but it means a lot. It means lowering over-head, cutting wages."

"What's that got to do with our getting out the plates tonight?" said Buckley.

"Coming, coming! Just a second, will you? Listen! The big boys have lost their money, haven't they? They'll try to get it back, won't they? Who'll pay them? We! How? Through the nose! For if this stock crash goes deep enough we'll lose, in a few short months, all the ground that we've gained by years of fighting."

"Now speak English," said Buckley, taking the lead again. "How do you figure that out?"

"Well, look at the facts. Every time there's been a crisis or a panic, who gets squeezed and pays for it? We do, the working class. I shouldn't have to tell you this, because you men ought to know it. But you don't. You know damn little about anything except racing sheets and baseball returns. But if hard times come on the tail of this stock crash, the layoffs you'll get will give you plenty of time to think, for then you'll be men of leisure." [489/490]

"Now you're making fun of us," muttered a few men.

"Like hell I am! I'm talking plain facts. Listen: how many of you know that four million people are out of work in this country right now, with machines putting still more fellows out on the street every day? And as for ourselves, don't think that just because we licked Max'l on the Big Smasher we've beaten him forever. Hell no! He'll find other ways of getting back at us. So we've got to get next to ourselves and start to do some thinking. We can't afford to feel sorry for a nice-looking old man just because he stands on a stage speak-ing in a shaky voice and starts to cry. What do you think he was crying about, anyway? For the uncertain future of his employees, or for the load of dollars that he dropped in Wall Street?"

The electrotypers stood heavy as trees, listening. Karl began to hammer facts into them.

"Why, dammit, men, think, think! You can't expect to coast along like this forever. Something is happening in this country and if you don't wake up to the facts you'll be going to your own economic fu-neral. The trouble with you men is that you're boss-conscious, all right, but you're not class-conscious. You hate the three partners in the office because you know they're squeezing you and you know they'll throw you on the junk pile as soon as you start to weaken, but that's as far as you see, you're afraid to peep over the wall of your little craft union. But it's time you started to wake up to the fact that the labor movement is something bigger than our own little local, it's time you started to realize that it takes in everybody, yes, even the workers down in the plant below."

At these words an uneasy movement ran through the men. "Those scabs? To hell with 'em!"

"What do you man, scabs? Don't talk like that! There [490/491] are no scabs, only unorganized workers. One thing drives men to break ranks and get work wherever they are able—bread. Men have got to eat, you can't stare that fact down. So what do you mean scabs? Those men downstairs are not bad fellows. But they're working for a foxy old man who knows how to pull the wool over their eyes, and we've got to get them wise to themselves. Why do you think I staged my little act tonight? Do you think I give a damn if the old guy gets his plates on his presses tonight or not? Do you?"

The men stood quiet, not stirring.

"Of course not! To hell with him! But when I bargained up and back with the old fox, I set every non-union man in the house thinking, I made him realize that if he belonged to an organization he could bargain, too."

The men began to grin.

"No, it's not funny," said Heitman. "Those people are working for a cunning man who drugs them with speeches about co-operation and all that happy family business. That old guy tells them how glorious it is to work unrestricted by unions, because a union hurts the initiative. And what's the result? They work eight hours a week longer than we do, they get far less pay, but worse than that they keep the open shop going and menace our own future. So don't go hating those fellows downstairs because if you do you'll be playing into the hand of that old bastard and nothing makes a big employer feel so good as finding out that workingmen hate each other. They get fat on that stuff."

"What do you want us to do?" asked someone. "Become organizers and business agents?"

Heitman threw up his hands, "Of course not, man! But what harm is there, when you're sitting next to one of these [491/492] fellows, in talking about our union, about our forty-four-hour week and how we stick together? What harm is there once in a while in telling them that, though we haven't got any house organs or shop orchestra, we get better pay and haven't got a man standing behind us with a stop-watch when we work? Is there any harm in that?"

No, the men could see no harm in that. Still——

"Listen," said Karl. "If the plant downstairs lays off half its help because of no business, Max'l will have to lay off some of us. Everything interlocks in this country, union and non-union. We feed on the plant. When they get no orders, we get no orders. So that old fox downstairs comes into our picture after all. Don't underestimate him. He's an old man hard to beat. He knows the ropes. And he doesn't stop at hypocrisy. He forbids his men to organize, but he hasn't the honesty to call his plant an open shop, so he wraps the American flag around his middle and calls it working on 'the American plan.' He's a patriot! But wait a minute! When I said that he forbids his employees to organize, did I say that he meets them half way by agreeing not to organize with other open-shop bosses? Did I?"

The men smiled grimly.

"Of course not! He makes no promises to his employees at all. Just look him up in the directories and you'll find that he belongs to every printing trades employers' association in the country; you'll find that while he bars his own employees from getting together and doing any collective bargaining, nothing stops him from getting together with other fellows like himself and pulling off some pretty shady bargains on the sly."

Heitman stopped talking, taking a breather. He had been going so hard that his forehead had grown shiny. [492/493]

"Am I boring you?" he asked firmly.

"No," they said.

"All right, I'm glad to hear it; I won't keep the molders much longer. I say again that I didn't want to make a spiel, but I had to get this out of my system. I just had to. The stock crash is upon us, and Christ knows what'll happen to us. Maybe the four million people out of work will grow to eight million, to twelve million, and then there'll be enough misery for everybody. The trouble is, too many men like yourselves don't know what the hell's happening. None of you seem to realize that a war is going on, that it has been going on for over a hundred years, ever since the first factory opened up and the owner said to a few men: 'Now you go in there and work for me, I'll see how much you can do and then I'll figure out a wage I can pay you so that I can make a good profit.'"

The men broke into smiles. Heitman frowned back. "All right," he said, "I'm finished." Then he looked at the clock and started shouting: "Brown, step up the dynamos! And you molders, get going on the type forms! Come on, step, step! Now, here!" he said, imitating Max'l, "let's get going there!"

The meeting broke up. Pojac, kicking up his heels, trotted back to the rear. Brown turned smartly, spitting at a post.

In another minute the finishers, sitting in silence, could hear the deep hum, low at first, as Brown turned on the dynamos. They listened to it, hearing the motors climb. They listened, also, as the tank men walked over the air pump and turned on the pressure. They sat on their stools, their tired hands between their thighs, and heard the song of the foundry rising from the floor. [493]

UPTON SINCLAIR

Sacco and Vanzetti

CORNELIA LAY in bed, a reaction from the long strain. The Negro maid brought her coffee and toast, but she could not eat; she lay like one dead. It was all over for her; she had done all she could, struggled all she could—so she told herself. The young people might go on, Joe might write newspaper stories, trying to rouse a heedless public; Betty might organize mass meetings and speeches on the Common, but the runaway grandmother's race was run.

She had to lie there and bring herself to face the thought of the electric chair. Through all these seven dreadful years, she had refused to face it—a game of self-deception; but Bart and Nick had been right all along—they had known that the thought must be faced, and they had done it. They had the will, and the philosophy; they had been able to talk about it and joke. Now Cornelia must do the same thing. Remember what somebody had told her—it does not hurt, because the current destroys the brain before there is time for a sensation. And when it is over, it is really over; other persons may worry for you, but you don't worry for yourself. Also, you are a martyr, you have accomplished something for the cause of love.

That was what she must manage to realize. Persuade herself that there was a new generation coming, that would care where this one was indifferent; that would count it as something that two wops had denied themselves happiness so that justice might be born into the world! Think about those young persons of the future; lie here and shut your eyes, and let them come into your presence and speak to you; feel their gentle hands upon your forehead, bidding you to rest, your tense nerves to relax and your heart to stop pounding.

Cornelia lay wrestling thus; and into her mind came drifting words of comfort. "Now we are not a failure. This is our career and our triumph." Vanzetti speaking; where had she heard him say those

From Upton Sinclair, *Boston* (New York: Albert & Charles Boni, 1928), pp. 613–17, 645–53.

words? On a chair by her bedside was a scrap-book, full of letters, manuscripts, clippings. She was moved to sit [613/614] up and turn the pages; here it was. Shortly after Judge Thayer had sentenced the two men to die, Cornelia had persuaded a reporter for the Northern American Newspaper Alliance to go to Dedhan with her, and see what kind of men these alleged bandits were. Now, reading the interview, Cornelia recalled every detail of the scene; the prisoners coming down from their tier of cells, getting a glimpse of sunshine in the central hall, and lighting up with it—Nick, with his "kid's" grin, Bart with his mature and gentle smile. The reporter, Phil D. Stong, a big fellow, rather blond German face, well-fed and well-groomed —on an expense account, as he told Cornelia, with a laugh; tender-hearted, with the sentimentality of his race—and struck dumb by the discovery of the two men of this transparent sincerity and fine idealism in the shadow of the electric chair, face to face with their last enemy and not afraid of him. He had listened, while the victims did the talking; then he had gone away and tried to make a picture of the scene for the readers of a chain of newspapers.

"Both men expect to die. They say so, and the conviction is written in grave, serene characters on Vanzetti's face. Tears touch the young man 'Nick's' eyes for a moment, brightly, but his voice is steady. He is married to a sweet-faced little Italian woman. They have two children.

"In a moment, Nick, with his smooth pompadour, and his boy's face, is laughing with the deputy sheriff in argument about prison fare.

"Vanzetti regards one kindly, but appraisingly. A ferocious mustache covers an expressive, smiling mouth. The stamp of thought is in every feature; the marks of the man whom strong intelligence has made an anchorite."

And then a glimpse of prison life:

"Up from the shops comes a file of gray men, arms folded, faces expressionless—a rhythm of steps and faces.

" 'They been working.' Sacco's fingers move nervously. 'God, when I cannot work I almost go crazy. My fingers used to be busy. I beg, I argue—give me something to do—I shovel coal, anything. At last, they give me a brick to clean—after three years. You see me now? I gain a pound a day for thirty days.' The deputy sheriff nods confirmation.

" 'First they give me basket to weave, like children. Better [614/615] than nothing, but not much. Then I sit alone—seven years —thousands of days—and all for say man's nature can be perfect—

day after day—nothing do—breathe, eat, sit up, lie down—because I think man innerly noble—not beast—'

"Vanzetti interrupts his companion gently. He knows the two visitors believe in the enforced regulations which restrain fallible humanity.

" 'We're capitalists,' he says smiling, and pointing to the line of workers. (Men under sentence of death are given no work.) 'We have home, we eat, don't do no work. We're non-producers—live off other man's work. When libertarians make speech, they calling Nick and me names.'

"Sacco gurgles with amusement. The deputy sheriff appears significantly. Suddenly one realizes that these men are to die in a straight wooden chair, just as the world begins its summer holidays.

"Nick and Vanzetti see the new expression and understand. They smile, gravely, sympathetically, as men smile at a child's troubles.

" 'If it had not been for these thing,' says Vanzetti, 'I might have live out my life, talking at street corners to scorning men. I might have die, unmarked, unknown, a failure. Now we are not a failure. This is our career and our triumph. Never in our full life can we hope to do such work for tolerance, for joostice, for man's onderstanding of man, as now we do by an accident.

" 'Our words—our lives—our pains—nothing! The taking of our lives —lives of a good shoemaker and a poor fish-peddler—all! That last moment belong to us—that agony is our triumph!'

"Not declaimed, just said simply."

There were tears in Cornelia's eyes as she finished. "Oh, beautiful! Beautiful!" And when Joe came in, later in the day, she showed him the clipping. "Those are marvelous words—those two paragraphs at the end. I wonder if you couldn't quote them again, and get people to read them."

Joe said that he would try it. In order to give a touch of drama, he put a headline: "Vanzetti to his Judges." The two paragraphs were taken up and reproduced in labor papers, [615/616] and became, as it were, a spiritual testament of Vanzetti, an untheological prayer which his friends carried about with them, and read while he was dying, and afterwards. Because of the title, people assumed that the words had been a part of a speech in court; but this was not so, they were spoken, quite simply and casually, to a newspaper reporter, the every-day stuff of Vanzetti's mind.

History records that those who heard the Gettysburg address of Abraham Lincoln were ill pleased by it. They found it brief and inadequate, and gave all their praise to the flowery discourse of the great Edward Everett of Boston. But the future seldom chooses words which are flowery; it chooses those which have been wrung from the human heart in moments of great suffering, and which convey a gleam of spiritual illumination. When such words have been spoken, we discover what Paul meant when he wrote, "this mortal shall put on immortality." School children learn them by heart, and libraries are written to interpret them; they are graven upon marble and cast in bronze; armies carry them on banners, temples arise to glorify them, and civilizations are built in their image.

Pass on, Bartolomeo Vanzetti, your work is done! You have fought the good fight, you have finished the race! Fear not the executioner, nor yet the raging slanderer—they are powerless to harm you, for you have carried out your life-purposes—including that incidental one of becoming a great master of English prose! You have spoken the noblest words heard in America in the two generations since Abraham Lincoln died! You have achieved what is called the "grand manner," so rare in literature! That simplicity whereby men become as little children, and enter into the kingdom of heaven; that dignity which causes the critics to bow their haughty heads; that tenderness which touches the heart, that rapture which fires it, that sublimity which brings men to their knees!

In short, old Bart, you have brought the Commonwealth of Massachusetts back into the literary world again! After many years, New England has another great writer—for a short while only, until it has sent two thousand volts of electricity through his brain! What an odd freak of history, that this great one should be a despised wop! That, after all the millions [616/617] spent upon education, he should not be a graduate of a college, nor even of a high school! That he should not even be able to spell correctly, nor to pronounce correctly, the language of which he is to be the glory!

What a satire upon great endowments, the huge masses of steel and stone, the deans and professors of this and that long-winded subject! As a result of their labors, there are a million persons in the Commonwealth of Massachusetts, who understand the correct use of past participles, and would not say, "I might have live"; yet there is not a single one of these millions who can speak a sentence that stands a chance of living! There are ten thousand graduates of Harvard College, every one of whom knows better than to say "onderstand" or "joostice"; yet there is only a handful who understand justice, and not one who will die for it! . . . [617/645]

The case worked also upon the consciences of persons who were cursed with artistic temperaments. Such unfortunates read [645/646] the letters of Vanzetti and recognized a brother in distress. He who had made himself a master of English prose spoke to all other writers, now as in times to come. They gathered from far and near, anxious that a great soul and prophet should be recognized before he was dead.

There came Arturo Giovannitti, compatriot and fellow-victim of the "frame-up" system: one of those whom Captain Proctor had set out to "get," in the days of Proctor's prime, before his conscience began to trouble him. For more than a year Giovannitti had lain in Salem jail, and had written a haunting poem, "The Walker."

> *One-two-three-four: four paces and the wall;*
> *One-two-three-four: four paces and the iron gate.*

Now he walked a somewhat longer road in front of the State House with the golden dome; measured, not by paces, but by minutes— one-two-three-four-five-six-seven. He went to the Common, temple of free speech with elm-tree limbs for arches. "Fellow-workers," he began—being an I.W.W., that was his formula. "Break it up!" shouted "Mickey the Gunman." "You've said enough!" But the poet protested: "I haven't said anything yet! Wait till I finish before you arrest any one." "You're talking against the courts!" was the answer of the superintendent of police. "You're not allowed to talk against the courts!" The mounted troopers drove their reluctant horses into the crowd. "Break it up! Move along there!"

John Dos Passos came, playwright and novelist, genial, gentle, and bold as a young bull buffalo. A graduate of Harvard, he came to save the honor of his alma mater. "You have put your name and indirectly the name of the university to an infamous document"—so he wrote to President Lowell; and then, since no Boston paper would publish his letter, he went out on the picket-line and exposed his head to the policemen's clubs, and his skin to the vermin in the old Joy Street police station.

"Fair Harvard, thy sons to thy jubilee throng!" There thronged George L. Teeple, of the class of '97, and got himself arrested with the other pickets, and read a statement in court paying fifteen dollars extra for the privilege, because the judge [646/647] remarked that there might be an excuse for ignorant foreigners, but there was very little excuse for a Harvard man to violate the law.

Also Powers Hapgood, nephew of Norman and of Hutchins. His was not the sort of head the Boston police were used to breaking. He had completed four years' work at Harvard in three; he had "made" the Dickey and the Hasty Pudding Club, the varsity track squad and the Harvard "Crimson." He had been in the service abroad, and was one of the few undergraduates honored by election to the Harvard Memorial Society. He was one of those young Americans in whom readers of fiction refuse to believe; "unreal and made to order," they say, of a college youth who travels over the country working in coal mines, and becoming a leader of the left wing miners. Now he came to express his opinion of President Lowell, and the opinion was such that official Boston shut it up in the Psychopathic Hospital.

Heywood Broun was carrying on the same fight in New York as "colyumnist" of the *World*, at a salary of four hundred and fifty dollars a week. Broun had been "flunked out" of Harvard in his youth, and this may have made him feel disrespectful. "From now on," he wrote, "will the institution of learning at Cambridge which we once called Harvard be known as Hangman's House?" The *World* published that, but refused to publish the next articles, so the "colyumnist" went on a "permanent strike," which made an enormous sensation among the literati. An extraordinary thing, the way the case "got" the intelligentsia, even that portion which prides itself most upon being hard-boiled and immune to social emotions.

Also there came alumni of the University of Hard Knocks. Those foreign names which pleased the readers of Boston newspapers so little belonged to clothing-workers who had given up their jobs, and spent their savings to come and jeopardize their skulls; to sailors from the port, to iron-workers, barbers, bakers, and waiters; also to poets and writers who had educated themselves, and thus could understand the soul of Vanzetti. There came Michael Gold, a young Jew from the [647/648] slums of New York, who had been a newspaper reporter in Boston when not yet out of his teens, and had been one of that group of anarchist sympathizers whom Cornelia had seen, eleven years ago, accompanying Galleani to the Plymouth cordage strike.

Mike was now a playwright and editor of the *New Masses*, but resented being classified as an "intellectual," and wanted to remain a worker; so he dressed in khaki, which gave a shock to Boston. He wandered about, fascinated by the spectacle of a city gone mad with fear. He listened to the conversation of sleek clerks and stockbrokers of State Street, ex-football players of Harvard who wished they might have a chance to tackle the "Reds." He listened to taxidrivers and soda-jerkers, who knew what they had read in a capitalist newspaper, or learned from others who had read it in some other capitalist newspaper. On the afternoon of the "false execution" he joined the "death march" in front of the State House, and the same two iron-handed cops who grabbed Dorothy Parker the poet grabbed Mike Gold the playwright, and hauled them away to the oddly-named Joy Street police station. "Hang them! Hang the anarchists!" cried the straw-hatted mob; and Mike, who had written a life of John Brown, saw the ghost of William Lloyd Garrison going down the street with a rope about his waist, followed by the "mob in broadcloth," crying "Hang him! Hang the abolitionist!"

Those Boston merchants of a hundred years ago had been, some of them, the "bootleggers" of their day; smuggling "black ivory" from Africa, Negro slaves whose labor would be turned into molasses in Louisiana. The molasses would be brought to New England and made into rum, and the rum would go back to Africa, to make drunk the savage chiefs whose war-victims would compose the next bootleg cargo. Now the great-great-grandsons of those old merchants bore the same names, and looked so much like their ancestors that when they came up for election to the Somerset Club, the directors thought they were voting for the ancestors. These great-great-grandsons had imported hundreds of white niggers from the Mediterranean and Baltic lands, to operate their steam and electric machines, and had built a colossal system for the exploiting of this new slave labor. These new masters considered [648/649] themselves civilized, and were willing to install "welfare work," and have their wives "do charity." But at the same time they looked upon these foreign hordes with mingled contempt and fear, and dreaded the day when they might refuse obedience. To suggest this to them was the worst crime that could be committed in modern New England; the "black abolitionists" of 1831 had been replaced, as objects of ruling class hatred, by the "red scum" of 1927.

So it was that Boston was under what amounted to martial law, and there were more detectives watching strangers than there were strangers. Any one who wore a beard, or had a dark face, was liable to be halted on the street and ordered to give an account of himself. A messenger carrying a box of seidlitz powders had to stop for a chemical analysis. Helen Black and Ann Washington Craton—a descendant of the father of her country—were arrested and taken to the police station and cross-questioned for hours; the reason being that they "looked like New Yorkers." Six Italians arrived in an automobile, and two of them needed a shave, so they were held on a bombing charge.

Joe Randall, of course, was a marked man; the fact that he wrote articles for newspapers and posed as a reporter only made him worse than the other "Bolsheviks." Detectives followed him everywhere, in restaurants, in drug stores when he bought an ice cream

soda, in barber shops when he got a shave. He made trouble for
them by insisting upon talking with them, which was destructive of
morale and against the ethics of "shadowing." New "dicks" were
substituted, but Joe said you could always recognize them by their
blank and stupid faces; there was no other occupation by which
such low-grade persons could manage to be well-dressed and well-
fed.

Impossible to imagine anything more grotesque than the activities
of these anthropoid mentalities, trying to deal with a world of which
they had no gleam of understanding. Some of the things they did
were beyond the absurdities of musical comedy. Heywood Broun's
wife, Ruth Hale, came to Boston at the height of the tragedy. Two
sleuths of the city spent the night in a Ford car, keeping watch on
Hanover street, opposite defense headquarters, and in the morning a
newspaper man asked them what they had been doing, and the
answer [649/650] was, "We had a straight tip on a bomb-plot, and
we were watching for the bombers." "Who are they?" asked the
reporter. The reply was, "Two women from New York, Ruth Hale
and Dorothy Parker."

On Thursday, the eleventh, Justice Sanderson of the
Supreme Judicial Court allowed a bill of exceptions from his ruling
to go to the Full Court. Also Web Thayer was persuaded, for the
sake of appearance, to permit exceptions to his rulings to be carried
up. So there were two more hopes for salvation from the courts;
Massachusetts was going to lean over backwards in respecting the
legal rights of two convicted wops. Chief Justice Rugg was ill, and
Crosby was in Europe; Sanderson was barred from considering his
own ruling, so there were Braley, Wait, Carroll, and Pierce, with
Braley, oldest member, presiding. He issued a summons for a special
sitting on the following Tuesday, to listen to arguments of counsel.

Hope once more in the hearts of all believers in law and order.
Surely the ruling group was coming to its senses; it had realized the
frightful blunder it was making, and had chosen a dignified way to
back down! Patience now, and keep cool, and don't do anything to
excite public feeling, and make it harder for the learned justices!
Stop the wild talk, and keep the New York radicals off the streets
and out of the newspapers! Above all, no disorders on the Common,
nor in front of the State House! So argued the "respectables."

Was there really a chance? Or was it merely that those in charge
of affairs wanted it to seem that way? Quincy Thornwell came to
his Aunt Cornelia, bringing rumors: the Governor had talked with
So-and-so, and had said this and that. More important yet, Mr. Lowell was showing signs of weakening, he was defending himself, for

the first time in his long life. One of the "middle minds" had been to
see him, and he had argued until two o'clock in the morning, trying
to justify his decision; he had been so anxious about it that he had
followed his visitor downstairs in his pajamas, and out into the garden, flashing a torchlight into the bushes to make sure there
[650/651] were no bombers hiding. Quincy Thornwell chuckled over
the picture: assuredly the strangest sight ever witnessed by the
chaste nymphs who haunt the shades of the classic elms of Harvard!

And then the learned justices of the Supreme Judicial Court, actually giving signs of humanity! Justice Wait had made a speech,
defending the action of the court; and now here was the wife of another one, the presiding justice, Braley, telephoning to Mrs. Jessica
Henderson; a Leach of Bridgewater she was, a highly respected person, and twice she called up to say: "Don't worry, my dear, everything is coming out all right, I assure you. They are not going to let
them be executed, they will find some way out. The judge does not
believe in capital punishment." What could have been the meaning
of that? Could it be that these old boys were fooling their own
wives, in the effort to cheer them up and keep peace in the family?
Or were they using the wives to lull the defense, and damp the dangerous agitation during the critical days? Impossible to guess.

In the Sacco-Vanzetti committee the never-ceasing struggle between those who wanted to be judicious and those who wanted to
make propaganda. Lawyers and college professors telephoning in, or
calling to make personal pleas: "Remember this is Boston, and keep
the New York nuts out of the limelight!" But the "New York nuts"
had something to say about that, and so had the Boston newspapers.
The visitors came hiking, wearing oil-cloth placards over their shoulders, getting cursed and nearly mobbed in each respectable town
they passed through. They came in sport-cars, with bootleg bottles
in their baggage. Girls came in pants, and men with no hats or neck-
ties. One brought a portable typewriter, ready for work, and when
he found no room in headquarters, he set himself up on the curb-
stone outside the Hotel Bellevue, and started writing letters for
Sacco and Vanzetti. The newspapers, of course, got pictures of him
at once. Also they eagerly interviewed a young man who announced
his intention of marching to Dedham jail to rescue Sacco and Vanzetti, and was disconcerted to learn that his campaign maps were
out of date. [651/652]

Such were the surface aspects of the invasion, easy to see and to
record. But there was another aspect, not so obvious to Boston news-
papermen, nor so diverting to their readers. The soul of the demonstration, a common feeling which animated all the participants, men

and women, old and young, rich and poor, educated and ignorant: a sense of black despair, of agonizing littleness in the face of a colossal evil; an impotent rage, a hatred, bitter as gall, rolling up in their minds, for this whole great city of greed masked by bigotry—smug and polite and treacherous, cultured and correct and deadly.

Very few of these agitators were professionals; not many of them had any training, any party to guide and support them. They came as individuals, hesitating and confused. They didn't like to do what they were doing; the women, and many of the men, felt like Lady Godiva riding through the town naked—worse even than she, because they had no certainty of accomplishing anything; perhaps they were making fools of themselves to no purpose at all.

They came because American labor would not come. Vanzetti had called for a million workers, and the million workers answered, "What the hell?" Most of them were content for Vanzetti to die—so that American prosperity might live; they were ready to make that sacrifice to Moloch, precisely as the mothers and fathers of Carthage were ready to put their infants into the red-hot iron arms of the god, so that Carthage might live. So, instead of the million workers, came one or two hundred poets, painters, dreamers and lovers of beauty, Greenwich Villagers, bums, bohemians—whatever names Boston, the correct and murderous, might choose to call them. A pitiful little group, throwing themselves against the iron battlements of American capitalism, with its machine-guns and poison gas bombs, its police in the front rank and army and navy in reserve.

And for every dreamer who came, there were thousands who stayed at home, chained by poverty, or a greater share of timidity; waiting, waiting, with a ghastly sense of uncertainty, feeling themselves more effectively imprisoned than Sacco and Vanzetti. Writing letters, but not knowing if they were read, sending telegrams—like shooting arrows into the dark! Unable to get any real news—a few bare events each day in the papers, [652/653] but no opinions, no guidance, no light. The radio grinding out its eternal silly thumping of drums and whining of saxophones—this greatest story in modern American history not worth a moment's attention! [653]

JOSEPH FREEMAN

From Bohemia to Russia

NEWSPAPER WORK now took up most of my time; but the impulse to
go to Soviet Russia, insistent since those Paris days when I had
urged a committee of American intellectuals to study the proletarian
republic, was becoming stronger than ever. I was convinced at this
time that Greta's departure from Moscow could have no influence
upon my own going there. This may have been a rationalization. If
so, objective facts helped my self-deception. Various friends who
had returned from the Soviet republic urged me to go there, among
them Michael Gold, Scott Nearing and Ruth Stout, the novelist's
sister, then secretary of the *New Masses* editorial staff.

I resigned from my job, and borrowed six hundred dollars from a
generous friend. Then I signed up as supercargo with a small freighter bound for Batum. It was the first ship flying the American flag
which went to Russia after the October Revolution. It carried no
passengers, only a crew of twenty-eight men.

Batum would give me a chance to enter Soviet Russia through the
back door, so to speak. I would see large sections of the country before I reached the official atmosphere of Moscow. And for thirty
days I would live with American workers on their job at sea. I
would come to proletarian Russia not from bohemian America but
from proletarian America. The freighter would be my bridge from
radical bohemia to Bolshevik Russia, from romance and rebellion to
revolutionary reality—a reality which had hitherto come to me only
through reports as various as Anton's and Hapgood's, Nearing's and
Mayakovsky's, Eastman's and Mike Gold's.

I went to say good-by to my family. They now lived in a three-
story, seventeen-room house in an exclusive section of Flatbush. Its
previous owner was a nationally known manufacturer high in American society.

As always, my father told me nothing about his business. From

From Joseph Freeman, *An American Testament: A Narrative of Rebels and
Romantics* (New York: Farrar & Rinehart, 1936), pp. 408–16.

friends I heard he had made somewhere between a million and two million dollars during the building boom.

In front of the house stood his big green Cadillac. The Negro chauffeur waved his hand and grinned.

"Hello, Joe, where in hell have you been keeping yourself? What have you been doing?"

"Chasing rainbows. And you, Roy?"

"Chasing women! Ha-ha-ha-ha!" [408/409]

I went through the vast, glass-enclosed porch with its grass rug and wicker chairs, the vestibule, the dining room with its heavy oak furniture and expensive cut glass. The kitchen door swung open; my mother came out in a neat print apron. She embraced me, kissed my cheek and said in Yiddish:

"Ach, my dear one! It's years since we've seen you. Where do you keep yourself? We were terrible worried—maybe you are sick or something."

"I've been busy," I replied in Yiddish. "How are you, darling?"

"You must excuse my appearance. I've been working in the kitchen. These cooks are all right, but they can't make *gefillte fish* properly."

"You look fine, mother. Here are some flowers for you. Where is dad?"

"Upstairs, reading the paper in the Rose Room. Go and talk to him, my son. I'll call you for supper. The children will be here soon."

The Rose Room was on the second floor. It was an immense oblong which ran the length of the house. On three sides it was enclosed by a series of windows, thirty of them, through which the bright afternoon light poured munificently. It got its name from the rose-colored carpet and plush furniture which my father had taken over with the house.

The radio was playing Russian music. My father sat in a big rose-colored plush armchair with a newspaper in his hand, his feet on a rose-colored footstool. He looked up through his reading glasses. I noticed he was getting bald, but his clean-shaven face was still young, fresh and powerful. He was dressed in a silk shirt, a bright new tie, and expensive gray suit. His ankles were covered by dark gray spats.

"Aw, *borukh habo!*" he said. As he spoke it, the ancient Hebrew greeting sounded half tender, half ironical. Then he added in English: "I thought you were dead, honest. I've been reading about this Passaic strike of yours, and I said to myself, maybe the police broke his neck. It will do him good, teach him a lesson not to stick his nose in where he doesn't belong. But I see you are alive. Well, some people have more luck than brains."

He went to a small closet, took out a bottle of Scotch and filled two glasses.

"Here," he said, pushing one of the glasses toward me. "But wait a minute, maybe I'll get you in trouble. Does your Radek allow you to drink?" [409/410]

"He's not interested in my private habits."

"Thank heaven for small favors," my father said. "And now tell me, to what do we owe the honor of this visit?"

"I've come to say good-by. I'm going to Russia."

"Crazier and crazier, day by day." He filled my empty glass. "Do you have to go ten thousand miles to starve to death? I thought you were starving to death in New York quite successfully."

I should never have told him that story: Last year I looked for a job; I was broke and walked from my rented room to the Pulitzer Building. It was a hot summer day, but I had to walk back. As I passed Brooklyn Bridge, I saw my father's green limousine swing into Manhattan. I was too proud to hail him, and walked home. He had kidded me about it ever since I had told him.

"I haven't starved in New York," I said, "and I won't starve in Russia."

"The papers say it's a terrible country."

"What papers? Do you have to believe their propaganda? You can afford to travel. Why don't you go and see your home town? Maybe you'll change your mind about the bolsheviks."

"No, siree!" my father said emphatically. "I don't want to travel. I don't care about France or England or Russia. America is plenty good enough for me—even Brooklyn. I wouldn't live in Europe for anything, especially Russia."

"Tastes differ," I said. "I like America, but it's not your America. And I'd like to see Russia too. At least the people there are interested in something else than making money." I could not understand why I was talking like a book, why I wasn't saying what I really felt.

"Listen, my son," father said tenderly, putting his hand on my knee. "Why don't you give up this foolishness? Why do you worry about mankind? Does mankind worry about you? Does mankind care whether or not you have a pair of shoes or a suit of clothes or a roof over your head? Worry about yourself a little. Believe me, if you should be dying of hunger, the bolsheviks wouldn't care."

"I don't expect them to."

"Why don't you settle down? If you had sense, you would have studied law. But at least do something practical now. You have wonderful opportunities. America is the richest country in the world. Look at me. We came from a little Russian village, poor and perse-cuted. We lived in a dirty hole in the ghetto here. We didn't have a piece of bread. Now, thank heaven, we have everything." [410/411]

I said nothing. I could see his point of view, but he could not see mine. I thought I understood the gratitude and triumph he felt in succeeding by the prevailing standards, but I could not explain my own attitude in personal terms without sounding like a prig, even to myself.

"Look at your friend Robert Smith," my father went on. "He was a lunatic like you once. Another one of those crazy socialists—wanted to save the world. Now he is married, has children, a house of his own, servants, a good car. They say he made half a million in real estate—may God grant the same to you. I have a good business; I'm getting on in years and I have no one to succeed me. Why don't you use some of that brain you think you have?"

"I'm not interested in business."

"All right: if you want to scribble, at least be like Elmer Rice. Write a Broadway hit like *On Trial*. Be a success."

"It's too late to change now, dad. I couldn't write a Broadway hit if I wanted to, and I don't want to." Noble youth. I felt more like a prig every minute.

"Look at Louis Smith," my father went on inexorably. "A labor or-ganizer, a socialist. Why, he made you a socialist—your teacher! And now he's in business too. Doing nicely in insurance. Your friend Max W. studies to be a doctor; Max G. edits a Wall Street paper. Edman, what's his name, is a professor. All your friends have settled down. They are making money, a name, a position. And you? Going around with people that get put in prison. Why am I cursed that my chil-dren should be different from other people's?"

His voice broke a little. Our family had indeed undergone extraor-dinary changes. Starting as a conventional, religious Jewish family in a little Ukrainian village, it had broken up under the impact of American life. The energy and egoism we had inherited from our fa-ther, the love which our mother had lavished on us, the conflicting values of the new American world had hurled us out of our original groove. My father had long since abandoned the ideals of the van-ished village. He was a successful American businessman. I was in the radical movement. The sister next to me had gone into the the-ater and—worse still, from my father's viewpoint—had married a gentile. My younger brother, just out of Cornell, hesitated for a brief moment between my father's ideals and my own, and was now working with Scott Nearing and the *New Masses*. The feudal past, the capitalist present and the [411/412] socialist future were colliding in our home, tearing it apart, straining hearts passionately devoted to one another.

"Don't you think I have your own good in mind?" my father continued. "Where will this communism lead you? You'll be an outcast from decent society."

"I don't care about decent society. Ninety per cent of humanity is an outcast from decent society—which it supports. It's that ninety per cent I care about, not the ten per cent that oppresses and exploits it."

"Then I'm an oppressor and exploiter too!" my father cried ironically. "I'm a capitalist. I own property. I employ labor. That's what you are saying: you are calling your own father an oppressor and exploiter. But ask anyone downtown: I pay my workers the highest wages; I've never had a strike on my hands."

"Please, dad, don't make this a personal quarrel. I like you. Our quarrel is not with individuals but with a social system." What could I say? My father talked out of his life; I talked out of books, repeating abstractions as if I did not realize what America meant to him, as if I were unaware of his long and bitter struggle for the security, comfort, respect and authority which he now enjoyed.

"I know you like me," he said, "but if you had a bolshevik revolution in this country you would confiscate my property just the same!"

"We can't make any exceptions. But don't worry, your property will be confiscated before that."

"How do you mean?"

"You're not a big capitalist. You're not a Morgan, Rockefeller or Schwab. You are a middleman. Don't be deceived by this prosperity. There's going to be a crisis worse than nineteen-seven. Then we'll have what Germany has had—inflation, unemployment, and the expropriation of the middle classes." That was the line of the Comintern.

"You mean we will lose the money for which we worked all these years?" my father asked.

"I'm sorry to tell you this, but it's a fact. Not this year, not next, or the one after the next. But sometime soon Wall Street will confiscate your property. The middle classes will be robbed along with the working classes. That's the kind of system in which we live."

My father leaned back and laughed.

"Ah, my son, my son, these bolsheviks have really made you crazy. You're all as crazy as bedbugs. We know these prophecies of yours. Where is Lenin's world revolution?" [412/413]

"We are not stock market speculators," I said bitterly. "We don't operate with minutes. History takes years. The world revolution will come—maybe not this decade or the next, but it will come."

"Yes, I know, everything is in the future—the collapse of capitalism, the world revolution—it will come some fine day. So will the
Messiah on a white horse. And by that time you'll be so dead that
you won't be able to stand up on Resurrection Day. So why waste
your time on it?"

"I don't expect to get anything out of it for myself."

"An idealist!" my father said ironically.

"No, not really. It gives me much more than I give it."

"Surely, with a home like this to come back to, with your opportunities, you're not doing this work for the couple of lousy dollars you
make. I know you've never understood the value of money and
never will, but at least get some glory, something sensible."

"You don't understand, dad. Look at Scott Nearing. He was doing
very nicely at a big university. No one compelled him to attack the
exploitation of children in industry, to lose his job, except his own
sense of what is right. He works for the Cause without money or
glory; his own comrades sometimes make life miserable for him, yet
I am sure he would not change places with J. P. Morgan."

"Neither would I," my father said. "A man should not have too
much money. He should have just enough to live securely."

"You say that because you are a middleman. You fear poverty and
despise your economic superiors—but you will be compelled to go
chasing dollars. The appetite for money feeds on itself. You get ten
thousand and want twenty—you get twenty and want fifty. Look at
all your friends hysterically piling up their dunghills of gold. That's
Business for you. Then when you get to the top, like the Morgans
and Rockefellers, and own the country, you go abroad and pile up
more in colonies—and fight for the money of the world. You make
wars and kill millions of people for your profit."

"The bolsheviks are angels? They killed plenty people too."

"It's a pity man hasn't got beyond force," I said. "But there it is,
for the time being, an inexorable necessity. But it makes a difference
who kills whom and for what. If the Whites and the imperialists had
let Russia alone, the bolsheviks would have been glad enough to
avoid blood. You cannot blame them for defending the most important thing in the world today—the first workers' socialist republic. Besides, less people have been killed in the Russian Revolution than in
the [413/414] French Revolution or in the American Civil War. History will forgive the wrath of the revolution; it will applaud its enormous advances. It will appreciate the pioneers of our own generation who give their lives for the future classless society."

"So you are working for future glory"—my father laughed—"like the pious Jew who gives up joys on this earth so that he may enjoy the glory of the World to Come? Your Nearings and Baldwins and Hapgoods and the rest of them are investing in the applause of posterity? Then you are all even crazier than I thought."

"No, they are not. None of them will be remembered, and they know it. Their satisfaction is an immediate one; it's the satisfaction of being right, of being on the side of progress."

"But why should you people worry about it? I can understand a worker being a radical. What has he got to lose? I can even understand a Lenin. It must be nice to leap from obscurity to fame, to be in history together with Napoleon and Washington. But you people —you will never be Napoleons or Lenins. What gnaws, what drives you to this silly agitation?"

"I think I can tell you about the workers. They are the ones who have nothing to lose. That is why they are the ones who make the revolution. But we are bound to help them. We have had the misfortune to take our education seriously, to acquire a historic sense. When you don't see what is right and true, you are free to follow your little egotistical interests. You can chase after money and women and glory. But when you do see the right thing, you must either fight for it or go to pieces. If you don't see the truth, you are merely blind. But if you see it and do not support it, you become corrupt."

"Ah, my dear philosopher," my father said gently, "a great help you must be to the communist movement. They need practical people too and you are nothing but a dreamer."

"There you are right, dad. I'm not good in practical enterprises. But Trotsky says that revolution will conquer for everyone not only the right to bread, but also the right to poetry. Those who have the talent for it fight for bread. I'll stick to the poetry."

"Sonny, the bolsheviks are not half as foolish as you. Bread I can understand, but who needs poetry?"

"Man lives not by bread alone. A Jew said that—Jesus."

"You can't eat ideals."

"You can't live without them. You have ideals too. The family is [414/415] your ideal. You have given every ounce of your energy and love and hope to it. But it's an old ideal. It's based on the individual, and we need a new civilization based on co-operative effort."

"Don't be a child," my father said. "You think Radek and them other fellows don't believe in the individual?"

"Sure. But they don't mean one individual out of a million, the way the businessman does. They mean every individual."

"Nonsense, my boy. Every man looks out for Number One. I

read in the papers that Trotsky is having a fight with his pals, who should play first fiddle in Russia. What's the difference between that and Morgan?"

"The aim. The bolsheviks don't fill their pockets with the people's money. Their fight for leadership is a fight for principles, for policy. The personal ambition is secondary."

"I read in the papers that your friend Max Eastman claims the Soviet government has fallen into the hands of crooks. You see, human nature doesn't change. When people get power, they lose their ideals." My father put his finger on the sorest spot of all. I was bitter that he should be able to cite a man reputed to be a communist to prove the degeneration of the Soviet system.

"Trotsky says Eastman lies," I said.

"How do you know he lies?"

"Even if what he says is true, it makes little difference. The revolution is bigger than any man. The leaders of the French Revolution guillotined each other—but that revolution was later called by everybody the most progressive historic event since the rise of Christianity. The Russian Revolution is an even greater event—and the Russian leaders will not guillotine each other. The quarrels are part of the vast growing pains of a vast social transformation. What is our alternative? Capitalism, war, unemployment, poverty for the mass of people. We live in an inferno. Think what life has meant for most people in our times. The bolsheviks may be hard, they may make mistakes—but they are building a better world."

"All right, son. Go ahead with these noble fantasies. You're old enough to know what you're doing. Everyone in America is making money and living a normal life—and you are wasting your life on a wild-goose chase."

"Is everyone making money? I've just come from Passaic."

"Of course there are poor people. But the smart ones don't have to be poor." [415/416]

"Most human beings are poor and wretched. They slave, they starve, they are sent on the breadline and to the trenches, and their bosses grow fat on the wealth these millions of slaves produce. To hell with that kind of world. It's unnecessary. We have the machines, the knowledge, the science to make a decent world for all. All we need is the proper social organization for it. The bolsheviks have found that. I'd rather work for such a new world than for anything else. Nothing else means anything to me."

My mother's voice came up the stairs.

"Come on, boys, the supper is getting cold."

Below the children were gathered around the table, the youngest now twelve. How much cleverer they were. They never argued with

my parents. My father did not even know that my younger brother
was engaged in the same work as myself, just as my youngest sister
went about quietly doing those very things for which my older sister
had to leave home. I often thought then and afterward that such is
the relation between all pioneers and epigoni, in the family as in society at large. The pioneers make the noise, fight the authorities,
wear themselves out battling for something new, then that new
thing becomes the old, the taken-for-granted; the epigoni do nor-
mally and naturally what we preached and suffered for in anger and
pain. No wonder some of the older Russian bolsheviks could not understand the new Soviet generation, which had not known czarism,
which grew up in a socialist-minded world as if it had existed from
the first hour of creation. But I had not forgotten my classics: the
epigoni, or "descendants," were the sons of the seven heroes who
fought against Thebes. Ten years later, to avenge their fathers, the
epigoni undertook a second expedition which was completely successful.

The Friday evening candles glowed about the white tablecloth.
My father mumbled the prayer over the wine—the *kiddush*—in a
very perfunctory way, without rising. He had long since ceased to
take the ritual seriously, and now ate ham and drank milk with his
meat. The servant brought in the bright yellow soup with noodles,
and the children broke into chorus—it was Greta's favorite:

> I'm sitting on top of the world
> Just rolling along, just rolling along [416]

JOHN STEINBECK

A Truce in the Battle

THE SOUND of a motor came up the road and stopped. Outside the tent there was a sudden swell of voices, and [242/243] then quiet again. Sam stuck his head into the tent. "London here?" he demanded.

"No. What's the matter?"

"There's a dressed-up son-of-a-bitch in a shiny car wants to see the boss."

"What about?"

"I don't know. Says he wants to see the chief of the strikers."

Mac said, "London's over by the pit. Tell him to come over. The guy probably wants to talk things over."

"O.K. I'll tell him."

In a moment London came into the tent, and the stranger followed him, a chunky, comfortable-looking man dressed in a grey business suit. His cheeks were pink and shaven, his hair nearly white. Wrinkles of good nature radiated from the corners of his eyes. On his mouth an open, friendly smile appeared every time he spoke. To London he said, "Are you the chairman of the camp?"

"Yeah," said London suspiciously. "I'm the elected boss."

Sam came in and took his place just behind London, his face dark and sullen. Mac squatted down on his haunches and balanced himself with his fingers. The newcomer smiled. His teeth were white and even. "My name's Bolter," he said simply. "I own a big orchard. I'm the new president of the Fruit Growers' Association of this valley."

"So what?" said London. "Got a good job for me if I'll sell out?"

The smile did not leave Bolter's face, but his clean, pink hands closed gently at his sides. "Let's try to get a better start than that," he begged. "I told you I was the *new* [243/244] president. That means there's a change in policy. I don't believe in doing things the

From John Steinbeck, *In Dubious Battle* (New York: The Modern Library, n.d.), pp. 242–51. [Originally published in 1936.]

way they were being done." While he spoke Mac looked not at Bolter, but at London.

Some of the anger left London's face. "What you got to say?" he asked. "Spill it out."

Bolter looked around for something to sit on, and saw nothing. He said, "I never could see how two men could get anything done by growling at each other. I've always had an idea that no matter how mad men were, if they could only get together with a table between them, something good would come out of it."

London snickered. "We ain't got a table."

"You know what I mean," Bolter continued. "Everybody in the Association said you men wouldn't listen to reason, but I told them I know American working men. Give American working men something reasonable to listen to, and they'll listen."

Sam spat out, "Well, we're listenin', ain't we? Go on an' give us somethin' reasonable."

Bolter's white teeth flashed. He looked around appreciatively. "There, you see? That's what I told them. I said, 'Let me lay our cards down on the table,' and then let them lay theirs down, and see if we can't make a hand. American working men aren't animals."

Mac muttered, "You ought to run for Congress."

"I beg your pardon?"

"I was talkin' to this here guy," said Mac. London's face had grown hard again.

Bolter went on, "That's what I'm here for, to lay our cards on the table. I told you I own an orchard, but don't think because of that I haven't your interests at heart. [244/245] All of us know we can't make money unless the working man is happy." He paused, waiting for some kind of answer. None came. "Well, here's the way I figure it; you're losing money and we're losing money because we're sitting growling at each other. We want you to come back to work. Then you'll get your wages, and we'll get our apples picked. That way we'll both be happy. Will you come back to work? No questions, no grudges, just two people who figured things out over the table?"

London said, "Sure we'll go back to work, mister. Ain't we American working men? Just give us the raise we want and kick out the scabs and we'll be up in those old trees tomorrow morning."

Bolter smiled around at them, one at a time, until his smile had rested on each face. "Well, I think you ought to have a raise," he said. "And I told everybody I thought so. Well, I'm not a very good business man. The rest of the Association explained it all to me. With the price of apples what it is, we're paying the top price we can. If we pay any more, we lose money."

Mac grinned, "I guess we ain't American workin' men after all," he said. "None of this sounds reasonable to me. So far it's sounded like a sock full of crap."

Jim said, "The reason they can't pay the raise is because that'd mean we win the strike; and if we did that, a lot of other poor dev-ils'd go on strike. Isn't that it, mister?"

Bolter's smile remained. "I thought from the first you deserved a raise, but I didn't have any power. I still believe it, and I'm the pres-ident of the Association. Now I've told the Association what I'm going to do. Some of 'em don't like it, but I insisted you men have to have a [245/246] raise. I'm going to offer you twenty cents, and no questions and no grudges. And we'll expect you back at work tomor-row morning."

London looked around at Sam. He laughed at Sam's scowling face, and slapped the lean man on the shoulder. "Mr. Bolter," he said, "like Mac says, I guess we ain't American workin' men. You wanted cards laid down, and then you laid yours down backs up. Here's ours, and by Christ, she's a full house. Your God-damn apples got to be picked and we ain't picking 'em without our raise. Nor nei-ther is nobody else pickin' 'em. What do you think of that, Mister Bolter?"

At last the smile had faded from Bolter's face. He said gravely, "The American nation has become great because everybody pitched in and helped. American labor is the best labor in the world, and the highest paid."

London broke in angrily, "S'pose Chink does get half a cent a day, if he can eat on it? What the hell do we care how much we get, if we got to go hungry?"

Bolter put on his smile again. "I have a home and children," he said. "I've worked hard. You think I'm different from you. I want you to look on me as a working man, too. I've worked for everything I've got. Now we've heard that radicals are working among you. I don't believe it. I don't believe American men, with American ideals, will listen to radicals. All of us are in the same boat. Times are hard. We're all trying to get along, and we've got to help each other."

Suddenly Sam yelled, "Oh, for Christ's sake, lay off. If you got somethin' to say, say it; only cut out this God-damn speech."

Bolter looked very sad. "Will you accept half?" [246/247]

"No," said London. "You woudn't offer no half unless you was pressed."

"How do you know the men wouldn't accept, if you put it to a vote?"

"Listen, mister," London said, "them guys is so full of piss and vinegar they'll skin you if you show that slick suit outside. We're strikin' for our raise. We're picketin' your God-damn orchards, and we're kickin' hell out of any scabs you run in. Now come on through with your 'or else.' Turn your damn cards over. What you think you're goin' to do if we don't go back?"

"Turn the vigilantes loose," said Mac.

Bolter said hurriedly, "We don't know anything about any vigilantes. But if the outraged citizens band together to keep the peace, that's their affair. The Association knows nothing about that." He smiled again. "Can't you men see that if you attack our homes and our children we have to protect them? Wouldn't you protect your own children?"

"What the hell do you think we're doin'?" London cried. "We're trying to protect 'em from starving. We're usin' the only way a workin' stiff's got. Don't you go talkin' about no children, or we'll show you something."

"We only want to settle this thing peacefully," said Bolter. "American citizens demand order, and I assure you men we're going to have order if we have to petition the governor for troops."

Sam's mouth was wet. He shouted, "And you get order by shootin' our men from windows, you yellow bastard. And in 'Frisco you got order by ridin' down women. An' the newspapers says, 'This mornin' a striker was killed when he threw himself on a bayonet.' *Threw himself!*" [247/248]

London wrapped his arm about the furious man and forced him slowly away from Bolter. "Lay off, Sam. Stop it, now. Just quiet yourself."

"Th' hell with you," Sam cried. "Stand there and take the lousy crap that big baloney hands you!"

London stiffened suddenly. His big fist lashed out and cracked into Sam's face, and Sam went down. London stood looking at him. Mac laughed hysterically. "A striker just threw himself into a fist," he said.

Sam sat up on the ground, "O.K., London. You win. I won't make no more fuss, but you wasn't in 'Frisco on Bloody Thursday."

Bolter stood where he was. "I hoped you would listen to reason," he said. "We have information that you're being influenced by radicals, sent here by red organizations. They are misleading you, telling you lies. They only want to stir up trouble. They're professional troublemakers, paid to cause strikes."

Mac stood up from his haunches. "Well, the dirty rats," he said. "Misleadin' American workin' men, are they? Prob'ly gettin' paid by Russia, don't you think, Mr. Bolter?"

The man looked back at him for a long time, and the healthy red was gone from his cheeks. "You're going to make us fight, I guess," he said. "I'm sorry. I wanted peace. We know who the radicals are, and we'll have to take action against them." He turned imploringly

to London. "Don't let them mislead you. Come back to work. We
only want peace."

London was scowling. "I had enough o' this," he said. "You want
peace. Well, what we done? Marched in two parades. An' what you
done? Shot three of our men, [248/249] burned a truck and a lunch
wagon and shut off our food supply. I'm sick o' your God-damned
lies, mister. I'll see you get out without Sam gets his hands on you,
but don't send nobody else again till you're ready to talk straight."

Bolter shook his head sadly. "We don't want to fight you men," he
said. "We want you to come back to work. But if we do have to
fight, we have weapons. The health authorities are pretty upset
about this camp. And the government doesn't like uninspected meat
moving in this county. The citizens are pretty tired of all this riot.
And of course we may have to call troops, if we need them."

Mac got up and went to the tent-flaps and looked out. Already the
evening was coming. The camp was quiet, for the men stood watching London's tent. All the faces, white in the gathering evening,
were turned in toward the tent. Mac yelled, "All right, boys. We
ain't goin' to sell you out." He turned back into the tent. "Light the
lamp, London, I want to tell this friend of man a few things."

London set a match to the tin lantern and hung it on the tent-
pole, where it cast a pale, steady light. Mac took up a position in
front of Bolter, and his muscled face broke into a derisive grin. "All
right, Sonny Boy," he said. "You been talkin' big, but I know you
been wettin' your pants the whole time. I admit you can do all the
things you say you can, but look what happens after. Your health
service burned the tents in Washington. And that was one of the
reasons that Hoover lost the labor vote. You called out guardsmen
in 'Frisco, and damn near the whole city went over to the strikers. Y' had to have the cops stop food from comin' in to turn public
opinion against the strike. I'm not talkin' right an' wrong [249/250]
now, mister. I'm tellin' you what happens." Mac stepped back a
pace. "Where do you think we're gettin' food and blankets an' medicine an' money? You know damn well where we're gettin' 'em. Your
valley's lousy with sympathizers. Your 'outraged citizens' are a little
bit outraged at you babies, and you know it. And you know, if you
get too tough, the unions 'll go out. Truck drivers and restaurant
men and field hands, everybody. And just because you do know it,
you try to throw a bluff. Well, it don't work. This camp's cleaner'n
the lousy bunk houses you keep for us on your ranches. You come
here to try to scare us, an' it don't work."

Bolter was very pale. He turned away from Mac and faced London. "I've tried to make peace," he said. "Do you know that this man
was sent out by red headquarters to start this strike? Watch out that

when he goes to jail you don't go too. We have a right to protect our property, and we'll do it. I've tried to deal man to man with you, and you won't deal. From now on the roads are closed. An ordinance will go through tonight forbidding any parading on the county roads, or any gathering. The sheriff will deputize a thousand men, if he needs them."

London glanced quickly at Mac, and Mac winked at him. London said, "Jesus, mister, I hope we can get you out of here safe. When the guys out there hear what you just said, why they'll want to take you to pieces."

Bolter's jaw tightened and his eyelids drooped. He straightened his shoulders. "Don't get the idea you can scare me," he said. "I'll protect my home and my children with my life if I have to. And if you lay a hand on me we'll wipe out your strike before morning."

London's arms doubled, and he stepped forward, but [250/251] Mac jumped in his way. "The guy's right, London. He don't scare. Plenty do, but he don't." He turned around. "Mister Bolter, we'll see you get out of the camp. We understand each other now. We know what to expect from you. And we know how careful you have to be when you use force. Don't forget the thousands of people that are sending us food and money. They'll do other things, if they have to. We been good, Mr. Bolter, but if you start any funny business, we'll show you a riot you'll remember."

Bolter said coldly, "That seems to be all. I'm sorry, but I'll have to report that you won't meet us halfway."

"Halfway?" Mac cried. "There ain't no halfway to nowhere." His voice dropped to softness. "London, you get on one side of him, and Sam on the other, and see that he gets away all right. Then I guess you'd better tell the guys what he said. But don't let 'em get out of hand. Tell 'em to tighten up the squads for trouble."

They surrounded Bolter and took him through the press of silent men, saw him into his coupe and watched him drive away down the road.... [251]

4
A Majority of One

UNLIKE THE SELECTIONS in "The Subversive Tradition," which, for the most part, make dissenting comments on particular features of the moral structure of society, and those in "Radicals and Reformers," which touch upon political and economic issues, the selections in this section are statements reflecting a rebellion stemming from an almost complete alienation from the values of society. The writers, or the characters about whom they write, may be called misfits, outsiders, malcontents. They are not reformers; they wave no banners, shout no slogans, promise no new world. Rather, they have visions— however indistinct—of the possibilities of a way of life better than the one offered by the society about them, and they choose to go their private ways. In the words of Emily Dickinson, they select their own society, then shut the door; their vote for their own way of life carries the overwhelming weight of the majority of one.

Their own ways of life are, of course, various. Some, like the Transcendentalists discussed in Emerson's essay, step aside from the currents of the world and "hold themselves aloof," believing that what the world has to offer them is not worth accepting. They ask more of their fellow man, collectively and individually, than he is willing to give. Feeling rejected, they in turn reject. In Emerson's time the more socially minded of them gathered for a few years at Brook Farm to form an ideal society. The more individualistic, like Thoreau, conducted a private experiment. Spurning the world of sham and delusion, the world that is generally called the real world, Thoreau declared his personal independence on July 4, 1845, by moving into his newly erected cabin on the shore of Walden Pond. He was seeking, as he states in the chapter from *Walden* included below, the "hard bottom" of *reality*, a stratum of existence deeper than the sandy bottom of the stream of time, which he regarded as suitable for fishing in but too shallow for serious mining. During his two years at Walden Pond, Thoreau succeeded in his determination "to live deliberately, to front only the essential facts of life."

The essential facts of life for one man, however, are not necessarily those for another. While Thoreau was tending his bean field on the shore of Walden Pond, Herman Melville was writing of his experience in forsaking all shores, seeking in the vastness of the oceans of the world some cure for the "damp, drizzly November" in his soul, a restless dissatisfaction that almost drove him—or his persona, Ishmael—to go about the street knocking off people's hats. Like Melville's Bulkington, Ishmael sought the "mortally intolerable truth" that resides far from land, in the "howling infinite" rather than at the hearth. Though man might be destroyed in the search, wrote Melville, it was a search better befitting the nature of man than the quest for the goals of society.

The rebellious spirit that underlay Thoreau's sojourn at Walden Pond and impelled Melville toward the sea drove Emily Dickinson into the seclusion of her home in Amherst, Massachusetts. There she kept her private church and made her own society, judging harshly the world that was judging her. "Much madness," she could say, "is divinest sense / To a discerning eye; / Much sense the starkest madness."

In "The Transcendentalist" Emerson predicted that those who know "these seething brains, these admirable radicals, these unsocial worshippers, these talkers who talk the sun and moon away, will believe that this heresy cannot pass away without leaving its mark." In the century and a quarter that has passed since Emerson made this prediction, the mark has been an indelible one, if sometimes irregular and often hazy in outline. The search for a setting, either in the mind or on the earth, to express one's private vision, or at least to escape from the pressure imposed by society, has taken many directions. The selections below can illustrate only a few. In the present century it has led to Europe, where the expatriates following World War I, taking their clue from Ernest Hemingway's *The Sun Also Rises*, pursued lives of sensual enjoyment and artistic fulfillment and defined immorality as "things that made you disgusted afterward." Depending on one's capacity for disgust, morality could thus cover a wide range of activities, broader by far than those permitted by the Boston society from which Harry Crosby catapulted himself to his tawdry and pointless suicide. Malcolm Cowley's analysis of the forces at work on, or within, Crosby underscores the human tragedy possible when the escape from the conventions of society is complete. Though much madness may be divinest sense, Cowley suggests that the irrational search to express one's private vision may unfortunately lead to madness that is only madness.

Yet the seeker abroad had the vantage point of a distant, perhaps a fuller, perspective on American life. At Epidaurus, for example, Henry Miller could glimpse a purer world much like the one Thoreau found at Walden Pond. The similarity between the observations of the two writers points up the vitality of the belief of the Transcendentalists a century before that the only worthwhile rebellion is the complete one. Emerson argued that society could not be changed unless individuals were changed. Miller makes the same point: "It is not enough to overthrow governments, masters, tyrants: one must overthrow his own preconceived ideas of right and wrong, good and bad, just and unjust." In the huge amphitheater at Epidaurus, lulled by its peace and quiet, Miller found what Thoreau had found at Walden Pond, the source of energy that permits men to "live only miraculously, think only miraculously, die miraculously." The search has not always led, however, to such exoticism as sun worship in Paris or to the classic monuments of Western civilization. Shortly after the end of World War II, in New York's Greenwich Village and San Francisco's North Beach, rebels against materialistic success, conventional moral behavior, cultural mediocrity, and anemic and academic literature emerged as hipsters, members of the "beat generation." An amorphous label to identify an amorphous rebellion, the team "beat" has been variously defined with reference to rhythm, to fatigue, and to beatific. The "beatniks"—the term was coined by Herb Caen, a San Francisco columnist—dramatized the rebellion present since the time of Emerson and Thoreau by the impressiveness of their number, their attractiveness to tourists and news media, and their intent to outrage and flout society by their outlandish appearance, poverty, sexual license, freedom of expression, exotic music and religions, and devotion to wine. The use of drugs or mind-expanding agents characterizes the latest "hippie" phase of the rebellion. Underlying the social protest, however, is the quest that motivated Thoreau, whom they look to as the prototype of the American social rebel. Like Thoreau, they are alienated, disengaged, disaffiliated from a society which they feel is dominated by nonessentials, by shams and delusions—a society of "squares."

The social rebels described in the final three selections illustrate different aspects of the "hipster" as he appears in contemporary American literature. Norman Mailer's Pierrot in "The Patron Saint of MacDougal Alley," written in 1951, before the "beat" label came into existence, is the young man who cannot get in step with society, who is not so much in contempt of social conventions as innocent of them. Mailer views him with an ironic sympathy, even a humor mixed with exasperation, as the type of apparently irresponsible person in whom—it is just barely possible, Mailer humorously suggests—may reside the salvation of the world. Jack Kerouac romanticizes his hero, Dean Moriarty, the social delinquent whose restless energies do not always find expression within the law, as "the father we never found." Moriarty's search for experience, as an end in itself, requires more of life than illusion; Moriarty seeks his "portion under the sun," not merely the goals of his society. The world about which LeRoi Jones writes in "The Screamers" is the night world of jazz music, which functions as a route for its devotees to leave America "on the first fast boat." Contrasted with the society of Sunday-night Baptists, pulp magazines, and "clean politicians," the world of the screaming horn is the world of the hippies, of excess and extremes of emotion, of no compromise. A hundred years from Walden Pond and Thoreau, Lynn Hope and his followers in the Graham still strive, in their different ways, "to save whatever it was each of us thought we loved." From Thoreau to Lynn Hope, the common denominator that binds these rebels is not society but the private definition of values and the majority vote of the individual.

RALPH WALDO EMERSON

The Transcendentalist

THE FIRST THING we have to say respecting what are called *new views* here in New England, at the present time, is, that they are not new, but the very oldest of thoughts cast into the mould of these new times. The light is always identical in its composition, but it falls on a great variety of objects, and by so falling is first revealed to us, not in its own form, for it is formless, but in theirs; in like manner, thought only appears in the objects it classifies. What is popularly called Transcendentalism among us, is Idealism; Idealism as it appears in 1842. As thinkers, mankind have ever divided into two sects, Materialists and Idealists; the first class founding on experience, the second on consciousness; the first class beginning to think from the data of the senses, the second class perceive that the senses are not final, and say, The senses give us representations of things, but what are the things themselves, they cannot tell. The materialist insists on facts, on history, on the force of circumstances and the animal wants of man; the idealist on the power [329/330] of Thought and of Will, on inspiration, on miracle, on individual culture. These two modes of thinking are both natural, but the idealist contends that his way of thinking is in higher nature. He concedes all that the other affirms, admits the impressions of sense, admits their coherency, their use and beauty, and then asks the materialist for his grounds of assurance that things are as his senses represent them. But I, he says, affirm facts not affected by the illusions of sense, facts which are of the same nature as the faculty which reports them, and not liable to doubt; facts which in their first appearance to us assume a native superiority to material facts, degrading these into a language by which the first are to be spoken; facts which it only needs a retire-

Ralph Waldo Emerson, "The Transcendentalist," in *The Complete Works of Ralph Waldo Emerson,* ed. Edward Waldo Emerson (Boston and New York: Houghton Mifflin Company, 1903–1904), I, 329–59. [Originally delivered as an address in Boston in January 1842 and first published in *The Dial,* January 1843.]

ment from the senses to discern. Every materialist will be an idealist; but an idealist can never go backward to be a materialist.

The idealist, in speaking of events, sees them as spirits. He does
not deny the sensuous fact: by no means; but he will not see that
alone. He does not deny the presence of this table, this chair, and
the walls of this room, but he looks at these things as the reverse
side of the tapestry, as the *other end,* each being a sequel or completion of a spiritual fact which nearly [330/331] concerns him. This
manner of looking at things transfers every object in nature from an
independent and anomalous position without there, into the consciousness. Even the materialist Condillac, perhaps the most logical
expounder of materialism, was constrained to say, "Though we
should soar into the heavens, though we should sink into the abyss,
we never go out of ourselves; it is always our own thought that we
perceive." What more could an idealist say?

The materialist, secure in the certainty of sensation, mocks at fine-
spun theories, at stargazers and dreamers, and believes that his life
is solid, that he at least takes nothing for granted, but knows where
he stands, and what he does. Yet how easy it is to show him that he
also is a phantom walking and working amid phantoms, and that he
need only ask a question or two beyond his daily questions to find
his solid universe growing dim and impalpable before his sense. The
sturdy capitalist, no matter how deep and square on blocks of
Quincy granite he lays the foundations of his banking-house or Exchange, must set it, at last, not on a cube corresponding to the an-
gles of his structure, but on a mass of unknown materials and solid-
ity, red-hot or white-hot perhaps at the core, which [331/332] rounds
off to an almost perfect sphericity, and lies floating in soft air, and
goes spinning away, dragging bank and banker with it at a rate of
thousands of miles the hour, he knows not whither,—a bit of bullet,
now glimmering, now darkling through a small cubic space on the
edge of an unimaginable pit of emptiness. And this wild balloon, in
which his whole venture is embarked, is just a symbol of his whole
state and faculty. One thing at least, he says, is certain, and does not
give me the headache, that figures do not lie; the multiplication
table has been hitherto found unimpeachable truth; and, moreover,
if I put a gold eagle in my safe, I find it again to-morrow;—but for
these thoughts, I know not whence they are. They change and pass
away. But ask him why he believes that an uniform experience will
continue uniform, or on what grounds he founds his faith in his figures, and he will perceive that his mental fabric is built up on just as
strange and quaking foundations as his proud edifice of stone.

In the order of thought, the materialist takes his departure from
the external world, and esteems a man as one product of that. The

idealist takes his departure from his consciousness, [332/333] and reckons the world an appearance. The materialist respects sensible masses, Society, Government, social art and luxury, every establishment, every mass, whether majority of numbers, or extent of space, or amount of objects, every social action. The idealist has another measure, which is metaphysical, namely the *rank* which things themselves take in his consciousness; not at all the size or appearance. Mind is the only reality, of which men and all other natures are better or worse reflectors. Nature, literature, history, are only subjective phenomena. Although in his action overpowered by the laws of action, and so, warmly cooperating with men, even preferring them to himself, yet when he speaks scientifically, or after the order of thought, he is constrained to degrade persons into representatives of truths. He does not respect labor, or the products of labor, namely property, otherwise than as a manifold symbol, illustrating with wonderful fidelity of details the laws of being; he does not respect government, except as far as it reiterates the law of his mind; nor the church, nor charities, nor arts, for themselves; but hears, as at a vast distance, what they say, as if his consciousness would speak to him through a pantomimic [333/334] scene. His thought, —that is the Universe. His experience inclines him to behold the procession of facts you call the world, as flowing perpetually outward from an invisible, unsounded centre in himself, centre alike of him and of them, and necessitating him to regard all things as having a subjective or relative existence, relative to that aforesaid Unknown Centre of him.

From this transfer of the world into the consciousness, this beholding of all things in the mind, follow easily his whole ethics. It is simpler to be self-dependent. The height, the deity of man is to be self-sustained, to need no gift, no foreign force. Society is good when it does not violate me, but best when it is likest to solitude. Everything real is self-existent. Everything divine shares the self-existence of Deity. All that you call the world is the shadow of that substance which you are, the perpetual creation of the powers of thought, of those that are dependent and of those that are independent of your will. Do not cumber yourself with fruitless pains to mend and remedy remote effects; let the soul be erect, and all things will go well. You think me the child of my circumstances: I make my circumstance. Let any [334/335] thought or motive of mine be different from that they are, the difference will transform my condition and economy. I—this thought which is called I—is the mould into which the world is poured like melted wax. The mould is invisible, but the world betrays the shape of the mould. You call it the power of circumstance, but it is the power of me. Am I in harmony with myself? my position will seem to you just and commanding. Am I vicious and insane? my fortunes will seem to you obscure and descending. As I am, so shall I associate, and so shall I act; Cæsar's history will paint out Cæsar. Jesus acted so, because he thought so. I do not wish to overlook or to gainsay any reality; I say I make my circumstance; but if you ask me, Whence am I? I feel like other men my relation to that Fact which cannot be spoken, or defined, nor even thought, but which exists, and will exist.

The Transcendentalist adopts the whole connection of spiritual doctrine. He believes in miracle, in the perpetual openness of the human mind to new influx of light and power; he believes in inspiration, and in ecstasy. He wishes that the spiritual principle should be suffered to demonstrate itself to the end, in all possible [335/336] applications to the state of man, without the admission of anything unspiritual; that is, anything positive, dogmatic, personal. Thus the spiritual measure of inspiration is the depth of the thought, and never, who said it? And so he resists all attempts to palm other rules and measures on the spirit than its own.

In action he easily incurs the charge of antinomianism by his avowal that he, who has the Law-giver, may with safety not only neglect, but even contravene every written commandment. In the play of Othello, the expiring Desdemona absolves her husband of the murder, to her attendant Emilia. Afterwards, when Emilia charges him with the crime, Othello exclaims,

> "You heard her say herself it was not I."

Emilia replies,

> "The more angel she, and thou the blacker devil."

Of this fine incident, Jacobi, the Transcendental moralist, makes use, with other parallel instances, in his reply to Fichte. Jacobi, refusing all measure of right and wrong except the determinations of the private spirit, remarks that there is no crime but has sometimes been a virtue. "I," he says, "am that atheist, that godless person who, in opposition to an imaginary [336/337] doctrine of calculation, would lie as the dying Desdemona lied; would lie and deceive, as Pylades when he personated Orestes; would assassinate like Timoleon; would perjure myself like Epaminondas and John de Witt; I would resolve on suicide like Cato; I would commit sacrilege with David; yea, and pluck ears of corn on the Sabbath, for no other reason than that I was fainting for lack of food. For I have assurance in myself that in pardoning these faults according to the letter, man exerts the sovereign right which the majesty of his being confers on him; he sets the seal of his divine nature to the grace he accords."

In like manner, if there is anything grand and daring in human thought or virtue, any reliance on the vast, the unknown; any presentiment, any extravagance of faith, the spiritualist adopts it as most in nature. The oriental mind has always tended to this largeness. Buddhism is an expression of it. The Buddhist, who thanks no man, who says, "Do not flatter your benefactors," but who, in his conviction that every good deed can by no possibility escape its reward, will not deceive the benefactor by pretending that he had done more than he should, is a Transcendentalist. [337/338]

You will see by this sketch that there is no such thing as a Transcendental *party;* that there is no pure Transcendentalist; that we know of none but prophets and heralds of such a philosophy; that all who by strong bias of nature have leaned to the spiritual side in doctrine, have stopped short of their goal. We have had many harbingers and forerunners; but of a purely spiritual life, history has afforded no example. I mean we have yet no man who has leaned entirely on his character, and eaten angels' food; who, trusting to his sentiments, found life made of miracles; who, working for universal aims, found himself fed, he knew not how; clothed, sheltered, and weaponed, he knew not how, and yet it was done by his own hands. Only in the instinct of the lower animals we find the suggestion of the methods of it, and something higher than our understanding. The squirrel hoards nuts and the bee gathers honey, without knowing what they do, and they are thus provided for without selfishness or disgrace.

Shall we say then that Transcendentalism is the Saturnalia or excess of Faith; the presentiment of a faith proper to man in his integrity, excessive only when his imperfect obedience [338/339] hinders the satisfaction of his wish? Nature is transcendental, exists primarily, necessarily, ever works and advances, yet takes no thought for the morrow. Man owns the dignity of the life which throbs around him, in chemistry, and tree, and animal, and in the involuntary functions of his own body; yet he is balked when he tries to fling himself into this enchanted circle, where all is done without degradation. Yet genius and virtue predict in man the same absence of private ends and of condescension to circumstances, united with every trait and talent of beauty and power.

This way of thinking, falling on Roman times, made Stoic philosophers; falling on despotic times, made patriot Catos and Brutuses; falling on superstitious times, made prophets and apostles; on popish times, made protestants and ascetic monks, preachers of Faith against the preachers of Works; on prelatical times, made Puritans and Quakers; and falling on Unitarian and commercial times, makes the peculiar shades of Idealism which we know.

It is well known to most of my audience that the Idealism of the present day acquired the name of Transcendental from the use of that term by Immanuel Kant, of Königsberg, who [339/340] replied to the skeptical philosophy of Locke, which insisted that there was nothing in the intellect which was not previously in the experience of the senses, by showing that there was a very important class of ideas or imperative forms, which did not come by experience, but through which experience was acquired; that these were intuitions of the mind itself; and he denominated them *Transcendental* forms. The extraordinary profoundness and precision of that man's thinking have given vogue to his nomenclature, in Europe and America, to that extent that whatever belongs to the class of intuitive thought is popularly called at the present day *Transcendental*.

Although, as we have said, there is no pure Transcendentalist, yet the tendency to respect the intuitions and to give them, at least in our creed, all authority over our experience, has deeply colored the conversation and poetry of the present day; and the history of genius and of religion in these times, though impure, and as yet not incarnated in any powerful individual, will be the history of this tendency.

It is a sign of our times, conspicuous to the coarsest observer, that many intelligent and religious persons withdraw themselves from the [340/341] common labors and competitions of the market and caucus, and betake themselves to a certain solitary and critical way of living, from which no solid fruit has yet appeared to justify their separation. They hold themselves aloof: they feel the disproportion between their faculties and the work offered them, and they prefer to ramble in the country and perish of ennui, to the degradation of such charities and such ambitions as the city can propose to them. They are striking work, and crying out for somewhat worthy to do! What they do is done only because they are overpowered by the humanities that speak on all sides; and they consent to such labor as is open to them, though to their lofty dream the writing of Iliads or Hamlets, or the building of cities or empires seems drudgery.

Now every one must do after his kind, be he asp or angel, and these must. The question which a wise man and a student of modern history will ask, is, what that kind is? And truly, as in ecclesiastical history we take so much pains to know what the Gnostics, what the Essenes, what the Manichees, and what the Reformers believed, it would not misbecome us to inquire nearer home, what these companions and contemporaries of ours think and do, at least so far as

[341/342] these thoughts and actions appear to be not accidental and personal, but common to many, and the inevitable flower of the Tree of Time. Our American literature and spiritual history are, we confess, in the optative mood; but whoso knows these seething brains, these admirable radicals, these unsocial worshippers, these talkers who talk the sun and moon away, will believe that this heresy cannot pass away without leaving its mark.

They are lonely; the spirit of their writing and conversation is lonely; they repel influences; they shun general society; they incline to shut themselves in their chamber in the house, to live in the country rather than in the town, and to find their tasks and amusements in solitude. Society, to be sure, does not like this very well; it saith, Whoso goes to walk alone, accuses the whole world; he declares all to be unfit to be his companions; it is very uncivil, nay, insulting; Society will retaliate. Meantime, this retirement does not proceed from any whim on the part of these separators; but if any one will take pains to talk with them, he will find that this part is chosen both from temperament and from principle; with some unwillingness too, and as a choice of the less of two evils; for these persons [342/343] are not by nature melancholy, sour, and unsocial,—they are not stockish or brute,—but joyous, susceptible, affectionate; they have even more than others a great wish to be loved. Like the young Mozart, they are rather ready to cry ten times a day, "But are you sure you love me?" Nay, if they tell you their whole thought, they will own that love seems to them the last and highest gift of nature; that there are persons whom in their hearts they daily thank for existing,—persons whose faces are perhaps unknown to them, but whose fame and spirit have penetrated their solitude,—and for whose sake they wish to exist. To behold the beauty of another character, which inspires a new interest in our own; to behold the beauty lodged in a human being, with such vivacity of apprehension that I am instantly forced home to inquire if I am not deformity itself; to behold in another the expression of a love so high that it assures itself,—assures itself also to me against every possible casualty except my unworthiness;—these are degrees on the scale of human happiness to which they have ascended; and it is a fidelity to this sentiment which has made common association distasteful to them. They wish a just and even fellowship, or none. They cannot [343/344] gossip with you, and they do not wish, as they are sincere and religious, to gratify any mere curiosity which you may entertain. Like fairies, they do not wish to be spoken of. Love me, they say, but do not ask who is my cousin and my uncle. If you do not need to hear my thought, because you can read it in my face and behavior, then I will tell it you from sunrise to sunset. If you cannot divine it, you would not understand what I say. I will not molest myself for you. I do not wish to be profaned.

And yet, it seems as if this loneliness, and not this love, would prevail in their circumstances, because of the extravagant demand they make on human nature. That, indeed, constitutes a new feature in their portrait, that they are the most exacting and extortionate critics. Their quarrel with every man they meet is not with his kind, but with his degree. There is not enough of him,—that is the only fault. They prolong their privilege of childhood in this wise; of doing nothing, but making immense demands on all the gladiators in the lists of action and fame. They make us feel the strange disappointment which overcasts every human youth. So many promising youths, and never a finished man! The profound nature will have [344/345] a savage rudeness; the delicate one will be shallow, or victim of sensibility; the richly accomplished will have some capital absurdity; and so every piece has a crack. 'T is strange, but this masterpiece is the result of such an extreme delicacy that the most unobserved flaw in the boy will neutralize the most aspiring genius, and spoil the work. Talk with a seaman of the hazards to life in his profession and he will ask you, 'Where are the old sailors? Do you not see that all are young men?' And we, on this sea of human thought, in like manner inquire, Where are the old idealists? where are they who represented to the last generation that extravagant hope which a few happy aspirants suggest to ours? In looking at the class of counsel, and power, and wealth, and at the matronage of the land, amidst all the prudence and all the triviality, one asks, Where are they who represented genius, virtue, the invisible and heavenly world, to these? Are they dead,—taken in early ripeness to the gods, —as ancient wisdom foretold their fate? Or did the high idea die out of them, and leave their unperfumed body as its tomb and tablet, announcing to all that the celestial inhabitant, who once gave them beauty, had departed? Will it be [345/346] better with the new generation? We easily predict a fair future to each new candidate who enters the lists, but we are frivolous and volatile, and by low aims and ill example do what we can to defeat this hope. Then these youths bring us a rough but effectual aid. By their unconcealed dissatisfaction they expose our poverty and the insignificance of man to man. A man is a poor limitary benefactor. He ought to be a shower of benefits—a great influence, which should never let his brother go, but should refresh old merits continually with new ones; so that though absent he should never be out of my mind, his name never far from my lips; but if the earth should open at my side, or my last hour were come, his name should be the prayer I should utter to the Universe. But in our experience, man is cheap and friendship wants its deep sense. We affect to dwell with our friends in their absence, but we do not; when deed, word, or letter comes not, they let us go. These exacting children advertise us of our wants. There is no compliment, no smooth speech with them; they pay you only this one compliment, of insatiable expectation; they aspire, they severely exact, and if they only stand fast in this watch-tower, and [346/347] persist in demanding unto the end, and without end, then are they terrible friends, whereof poet and priest cannot choose but stand in awe; and what if they eat clouds, and drink wind, they have not been without service to the race of man.

With this passion for what is great and extraordinary, it cannot be wondered at that they are repelled by vulgarity and frivolity in people. They say to themselves, It is better to be alone than in bad company. And it is really a wish to be met,—the wish to find society for their hope and religion,—which prompts them to shun what is called society. They feel that they are never so fit for friendship as when they have quitted mankind and taken themselves to friend. A picture, a book, a favorite spot in the hills or the woods which they can people with the fair and worthy creation of the fancy, can give them often forms so vivid that these for the time shall seem real, and society the illusion.

But their solitary and fastidious manners not only withdraw them from the conversation, but from the labors of the world; they are not good citizens, not good members of society; unwillingly they bear their part of the public and private burdens; they do not willingly [347/348] share in the public charities, in the public religious rites, in the enterprises of education, of missions foreign and domestic, in the abolition of the slave-trade, or in the temperance society. They do not even like to vote. The philanthropists inquire whether Transcendentalism does not mean sloth: they had as lief hear that their friend is dead, as that he is a Transcendentalist; for then is he paralyzed, and can never do anything for humanity. What right, cries the good world, has the man of genius to retreat from work, and indulge himself? The popular literary creed seems to be, 'I am a sublime genius; I ought not therefore to labor.' But genius is the power to labor better and more availably. Deserve thy genius: exalt it. The good, the illuminated, sit apart from the rest, censuring their dullness and vices, as if they thought that by sitting very grand in their chairs, the very brokers, attorneys, and congressmen would see the error of their ways, and flock to them. But the good and wise must learn to act, and carry salvation to the combatants and demagogues in the dusty arena below.

On the part of these children it is replied that life and their fac- ulty seem to them gifts too rich to be squandered on such trifles as you propose [348/349] to them. What you call your fundamental insti- tutions, your great and holy causes, seem to them great abuses, and, when nearly seen, paltry matters. Each 'cause' as it is called,—say Abolition, Temperance, say Calvinism, or Unitarianism,—becomes speedily a little shop, where the article, let it have been at first never so subtle and ethereal, is now made up into portable and con- venient cakes, and retailed in small quantities to suit purchasers. You make very free use of these words 'great' and 'holy,' but few things appear to them such. Few persons have any magnificence of nature to inspire enthusiasm, and the philanthropies and charities have a certain air of quackery. As to the general course of living, and the daily employments of men, they cannot see much virtue in these, since they are parts of this vicious circle; and as no great ends are answered by the men, there is nothing noble in the arts by which they are maintained. Nay, they have made the experiment and found that from the liberal professions to the coarsest manual labor, and from the courtesies of the academy and the college to the con- ventions of the cotillon-room and the morning call, there is a spirit of cowardly compromise and seeming which intimates a frightful [349/350] skepticism, a life without love, and an activity without an aim.

Unless the action is necessary, unless it is adequate, I do not wish to perform it. I do not wish to do one thing but once. I do not love routine. Once possessed of the principle, it is equally easy to make four or forty thousand applications of it. A great man will be content to have indicated in any the slightest manner his perception of the reigning Idea of his time, and will leave to those who like it the multiplication of examples. When he has hit the white, the rest may shatter the target. Every thing admonishes us how needlessly long life is. Every moment of a hero so raises and cheers us that a twelve- month is an age. All that the brave Xanthus brings home from his wars is the recollection that at the storming of Samos, "in the heat of the battle, Pericles smiled on me, and passed on to another detach- ment." It is the quality of the moment, not the number of days, of events, or of actors, that imports.

New, we confess, and by no means happy, is our condition: if you want the aid of our labor, we ourselves stand in greater want of the labor. We are miserable with inaction. We perish of rest and rust: but we do not like your work. [350/351]

'Then,' says the world, 'show me your own.'

'We have none.'

'What will you do, then?' cries the world.

'We will wait.'

'How long?'

'Until the Universe beckons and calls us to work.'

'But whilst you wait, you grow old and useless.'

'Be it so: I can sit in a corner and *perish* (as you call it), but I will not move until I have the highest command. If no call should come for years, for centuries, then I know that the want of the Universe is the attestation of faith by my abstinence. Your virtuous projects, so called, do not cheer me. I know that which shall come will cheer me. If I cannot work, at least I need not lie. All that is clearly due today is not to lie. In other places other men have encountered sharp trials, and have behaved themselves well. The martyrs were sawn asunder, or hung alive on meat-hooks. Cannot we screw our courage to patience and truth, and without complaint, or even with good-humor, await our turn of action in the Infinite Counsels?'

But to come a little closer to the secret of [351/352] these persons, we must say that to them it seems a very easy matter to answer the objections of the man of the world, but not so easy to dispose of the doubts and objections that occur to themselves. They are exercised in their own spirit with queries which acquaint them with all adversity, and with the trials of the bravest heroes. When I asked them concerning their private experience, they answered somewhat in this wise: It is not to be denied that there must be some wide difference between my faith and other faith; and mine is a certain brief experience, which surprised me in the highway or in the market, in some place, at some time,—whether in the body or out of the body, God knoweth,—and made me aware that I had played the fool with fools all this time, but that law existed for me and for all, that to me belonged trust, a child's trust and obedience, and the worship of ideas, and I should never be fool more. Well, in the space of an hour probably, I was let down from this height; I was at my old tricks, the selfish member of a selfish society. My life is superficial, takes no root in the deep world; I ask, When shall I die and be relieved of the responsibility of seeing an Universe which I do not use? I wish to exchange this flash-of-lightning [352/353] faith for continuous daylight, this fever-glow for a benign climate.

These two states of thought diverge every moment, and stand in wild contrast. To him who looks at his life from these moments of illumination, it will seem that he skulks and plays a mean, shiftless and subaltern part in the world. That is to be done which he has not skill to do, or to be said which others can say better, and he lies by, or occupies his hands with some plaything, until his hour comes again. Much of our reading, much of our labor, seems mere waiting: it was not that we were born for. Any other could do it as well or better. So little skill enters into these works, so little do they mix with the divine life, that it really signifies little what we do, whether we turn a grindstone, or ride, or run, or make fortunes, or govern the state. The worst feature of this double consciousness is, that the two lives, of the understanding and of the soul, which we lead, really show very little relation to each other; never meet and measure each other: one prevails now, all buzz and din; and the other prevails then, all infinitude and paradise; and, with the progress of life, the two discover no greater disposition to reconcile themselves. [353/354] Yet, what is my faith? What am I? What but a thought of serenity and independence, an abode in the deep blue sky? Presently the clouds shut down again; yet we retain the belief that this petty web we weave will at last be overshot and reticulated with veins of the blue, and that the moments will characterize the days. Patience, then, is for us, is it not? Patience, and still patience. When we pass, as presently we shall, into some new infinitude, out of this Iceland of negations, it will please us to reflect that though we had few virtues or consolations, we bore with our indigence, nor once strove to repair it with hypocrisy or false heat of any kind.

But this class are not sufficiently characterized if we omit to add that they are lovers and worshippers of Beauty. In the eternal trinity of Truth, Goodness, and Beauty, each in its perfection including the three, they prefer to make Beauty the sign and head. Something of the same taste is observable in all the moral movements of the time, in the religious and benevolent enterprises. They have a liberal, even an æsthetic spirit. A reference to Beauty in action sounds, to be sure, a little hollow and ridiculous in the ears of the old church. In politics, it has [354/355] often sufficed, when they treated of justice, if they kept the bounds of selfish calculation. If they granted restitution, it was prudence which granted it. But the justice which is now claimed for the black, and the pauper, and the drunkard, is for Beauty,—is for a necessity to the soul of the agent, not of the beneficiary. I say this is the tendency, not yet the realization. Our virtue totters and trips, does not yet walk firmly. Its representatives are austere; they preach and denounce; their rectitude is not yet a grace. They are still liable to that slight taint of burlesque which in our strange world attaches to the zealot. A saint should be as dear as the apple of the eye. Yet we are tempted to smile, and we flee from the working to the speculative reformer, to escape that same slight ridicule. Alas for these days of derision and criticism! We call the Beautiful the highest, because it appears to us the golden mean, escaping the dowdiness of the good and the heartlessness of the true. They are lovers of nature also, and find an indemnity in the inviolable order of the world for the violated order and grace of man.

There is, no doubt, a great deal of well-founded objection to be spoken or felt against the sayings and doings of this class, some of [355/356] whose traits we have selected; no doubt they will lay themselves open to criticism and to lampoons, and as ridiculous stories will be to be told of them as of any. There will be cant and pretension; there will be subtilty and moonshine. These persons are of unequal strength, and do not all prosper. They complain that everything around them must be denied; and if feeble, it takes all their strength to deny, before they can begin to lead their own life. Grave seniors insist on their respect to this institution and that usage; to an obsolete history; to some vocation, or college, or etiquette, or beneficiary, or charity, or morning or evening call, which they resist as what does not concern them. But it costs such sleepless nights, alienations and misgivings,—they have so many moods about it; these old guardians never change *their* minds; they have but one mood on the subject, namely, that Antony is very perverse,—that it is quite as much as Antony can do to assert his rights, abstain from what he thinks foolish, and keep his temper. He cannot help the reaction of this injustice in his own mind. He is braced-up and stilted; all freedom and flowing genius, all sallies of wit and frolic nature are quite out of the question; it is well [356/357] if he can keep from lying, justice, and suicide. This is no time for gaiety and grace. His strength and spirits are wasted in rejection. But the strong spirits overpower those around them without effort. Their thought and emotion comes in like a flood, quite withdraws them from all notice of these carping critics; they surrender themselves with glad heart to the heavenly guide, and only by implication reject the clamorous nonsense of the hour. Grave seniors talk to the deaf,—church and old book mumble and ritualize to an unheeding, preoccupied and advancing mind, and thus they by happiness of greater momentum lose no time, but take the right road at first.

But all these of whom I speak are not proficients; they are novices; they only show the road in which man should travel, when the soul has greater health and prowess. Yet let them feel the dignity of their charge, and deserve a larger power. Their heart is the ark in which the fire is concealed which shall burn in a broader and universal flame. Let them obey the Genius then most when his impulse is wildest; then most when he seems to lead to uninhabitable deserts of thought and life; for the path which the hero travels alone is the highway of health [357/358] and benefit to mankind. What is the privilege and nobility of our nature but its persistency, through its power to attach itself to what is permanent?

Society also has its duties in reference to this class, and must behold them with what charity it can. Possibly some benefit may yet accrue from them to the state. In our Mechanics' Fair, there must be not only bridges, ploughs, carpenters' planes, and baking troughs, but also some few finer instruments,—rain-gauges, thermometers, and telescopes; and in society, besides farmers, sailors, and weavers, there must be a few persons of purer fire kept specially as gauges and meters of character; persons of a fine, detecting instinct, who note the smallest accumulations of wit and feeling in the bystander. Perhaps too there might be room for the exciters and monitors; collectors of the heavenly spark, with power to convey the electricity to others. Or, as the storm-tossed vessel at sea speaks the frigate or 'line packet' to learn its longitude, so it may not be without its advantage that we should now and then encounter rare and gifted men, to compare the points of our spiritual compass, and verify our bearings from superior chronometers. [358/359]

Admidst the downward tendency and proneness of things, when every voice is raised for a new road or another statute or a subscription of stock; for an improvement in dress, or in dentistry; for a new house or a larger business; for a political party, or the division of an estate;—will you not tolerate one or two solitary voices in the land, speaking for thoughts and principles not marketable or perishable? Soon these improvements and mechanical inventions will be superseded; these modes of living lost out of memory; these cities rotted, ruined by war, by new inventions, by new seats of trade, or the geologic changes:—all gone, like the shells which sprinkle the sea-beach with a white colony to-day, forever renewed to be forever destroyed. But the thoughts which these few hermits strove to proclaim by silence as well as by speech, not only by what they did, but by what they forebore to do, shall abide in beauty and strength, to reorganize themselves in nature, to invest themselves anew in other, perhaps higher endowed and happier mixed clay than ours, in fuller union with the surrounding system. [359]

HENRY DAVID THOREAU

Where I Lived, and
What I Lived For

AT A CERTAIN season of our life we are accustomed to consider every
spot as the possible site of a house. I have thus surveyed the country
on every side within a dozen miles of where I live. In imagination I
have bought all the farms in succession, for all were to be bought,
and I knew their price. I walked over each farmer's premises, tasted
his wild apples, discoursed on husbandry with him, took his farm at
his price, at any price, mortgaging it to him in my mind; even put a
higher price on it,—took everything but a deed of it,—took his word
for his deed, for I dearly love to talk,—cultivated it, and him too
to some extent, I trust, and withdrew when I had enjoyed it long
enough, leaving him to carry it on. This experience entitled me to be
regarded as a sort of real-estate broker by my friends. Wherever I
sat, there I might live, and the landscape radiated from me accordingly. [128/129] What is a house but a *sedes,* a seat?—better if a
country seat. I discovered many a site for a house not likely to be soon
improved, which some might have thought too far from the village,
but to my eyes the village was too far from it. Well, there I might
live, I said; and there I did live, for an hour, a summer and a winter
life; saw how I could let the years run off; buffet the winter through,
and see the spring come in. The future inhabitants of this region,
wherever they may place their houses, may be sure that they have
been anticipated. An afternoon sufficed to lay out the land into orchard, woodlot, and pasture, and to decide what fine oaks or pines
should be left to stand before the door, and whence each blasted
tree could be seen to the best advantage; and then I let it lie; fallow
perchance, for a man is rich in proportion to the number of things
which he can afford to let alone.

Henry David Thoreau, "Where I Lived, and What I Lived For," in *Walden,*
The Writings of Henry David Thoreau (Boston and New York: Houghton,
Mifflin and Company, 1893), II, 128–55. [Originally published in 1854.]

My imagination carried me so far that I even had the refusal of several farms,— the refusal was all I wanted,—but I never got my fingers burned by actual possession. The nearest that I came to actual possession was when I bought the Hollowell place, [129/130] and had begun to sort my seeds, and collected materials with which to make a wheelbarrow to carry it on or off with; but before the owner gave me a deed of it, his wife—every man has such a wife—changed her mind and wished to keep it, and he offered me ten dollars to release him. Now, to speak the truth, I had but ten cents in the world, and it surpassed my arithmetic to tell, if I was the man who had ten cents, or who had a farm, or ten dollars, or all together. However, I let him keep the ten dollars and the farm too, for I had carried it far enough; or rather, to be generous, I sold him the farm for just what I gave for it, and, as he was not a rich man, made him a present of ten dollars, and still had my ten cents, and seeds, and materials for a wheelbarrow left. I found thus that I had been a rich man without any damage to my poverty. But I retained the landscape, and I have since annually carried off what it yielded without a wheelbarrow. With respect to landscapes,—

> "I am monarch of all I *survey*,
> My right there is none to dispute."

I have frequently seen a poet withdraw, having enjoyed the most valuable part of a [130/131] farm, while the crusty farmer supposed that he had got a few wild apples only. Why, the owner does not know it for many years when a poet has put his farm in rhyme, the most admirable kind of invisible fence, has fairly impounded it, milked it, skimmed it, and got all the cream, and left the farmer only the skimmed milk.

The real attractions of the Hollowell farm, to me, were: its complete retirement, being about two miles from the village, half a mile from the nearest neighbor, and separated from the highway by a broad field; its bounding on the river, which the owner said protected it by its fogs from frosts in the spring, though that was nothing to me; the gray color and ruinous state of the house and barn, and the dilapidated fences, which put such an interval between me and the last occupant; the hollow and lichen-covered apple trees, gnawed by rabbits, showing what kind of neighbors I should have; but above all, the recollection I had of it from my earliest voyages up the river, when the house was concealed behind a dense grove of red maples, through which I heard the house-dog bark. I was in haste to buy it, before the proprietor finished getting out some [131/132] rocks, cutting down the hollow apple trees, and grubbing up some young birches which had sprung up in the pasture, or, in short, had made any more of his improvements. To enjoy these advantages I was ready to carry it on; like Atlas, to take the world on my shoulders,—I never heard what compensation he received for that,—and do all those things which had no other motive or excuse but that I might pay for it and be unmolested in my possession of it; for I knew all the while that it would yield the most abundant crop of the kind I wanted if I could only afford to let it alone. But it turned out as I have said.

All that I could say, then, with respect to farming on a large scale, (I have always cultivated a garden,) was, that I had had my seeds ready. Many think that seeds improve with age. I have no doubt that time discriminates between the good and the bad; and when at last I shall plant, I shall be less likely to be disappointed. But I would say to my fellows, once for all, As long as possible live free and uncommitted. It makes but little difference whether you are committed to a farm or the county jail.

Old Cato, whose "De Re Rusticâ" is my [132/133] "Cultivator," says, and the only translation I have seen makes sheer nonsense of the passage, "When you think of getting a farm turn it thus in your mind, not to buy greedily; nor spare your pains to look at it, and do not think it enough to go round it once. The oftener you go there the more it will please you, if it is good." I think I shall not buy greedily, but go round and round it as long as I live, and be buried in it first, that it may please me the more at last.

The present was my next experiment of this kind, which I purpose to describe more at length, for convenience, putting the experience of two years into one. As I have said, I do not propose to write an ode to dejection, but to brag as lustily as chanticleer in the morning, standing on his roost, if only to wake my neighbors up.

When first I took up my abode in the woods, that is, began to spend my nights as well as days there, which, by accident, was on Independence day, or the fourth of July, 1845, my house was not finished for winter, but was merely a defence against the rain, without plastering or chimney, the walls being of rough weather-stained boards, with [133/134] wide chinks, which made it cool at night. The upright white hewn studs and freshly planed door and window casings gave it a clean and airy look, especially in the morning, when its timbers were saturated with dew, so that I fancied that by noon some sweet gum would exude from them. To my imagination it retained throughout the day more or less of the auroral character, reminding me of a certain house on a mountain which I had visited a year before. This was an airy and unplastered cabin, fit to entertain a travelling god, and where a goddess might trail her garments. The winds which passed over my dwelling were such as sweep over the ridges of mountains, bearing the broken strains, or celestial parts only, of terrestrial music. The morning wind forever blows, the poem of creation is uninterrupted; but few are the ears that hear it. Olympus is but the outside of the earth everywhere.

The only house I had been the owner of before, if I except a boat, was a tent, which I used occasionally when making excursions in the summer, and this is still rolled up in my garret; but the boat, after passing from hand to hand, has gone down the stream of [134/135] time. With this more substantial shelter about me, I had made some progress toward settling in the world. This frame, so slightly clad, was a sort of crystallization around me, and reacted on the builder. It was suggestive somewhat as a picture in outlines. I did not need to go out doors to take the air, for the atmosphere within had lost none of its freshness. It was not so much within doors as behind a door where I sat, even in the rainiest weather. The Harivansa says, "An abode without birds is like a meat without seasoning." Such was not my abode, for I found myself suddenly neighbor to the birds; not by having imprisoned one, but having caged myself near them. I was not only nearer to some of those which commonly frequent the garden and the orchard, but to those wilder and more thrilling song-sters of the forest which never, or rarely, serenade a villager,—the wood-thrush, the veery, the scarlet tanager, the field-sparrow, the whippoorwill, and many others.

I was seated by the shore of a small pond, about a mile and a half south of the village of Concord and somewhat higher than it, in the midst of an extensive wood [135/136] between that town and Lin-coln, and about two miles south of that our only field known to fame, Concord Battle Ground; but I was so low in the woods that the op-posite shore, half a mile off, like the rest, covered with wood, was my most distant horizon. For the first week, whenever I looked out on the pond it impressed me like a tarn high up on the side of a mountain, its bottom far above the surface of other lakes, and, as the sun arose, I saw it throwing off its nightly clothing of mist, and here and there, by degrees, its soft ripples or its smooth reflecting surface was revealed, while the mists, like ghosts, were stealthily withdraw-ing in every direction into the woods, as at the breaking up of some nocturnal conventicle. The very dew seemed to hang upon the trees later into the day than usual, as on the sides of mountains.

This small lake was of most value as a neighbor in the intervals of a gentle rain storm in August, when, both air and water being per-fectly still, but the sky overcast, mid-afternoon had all the serenity of evening, and the wood-thrush sang around, and was heard from shore to shore. A lake like this is never smoother than at such a time; [136/137] and the clear portion of the air above it being shallow and darkened by clouds, the water, full of light and reflections, becomes a lower heaven itself so much the more important. From a hill top near by, where the wood had been recently cut off, there was a pleasing vista southward across the pond, through a wide indentation in the hills which form the shore there, where their opposite sides sloping toward each other suggested a stream flowing out in that direction through a wooded valley, but stream there was none. That way I looked between and over the near green hills to some distant and higher ones in the horizon, tinged with blue. Indeed, by standing on tiptoe I could catch a glimpse of some of the peaks of the still bluer and more distant mountain ranges in the north-west, those true-blue coins from heaven's own mint, and also of some portion of the village. But in other directions, even from this point, I could not see over or beyond the woods which surrounded me. It is well to have some water in your neighborhood, to give buoyancy to and float the earth. One value even of the smallest well is, that when you look into it you see that earth is not continent [137/138] but insular. This is as important as that it keeps butter cool. When I looked across the pond from this peak toward the Sudbury meadows, which in time of flood I distinguished elevated perhaps by a mirage in their seething valley, like a coin in a basin, all the earth beyond the pond appeared like a thin crust insulated and floated even by this small sheet of intervening water, and I was reminded that this on which I dwelt was but *dry land*.

Though the view from my door was still more contracted, I did not feel crowded or confined in the least. There was pasture enough for my imagination. The low shrub-oak plateau to which the opposite shore arose, stretched away toward the prairies of the West and the steppes of Tartary, affording ample room for all the roving families of men. "There are none happy in the world but beings who enjoy freely a vast horizon,"—said Damodara, when his herds required new and larger pastures.

Both place and time were changed, and I dwelt nearer to those parts of the universe and to those eras in history which had most attracted me. Where I lived was as far off as many a region viewed nightly by astronomers. [138/139] We are wont to imagine rare and delectable places in some remote and more celestial corner of the system, behind the constellation of Cassiopeia's Chair, far from noise and disturbance. I discovered that my house actually had its site in such a withdrawn, but forever new and unprofaned, part of the universe. If it were worth the while to settle in those parts near to the Pleiades or the Hyades, to Aldebaran or Altair, then I was really there, or at an equal remoteness from the life which I had left behind, dwindled and twinkling with as fine a ray to my nearest neighbor, and to be seen only in moonless nights by him. Such was that part of creation where I had squatted;—

> "There was a shepherd that did live,
>   And held his thoughts as high
> As were the mounts whereon his flocks
>   Did hourly feed him by."

What should we think of the shepherd's life if his flocks always wandered to higher pastures than his thoughts?

Every morning was a cheerful invitation to make my life of equal simplicity, and I may say innocence, with Nature herself. I have been as sincere a worshipper of Aurora [139/140] as the Greeks. I got up early and bathed in the pond; that was a religious exercise, and one of the best things which I did. They say that characters were engraven on the bathing tub of king Tching-thang to this effect: "Renew thyself completely each day; do it again, and again, and forever again." I can understand that. Morning brings back the heroic ages. I was as much affected by the faint hum of a mosquito making its invisible and unimaginable tour through my apartment at earliest dawn, when I was sitting with door and windows open, as I could be by any trumpet that ever sang of fame. It was Homer's requiem; itself an Iliad and Odyssey in the air, singing its own wrath and wanderings. There was something cosmical about it; a standing advertisement, till forbidden, of the everlasting vigor and fertility of the world. The morning, which is the most memorable season of the day, is the awakening hour. Then there is least somnolence in us; and for an hour, at least, some part of us awakes which slumbers all the rest of the day and night. Little is to be expected of that day, if it can be called a day, to which we are not awakened by our Genius, but by the mechanical [140/141] nudgings of some servitor, are not awakened by our newly-acquired force and aspirations from within, accompanied by the undulations of celestial music, instead of factory bells, and a fragrance filling the air—to a higher life than we fell asleep from; and thus the darkness bear its fruit, and prove itself to be good, no less than the light. That man who does not believe that each day contains an earlier, more sacred, and auroral hour than he has yet profaned, has despaired of life, and is pursuing a descending and darkening way. After a partial cessation of his sensuous life, the soul of man, or its organs rather, are reinvigorated each day, and his Genius tries again what noble life it can make. All memorable events, I should say, transpire in morning time and in a morning atmosphere. The Vedas say, "All intelligences awake with the morning." Poetry and art, and the fairest and most memorable of the actions of men, date from such an hour. All poets and heroes, like Memnon, are the children of Aurora, and emit their music at sunrise. To him whose elastic and vigorous thought keeps pace with the sun, the day is a perpetual morning. It matters not what the clocks say or the attitudes [141/142] and labors of men. Morning is when I am awake and there is a dawn in me. Moral reform is the effort to throw off sleep. Why is it that men give so poor an account of their day if they have not been slumbering? They are not such poor calculators. If they had not been overcome with drowsiness they would have performed something. The millions are awake enough for physical labor; but only one in a million is awake enough for effective intellectual exertion, only one in a hundred millions to a poetic or divine life. To be awake is to be alive. I have never yet met a man who was quite awake. How could I have looked him in the face?

We must learn to reawaken and keep ourselves awake, not by mechanical aids, but by an infinite expectation of the dawn, which does not forsake us in our soundest sleep. I know of no more encouraging fact than the unquestionable ability of man to elevate his life by a conscious endeavor. It is something to be able to paint a particular picture, or to carve a statue, and so to make a few objects beautiful; but it is far more glorious to carve and paint the very atmosphere and medium through which we look, which morally [142/143] we can do. To affect the quality of the day, that is the highest of arts. Every man is tasked to make his life, even in its details, worthy of the contemplation of his most elevated and critical hour. If we refused, or rather used up, such paltry information as we get, the oracles would distinctly inform us how this might be done.

I went to the woods because I wished to live deliberately, to front only the essential facts of life, and see if I could not learn what it had to teach, and not, when I came to die, discover that I had not lived. I did not wish to live what was not life, living is so dear; nor did I wish to practise resignation, unless it was quite necessary. I wanted to live deep and suck out all the marrow of life, to live so sturdily and Spartan-like as to put to rout all that was not life, to cut a broad swath and shave close, to drive life into a corner, and reduce it to its lowest terms, and, if it proved to be mean, why then to get the whole, and genuine meanness of it, and publish its meanness to the world; or if it were sublime, to know it by experience, and be able to give a true account of it in my next excursion. For most men, it appears to me, are in a strange uncertainty [143/144] about it, whether it is of the devil or of God, and have *somewhat hastily* concluded that it is the chief end of man here to "glorify God and enjoy him forever."

Still we live meanly, like ants; though the fable tells us that we were long ago changed into men; like pygmies we fight with cranes; it is error upon error, and clout upon clout, and our best virtue has for its occasion a superfluous and evitable wretchedness. Our life is frittered away by detail. An honest man has hardly need to count more than his ten fingers, or in extreme cases he may add his ten toes, and lump the rest. Simplicity, simplicity, simplicity! I say, let your affairs be as two or three, and not a hundred or a thousand; instead of a million count half a dozen, and keep your accounts on your thumb nail. In the midst of this chopping sea of civilized life, such are the clouds and storms and quicksands and thousand-and-one items to be allowed for, that a man has to live, if he would not founder and go to the bottom and not make his port at all, by dead reckoning, and he must be a great calculator indeed who succeeds. Simplify, simplify. Instead of three meals a day, if it be necessary eat [144/145] but one; instead of a hundred dishes, five; and reduce other things in proportion. Our life is like a German Confederacy, made up of petty states, with its boundary forever fluctuating, so that even a German cannot tell you how it is bounded at any moment. The nation itself, with all its so-called internal improvements, which, by the way are all external and superficial, is just such an unwieldy and overgrown establishment, cluttered with furniture and tripped up by its own traps, ruined by luxury and heedless expense, by want of calculation and a worthy aim, as the million households in the land; and the only cure for it as for them is in a rigid economy, a stern and more than Spartan simplicity of life and elevation of purpose. It lives too fast. Men think that it is essential that the *Nation* have commerce, and export ice, and talk through a telegraph, and ride thirty miles an hour, without a doubt, whether *they* do or not; but whether we should live like baboons or like men, is a little uncertain. If we do not get out sleepers, and forge rails, and devote days and nights to the work, but go to tinkering upon our *lives* to improve *them,* who will build railroads? And if railroads are [145/146] not built, how shall we get to heaven in season? But if we stay at home and mind our business, who will want railroads? We do not ride on the railroad; it rides upon us. Did you ever think what those sleepers are that underlie the railroad? Each one is a man, an Irishman, or a Yankee man. The rails are laid on them, and they are covered with sand, and the cars run smoothly over them. They are sound sleepers, I assure you. And every few years a new lot is laid down and run over; so that, if some have the pleasure of riding on a rail, others have the misfortune to be ridden upon. And when they run over a man that is walking in his sleep, a supernumerary sleeper in the wrong position, and wake him up, they suddenly stop the cars, and make a hue and cry about it, as if this were an exception. I am glad to know that it takes a gang of men for every five miles to keep the sleepers down and level in their beds as it is, for this is a sign that they may sometime get up again.

Why should we live with such hurry and waste of life? We are determined to be starved before we are hungry. Men say that a stitch in time saves nine, and so they [146/147] take a thousand stitches to-day to save nine to-morrow. As for *work*, we haven't any of consequence. We have the Saint Vitus' dance, and cannot possibly keep our heads still. If I should only give a few pulls at the parish bell-rope, as for a fire, that is, without setting the bell, there is hardly a man on his farm in the outskirts of Concord, notwithstanding that press of engagements which was his excuse so many times this morning, nor a boy, nor a woman, I might almost say, but would forsake all and follow that sound, not mainly to save property from the flames, but, if we will confess the truth, much more to see it burn, since burn it must, and we, be it known, did not set it on fire,—or to see it put out, and have a hand in it, if that is done as handsomely; yet, even if it were the parish church itself. Hardly a man takes a half hour's nap after dinner, but when he wakes he holds up his head and asks, "What's the news?" as if the rest of mankind has stood his sentinels. Some give directions to be waked every half hour, doubtless for no other purpose; and then, to pay for it, they tell what they have dreamed. After a night's sleep the news is as indispensable [147/148] as the breakfast. "Pray tell me anything new that has happened to a man anywhere on this globe,"—and he reads it over his coffee and rolls, that a man has had his eyes gouged out this morning on the Wachito River; never dreaming the while that he lives in the dark unfathomed mammoth cave of this world, and has but the rudiment of an eye himself.

For my part, I could easily do without the post-office. I think that there are very few important communications made through it. To speak critically, I never received more one or two letters in my life —I wrote this some years ago—that were worth the postage. The penny-post is, commonly, an institution through which you seriously offer a man that penny for his thoughts which is so often safely offered in jest. And I am sure that I never read any memorable news in a newspaper. If we read of one man robbed, or murdered, or killed by accident, or one house burned, or one vessel wrecked, or one steamboat blown up, or one cow run over on the Western Rail-

road, or one mad dog killed, or one lot of grasshoppers in the winter,—we never need read of another. One is enough. If you are acquainted with [148/149] the principle, what do you care for a myriad
instances and applications? To a philosopher all *news*, as it is called,
is gossip, and they who edit and read it are old women over their
tea. Yet not a few are greedy after this gossip. There was such a
rush, as I hear, the other day at one of the offices to learn the foreign news by the last arrival, that several large squares of plate glass
belonging to the establishment were broken by the pressure,—news
which I seriously think a ready wit might write a twelvemonth or
twelve years beforehand with sufficent accuracy. As for Spain, for
instance, if you know how to throw in Don Carlos and the Infanta,
and Don Pedro and Seville and Granada, from time to time in the
right proportions,—they may have changed the names a little since I
saw the papers,—and serve up a bull-fight when other entertain-
ments fail, it will be true to the letter, and give us as good an idea
of the exact state or ruin of things in Spain as the most succinct and
lucid reports under this head in the newspapers: and as for England, almost the last significant scrap of news from that quarter
was the revolution of 1649; and if you have learned the history of her
crops for an [149/150] average year, you never need attend to that
thing again, unless your speculations are of a merely pecuniary character. If one may judge who rarely looks into the newspapers, nothing new does ever happen in foreign parts, a French revolution not
excepted.

What news! how much more important to know what that is
which was never old! "Kieou-he-yu (great dignitary of the state of
Wei) sent a man to Khoung-tseu to know his news. Khoung-tseu
caused the messenger to be seated near him, and questioned him in
these terms: What is your master doing? The messenger answered
with respect: My master desires to diminish the number of his
faults, but he cannot come to the end of them. The messenger being
gone, the philosopher remarked: What a worthy messenger! What a
worthy messenger!" The preacher, instead of vexing the ears of
drowsy farmers on their day of rest at the end of the week,—for Sunday is the fit conclusion of an ill-spent week, and not the fresh and
brave beginning of a new one,—with this one other draggle-tail of a
sermon, should shout with thundering voice,—"Pause! Avast! Why so
seeming fast, but deadly slow?" [150/151]

Shams and delusions are esteemed for soundest truths, while reality is fabulous. If men would steadily observe realities only, and not
allow themselves to be deluded, life, to compare it with such things
as we know, would be like a fairy tale and the Arabian Nights' En-
tertainments. If we respected only what is inevitable and has a right

to be, music and poetry would resound along the streets. When we are unhurried and wise, we perceive that only great and worthy things have any permanent and absolute existence,—that petty fears and petty pleasures are but the shadow of the reality. This is always exhilarating and sublime. By closing the eyes and slumbering, and consenting to be deceived by shows, men establish and confirm their daily life of routine and habit everywhere, which still is built on purely illusory foundations. Children, who play life, discern its true law and relations more clearly than men, who fail to live it worthily, but who think that they are wiser by experience, that is, by failure. I have read in a Hindoo book, that "there was a king's son, who, being expelled in infancy from his native city, was brought up by a for-ester, and, growing up to maturity in that state, [151/152] imagined himself to belong to the barbarous race with which he lived. One of his father's ministers having discovered him, revealed to him what he was, and the misconception of his character was removed, and he knew himself to be a prince. So soul," continues the Hindoo philoso-pher, "from the circumstances in which it is placed, mistakes its own character, until the truth is revealed to it by some holy teacher, and then it knows itself to be *Brahme*." I perceive that we inhabitants of New England live this mean life that we do because our vision does not penetrate the surface of things. We think that that *is* which *ap-pears* to be. If a man should walk through this town and see only the reality, where, think you, would the "Mill-dam" go to? If he should give us an account of the realities he beheld there, we should not recognize the place in his description. Look at a meeting-house, or a courthouse, or a jail, or a shop, or a dwelling-house, and say what that thing really is before a true gaze, and they would all go to pieces in your account of them. Men esteem truth remote, in the outskirts of the system, behind the farthest star, before Adam and after the last man. In eternity there is indeed [152/153] something true and sublime. But all these times and places and occasions are now and here. God himself culminates in the present moment, and will never be more divine in the lapse of all the ages. And we are enabled to apprehend at all what is sublime and noble only by the perpetual instilling and drenching of the reality that surrounds us. The universe constantly and obediently answers to our conceptions; whether we travel fast or slow, the track is laid for us. Let us spend our lives in conceiving then. The poet or the artist never yet had so fair and noble a design but some of his posterity at least could ac-complish it.

Let us spend one day as deliberately as Nature, and not be thrown off the track by every nutshell and mosquito's wing that falls on the rails. Let us rise early and fast, or break fast, gently and without perturbation; let company come and let company go, let the bells ring and the children cry,—determined to make a day of it. Why should we knock under and go with the stream? Let us not be upset and overwhelmed in that terrible rapid and whirlpool called a dinner, situated in the meridian shallows. Weather this danger and you are safe, for the rest [153/154] of the way is down hill. With unrelaxed nerves, with morning vigor, sail by it, looking another way, tied to the mast like Ulysses. If the engine whistles, let it whistle till it is hoarse for its pains. If the bell rings, why should we run? We will consider what kind of music they are like. Let us settle ourselves, and work and wedge our feet downward through the mud and slush of opinion, and prejudice, and tradition, and delusion, and appearance, that alluvion which covers the globe, through Paris and London, through New York and Boston and Concord, through church and state, through poetry and philosophy and religion, till we come to a hard bottom and rocks in place, which we can call *reality*, and say, This is, and no mistake; and then begin, having a *point d'appui*, below freshet and frost and fire, a place where you might found a wall or a state, or set a lamp-post safely, or perhaps a gauge, not a Nilometer, but a Realometer, that future ages might know how deep a freshet of shams and appearances had gathered from time to time. If you stand right fronting and face to face to a fact, you will see the sun glimmer on both its surfaces, as if it were a cimeter, and feel [154/155] its sweet edge dividing you through the heart and marrow, and so you will happily conclude your mortal career. Be it life or death, we crave only reality. If we are really dying, let us hear the rattle in our throats and feel cold in the extremities; if we are alive, let us go about our business.

Time is but the stream I go a-fishing in. I drink at it; but while I drink I see the sandy bottom and detect how shallow it is. Its thin current slides away, but eternity remains. I would drink deeper; fish in the sky, whose bottom is pebbly with stars. I cannot count one. I know not the first letter of the alphabet. I have always been regretting that I was not as wise as the day I was born. The intellect is a cleaver; it discerns and rifts its way into the secret of things. I do not wish to be any more busy with my hands than is necessary. My head is hands and feet. I feel all my best faculties concentrated in it. My instinct tells me that my head is an organ for burrowing, as some creatures use their snout and fore-paws, and with it I would mine and burrow my way through these hills. I think that the richest vein is somewhere hereabouts; so by the divining rod and thin rising vapors I judge; and here I will begin to mine. [155]

HERMAN MELVILLE

From Moby-Dick

LOOMINGS

CALL ME ISHMAEL. Some years ago—never mind how long precisely—
having little or no money in my purse, and nothing particular to interest me on shore, I thought I would sail about a little and see the
watery part of the world. It is a way I have of driving off the spleen,
and regulating the circulation. Whenever I find myself growing grim
about the mouth; whenever it is a damp, drizzly November in my
soul; whenever I find myself involuntarily pausing before coffin
warehouses, and bringing up the rear of every funeral I meet; and
especially whenever my hypos get such an upper hand of me, that it
requires a strong moral principle to prevent me from deliberately
stepping into the street, and methodically knocking people's hats off
—then, I account it high time to get to sea as soon as I can. This is
my substitute for pistol and ball. With a philosophical flourish Cato
throws himself upon his sword; I quietly take to the ship. There is
nothing surprising in this. If they but knew it, almost all men in
their degree, some time or other, cherish very nearly the same feelings toward the ocean with me.

There now is your insular city of the Manhattoes, belted round by
wharves as Indian isles by coral reefs—commerce surrounds it with
her surf. Right and left, the streets take you waterward. Its extreme
down-town is the battery, where that noble mole is washed by
waves, and [1/2] cooled by breezes, which a few hours previous
were out of sight of land. Look at the crowds of water-gazers there.

Circumambulate the city of a dreamy Sabbath afternoon. Go from
Corlears Hook to Coenties Slip, and from thence, by Whitehall,
northward. What do you see?—Posted like silent sentinels all around
the town, stand thousands upon thousands of mortal men fixed in

From Herman Melville, *Moby-Dick, The Works of Herman Melville,* Standard
Edition (New York: Russell & Russell, 1963), VII, 1–7, 132–33. [Chapters 1
and 23 of *Moby-Dick,* originally published in 1851.]

ocean reveries. Some leaning against the spiles; some seated upon
the pier-heads; some looking over the bulwarks of ships from China;
some high aloft in the rigging, as if striving to get a still better sea-
ward peep. But these are all landsmen; of week days pent up in lath
and plaster—tied to counters, nailed to benches, clinched to desks.
How then is this? Are the green fields gone? What do they here?

But look! here come more crowds, pacing straight for the water,
and seemingly bound for a dive. Strange! Nothing will content them
but the extremest limit of the land; loitering under the shady lee of
yonder warehouses will not suffice. No. They must get just as nigh
the water as they possibly can without falling in. And there they
stand—miles of them—leagues. Inlanders all, they come from lanes
and alleys, streets and avenues—north, east, south, and west. Yet
here they all unite. Tell me, does the magnetic virtue of the needles of
the compasses of all those ships attract them thither?

Once more. Say, you are in the country; in some high land of
lakes. Take almost any path you please, and ten to one it carries you
down in a dale, and leaves you there by a pool in the stream. There
is magic in it. Let the most absent-minded of men be plunged in his
deepest reveries—stand that man on his legs, set his feet a-going,
and he will infallibly lead you to water, if water there be in all that
region. Should you ever be athirst in the great American desert, try
this experiment, if your [2/3] caravan happen to be supplied with a
metaphysical professor. Yes, as everyone knows, meditation and
water are wedded forever.

But here is an artist. He desires to paint you the dreamiest, shad-
iest, quietest, most enchanting bit of romantic landscape in all the
valley of the Saco. What is the chief element he employs? There
stand his trees, each with a hollow trunk, as if a hermit and a crucifix were within; and here sleeps his meadow, and there sleep his cattle; and up from yonder cottage goes a sleepy smoke. Deep into distant woodlands winds a mazy way, reaching to overlapping spurs of
mountains bathed in their hillside blue. But though the picture lies
thus tranced, and though this pine-tree shakes down its sighs like
leaves upon this shepherd's head, yet all were vain, unless the shepherd's eye were fixed upon the magic stream before him. Go visit the
Prairies in June, when for scores on scores of miles you wade knee-
deep among tiger-lilies—what is the one charm wanting?—Water—
there is not a drop of water there! Were Niagara but a cataract of
sand, would you travel your thousand miles to see it? Why did the
poor poet of Tennessee, upon suddenly receiving two handfuls of
silver, deliberate whether to buy him a coat, which he sadly needed,
or invest his money in a pedestrian trip to Rockaway Beach? Why is
almost every robust healthy boy with a robust healthy soul in him,

at some time or other crazy to go to sea? Why upon your first voyage as a passenger, did you yourself feel such a mystical vibration, when first told that you and your ship were now out of sight of land? Why did the old Persians hold the sea holy? Why did the Greeks give it a separate deity, and own brother of Jove? Surely all this is not without meaning. And still deeper the meaning of that story of Narcissus, who because he could not grasp the tormenting, mild [3/4] image he saw in the fountain, plunged into it and was drowned. But that same image, we ourselves see in all rivers and oceans. It is the image of the ungraspable phantom of life; and this is the key to it all.

Now, when I say that I am in the habit of going to sea whenever I begin to grow hazy about the eyes, and begin to be over conscious of my lungs, I do not mean to have it inferred that I ever go to sea as a passenger. For to go as a passenger you must needs have a purse, and a purse is but a rag unless you have something in it. Besides, passengers get sea-sick—grow quarrelsome—don't sleep of nights—do not enjoy themselves much, as a general thing;—no, I never go as a passenger; nor, though I am something of a salt, do I ever go to sea as a Commodore, or a Captain, or a Cook. I abandon the glory and distinction of such offices to those who like them. For my part, I abominate all honourable respectable toils, trials, and tribulations of every kind whatsoever. It is quite as much as I can do to take care of myself without taking care of ships, barques, brigs, schooners, and what not. And as for going as cook,—though I confess there is considerable glory in that, a cook being a sort of officer on shipboard—yet, somehow, I never fancied broiling fowls;— though once broiled, judiciously buttered, and judgmatically salted and peppered, there is no one who will speak more respectfully, not to say reverentially, of a broiled fowl than I will. It is out of the idolatrous dotings of the old Egyptians upon broiled ibis and roasted river horse, that you see the mummies of those creatures in their huge bake-houses the pyramids.

No, when I go to sea, I go as a simple sailor, right before the mast, plumb down into the forecastle, aloft there to the royal masthead. True, they rather order me about some, and make me jump from spar to spar, [4/5] like a grasshopper in a May meadow. And at first, this sort of thing is unpleasant enough. It touches one's sense of honor, particularly if you come of an old established family in the land, the Van Rensselaers, or Randolphs, or Hardicanutes. And more than all, if just previous to putting your hand into the tar-pot, you have been lording it as a country schoolmaster, making the tallest boys stand in awe of you. The transition is a keen one, I assure you, from a schoolmaster to a sailor, and requires a strong decoction of Seneca and the Stoics to enable you to grin and bear it. But even this wears off in time.

What of it, if some old hunks of a sea-captain orders me to get a broom and sweep down the decks? What does that indignity amount to, weighed, I mean, in the scales of the New Testament? Do you think the archangel Gabriel thinks anything the less of me, because I promptly and respectfully obey the old hunks in that particular instance? Who ain't a slave? Tell me that. Well, then, however the old sea-captains may order me about—however they may thump and punch me about, I have the satisfaction of knowing that it is all right; that everybody else is one way or other served in much the same way—either in a physical or metaphysical point of view, that is; and so the universal thump is passed round, and all hands should rub each other's shoulder-blades, and be content.

Again, I always go to sea as a sailor, because they make a point of paying me for my trouble, whereas they never pay passengers a single penny that I ever heard of. On the contrary, passengers themselves must pay. And there is all the difference in the world between paying and being paid. The act of paying is perhaps the most uncomfortable infliction that the two orchard thieves entailed upon us. But *being paid*,—what will compare [5/6] with it? The urbane activity with which a man receives money is really marvellous, considering that we so earnestly believe money to be the root of all earthly ills, and that on no account can a monied man enter heaven. Ah! how cheerfully we consign ourselves to perdition!

Finally, I always go to sea as a sailor, because of the wholesome exercise and pure air of the forecastle deck. For as in this world, head-winds are far more prevalent than winds from astern (that is, if you never violate the Pythagorean maxim), so for the most part the commodore on the quarter-deck gets his atmosphere at second hand from the sailors on the forecastle. He thinks he breathes it first; but not so. In much the same way do the commonalty lead their leaders in many other things, at the same time that the leaders little suspect it. But wherefore it was that after having repeatedly smelt the sea as a merchant sailor, I should now take it into my head to go on a whaling voyage; this the invisible police-officer of the Fates, who has the constant surveillance of me, and secretly dogs me, and influences me in some unaccountable way—he can better answer than any one else. And, doubtless, my going on this whaling voyage formed part of the grand programme of Providence that was drawn up a long time ago. It came in as a sort of brief interlude and solo between more extensive performances. I take it that this part of the bill must have run something like this:—

*'Grand Contested Election for the Presidency of the
United States.*
'WHALING VOYAGE BY ONE ISHMAEL.
'BLOODY BATTLE IN AFGHANISTAN.'

Though I cannot tell why it was exactly that those stage managers, the Fates, put me down for this shabby [6/7] part of a whaling
voyage, when others were set down for magnificent parts in high
tragedies, and short and easy parts in genteel comedies, and jolly
parts in farces—though I cannot tell why this was exactly; yet, now
that I recall all the circumstances, I think I can see a little into the
springs and motives which, being cunningly presented to me under
various disguises, induced me to set about performing the part I did,
besides cajoling me into the delusion that it was a choice resulting
from my own unbiased freewill and discriminating judgment.

Chief among these motives was the overwhelming idea of the
great whale himself. Such a portentous and mysterious monster
roused all my curiosity. Then the wild and distant seas where he
rolled his island bulk; the undeliverable, nameless perils of the
whale; these, with all the attending marvels of a thousand Patago-
nian sights and sounds, helped to sway me to my wish. With other
men, perhaps, such things would not have been inducements; but as
for me, I am tormented with an everlasting itch for things remote. I
love to sail forbidden seas, and land on barbarous coasts. Not ignoring what is good, I am quick to perceive a horror, and could still be
social with it—would they let me—since it is but well to be on
friendly terms with all the inmates of the place one lodges in.

By reason of these things, then, the whaling voyage was welcome;
the great flood-gates of the wonder-world swung open, and in the
wild conceits that swayed me to my purpose, two and two there
floated into my inmost soul, endless processions of the whale, and,
midmost of them all, one grand hooded phantom, like a snow hill in
the air. [7]

THE LEE SHORE

Some chapters back, one Bulkington was spoken of, a tall, new-
landed mariner, encountered in New Bedford at the inn.

When on that shivering winter's night the *Pequod* thrust her vindictive bows into the cold malicious waves, who should I see standing at her helm but Bulkington! I looked with sympathetic awe and
fearfulness upon the man, who in mid-winter just landed from a four

years' dangerous voyage, could so unrestingly push off again for still another tempestuous term. The land seemed scorching to his feet. Wonderfullest things are ever the unmentionable; deep memories yield no epitaphs; this six-inch chapter is the stoneless grave of Bulkington. Let me only say that it fared with him as with the storm-tossed ship, that miserably drives along the leeward land. The port would fain give succour; the port is pitiful; in the port is safety, comfort, hearthstone, supper, warm blankets, friends, all that's kind to our mortalities. But in that gale, the port, the land, is that ship's direst jeopardy; she must fly all hospitality; one touch of land, though it but graze the keel, would make her shudder through and through. With all her might she crowds all sail off shore; in so doing, fights 'gainst the very winds that fain would blow her homeward; seeks all the lashed sea's landlessness again; for refuge's sake forlornly rushing into peril; her only friend her bitterest foe!

Know ye, now, Bulkington? Glimpses do ye seem to [132/133] see of that mortally intolerable truth; that all deep, earnest thinking is but the intrepid effort of the soul to keep the open independence of her sea; while the wildest winds of heaven and earth conspire to cast her on the treacherous, slavish shore?

But as in landlessness alone resides the highest truth, shoreless, indefinite as God—so, better is it to perish in that howling infinite, than be ingloriously dashed upon the lee, even if that were safety! For worm-like, then, oh! who would craven crawl to land! Terrors of the terrible! is all this agony so vain? Take heart, take heart, O Bulkington! Bear thee grimly, demigod! Up from the spray of thy ocean-perishing—straight up, leaps thy apotheosis! [133]

EMILY DICKINSON

—◆—

Three Poems

Much madness is divinest sense
To a discerning eye;
Much sense the starkest madness. [7/8]
'Tis the majority
In this, as all, prevails.
Assent, and you are sane;
Demur,—you're straightway dangerous,
And handled with a chain. [8]

The soul selects her own society,
Then shuts the door;
On her divine majority
Obtrude no more.

Unmoved, she notes the chariot's pausing
At her low gate;
Unmoved, an emperor is kneeling
Upon her mat.

I've known her from an ample nation
Choose one;
Then close the valves of her attention
Like stone. [8]

From *Poems by Emily Dickinson*, ed. Martha Dickinson Bianchi and Alfred Leete Hampson (Boston: Little, Brown and Company, 1937), pp. 7–8, 95.

Some keep the Sabbath going to church;
I keep it staying at home,
With a bobolink for a chorister,
And an orchard for a dome.

Some keep the Sabbath in surplice;
I just wear my wings,
And instead of tolling the bell for church,
Our little sexton sings.

God preaches,—a noted clergyman,—
And the sermon is never long;
So instead of getting to heaven at last,
I'm going all along! [95]

MALCOLM COWLEY

Echoes of a Suicide

1: LETTER LEFT ON A DRESSING TABLE

HARRY CROSBY and his wife arrived in New York during the first week of December 1929 and Hart Crane gave a party for them in his room on Brooklyn Heights. It was a good party, too; Harry smiled a lot—you remembered his very white teeth—and had easy manners and, without talking a great deal, he charmed everyone. On the afternoon of December 10 he borrowed the keys to a friend's studio in the Hotel des Artistes. When he failed to answer the telephone or the doorbell that evening, the friend had the door broken down and found Harry's body with that of a young society woman, Mrs. Josephine Bigelow.

The double suicide was a front-page story, but the newspapers could find no reason for it and the police had no explanation to offer. Harry was young, just six months past his thirty-first birthday; he was rich, happily married and, except for a slight infection of the throat, in the best of health. All the usual motives were lacking. He had lost a little money in the stock market but did not brood about it; he had love affairs but spoke of breaking them off; he was not dissatisfied with his progress as a poet and a publisher. Nor did he suffer from any sense of [246/247] inferiority: people had always liked him, all his life had moved in pleasant ways; and he lay there now beside a dead woman in a borrowed studio.

He left behind him no letter, not even a final scrawl.

This deliberate silence seemed strange to the police. They knew that suicides usually give some explanation, often in the shape of a long document addressed to wife, mother or husband, insisting that they had done the wisest thing, justifying themselves before and accusing society. Poets in particular, among whom suicide is almost an

From Malcolm Cowley, "Echoes of a Suicide," *Exile's Return: A Literary Odyssey of the 1920's* (New York: The Viking Press, 1951), pp. 246–53, 255–62, 265–72. [A revision of the 1934 original edition.]

occupational disease, are likely to write final messages to the world
that neglected them. They insist on this last word—and if Harry
Crosby left none, he must have believed that his message was already written.

He had been keeping a diary—later published in three volumes by
the Black Sun Press in Paris—and, in effect, it takes the place of a
letter slipped into the frame of the mirror or left on the dressing
table under a jar of cold cream. It does not explain the immediate
occasion, does not tell why he chose to die on that particular afternoon after keeping a rendezvous and sharing a bottle of Scotch
whisky. But the real causes of his deed can be clearly deciphered
from this record of things done, books read and ideas seized upon
for guidance.

And something more can be deciphered there. It happens that his
brief and not particularly distinguished literary life of seven years
included practically all the themes I have been trying to develop—
the separation from home, the effects of service in the ambulance
corps, the exile in France, then other themes, bohemianism, the religion of art, the escape from society, the effort to defend one's individuality even at the cost of sterility and madness, then the final period of demoralization when the whole philosophical structure crum-
bled from within, just at the moment when bourgeois society was
beginning to crumble after its greatest outpouring of luxuries, its
longest debauch—all this [247/248] is suggested in Harry Crosby's life
and is rendered fairly explicit in his diary. But it is not my only reason for writing about him. Harry was wealthier than the other pure
poets and refugees of art: he had means and leisure to carry his
ideas to their conclusion while most of the others were being turned
aside, partly by the homely skepticism that is instilled into the middle classes and partly by the daily business of earning a living. He
was not more talented than his associates, but he was more single-
minded, more literal, and was not held back by the fear of death or
ridicule from carrying his principles to their extremes. As a result,
his life had the quality of a logical structure. His suicide was the last
term of a syllogism; it was like the signature to a second-rate but honest and exciting poem.

But there is one question raised by his life that his diary doesn't
answer. How did he first become entangled in the chain of events and
ambitions that ended in the Hotel des Artistes? His background
seemed to promise an entirely different career.

Henry Grew Crosby was born in Boston on June 4, 1898; his parents lived toward the lower end of Beacon Street. His father, Stephen Van Rensselaer Crosby, was a banker; his mother, born Hen-
rietta Grew, was the sister of Mrs. J. Pierpont Morgan. Harry at-

tended St.Mark's, an Episcopalian preparatory school, where, being
too light for football, he ran on the cross-country team. He graduated
in June 1917. With several of his classmates he immediately volunteered for the American Ambulance Service in France. . . . Boys
with this background had an easy path to follow. St. Mark's was
popularly supposed to lead, after four years at Harvard, to Kid-
der, Peabody and Company, the Boston bankers (just as Groton
School led to Lee, Higginson). Then, after a proper apprenticeship,
the young man moved on to New York, where his parents bought
him a seat on the Stock Exchange; he might end as a Morgan partner. Alternatively, [248/249] he might study law and become the at-
torney for a big public utility; or he might enter the diplomatic service and rise to an ambassadorship, like Harry's cousin Joseph
Grew; or he might retire at the age of thirty-five and live on his in-
come and buy pictures. The American high bourgeoisie takes care of
its sons, provided only that they make a proper marriage and don't
drink too much. What was it that turned Harry aside from the
smooth road in front of him?

I think the answer lies in what happened to him during the war,
and particularly in one brief experience to which he alludes several
times in his diary, but without explaining it fully. The whole story is
told in his war letters, privately printed by his parents—incidentally
they are exactly like the war letters of fifty other nice American boys
of good families which were printed in the same pious fashion. On
November 22, 1917, Harry was at a dressing station in the hills near
Verdun. While he was waiting to drive an ambulance full of
wounded men to the field hospital at Bras, a shell burst in the road;
the boy standing next to him was seriously wounded. Harry helped
to put him into the ambulance and drove back toward Bras through
a German barrage. There was one especially bad moment when the
road was blocked by a stalled truck and Harry had to wait for minute after minute while shells rained down on either side of the road.

> The hills of Verdun [he noted in his diary on the tenth anniversary
> of the adventure] and the red sun setting back of the hills and the
> charred skeletons of trees and the river Meuse and the black shells
> spouting up in columns along the road to Bras and the thunder of the
> barrage and the wounded and the ride through red explosions and the
> violent metamorphose from boy into man.

There was indeed a violent metamorphosis, but not from boy into
man: rather, it was from life into death. What really happened
[249/250] was that Harry died in those endless moments when he
was waiting for the road to be cleared. In his heart he felt that he

belonged with his good friends Aaron Davis Weld and Oliver Ames, Jr., both killed in action. Bodily he survived, and with a keener appetite for pleasure, but only to find that something was dead inside him—his boyhood, Boston, St. Mark's, the Myopia Hunt, a respectable marriage, an assured future as a banker, everything that was supposed to lead him toward a responsible place in the world.

At first he didn't realize what had happened. He went back to Boston after the war and tried to resume his old life. He entered Harvard in the fall of 1919; he made the cross-country squad and was almost automatically elected to the societies, waiting clubs and final clubs which a young man of good family was supposed to join—Institute of 1770, D.K.E., Hasty Pudding, S. K. Club, A. D. Club. But he wasn't much interested, he wasn't a nice boy any longer, and after two years he seized the opportunity of being graduated with a wartime degree, *honoris causa*. Under protest, he took a position in a bank, but stayed away from it as much as possible and drank enough to insure himself against the danger of being promoted. He read, he fell in love, he gambled, and on January 1, 1922, he began his diary.

"New York," the first brief entry reads, "New York and all day in bed all arms around while the snow falls silently outside and all night on the train alone to Boston." He went back to this abhorrent desk—then, on February 7, "Mamma gave me a hundred dollars for going a month without drinking. Wasn't worth it." On March 12, "Have not been to the Bank for five days." On March 14, "Resigned from the Bank," and on March 21:

> Mamma has secured for me a position in the Bank in Paris. Happier —One of my wild days where I threw all care to the wind [250/251] and drank to excess with 405—Result of being happier. At midnight drove old Walrus's new automobile down the Arlington Street subway until we crashed slap-bang into an iron fence. A shower of broken glass, a crushed radiator, a bent axle, but no one hurt. Still another episode to add to my rotten reputation.

Shadows of the Sun—the title under which the diary was published—is better than these early notes suggest, but it won't ever be ranked as one of the great autobiographies. Such works have usually been distinguished either by the author's outward observation of people or else by his ability to look inward into his heart. Harry Crosby looked hard in neither direction. Like so many other poets of our age he was self-centered without being at all introspective, and was devoted to his friends without being sympathetic—he did not feel with people or feel into them. The figures that recur in his diary—Joyce, D. H. Lawrence, Hart Crane, Archibald MacLeish, Caresse (his wife), his parents, the Fire Princess, the Sorceress, E. E. Cummings, Kay Boyle—all remain as wooden as marionettes: they *do* things, they move their arms, raise glasses to their lips, utter judgments about one another, but you cannot see the motives behind the actions and the words. Rather than the people, it is the background that finally comes alive.

But this rule has one exception. Harry Crosby himself, though at first he seems as mechanical as the other figures presented in his story, ends in an unexpected fashion by impressing his personality upon you and half-winning your affection. You begin with the conviction that he was a bad poet, a man who dramatized himself, and most of all a fool. Without ever abandoning these ideas you gradually revise them, and are glad to admit that he was an appealing fool, a gallant fool, a brave, candid, single-minded and fanatically generous fool who bore nobody malice. His was not a weakling. Indeed, you come to feel that [251/252] his strength was what killed him: a weaker man would have been prudent enough to survive. He had gifts that would have made him an explorer, a soldier of fortune, a revolutionist: they were qualities fatal to a poet.

Yet even in this profession where he didn't belong, he wasn't altogether a failure. It is true that his early poems were naïve, awkward, false, unspeakably flat; it is true that he never acquired, even at the end, a sense of the value of words. But he was beginning to develop something else, a quality of speed, intensity, crazy vigor—and a poem need not have all the virtues to survive; sometimes one virtue is enough. As for his diary, I think there is no doubt that it will continue to be read by those lucky enough to get hold of it. It isn't a great autobiography, no, but it is a valuable record of behavior and a great source document for the manners of the age that was ours.

And it is something else besides, an interesting story. It tells how a young man from Back Bay adjusted himself to another world—how he got married, went to Paris and threw up his job in an American bank there—how he traveled through southern Europe and northern Africa, observing the landscapes, if not the people, with a sure eye —how he lived in an old mill near Paris and entertained everybody, poets, Russian refugees, hopheads, pederasts, artists and princes royal —how he returned to New York, lived too feverishly, became completely demoralized. . . . But it is not the mere story of his life with which we are concerned. Let us see what his problems were, and how he tried to solve them, and how the answers that he found led him inevitably toward one conclusion. [252/253]

2: CITY OF THE SUN

His boyhood and its easy aspirations being dead within him, Harry Crosby was left after the war with nothing to live for and no desires except an immoderate thirst for enjoyment, the sort of thirst that parches young men when they feel that any sip of pleasure may be their last. But his boyhood life, though dead, had not been buried. He was like a blackboard from which something had been partly erased: the old words had to be wiped clean before new ones could be written; all that Boston implied had to be eradicated. Then, too, he had to find a new home to take the place of the one he was bent on losing. His war experience had to be integrated into his life after the war. . . . Problems like these were difficult, but they could be solved *ambulando*, as he went along. His really urgent problem was to find immediately a new ideal, a reason for living.

He tried to find it in books. In the midst of banking, lovemaking and drinking, he read devotedly, with the sense of new vistas opening out before him. And almost all the books he admired were those belonging to the Symbolist tradition and to what I have called the religion of art. . . . [253/255]

Gradually out of his favorite books the materials for a new ideal of life were being assembled: he wrote that he was beginning "to lay the foundation for my castle of philosophy (not to be confounded with my inner or *inmost* (to be exact) Castle of Beauty)":

> Life is pathetic, futile save for the development of the soul; memories, passionate memories are the utmost gold; poetry is religion (for me); silence invariably has her compensation; thought-control is a necessity (but is disloyal in affairs of love); simplicity is strengthening (the strength of the Sun); fanatic faith in the Sun is essential (for the utmost Castle of Beauty).

Outside the ivory walls of this castle was a landscape devastated as if by a hostile army. "Machinery has stamped its heel of ugliness upon the unromantic world." America in particular was pustulant with "civic federations . . . boy-scout clubs . . . educational toys and its Y.M.C.A. and its congregational baptist churches and all this smug self-satisfaction. Horribly bleak, horribly depressing."—"This damn country" seemed to be run for children and "smelt, stank rather, of bananas and Coca Cola and ice cream." Even Europe was falling before the invader. "Industrialism is triumphant and ugliness, sordid ugliness, is everywhere destroying beauty, which has fled to

the museums (dead) or into the dark forests of the soul (alive)."
The only safety lay in strengthening one's defenses. "The gorgeous
flame of poetry is the moat and beyond, the monstrous (and men-
struous) world, the world that must be continually beaten back, the
world that is always laying siege to the castle of the soul."

Whatever happened in the outside world (with the exception
[255/256] of a few heroic and individual feats, like Lindbergh's flight
and Alain Gerbault's voyage in an open boat) was absolutely without interest to the soul inside its castle. Harry didn't even read newspapers (sometimes he glanced at *Paris-Sport* to learn the racing results). He was "bored by politics (full of sound and signifying nothing)." So strong were his defenses that not only machinery and mediocrity but also the commonest human emotions were barred out.
No living impulse, no creative force, could cross his moat of fire. In
his safe donjon where the larders were stocked with golden memories and bank dividends, he threatened to be transformed into something not so much superhuman as dehumanized. . . . [256/257] . . .
The religion of art was not without having its political sequels.

It also had its sequels in action: of this there can be no doubt
whatever. Long ago, in the course of the prolonged debate about
life and literature and censorship, it used to be said that art and
morality existed in different worlds, that nobody was ever improved
or corrupted by reading a book. But Harry advanced a different
idea in a bad sonnet to Baudelaire:

> Within my soul you've set your blackest flag
> And made my disillusioned heart your tomb,
> My mind which once was young and virginal
> Is now a swamp, a spleenfilled pregnant womb.

His disillusioned heart and spleen-filled mind were delighted with
The Picture of Dorian Gray, which he read for a second time. He
particularly enjoyed

> . . . its sparkling cynicism, its color idealism and its undercurrent of
> dangerous philosophy. . . . "Every impulse that we strive to strangle
> broods in the mind and poisons us. The body sins once and is done
> with its sin, for action is a mode of purification. . . . The only way to
> get rid of a temptation is to yield to it" (tempest of applause).

This was written on July 19, 1924. On July 21 came the sequel:

> The sun is streaming through the bedroom window, it is eleven
> o'clock and I know by my dirty hands, by the torn banknotes on the
> dressing table, by the clothes and matches and small change scattered

over the floor that last night I was drunk. . . . This the result of reading Wilde. Blanche. Rhymes with Avalanche. [257/258]

His reading of Baudelaire and Wilde was of course not the only or the principal cause of his wining and wenching and gambling for high stakes: the war had already given him a taste for strong pleasures. What his reading did was to supply him with moral justification for a course he might have followed in any case. It also supplied him with maxims: Live dangerously! Seize the day! Be in all things extravagant! Money troubles are never fatal, *une plaie d'argent ne tue jamais* (not even when starving? Harry wondered, but put his doubts aside). Finally his reading supplied him with a goal to be attained by debauches—ecstasy! "The human soul belongs to the spiritual world and is ever seeking to be reunited to its source (the Sun). Such union is hindered by the bodily senses, but though not permanently attainable until death, it can be enjoyed at times in the state called ecstasy when the veil of sensual perception is rent asunder and the soul is merged in God (in the Sun)." Stimulants were an aid in achieving that condition: alcohol, hashish, love and opium were successive rites that led toward a vast upsoaring of the spirit; they served as a Eucharist.

Such was the religion of art, not as it was found at its best in the books of a great writer like Joyce or Valéry or Proust, but as it existed more typically in the mind of a young man home from the war, whose education had been interrupted and whose talent was for action rather than contemplation. Even to Harry Crosby, it was not entirely harmful: it gave him a sort of discipline in his debaucheries; it even ended by teaching him to write. But it prevented his interests from expanding, his life from broadening out; it protected him from any new, reinvigorating currents that might have come to him from any other social classes than his own tired class; it condemned him to move in only one direction, toward greater intensity, isolation, frenzy, and finally toward madness. For that, too, was imposed on him by the religion of art. "I believe," he wrote in the midst of a short [258/259] credo, "in the half-sane half-insane madness and illuminism of the seer." He quoted from Symons and from a résumé of Schopenhauer: "Social rules are made by normal people for normal people, and the man of genius is fundamentally abnormal."—"The direct connection of madness and genius is established by the biographies of great men, such as Rousseau, Byron, Poe, etc. Yet in these semi-madmen, these geniuses, lies the true aristocracy of mankind."—"Applause," he added, "of Suns crashing against Suns." He had set himself the goal of going crazy in order to become a genius. He was the boy apprenticed to a lunatic. . . . [259/260]

In the search for that fatherland where everything was best, he traveled through Brittany, the Basque coast, Italy and Spain. At Biskra, on the northern edge of the African desert, it seemed to him that he had finally escaped from ugliness and industrialism:

> There are Arabs coming into town on diminutive donkeys (not coming into town in diminutive Fords) and there is a tiny Tofla tending her goats in a deserted palm garden and there are crumbling walls and sun-baked houses and a certain sluggishness and it never [260/261] rains and the sun gives health and all one needs are dried dates and bread and coffee (and of course hashish) and a straw mat in a bare room of stone ("a man's wealth should be estimated by what he can do without") and we walk to the Café Maure and smoke hashish (to the amusement of the *indigènes*) and we see the village sheik in a black and white burnous and a little Negress *accroupie* in his path (no self-consciousness here). . . .

That evening Harry and Caresse went to a house opening off a dark alleyway to watch a little naked Arab girl do a *danse du ventre:*

> . . . little Zora removing layer after layer of the most voluminous garments, the last piece being a pair of vast cotton drawers such as clowns wear, and which was gathered about her slender waist by a huge halyard. Then she begins to dance, slowness at first with curious rhythms of her ventre and then convulsive shiverings (two matchless breasts like succulent fruit) and wilder the music and more serpentine her rhythms and her head moves forward and backward and her body weaves an invitation and we went home to the hotel and O God when shall we ever cast off the chains of New England?

The following morning he wrote, "And the chains of New England are broken and unbroken—the death of conscience is not the death of self-consciousness." Biskra had not produced the desired effect. Eight days later he was back in Paris—"Paris, and all other lands and cities dwindle into Nothingness. Paris the City of the Sun."

Here, he decided, he would spend his days; this Sun-City would be his spiritual home. In June he faithfully attended the races; in August he went driving off to Deauville to play baccarat and bask on the beach; in October, his favorite month, there was racing again near Paris; there were visits to booksellers and picture galleries, and long exhilarating walks in the Bois, and [261/262] friends in for cocktails— he was entering into the life of the city and meeting not only exiles like himself, young writers like Hemingway, MacLeish, Kay Boyle and Hart Crane, but also French artists and noblemen. As the years passed by he saw less often the little stone farmhouse near Annisquam and heard less often "the sound of the Fog Horn booming through the Fog"; there was nothing to remind him of his dead boyhood. Yet he was beginning again to be restless and dissatisfied. . . . [262/265]

This was the world and the city that Harry Crosby had chosen for home. He never quite belonged to it. He too was marked for death, but he was not yet a thing of bones and paper; he had too much sinew not to grow tired of his fellow townsmen. Toward the end, a note of fatigue and disgust with Paris began to creep into his diary; he was beginning to be irritated by the people always crowding about him. "Really the stupidity of the French is beyond imagination."—"And I hate the English Jesus how I hate the English so damn bourgeois and banal."—"I like New York much better than Paris." It was becoming evident that the home he had so joyously chosen, after destroying the traces of his boyhood, was not to be his home after all. Perhaps he could find a new home in New York. Or else, if that failed him—[265/266]

He had meanwhile still another problem to solve. In addition to a way of living and a home that had served him temporarily, he needed also a faith and a ritual. Poetry in itself was not enough: he wanted something beyond it, a transcendent symbol he could celebrate and adore.

The symbol he chose for himself was the Sun.

I don't know how he came to make this choice. He may have done so arbitrarily, during his boyhood; in any case he already regarded himself as a sun-worshiper before beginning his diary. He tried from the beginning to dignify his faith by finding historical parallels, and was delighted to learn that the Peruvians, the Persians, the Egyptians and many other ancient peoples had also worshiped the sun; he memorized the names of their sun-gods and adopted some of their rituals. In those religions, however, the sun had usually represented a principle of fertility; it was what caused the wheat and maize to grow and thus preserved and symbolized the life of the tribe or nation. Harry's sun-worship was something different, a wholly individual matter, a bloodless, dehumanized religion without community or fraternity or purpose. Yet he fanatically clung to it and, at least toward the end, believed in it sincerely.

It seems to have stood for many different things. Sometimes it was nature-worship—"I am a mystic and religion is not a question of sermons and churches but rather it is an understanding of the infinite through nature (Sun, Moon and Stars)." Sometimes it seemed to be light-worship. Sometimes it was plainly self-worship, Harry himself becoming a sun-symbol—"Today read in Schopenhauer that the center of gravity (for me the Sun) should fall entirely and absolutely within oneself." It was often body-worship—one of the rites that Harry invented for himself was sun-bathing, preferably on top of a tower, until his whole body was "sunnygolden" and until he "exploded into the Sun." Still oftener it was sex-worship—"My soul today is a young phallus [266/267] thrusting upwards to possess the young goddess of the Sun." He gave sun-names to the women he loved, so that his union with them symbolized a union with the sun itself.

His faith was also a refuge from ugliness and industrialism—"I belive in the Sun because the Sun is the only thing in life that does not disillusion."

But his transcendent symbol was something else besides, something that wasn't clear in his own mind but stands forth unmistakably to the reader of his diary. Because the Sun was at the center of his life—because the center of his life was empty, no living impulse being able to cross the moat of fire with which he had surrounded himself, and because, ever since that day at Verdun, death ruled as master in his inmost castle—because of all this, and by a simple process of transference, the sun became a cold abyss, a black sun, a gulf of death into which he would some day hurl himself ecstatically, down, down, downwards, falling "into the Red-Gold (night) of the Sun . . . SUNFIRE!" His worship of the Sun became the expectation of, the strained desire for, "a Sun-Death into Sun."

The truly extraordinary feature of Harry Crosby's life, the quality that gave it logic and made it resemble a clear syllogism, was the fashion in which all the different strands of it were woven together into the single conception of a sun-death.

Take the first strand of all: take the war. Harry often mentions it in his diary; he dwells on it with a horrified fascination that becomes almost love. Yet he never mentions the historical causes or results of it, never seems to regard it as a struggle among nations for survival and among industries for markets. To him it was a blind, splendid catastrophe that meant only one thing, death. It was kept fresh in his mind by symbols like his dead friends, his nearly fatal adventure at Verdun, the Unknown Soldier, the military graveyards, always by corpses—and since these [267/268] deaths were fine and courageous, were good deaths, the war itself was good.

Here are a few of his reflections on it:

February 1, 1925.—Above all, we who have known war must never forget war. And that is why I have the picture of a soldier's corpse nailed to door of my library.

November 22, 1925.—All day in the streets the hawkers hawk their wares . . . and at night in a glass of brandy a toast in honor of the day (the day of the barrage at Verdun, the day S was wounded).

There will always be war.

November 11, 1927.—Armistice Day day that for me is the most significant day of the year ... before going to bed I smoked my pipe and drank two glasses of brandy, To Oliver Ames Junior (killed in action) to Aaron Davis Weld (killed in action).

One Fourth of July in Paris, he attended the unveiling of a statue to Alan Seeger and heard the reading of his "Rendezvous with Death":

At the end, to the triumphant sound of trumpets, troops at attention defiled past the grandstand: Foch, Pétain, Joffre, Mangin, Poincaré, Millerand and our uninspiring Ambassador. Very impressive, very significant, as all such things are to those who went to war. Stood with the small contingent of members of the Field Service, and afterwards we were invited to the Elysée Palace to meet Millerand and Mangin (how the poilus used to shake their fists at him and call him *le Boucher*).

This comment is, in Harry's own words, "very impressive, very significant." He had more or less consciously taken the side [268/269] of Mangin the Butcher against the common soldiers whose lives were wasted at Mangin's orders, whose bodies were melted down into the row of medals that Mangin wore on his left breast. He had taken the side of death against life; now he was preparing to act upon his choice. By committing suicide, he was rejoining his dead friends, his only true friends, and was fulfilling the destiny marked out for him at Verdun.

But just as his war service led him toward this end, so too did his study of the Symbolist poets and philosophers; they were still his guides. Out of his reading came the idea that the achievement of individuality was the purpose to seek above all others—the highest expression of the self was in the act of self-annihilation. Out of his reading came the idea that ecstasy was to be attained at any price—death was the last ecstasy. Out of his reading he learned to admire and seek madness—what could be crazier than killing oneself?—and learned that life itself might be transformed into a work of art rising to a splendid climax—"to die at the right time." His suicide would be the last debauch, the final extravagance, the boldest act of sex, the supreme gesture of defiance to the world he despised.

He had been seeking a home without really finding it. Death was his permanent home.

Even the religion of his boyhood resumed a place in his life when he learned that the birthday and high feast of Christianity was really the winter solstice, the birthday of the sun, and reflected that

Jesus Christ, in a sense, had committed suicide. In the pursuit of death, all the strands united, aphelion and perihelion, boyhood and manhood, Boston and Paris, peace and war—all his conflicts were resolved. For the first time Harry Crosby became fully integrated, self-sufficient, complete.

During the summer of 1928 he spent a month at the Lido. All afternoon he would swim or lie basking in the sun among the [269/270] almost naked pretty girls; at night he danced or drank champagne or read. His reading, like his dissipation, had now acquired a purpose; all of it pointed in one direction, thus:

> July 2.—A reading about Van Gogh and the delirium of his vision . . . Van Gogh the example of triumphant individuality Van Gogh the painter of suns the painter of that Sun which consumed him and which was responsible for his final madness and suicide. A Sun-Death into Sun!
>
> July 6.—Tonight in Nietzsche I read a significant passage: "Die at the right time." Die at the right time, so teacheth Zarathustra and again the direct 31–10–42. Clickety-click clickety-click the express train into Sun.

It must have been during the same exalted month that he wrote a prose poem, "Hail: Death!" which was published in the September 1928 issue of *transition:*

> Take Cleopatra! Take the Saints and Martyrs! . . . Take Nietzsche: "Die at the right time," no matter where you are, in the depths of the coal pit, in the crowded streets of the city, among the dunes of the desert, in cocktail bars, or in the perfumed corridors of the Ritz, at the right time, when your entire life, when your soul and your body, your spirit and your senses are concentrated, are reduced to a pinpoint, the ultimate gold point, the point of finality, irrevocable as the sun, sun-point, then is the time, and not until then, and not after then (O horrors of anti-climax from which there is no recovering!) for us to penetrate into the cavern of the somber Slave-Girl of Death . . . in order to be reborn, in order to become what you wish to become, tree or flower or star or sun, or even dust and nothingness, for it is stronger to founder in the Black Sea of Nothingness, like a ship going down with flags, than to crawl like a Maldoror into the malodorous whorehouse of evil and old age. [270/271]

In those days Harry Crosby seemed at the greatest possible distance from old age and decay, at the very perihelion of his youth. His physical condition was excellent, in spite of dissipation: he was all muscle and sinew and his skin was burned so red that French-

men took him for a Red Indian. He was taut with energy, burning
with desire; he was swimming, dancing, drinking, making love, writing mad poems; and all the time he was laying plans for his final
extinction. It was to take place on October 31, 1942—this date had acquired a symbolic meaning. With Caresse he was to fly an airplane
over a forest and jump out. There was to be no funeral—"I do not
want to be buried in the ground. I want to be cremated. . . . Take
my ashes clean and white, ascend above New York at dawn and
scatter them to the four winds."

All during the summer and autumn of 1928 these plans were taking
shape. And during the same months, Harry was enjoying himself
with terrifying gusto:

> September 4.—Read about the Synapothanomenos or band of those
> who wanted to die together formed by Anthony and Cleopatra after the
> battle of Actium and I should like to have influence strong enough to
> lead a band of followers into the Sun-Death.

> November 7.—Perhaps in my soul I shall become great because I
> have Sun-Thoughts and this autumn I am very happy. It is very rare to
> be so very happy.

> December 22.—I read in my notebook . . . that Aphelion in astron-
> omy is the point of the orbit of a planet at which it is most distant from
> the Sun (the City of Dreadful Night); that the most simple Sun-Death
> is from an aeroplane over a forest (31–10–42) down down down
> down Bang! the body is dead—up up up up Bang!!!! the Soul explodes
> into the Bed of Sun (pull over us the gold sheets Dear). [271/272]

One of his friends, a gifted poet, said that he could no longer bear
to shake his hand. Harry had so definitely fixed the date of his
death, had made up his mind so firmly, had died in anticipation so
many times, that he was like Lazarus with the death-smell about
him: shaking his hand was like shaking hands with a corpse—and
yet what a lively, lustful, laughter-seeking corpse, with gold pieces
in his pocket, hands always moving, teeth gleaming white and the
glint of sun on his skin—a corpse already in winding-sheets, pleading
for faster music as he screamed his triumphant dirge:

> For the Seekers after Fire and the Seers and the Prophets and the
> Worshipers of the Sun, life ends not with a whimper, but with a Bang
> —a violent explosion mechanically perfect . . . while we, having set fire
> to the powderhouse of our souls, explode (suns within suns and cata-
> racts of gold) into the frenzied fury of the Sun, into the madness of the
> Sun into the hot gold arms and hot gold eyes of the Goddess of the
> Sun! [272]

HENRY MILLER

Epidaurus

WE AWOKE EARLY and hired a car to take us to Epidaurus. The day began in sublime peace. It was my first real glimpse of the Peloponnesus. It was not a glimpse either, but a vista opening upon a hushed still world such as man will one day inherit when he ceases to indulge in murder and thievery. I wonder how it is that no painter has ever given us the magic of this idyllic landscape. Is it too undramatic, too idyllic? Is the light too ethereal to be captured by the brush? This I can say, and perhaps it will discourage the over-enthusiastic artist: there is no trace of ugliness here, either in line, color, form, feature or sentiment. It is [55/56] sheer perfection, as in Mozart's music. Indeed, I venture to say that there is more of Mozart here than anywhere else in the world. The road to Epidaurus is like the road to creation. One stops searching. One grows silent, stilled by the hush of mysterious beginnings. If one could speak one would become melodious. There is nothing to be seized or treasured or cornered off here: there is only a breaking down of the walls which lock the spirit in. The landscape does not recede, it installs itself in the open places of the heart; it crowds in, accumulates, dispossesses. You are no longer riding through something—call it Nature, if you will—but participating in a rout, a rout of the forces of greed, malevolence, envy, selfishness, spite, intolerance, pride, arrogance, cunning, duplicity and so on.

It is the morning of the first day of the great peace, the peace of the heart, which comes with surrender. I never knew the meaning of peace until I arrived at Epidaurus. Like everybody I had used the word all my life, without once realizing that I was using a counterfeit. Peace is not the opposite of war any more than death is the opposite of life. The poverty of language, which is to say the poverty

From Henry Miller, "Epidaurus and Mycenae," in *The Henry Miller Reader*, ed. Lawrence Durrell (Norfolk, Connecticut: New Directions, 1959), pp. 55–63. [From *The Colossus of Maroussi*, 1941.]

of man's imagination or the poverty of his inner life, has created an ambivalence which is absolutely false. I am talking of course of the peace which passeth all understanding. There is no other kind. The peace which most of us know is merely a cessation of hostilities, a truce, an interregnum, a lull, a respite, which is negative. The peace of the heart is positive and invincible, demanding no conditions, requiring no protection. It just is. If it is a victory it is a peculiar one because it is based entirely on surrender, a voluntary surrender, to be sure. There is no mystery in my mind as to the nature of the cures which were wrought at this great therapeutic center of the ancient world. Here the healer himself was healed, first and most important step in the development of the art, which is not medical but religious. Second, the patient was healed before ever he received the cure. The great physicians have always spoken of Nature as being the great healer. That is only partially true. Nature alone can do nothing. Nature can cure only when man [56/57] recognizes his place in the world, which is not in Nature, as with the animal, but in the human kingdom, the link between the natural and the divine.

To the infrahuman specimens of this benighted scientific age the ritual and worship connected with the art of healing as practiced at Epidaurus seems like sheer buncombe. In our world the blind lead the blind and the sick go to the sick to be cured. We are making constant progress, but it is a progress which leads to the operating table, to the poor house, to the insane asylum, to the trenches. We have no healers—we have only butchers whose knowledge of anatomy entitles them to a diploma which in turn entitles them to carve out or amputate our illnesses so that we may carry on in crippled fashion until such time as we are fit for the slaughter house. We announce the discovery of this cure and that but make no mention of the new diseases which we have created en route. The medical cult operates very much like the War Office—the triumphs which they broadcast are sops thrown out to conceal death and disaster. The medicos, like the military authorities, are helpless; they are waging a hopeless fight from the start. What man wants is peace in order that he may live. Defeating our neighbor doesn't give peace any more than curing cancer brings health. Man doesn't begin to live through triumphing over his enemy nor does he begin to acquire health through endless cures. The joy of life comes through peace, which is not static but dynamic. No man can really say that he knows what joy is until he has experienced peace. And without joy there is no life, even if you have a dozen cars, six butlers, a castle, a private chapel and a bomb-proof vault. Our diseases are our attachments, be they habits, ideologies, ideals, principles, possessions, phobias, gods, cults, religions, what you please. Good wages can be a disease just as much as bad wages. Leisure can be just as great a disease as work. Whatever we cling to, even if it be hope or faith, can be the disease which carries us off. Surrender is absolute: if you cling to even the tiniest crumb you nourish the germ which will devour you. As for clinging to God, God long ago abandoned us in order that we might realize the joy of [57/58]attaining godhood through our own efforts. All this whimpering that is going on in the dark, this insistent, piteous plea for peace which will grow bigger as the pain and the misery increase, where is it to be found? *Peace,* do people imagine that it is something to be cornered, like corn or wheat? Is it something which can be pounced upon and devoured, as with wolves fighting over a carcass? I hear people talking about peace and their faces are clouded with anger or with hatred or with scorn and disdain, with pride and arrogance. There are people who want to fight to bring about peace—the most deluded souls of all. There will be no peace until murder is eliminated from the heart and mind. Murder is the apex of the broad pyramid whose base is the self. That which stands will have to fall. Everything which man has fought for will have to be relinquished before he can begin to live as man. Up till now he has been a sick beast and even his divinity stinks. He is master of many worlds and in his own he is a slave. What rules the world is the heart, not the brain. In every realm our conquests bring only death. We have turned our backs on the one realm wherein freedom lies. At Epidaurus, in the stillness, in the great peace that came over me, I heard the heart of the world beat. I know what the cure is: it is to give up, to relinquish, to surrender, so that our little hearts may beat in unison with the great heart of the world.

I think that the great hordes who made the long trek to Epidaurus from every corner of the ancient world were already cured before they arrived there. Sitting in the strangely silent amphitheatre I thought of the long and devious route by which I had at last come to this healing center of peace. No man could have chosen a more circumlocuitous voyage than mine. Over thirty years I had wandered, as if in a labyrinth. I had tasted every joy, every despair, but I had never known the meaning of peace. En route I had vanquished all my enemies one by one, but the greatest enemy of all I had not even recognized—*myself*. As I entered the still bowl, bathed now in a marble light, I came to that spot in the dead center where the faintest whisper rises like a glad bird and vanishes over the shoulder of the low hill, as the [58/59] light of a clear day recedes before the velvet black of night. Balboa standing upon the peak of Darien could not have known a greater wonder than I at this moment. There was nothing more to conquer: an ocean of peace lay before me. To be free, as I then knew myself to be, is to realize that all conquest is vain, even the conquest of self, which is the last act of egotism. To be joyous is to carry the ego to its last summit and to deliver it triumphantly. To know peace is total: it is the moment after, when the surrender is complete, when there is no longer even the consciousness of surrender. Peace is at the center and when it is attained the voice issues forth in praise and benediction. Then the voice carries far and wide, to the outermost limits of the universe. Then it heals, because it brings light and the warmth of compassion.

Epidaurus is merely a place symbol: the real place is in the heart, in every man's heart, if he will but stop and search it. Every discovery is mysterious in that it reveals what is so unexpectedly immediate, so close, so long and intimately known. The wise man has no need to journey forth; it is the fool who seeks the pot of gold at the rainbow's end. But the two are always fated to meet and unite. They meet at the heart of the world, which is the beginning and the end of the path. They meet in realization and unite in transcendence of their roles.

The world is both young and old: like the individual, it renews itself in death and ages through infinite births. At every stage there is the possibility of fulfillment. Peace lies at any point along the line. It is a continuum and one that is just as undemonstrable by demarcation as a line is undemonstrable by stringing points together. To make a line requires a totality of being, of will and of imagination. What constitutes a line, which is an exercise in metaphysics, one may speculate on for eternity. But even an idiot can draw a line, and in doing so he is the equal of the professor for whom the nature of a line is a mystery beyond all comprehension.

The mastery of great things comes with the doing of trifles; the little voyage is for the timid soul just as formidable as the big voyage for the great one. Voyages are accomplished inwardly, [59/60] and the most hazardous ones, needless to say, are made without moving from the spot. But the sense of voyage can wither and die. There are adventurers who penetrate to the remotest parts of the earth, dragging to a fruitless goal an animated corpse. The earth pullulates with adventurous spirits who populate it with death: these are the souls who, bent upon conquest, fill the outer corridors of space with strife and bickering. What gives a phantasmal hue to life is this wretched shadow play between ghoul and ghost. The panic and confusion which grips the soul of the wanderer is the reverberation of the pandemonium created by the lost and the damned.

As I was basking on the steps of the amphitheatre the very natural thought came to my head to send a word of cheer to my friends.

I thought particularly of my psychoanalyst friends. I wrote out three cards, one to France, one to England, and one to America. I very gently urged these broken-down hacks who called themselves healers to abandon their work and come to Epidaurus for a cure. All three of them were in dire need of the healing art—saviors who were helpless to save themselves. One of them committed suicide before my word of cheer reached him; another died of a broken heart shortly after receiving my card; the third one answered briefly that he envied me and wished he had the courage to quit his work.

The analyst everywhere is fighting a hopeless fight. For every individual whom he restores to the stream of life, "adapted," as they put it, a dozen are incapacitated. There will never be enough analysts to go round, no matter how fast we turn them out. One brief war is enough to undo the work of centuries. Surgery of course will make new advances, though of what use these advantages are it is difficult to see. Our whole way of life has to alter. We don't want better surgical appliances, we want a better life. If all the surgeons, all the analysts, all the medicos could be withdrawn from their activity and gathered together for a spell in the great bowl at Epidaurus, if they could discuss in peace and quiet the immediate, drastic need of humanity at large, the [60/61] answer would be forthcoming speedily, and it would be unanimous: REVOLUTION. A world-wide revolution from top to bottom, in every country, in every class, in every realm of consciousness. The fight is not against disease: disease is a by-product. The enemy of man is not germs, but man himself, his pride, his prejudices, his stupidity, his arrogance. No class is immune, no system holds a panacea. Each one individually must revolt against a way of life which is not his own. The revolt, to be effective, must be continuous and relentless. It is not enough to overthrow governments, masters, tyrants: one must overthrow his own preconceived ideas of right and wrong, good and bad, just and unjust. We must abandon the hard-fought trenches we have dug ourselves into and come out into the open, surrender our arms, our possessions, our rights as individuals, classes, nations, peoples. A billion men seeking peace cannot be enslaved. We have enslaved ourselves, by our own petty, circumscribed view of life. It is glorious to offer one's life for a cause, but dead men accomplish nothing. Life demands that we offer something more—spirit, soul, intelligence, good will. Nature is ever ready to repair the gaps caused by death, but nature cannot supply the intelligence, the will, the imagination to conquer the forces of death. Nature restores and repairs, that is all. It is man's task to eradicate the homicidal instinct, which is infinite in its ramifications and manifestations. It is useless to call upon God, as it is futile to meet force with force. Every battle is a marriage conceived in blood and anguish, every war is a defeat to the human spirit. War is only a vast manifestation in dramatic style of the sham, hollow, mock conflicts, which take place daily everywhere even in so-called times of peace. Every man contributes his bit to keep the carnage going, even those who seem to be staying aloof. We are all involved, all participating, willy-nilly. The earth is our creation and we must accept the fruits of our creation. As long as we refuse to think in terms of world good and world goods, of world order, world peace, we shall murder and betray one another. It can go on till the crack of doom, if we wish it to be thus. Nothing can bring about a new and better world but [61/62] our own desire for it. Man kills through fear—and fear is hydra-headed. Once we start slaying there is no end to it. An eternity would not suffice to vanquish the demons who torture us. *Who put the demons there?* That is for each one to ask himself. Let every man search his own heart. Neither God nor the Devil is responsible, and certainly not such puny monsters as Hitler, Mussolini, Stalin, et alia. Certainly not such bugaboos as Catholicism, Capitalism, Communism. Who put the demons there in our heart to torture us? A good question, and if the only way to find out is to go to Epidaurus, then I urge you one and all to drop everything and go there—at once.

In Greece one has the conviction that *genius* is the norm, not mediocrity. No country has produced, in proportion to its numbers, as many geniuses as Greece. In one century alone this tiny nation gave to the world almost five hundred men of genius. Her art, which goes back fifty centuries, is eternal and incomparable. The landscape remains the most satisfactory, the most wondrous, that our earth has to offer. The inhabitants of this little world lived in harmony with their natural surroundings, peopling them with gods who were real and with whom they lived in intimate communion. The Greek cosmos is the most eloquent illustration of the unity of thought and deed. It persists even today, though its elements have long since been dispersed. The image of Greece, faded though it be, endures as an archetype of the miracle wrought by the human spirit. A whole people, as the relics of their achievements testify, lifted themselves to a point never before and never since attained. It was miraculous. It still is. The task of genius, and man is nothing if not genius, is to keep the miracle alive, to live always in the miracle, to make the miracle more and more miraculous, to swear allegiance to nothing, but live only miraculously, think only miraculously, die miraculously. It matters little how much is destroyed, if only the germ of the miraculous be preserved and nurtured. At Epidaurus you are confronted with and permeated by the intangible residue of the miraculous surge of the human spirit. It inundates you like the spray of a mighty wave which broke at last upon the farther [62/63] shore. Today our attention is centered upon the physical inexhaustibility of the universe; we *must* concentrate all our thought upon that solid fact because never before has man plundered and devastated to such a degree as today. We are therefore prone to forget that in the realm of the spirit there is also an inexhaustibility, that in this realm no gain is ever lost.When one stands at Epidaurus one *knows* this to be a fact. With malice and spite the world may buckle and crack but here, no matter into what vast hurricane we may whip our evil passions, lies an area of peace and calm, the pure distilled heritage of a past which is not altogether lost. [63]

NORMAN MAILER

The Patron Saint of MacDougal Alley

How CAN ONE describe Pierrot? It is impossible to understand him; one may only tell stories about him. Yet with every move he makes, he creates another story, so one cannot keep up. Pierrot is an original; he is unlike anyone else on the face of the earth .

I can describe how he looks. He is now nineteen, and of average height. He has dark hair, regular features, and a very pleasant smile. There are times when he grows a mustache, and there are times when he shaves it off. During those periods when he sports a few hairs beneath his nose, he looks a year or two younger; when he strips it, he is nineteen again. I suspect he will look nineteen a decade from now; what is worse I often have the suspicion that he looked the same when he was born. Pierrot will never change. He is absolutely predictable in the most unforeseen situations.

He is the son of my friend Jacques Battigny, who is a professor of Romance languages at a university in New York, and never were a father and son more related and less alike. Jacques is a gentleman of considerable culture; as a representative French intellectual it is somewhat intolerable to him to pass through [394/395] experience without comprehending it rationally. He demands order in every corner of his life. It is his cross that Pierrot is the eternal flux.

Father and son are thesis and antithesis. Put another way, Pierrot is Jacques turned inside out, the clothes-dummy of an intellectual. He has all the attributes of the French mind except its erudition; his greatest joy is to approach logically large bodies of experience about which he knows nothing. The first time I met him, Pierrot spoke to me for hours; he mentioned in passing, Marx, Freud, and Darwin; Heidegger, Kierkegaard, and Sartre; Lawrence and Henry Miller; Nietzsche and Spengler; Vico and Edmund Wilson; Jean Genet and Simone de Beauvoir; Leon Trotsky and Max Schachtman; Wilhelm

Norman Mailer, "The Patron Saint of MacDougal Alley," in *Advertisements for Myself* (New York: G. P. Putnam's Sons, 1959), pp. 394–402.

Reich, Gregory Zilboorg, and Karen Horney. There were two hundred other names of varied importance, and I do not believe he used a word which had less than four syllables. Therefore, it took some time for me to realize that Pierrot was an idiot.

In the hours between, he husked my brains. What did I think of Mr. Aldous Huxley? Pierrot would inquire, and long before I had reconstituted my recollections of Huxley's work and delivered them in some organized form, Pierrot was wondering how I evaluated Mr. Thomas Stearns Eliot. It seemed to me that I had never met an adolescent who was more intelligent: the breadth of his queries, the energy of his curiosity, and the quick reception which shone in his brown eyes, were quite impressive. Chaplin and Griffiths, Jackson Pollack and Hans Hofmann, did I like Berlioz and had I heard Benjamin Britten? Pierrot was tireless. Only when the afternoon had passed and my wife felt obliged to invite him for dinner, did I begin to suspect that Pierrot did not contribute as much as I.

A few minutes later in response to a discreet inquiry or two, Pierrot confessed to me with relish that he had never seen a single one of the pictures he mentioned, nor read one of the authors we spoke about. "You understand," he said to me, "it is so depressing. I want to amass the totality of knowledge, and consequently I don't know where to begin." He sighed. "I look at the books on my father's shelf. I say to myself, 'Is it in these books that I will find the termination, or even the beginning, of my philosophical quest?' You understand? What is the meaning to life? That is what obsesses me. And will these books give the answer? I look at them. They are [395/396] paper, they are cardboard. Is it possible that the essence of truth can be communicated to paper and ink?" He paused and smiled, "Reality and illusion. I think about history, and I wonder, 'Does Marxism take proper account of history?' Someone was telling me to read Engel's *Marriage and The Family*. Would you recommend it? I am very interested in the subject."

He was absolutely tireless. As dinner progressed, as the dishes were washed, the brunt of the conversation shifted from my tongue to Pierrot's. He sat with my wife and me through the evening, he discussed his ambitions, his depressions, his victories, his defeats. What did I think of his parents, he wanted to know, and immediately proceeded to tell me. Pierrot's mother had died, and his father had married again. Georgette was ten years younger than Jacques, and Pierrot found this disturbing. "You understand," he said to me cheerfully, "I look for love. I search for it in the midst of my family, and I do not find it. Between Georgette and me there is an attraction, I ask myself whether it is maternal or physical? I should like to bring matters to a head, but I am a virgin, and I should detest it if I could not satisfy her. Is it true that one must serve the apprentice-ship of love?" Long before I could have turned an answer, he had forgotten his question. "And then I wonder in the privacy of my thoughts if what I really seek is the conquest of Georgette, or if I am looking for her only to be my mother. I should like her to hold me close. You understand, I am masochistic. I feel so many things." He held his breast. "I am an infant and I am a lover. Which is my nature? Which do I desire to satisfy? You realize, I want to be close to my father, and yet I am repelled by him. It is like psychoanalysis. I think sometimes I wish to live *ménage à trois*, but then I decide I am destructive and desire to live in isolation. Is it man's nature to live in isolation? I feel so lonely at times. I wish to communicate. Communication is a problem which interests me. Does it you?"

At one o'clock in the morning, after numerous hints had failed, I was obliged to tell Pierrot that he must go home. He looked at me sadly, he told me that he knew he bored me, he left with an air of such dejection that my wife and I were ashamed of ourselves, and felt we had turned a waif into the streets. The next time I saw his father, I apologized for this, and was cut short.

"Apologize for nothing," Jacques shouted. "The boy is a monster. He has no conception whatsoever of time. If you had not [396/397] put him out, he would have stayed for a week." Jacques held his head. "I shall certainly go mad. There is nothing to do with him but to be completely rude. Listen to what has happened."

The story Jacques told was indeed painful. Battigny the senior is a lover of books. He loves to read, he declaims on the art of reading, he loves bindings, he loves type, he loves books separately and to-gether. It seems that Pierrot was once talking to a friend of Jacques', a somewhat distinguished professor. The professor, taken with the boy, loaned him a copy of Florio's translation of Montaigne's essays. It was not a first edition, but it was an old one, and of some value, beautifully tooled in leather, and handsomely printed. "Do you know how long ago that was?" Jacques demanded of me. "It was two years ago. Pierrot has kept it in his brief case for two years. Has he ever read a page?" The answer was that he had not. He had merely kept it, and in the course of keeping it, the cover-board had been sheared and the spine exposed. "I screamed at him," Jacques said softly, "it was indecent. I told him it was two years he had kept it, and he told me no, it was only a short period. He cannot compre-hend the passage of time. He is always about to dip into the book, to study it here and smell it there. It is shameful.

"It is intolerable," Jacques cried. "He torments me. I have talked to his English teacher at high school. He asks her if he should study *Beowulf,* and he cannot even pass the examinations. I do not care if he does not go to college, I am not a snob about it, but the boy is incapable of doing anything with his hands. He cannot even learn a trade."

I was to discover that Pierrot could not even learn to say yes or no. He was quite incapable of it, no matter to what brutal lengths I pursued him. Once in eating at my house, I asked him if he wished some bread and butter.

"I do not know," Pierrot said, "I ask myself."

"Pierrot, do you want bread and butter?" I cried out.

"Why do you wish me to eat?" he asked dreamily, as if my motive were sinister. "One eats to live, which supposes that life is worth while. But I ask myself: is life worth while?"

"Pierrot! Do you want bread and butter? Answer yes or no!"

Pierrot smiled sheepishly. "Why do you ask me a yes-and-no question?"

One could say anything to him, and he enjoyed it immensely. He had been making advances to my wife for quite some time. No [397/398] matter how she teased him, scolded him, or ignored him, he persisted. Yet once, when I took a walk with him, he launched into a long description of my virtues. I was handsome, I was attractive, he was stirred by me. And with that he pinched my bicep and said, "You are so strong."

"My God, Pierrot," I said in exasperation. "First you try to make love to my wife, and then you try to make love to me."

"Yes," he said morosely, "and I succeed with neither."

His father finally drove him from the house. He gave Pierrot two hundred dollars, and told him he was to find a job in the city and learn to live by his own labor. Jacques was penitent. "I am so cruel to the boy. But what is there to do? I cannot bear the sight of him. Have you ever watched him work? If he picks up a hammer, he smashes his thumb. He lays down the hammer, he sucks his finger, he loses the hammer, he forgets why he needed it in the first place, he tries to remember, he ends by falling asleep." Jacques groaned. "I dread to think of him out in the world. He is completely impractical. He will spend the two hundred dollars in a night on his bohemian friends."

Only a father could have been so wrong. Pierrot had the blood of a French peasant. The two hundred dollars lasted for six months. He lived with one friend, he lived with another; he lunched with an acquaintance and stayed for dinner. He drank beer in the Village; he was always to be found at Louis', at Minetta's, at the San Remo, but no one remembered when he had paid for a drink. He was pretty enough to be courted, and he had frequent adventures with homosexuals. They were always finding him in a bar, they would talk to him, he would talk to them. He would tell them his troubles, he would confide, he would admit warmly that he had never discovered anyone who understood him so well. He would end by going to the other's apartment. There Pierrot would drink, he would continue to talk, he would talk even as the friend removed his shirt and apologized for the heat. It was only at the penultimate moment that Pierrot would leave. "You understand," he would say, "I want to know you. But I am so confused. Do we have a basis to find a foundation of things in common?" And out he would skip through the door.

"Why do they always approach me?" he would ask in an innocent voice. [398/399]

I would make the mistake of being severe. "Because you solicit, Pierrot."

He would smile. "Ah, that is an interesting interpretation. I hope it is true. I would love to make my living in an anti-social manner. Society is so evil."

He lived with a girl who was a fair mate for him. She had a tic at one corner of her mouth, and she was a follower of Buddha. The girl was trying to start a Buddhist colony in America. It was all mixed somehow with a theory about the birth trauma which she explained to me one night at a party. The reason armies functioned in combat was because the noise of battle returned the ordinary soldier to the primal state of birth. At such a moment his officers came to represent the protecting mother, and the soldier would obey their will even if it meant death. She was proud of the theory, and snapped at Pierrot when he would attempt to discuss it with her.

"A wonderful girl," he told me once. "It is a most exciting affair. She is absolutely frigid."

It seemed that if he dropped his shoes upon the floor, she would not allow him to approach her. "There is such uncertainty. It recaptures the uncertainty of life. I think about it. People meet. Lives intersect. It is points on a plane. Would you say this is a fit topic for philosophical investigation?"

In the course of events the Buddhist threw him out. At any rate, metaphorically she threw him out. The affair ended, but since Pierrot had no place to live, he continued to stay with her while he looked for another friend to give him a bed. During this period he came to me to ask if I would put him up, but I refused. After making these requests, he would look so forlorn that I hated myself.

"I understand," he said. "One of my friends who is analyzing me by hypnosis has made me see that I exploit everyone. It is the influence of the culture, I would think. I have become very interested in the movements of political bodies. I see that previously I adopted too personal an attitude. What is your opinion of my new political approach?"

"We'll discuss it another time, Pierrot. I'm awfully sorry I can't put you up for the night."

"It is all right," he said sweetly. "I do not know where I shall sleep tonight, but it does not matter. I am an exploiter, and it is only proper that people should recognize this in me." He left with a [399/400] meek forgiving look. "I shall sleep. Do not worry about me," he said as the door closed.

Five minutes later I was still trying to put the matter from my mind when the doorbell rang. Pierrot was back. All night he had had a problem he wanted to discuss with me, but in the interest of our conversation, it had completely slipped his mind.

"What is it?" I asked coldly, annoyed at having been taken in.

He answered me in French. "*Tu sais, j'ai la chaude-pisse.*"

"Oh, Christ!"

He nodded. He had been to see a doctor, and it would be cleared up. There would be a wonder drug employed.

"Not by one of your friends, I hope?"

No, this was a bona-fide doctor. But he had another problem. The ailment had been provoked by the Buddhist. Of this, he was certain. At the moment, however, he was engaged in an affair with a young married woman, and he was curious to know whether he should tell her.

"You certainly should." I grasped him by the shoulder. "Pierrot, you have to tell her."

His brown eyes clouded. "You understand, it would be very difficult. It would destroy so much rapport between us. I would prefer to say nothing. Why should I speak? I am absolutely without morality," he declared with passion.

"Morality be damned," I said. "Do you realize that if you don't tell the girl, you will have to see the doctor again and again? Do you know how expensive that is?"

He sighed. This is what he had been afraid of. Like the peasant brought slowly and stubbornly to face some new and detestable reality, he agreed dourly. "In that case, I shall tell her. It is too bad."

Lately, I have hardly seen Pierrot. His two hundred dollars has run out, and he is now obliged to work. He has had eleven jobs in four months. I could not hope to describe them all. He has been let go, fired, dismissed, and has resigned. He was an office boy for two days, and on the second day, pausing to take a drink, he placed his letter basket on the lip of the water cooler. Somehow—he is convinced it is the fault of the cooler—the water ran over the papers. In attempting to wipe them, he dropped the basket, and the wet paper became dirty. Signatures ran, names became illegible, and to

[400/401] the fury of the office manager, Pierrot did not attempt to excuse himself but asked instead why Americans were so compulsive about business correspondence.

He also worked in a factory. He was very depressed after the first day of work had ended, and called me up in such a mournful voice that I felt obliged to see him. He was tired, he was disgusted. "I hold a piece of metal in my hand," he said to me, "and I touch it to an abrasive agent. Slowly square corners become round. Eight hours of such work I suffer. Can this be the meaning to existence?" His voice conveyed that he expected to continue the job until the end of time. "I search for my identity. It is lost. I am merely Agent 48."

At this point I rose upon him in wrath. I told him that he had two choices. He could work in order to live, or he could die. If he wished to die, I would not attempt to discourage him. In fact, I would abet him. "If you come to me, Pierrot, and ask for a gun, I will attempt to find you a gun. Until then, stop complaining." He listened to me with an enormous smile. His eyes shone at the vigor of my language. "You are marvelous," he said with admiration.

The very last I've heard is that Pierrot is soon to be drafted. Some of my friends are very upset about this. They say that the boy will be a mental case in a few weeks. Others insist that the army will be good for him. I am at odds with both of them.

I see Pierrot in the army. He will sleep late, curled in a little ball beneath his blankets. He will be certain to miss reveille. About eight o'clock in the morning he will stumble drowsily to the mess hall, his mess gear falling from his hand, and will look stupidly at the cook.

"Oh," he will say, "oh, I am late for breakfast."

"Get out of here," the cook will say.

"Oh, I go." Pierrot will nod. "I deserve to miss a meal. I have been negligent. Of course, I will be out all day on a march, and I will be very hungry, but it is my fault. And it does not matter. What is food?" He will be so unhappy that the cook no matter how he curses will scramble him some eggs. Pierrot will suggest toast, he will induce the cook to heat the coffee, he will engage him in a philosophical discussion. At eleven o'clock, Pierrot will leave to join his training platoon, and at two in the afternoon he will find them. Hours later, at retreat parade, the inspecting officer will discover that Pierrot has lost his rifle. [401/402]

That will be the beginning of the end. Pierrot will be assigned to K.P. for three days in a row. By the first morning he will so have misplaced and mis-washed the pots that the cooks will be forced to assist him, and will work harder than they have ever worked. By evening the mess sergeant will be begging the first sergeant never to put Pierrot on K.P. again.

The army cannot recover from such a blow. K.P. is its foundation, and when cooks ask to remove men from that duty, it can take only a few days before every soldier in the army will follow the trail blazed by Pierre Battigny. I see the army collapsing two months after Pierrot enters it.

At that moment I hope to influence the course of history. Together with such responsible individuals as I may find, I will raise a subscription to send Pierrot to the Soviet Union. Once he is there, the world is saved. He will be put in the army immediately, and before his first day is over, the Russians will have him up before a firing squad. Then Pierrot will rise to his true stature.

"I ask myself," he will say to the Russian soldiers, "am I not miserable? Is life not sad? Shoot me."

At this point the Russians will throw down their arms and begin to weep. "We do not enjoy ourselves either," they will sob. "Shoot us, too." In the grand Russian manner, the news will spread across the steppes. Soldiers everywhere will cast away their weapons. America and Russia will be disarmed in a night, and peace will come over the earth.

They will build a statue to Pierrot at the corner of Eighth Street and MacDougal. New generations will pass and spit at him. "He was Square," they will say. [402]

JACK KEROUAC

Dean Moriarty

I FIRST MET Dean not long after my wife and I split up. I had just gotten over a serious illness that I won't bother to talk about, except that it had something to do with the miserably weary split-up and my feeling that everything was dead. With the coming of Dean Moriarty began the part of my life you could call my life on the road. Before that I'd often dreamed of going West to see the country, always vaguely planning and never taking off. Dean is the perfect guy for the road because he actually was born on the road, when his parents were passing through Salt Lake City in 1926, in a jalopy, on their way to Los Angeles. First reports of him came to me through Chad King, who'd shown me a few letters [3/4] from him written in a New Mexico reform school. I was tremendously interested in the letters because they so naïvely and sweetly asked Chad to teach him all about Nietzsche and all the wonderful intellectual things that Chad knew. At one point Carlo and I talked about the letters and wondered if we would ever meet the strange Dean Moriarty. This is all far back, when Dean was not the way he is today, when he was a young jailkid shrouded in mystery. Then news came that Dean was out of reform school and was coming to New York for the first time; also there was talk that he had just married a girl called Marylou.

One day I was hanging around the campus and Chad and Tim Gray told me Dean was staying in a cold-water pad in East Harlem, the Spanish Harlem. Dean had arrived the night before, the first time in New York, with his beautiful little sharp chick Marylou; they got off the Greyhound bus at 50th Street and cut around the corner looking for a place to eat and went right in Hector's, and since then Hector's cafeteria has always been a big symbol of New York for Dean. They spent money on beautiful big glazed cakes and

From Jack Kerouac, *On The Road* (New York: The Viking Press, 1957), pp. 3–11, 305–10.

creampuffs.

All this time Dean was telling Marylou things like this: "Now, darling, here we are in New York and although I haven't quite told you everything that I was thinking about when we crossed Missouri and especially at the point when we passed the Booneville reformatory which reminded me of my jail problem, it is absolutely necessary now to postpone all those leftover things concerning our personal lovethings and at once begin thinking of specific worklife plans . . ." and so on in the way that he had in those early days.

I went to the cold-water flat with the boys, and Dean came to the door in his shorts. Marylou was jumping off the couch; Dean had dispatched the occupant of the apartment to the kitchen, probably to make coffee, while he proceeded with his loveproblems, for to him sex was the one and only holy and important thing in life, although he had to sweat and curse to make a living and so on. You saw that in the way he stood bobbing his head, always looking down, nodding, like a young boxer to instructions, to make you think he was listening to [4/5] every word, throwing in a thousand "Yeses" and "That's rights." My first impression of Dean was of a young Gene Autry—trim, thin-hipped, blue-eyed, with a real Oklahoma accent—a sideburned hero of the snowy West. In fact he'd just been working on a ranch, Ed Wall's in Colorado, before marrying Marylou and coming East. Marylou was a pretty blonde with immense ringlets of hair like a sea of golden tresses; she sat there on the edge of the couch with her hands hanging in her lap and her smoky blue country eyes fixed on a wide stare because she was in an evil gray New York pad that she'd heard about back West, and waiting like a longbodied emaciated Modigliani surrealist woman in a serious room. But, outside of being a sweet little girl, she was awfully dumb and capable of doing horrible things. That night we all drank beer and pulled wrists and talked till dawn, and in the morning, while we sat around dumbly smoking butts from ashtrays in the gray light of a gloomy day, Dean got up nervously, paced around, thinking, and decided the thing to do was to have Marylou make breakfast and sweep the floor. "In other words we've got to get on the ball, darling, what I'm saying, otherwise it'll be fluctuating and lack of true knowledge or crystallization of our plans." Then I went away.

During the following week he confided in Chad King that he absolutely had to learn how to write from him; Chad said I was a writer and he should come to me for advice. Meanwhile Dean had gotten a job in a parking lot, had a fight with Marylou in their Hoboken apartment—God knows why they went there—and she was so mad and so down deep vindictive that she reported to the police some false trumped-up hysterical crazy charge, and Dean had to lam from Hoboken. So he had no place to live. He came right out to Paterson, New Jersey, where I was living with my aunt, and one night while I was studying there was a knock on the door, and there was Dean, bowing, shuffling obsequiously in the dark of the hall, and saying, "Hel-lo, you remember me—Dean Moriarty? I've come to ask you to show me how to write."

"And where's Marylou?" I asked, and Dean said she'd apparently whored a few dollars together and gone back to Denver [5/6]—"the whore!" So we went out to have a few beers because we couldn't talk like we wanted to talk in front of my aunt, who sat in the living room reading her paper. She took one look at Dean and decided that he was a madman.

In the bar I told Dean, "Hell, man, I know very well you didn't come to me only to want to become a writer, and after all what do I really know about it except you've got to stick to it with the energy of a benny addict." And he said, "Yes, of course, I know exactly what you mean and in fact all those problems have occurred to me, but the thing that I want is the realization of those factors that should one depend on Schopenhauer's dichotomy for any inwardly realized . . ." and so on in that way, things I understood not a bit and he himself didn't. In those days he really didn't know what he was talking about; that is to say, he was a young jailkid all hung-up on the wonderful possibilities of becoming a real intellectual, and he liked to talk in the tone and using the words, but in a jumbled way, that he had heard from "real intellectuals"—although, mind you, he wasn't so naïve as that in all other things, and it took him just a few months with Carlo Marx to become completely *in there* with all the terms and jargon. Nonetheless we understood each other on other levels of madness, and I agreed that he could stay at my house till he found a job and furthermore we agreed to go out West sometime. That was the winter of 1947.

One night when Dean ate supper at my house—he already had the parking-lot job in New York—he leaned over my shoulder as I typed rapidly away and said, "Come on man, those girls won't wait, make it fast."

I said, "Hold on just a minute. I'll be right with you soon as I finish this chapter," and it was one of the best chapters in the book. Then I dressed and off we flew to New York to meet some girls. As we rode in the bus in the weird phosphorescent void of the Lincoln Tunnel we leaned on each other with fingers waving and yelled and talked excitedly, and I was beginning to get the bug like Dean. He was simply a youth tremendously excited with life, and though he was a con-man, he was only conning because he wanted so much to live and to [6/7] get involved with people who would otherwise pay no attention to him. He was conning me and I knew it (for room and board and "how-to-write," etc.), and he knew I knew (this has been the basis of our relationship), but I didn't care and we got along fine—no pestering, no catering; we tiptoed around each other like heartbreaking new friends. I began to learn from him as much as he probably learned from me. As far as my work was concerned he said, "Go ahead, everything you do is great." He watched over my shoulder as I wrote stories, yelling "Yes! That's right! Wow! Man!" and "Phew!" and wiped his face with his handkerchief. "Man, wow, there's so many things to do, so many things to write! How to even *begin* to get it all down and without modified restraints and all hung-up on like literary inhibitions and grammatical fears . . ."

"That's right, man, now you're talking." And a kind of holy lightning I saw flashing from his excitement and his visions, which he described so torrentially that people in buses looked around to see the "overexcited nut." In the West he'd spent a third of his time in the poolhall, a third in jail, and a third in the public library. They'd seen him rushing eagerly down the winter streets, bareheaded, carrying books to the poolhall, or climbing trees to get into the attics of buddies where he spent days reading or hiding from the law.

We went to New York—I forget what the situation was, two colored girls—there were no girls there; they were supposed to meet him in a diner and didn't show up. We went to his parking lot where he had a few things to do—change his clothes in the shack in back and spruce up a bit in front of a cracked mirror and so on, and then we took off. And that was the night Dean met Carlo Marx. A tremendous thing happened when Dean met Carlo Marx. Two keen minds that they are, they took to each other at the drop of a hat. Two piercing eyes glanced into two piercing eyes—the holy con-man with the shining mind, and the sorrowful poetic con-man with the dark mind that is Carlo Marx. From that moment on I saw very little of Dean, and I was a little sorry too. Their energies met head-on, I was a lout compared, I couldn't keep up with them. [7/8] The whole mad swirl of everything that was to come began then; it would mix ʼʋ all my friends and all I had left of my family in a big dust cloud ʼ the American Night. Carlo told him of Old Bull Lee, Elmer ʼ Jane: Lee in Texas growing weed, Hassel on Riker's Island, ʼdering on Times Square in a benzedrine hallucination, with ʼl in her arms and ending up in Bellevue. And Dean told ʼown people in the West like Tommy Snark, the ʼll rotation shark and cardplayer and queer saint. ʼJohnson, Big Ed Dunkel, his boyhood buddies,

his street buddies, his innumerable girls and sex-parties and porno-
graphic pictures, his heroes, heroines, adventures. They rushed
down the street together, digging everything in the early way they
had, which later became so much sadder and perceptive and blank.
But then they danced down the streets like dingledodies, and I
shambled after as I've been doing all my life after people who interest me, because the only people for me are the mad ones, the ones
who are mad to live, mad to talk, mad to be saved, desirous of everything at the same time, the ones who never yawn or say a commonplace thing, but burn, burn, burn like fabulous yellow roman
candles exploding like spiders across the stars and in the middle you
see the blue centerlight pop and everybody goes "Awww!" What did
they call such young people in Goethe's Germany? Wanting dearly
to learn how to write like Carlo, the first thing you know, Dean was
attacking him with a great amorous soul such as only a con-man can
have. "Now, Carlo, let *me* speak—here's what *I'm* saying . . ." I
didn't see them for about two weeks, during which time they ce-
mented their relationship to fiendish allday-allnight-talk proportions.

Then came spring, the great time of traveling, and everybody in
the scattered gang was getting ready to take one trip or another. I
was busily at work on my novel and when I came to the halfway
mark, after a trip down South with my aunt to visit my brother
Rocco, I got ready to travel West for the very first time.

Dean had already left. Carlo and I saw him off at the 34th Street
Greyhound station. Upstairs they had a place where [8/9] you
could make pictures for a quarter. Carlo took off his glasses and
looked sinister. Dean made a profile shot and looked coyly around. I
took a straight picture that made me look like a thirty-year-old Italian who'd kill anybody who said anything against his mother. This
picture Carlo and Dean neatly cut down the middle with a razor
and saved a half each in their wallets. Dean was wearing a real
Western business suit for his big trip back to Denver; he'd finished
his first fling in New York. I say fling, but he only worked like a dog
in parking lots. The most fantastic parking-lot attendant in the
world, he can back a car forty miles an hour into a tight squeeze
and stop at the wall, jump out, race among fenders, leap into another car, circle it fifty miles an hour in a narrow space, back swiftly
into tight spot, *bump,* snap the car with the emergency so that you
see it bounce as he flies out; then clear to the ticket shack, sprinting
like a track star, hand a ticket, leap into a newly arrived car before
the owner's half out, leap literally under him as he steps out, start
the car with the door flapping, and roar off to the next available
spot, arc, pop in, brake, out, run; working like that without pause

eight hours a night, evening rush hours and after-theater rush hours, in greasy wino pants with a frayed fur-lined jacket and beat shoes that flap. Now he'd bought a new suit to go back in; blue with pencil stripes, vest and all—eleven dollars on Third Avenue, with a watch and watch chain, and a portable typewriter with which he was going to start writing in a Denver rooming house as soon as he got a job there. We had a farewell meal of franks and beans in a Seventh Avenue Riker's, and then Dean got on the bus that said Chicago and roared off into the night. There went our wrangler. I promised myself to go the same way when spring really bloomed and opened up the land.

And this was really the way that my whole road experience began, and the things that were to come are too fantastic not to tell.

Yes, and it wasn't only because I was a writer and needed new experiences that I wanted to know Dean more, and because my life hanging around the campus had reached the [9/10] completion of its cycle and was stultified, but because, somehow, in spite of our difference in character, he reminded me of some long-lost brother; the sight of his suffering bony face with the long sideburns and his straining muscular sweating neck made me remember my boyhood in those dye-dumps and swim-holes and riversides of Paterson and the Passaic. His dirty workclothes clung to him so gracefully, as though you couldn't buy a better fit from a custom tailor but only earn it from the Natural Tailor of Natural Joy, as Dean had, in his stresses. And in his excited way of speaking I heard again the voices of old companions and brothers under the bridge, among the motorcycles, along the wash-lined neighborhood and drowsy doorsteps of afternoon where boys played guitars while their older brothers worked in the mills. All my other current friends were "intellectuals" —Chad the Nietzschean anthropologist, Carlo Marx and his nutty surrealist low-voiced serious staring talk, Old Bull Lee and his critical anti-everything drawl—or else they were slinking criminals like Elmer Hassel, with that hip sneer; Jane Lee the same, sprawled on the Oriental cover of her couch, sniffing at the *New Yorker*. But Dean's intelligence was every bit as formal and shining and complete, without the tedious intellectualness. And his "criminality" was not something that sulked and sneered; it was a wild yea-saying overburst of American joy; it was Western, the west wind, an ode from the Plains, something new, long prophesied, long a-coming (he only stole cars for joy rides). Besides, all my New York friends were in the negative, nightmare position of putting down society and giving their tired bookish or political or psychoanalytical reasons, but Dean just raced in society, eager for bread and love; he didn't care one way or the other, "so long's I can get that lil ole gal with that lil sumpin down there tween her legs, boy," and "so long's we can *eat,* son, y'ear me? I'm *hungry,* I'm *starving,* let's *eat right now!"*—and off we'd rush to *eat,* whereof, as saith Ecclesiastes, "It is your portion under the sun."

A western kinsman of the sun, Dean. Although my aunt warned me that he would get me in trouble, I could hear a new call and see a new horizon, and believe it at my young [10/11] age; and a little bit of trouble or even Dean's eventual rejection of me as a buddy, putting me down, as he would later, on starving sidewalks and sickbeds—what did it matter? I was a young writer and I wanted to take off.

Somewhere along the line I knew there'd be girls, visions, everything; somewhere along the line the pearl would be handed to me. [11] . . .

Dean drove from Mexico City and saw Victor again in Gregoria and pushed that old car all the way to Lake Charles, Louisiana, before the rear end finally dropped on the road as he had always known it would. So he wired Inez for airplane fare and flew the rest of the way. When he arrived in New York with the divorce papers in his hands, he and Inez immediately went to Newark and got married; and that night, telling her everything was all right and not to worry, and making logics where there was nothing but inestimable sorrowful sweats, he jumped on a bus and roared off again across the awful continent to San Francisco to rejoin Camille and the two baby girls. So now he was three times married, twice divorced, and living with his second wife. [305/306]

In the fall I myself started back home from Mexico City and one night just over Laredo border in Dilley, Texas, I was standing on the hot road underneath an arc-lamp with the summer moths smashing into it when I heard the sound of footsteps from the darkness beyond, and lo, a tall old man with flowing white hair came clomping by with a pack on his back, and when he saw me as he passed, he said, *"Go moan for man,"* and clomped on back to his dark. Did this mean that I should at last go on my pilgrimage on foot on the dark roads around America? I struggled and hurried to New York, and one night I was standing in a dark street in Manhattan and called up the window of a loft where I thought my friends were having a party. But a pretty girl stuck her head out the window and said, "Yes? Who is it?"

"Sal Paradise," I said, and heard my name resound in the sad and empty street.

"Come on up," she called. "I'm making hot chocolate." So I went up and there she was, the girl with the pure and innocent dear eyes that I had always searched for and for so long. We agreed to love each other madly. In the winter we planned to migrate to San Francisco, bringing all our beat furniture and broken belongings with us in a jalopy panel truck. I wrote to Dean and told him. He wrote back a huge letter eighteen thousand words long, all about his young years in Denver, and said he was coming to get me and personally select the old truck himself and drive us home. We had six weeks to save up the money for the truck and began working and counting every cent. And suddenly Dean arrived anyway, five and a half weeks in advance, and nobody had any money to go through with the plan.

I was taking a walk in the middle of the night and came back to my girl to tell her what I thought about during my walk. She stood in the dark little pad with a strange smile. I told her a number of things and suddenly I noticed the hush in the room and looked around and saw a battered book on the radio. I knew it was Dean's high-eternity-in-the-afternoon Proust. As in a dream I saw him tiptoe in from the dark hall in his stocking feet. He couldn't talk any more. He hopped [306/307] and laughed, he stuttered and fluttered his hands and said, "Ah—ah—you must listen to hear." We listened, all ears. But he forgot what he wanted to say. "Really listen—ahem. Look, dear Sal—sweet Laura—I've come—I'm gone—but wait—ah yes." And he stared with rocky sorrow into his hands. "Can't talk no more—do you understand that it is—or might be—But listen!" We all listened. He was listening to sounds in the night. "Yes!" he whispered with awe. "But you see—no need to talk any more—and further."

"But why did you come so soon, Dean?"

"Ah," he said, looking at me as if for the first time, "so soon, yes. We—we'll know—that is, I don't know. I came on the railroad pass—cabooses—old hard-bench coaches—Texas—played flute and wooden sweet potato all the way." He took out his new wooden flute. He played a few squeaky notes on it and jumped up and down in his stocking feet. "See?" he said. "But of course, Sal, I can talk as soon as ever and have many things to say to you in fact with my own little bangtail mind I've been reading and reading this gone Proust all the way across the country and digging a great number of things I'll never have TIME to tell you about and we STILL haven't talked of Mexico and our parting there in fever—but no need to talk. Absolutely, now, yes?"

"All right, we won't talk." And he started telling the story of what he did in LA on the way over in every possible detail, how he visited a family, had dinner, talked to the father, the sons, the sisters—what they looked like, what they ate, their furnishings, their thoughts, their interests, their very souls; it took him three hours of detailed elucidation, and having concluded this he said, "Ah, but you see what I wanted to REALLY tell you—much later—Arkansas, crossing on train—playing flute—play cards with boys, my dirty deck —won money, blew sweet-potato solo—for sailors. Long long awful trip five days and five nights just to SEE you, Sal."

"What about Camille?"

"Gave permission of course—waiting for me. Camille and I all straight forever-and-ever . . ."

"And Inez?" [307/308]

"I—I—I want her to come back to Frisco with me live other side of town—don't you think? Don't know why I came." Later he said in a sudden moment of gaping wonder, "Well and yes, of course, I wanted to see your sweet girl and you—glad of you—love you as ever." He stayed in New York three days and hastily made preparations to get back on the train with his railroad passes and again recross the continent, five days and five nights in dusty coaches and hard-bench crummies, and of course we had no money for a truck and couldn't go back with him. With Inez he spent one night explaining and sweating and fighting, and she threw him out. A letter came for him, care of me. I saw it. It was from Camille. "My heart broke when I saw you go across the tracks with your bag. I pray and pray you get back safe. . . . I do want Sal and his friend to come and live on the same street. . . . I know you'll make it but I can't help worrying—now that we've decided everything. . . . Dear Dean, it's the end of the first half of the century. Welcome with love and kisses to spend the other half with us. We all wait for you. [Signed] Camille, Amy, and Little Joanie." So Dean's life was settled with his most constant, most embittered, and best-knowing wife Camille, and I thanked God for him.

The last time I saw him it was under sad and strange circumstances. Remi Boncœur had arrived in New York after having gone around the world several times in ships. I wanted him to meet and know Dean. They did meet, but Dean couldn't talk any more and said nothing, and Remi turned away. Remi had gotten tickets for the Duke Ellington concert at the Metropolitan Opera and insisted Laura and I come with him and his girl. Remi was fat and sad now but still the eager and formal gentleman, and he wanted to do things the *right way,* as he emphasized. So he got his bookie to drive us to the concert in a Cadillac. It was a cold winter night. The Cadillac was parked and ready to go. Dean stood outside the windows with his bag, ready to go to Penn Station and on across the land.

"Good-by, Dean," I said. "I sure wish I didn't have to go to the concert." [308/309]

"D'you think I can ride to Fortieth Street with you?" he whispered. "Want to be with you as much as possible, m'boy, and besides it's so durned cold in this here New Yawk . . ." I whispered to Remi. No, he wouldn't have it, he liked me but he didn't like my idiot friends. I wasn't going to start all over again ruining his planned evenings as I had done at Alfred's in San Francisco in 1947 with Roland Major.

"Absolutely out of the question, Sal!" Poor Remi, he had a special necktie made for this evening; on it was painted a replica of the concert tickets, and the names Sal and Laura and Remi and Vicki, the girl, together with a series of sad jokes and some of his favorite sayings such as "You can't teach the old maestro a new tune."

So Dean couldn't ride uptown with us and the only thing I could do was sit in the back of the Cadillac and wave at him. The bookie at the wheel also wanted nothing to do with Dean. Dean, ragged in a motheaten overcoat he brought specially for the freezing temperatures of the East, walked off alone, and the last I saw of him he rounded the corner of Seventh Avenue, eyes on the street ahead, and bent to it again. Poor little Laura, my baby, to whom I'd told everything about Dean, began almost to cry.

"Oh, we shouldn't let him go like this. What'll we do?"

Old Dean's gone, I thought, and out loud I said, "He'll be all right." And off we went to the sad and disinclined concert for which I had no stomach whatever and all the time I was thinking of Dean and how he got back on the train and rode over three thousand miles over that awful land and never knew why he had come anyway, except to see me.

So in America when the sun goes down and I sit on the old broken-down river pier watching the long, long skies over New Jersey and sense all that raw land that rolls in one unbelievable huge bulge over to the West Coast, and all that road going, all the people dreaming in the immensity of it, and in Iowa I know by now the children must be crying in the land where they let the children cry, and tonight the stars'll be out, and don't you know that God is Pooh Bear? the evening star must be drooping and shedding her sparkler dims on the prairie, [309/310] which is just before the coming of complete night that blesses the earth, darkens all rivers, cups the peaks and folds the final shore in, and nobody, nobody knows what's going to happen to anybody besides the forlorn rags of growing old, I think of Dean Moriarty, I even think of Old Dean Moriarty the father we never found, I think of Dean Moriarty. [310]

LEROI JONES

The Screamers

LYNN HOPE adjusts his turban under the swishing red green yellow shadow lights. Dots. Suede heaven raining, windows yawning cool summer air, and his musicians watch him grinning, quietly, or high with wine blotches on four dollar shirts. A yellow girl will not dance with me, nor will Teddy's people, in line to the left of the stage, readying their *Routines*. Haroldeen, the most beautiful, in her pitiful dead sweater. Make it yellow, wish it whole. Lights. Teddy, Sonny Boy, Kenney & Calvin, Scram, a few of Nat's boys jamming long washed handkerchiefs in breast pockets, pushing shirts into home-made cummerbunds, shuffling lightly for any audience.
"The Cross-Over", Deen laughing at us all. And they perform in solemn unison a social tract of love. (With no music till Lynn finishes 'macking' with any big-lipped Esther screws across the stage. White and green plaid jackets his men wear, and that twisted badge, black turban on red string conked hair. (OPPRESSORS!) A greasy hipness, down-ness, nobody in our camp believed (having social worker mothers and postman fathers; or living squeezed in light skinned projects with adulterers and proud skinny ladies with soft voices). The theory, the spectrum, this sound backed inside their heads, and still rub sweaty against those lesser lights. Those niggers. Laundromat workers, beauticians, pregnant short haired jail bait separated all ways from 'us,' but in this vat we sweated gladly for each other. And rubbed. And Lynn could be a common hero, from whatever side we saw him. Knowing that energy, and its response. That drained silence we had to make with our hands, leaving actual love to Nat or Al or Scram. [290/291]

He stomped his foot, and waved one hand. The other hung loosely on his horn. And their turbans wove in among those shad-

LeRoi Jones, "The Screamers," in *The Moderns: An Anthology of New Writing in America*, ed. LeRoi Jones (New York: Corinth Books, 1963), pp. 290–96.

ows. Lynn's tighter, neater, and bright gorgeous yellow stuck with a green stone. Also, those green sparkling cubes dancing off his pinkies. A-boomp bahba bahba, A-boomp bahba bahba, A-boomp bahba bahba, A-boomp bahba bahba, the turbans sway behind him. And he grins before he lifts the horn, at deen or drunk becky, and we search the dark for girls.

Who would I get? (Not anyone who would understand this.) Some light girl who had fallen into bad times and ill-repute for dating Bubbles. And he fixed her later with his child, now she walks Orange st. wiping chocolate from its face. A disgraced white girl who learned to calypso in vocational school. Hence, behind halting speech, a humanity as paltry as her cotton dress. (And the big hats made a line behind her, stroking their erections, hoping for photographs to take down south). Lynn would oblige. He would make the most perverted hopes sensual and possible. Chanting at that dark crowd. Or some girl, a wino's daughter, with carefully vaselined bow legs would drape her filthy angora against the cardboard corinthian, eyeing past any greediness a white man knows, my soft tyrolean hat, pressed corduroy suit, and "B" sweater. Whatever they meant, finally to her, valuable shadows barely visible. Some stuck-up boy with "good" hair. And as a naked display of America, for I meant to her that same oppression. A stunted head of greased glass feathers, orange lips, brown pasted edge to the collar of her dying blouse. The secret perfume of poverty and ignorant desire. Arrogant too, at my disorder, which calls her smile mysterious. Turning to be eaten by the crowd. That mingled foliage of sweat and shadows: *Night Train* was what they swayed to. And smelled each other in The Grind, The Rub, The Slow Drag. From side to side, slow or jerked staccato as their wedding dictated. Big hats bent tight skirts, and some light girls' hair swept the resin on the floor. Respectable ladies put stiff arms on your waist to keep some light between, looking nervously at an ugly friend forever at the music's edge.

I wanted girls like Erselle, whose father sang on television, but my hair was not straight enough, and my father never learned how to drink. Our house sat lonely and large on a half-italian street, filled with important Negroes. (Though it is rumored they had a son, thin [291/292] with big eyes, they killed because he was crazy.) Surrounded by the haughty daughters of depressed economic groups. They plotted in their projects for mediocrity, and the neighborhood smelled of their despair. And only the wild or the very poor thrived in Graham's or could be roused by Lynn's histories and rhythms. America had choked the rest, who could sit still for hours under popular songs, or be readied for citizenship by slightly bohemian social workers. They rivaled pure emotion with wind-up record players that pumped Jo Stafford into Home Economics rooms. And these carefully scrubbed children of my parents' friends fattened on their rhythms until they could join the Urban League or Household Finance and hound the poor for their honesty.

I was too quiet to become a murderer, and too used to extravagance for their skinny lyrics. They mentioned neither cocaine nor Bach, which was my reading, and the flaw of that society. I disappeared into the slums, and fell in love with violence, and invented for myself a mysterious economy of need. Hence, I shambled anonymously thru Lloyd's, The Nitecap, The Hi-Spot, and Graham's desiring everything I felt. In a new english overcoat and green hat, scouring that town for my peers. And they were old pinch faced whores full of snuff and weak dope, celebrity fags with radio programs, mute bass players who loved me, and built the myth of my intelligence. You see, I left America on the first fast boat.

This was Sunday night, and the Baptists were still praying in their "fabulous" churches. Though my father sat listening to the radio, or reading pulp cowboy magazines, which I take in part to be the truest legacy of my spirit. God never had a chance. And I would be walking slowly towards The Graham, not even knowing how to smoke. Willing for any experience, any image, any further separation from where my good grades were sure to lead. Frightened of post offices, lawyer's offices, doctor's cars, the deaths of clean politicians. Or of the imaginary fat man, advertising cemeteries to his "good colored friends". Lynn's screams erased them all, and I thought myself intrepid white commando from the West. Plunged into noise and flesh, and their form become an ethic.

Now Lynn wheeled and hunched himself for another time. Fast dancers fanned themselves. Couples who practiced during the week talked over their steps. Deen and her dancing clubs readied avant-garde [292/293] routines. Now it was *Harlem Nocturne* which I whistled loudly one saturday in a laundromat, and the girl who stuffed in my khakis and stiff underwear asked was I a musician. I met her at Graham's that night and we waved, and I suppose she knew I loved her.

Nocturne was slow and heavy and the serious dancers loosened their ties. The slowly twisting lights made specks of human shadows, the darkness seemed to float around the hall. Any meat you clung to was yours those few minutes without interruption. The length of the music was the only form. And the idea was to press against each other hard, to rub, to shove the hips tight, and gasp at whatever passion. Professionals wore jocks against embarrassment. Amateurs, like myself, after the music stopped, put our hands quickly into our pockets, and retreated into the shadows. It was as meaningful as anything else we knew.

All extremes were popular with that crowd. The singers shouted, the musicians stomped and howled. The dancers ground each other past passion or moved so fast it blurred intelligence. We hated the popular song, and any freedman could tell you if you asked that white people danced jerkily, and were slower than our champions. One style, which developed as italians showed up with pegs, and our own grace moved towards bellbottom pants to further complicate the cipher, was the honk. The repeated rhythmic figure, a screamed riff, pushed in its insistence past music. It was hatred and frustration, secrecy and despair. It spurted out of the dipthong culture, and re-inforced the black cults of emotion. There was no compromise, no dreary sophistication, only the elegance of something that is too ugly to be described, and is diluted only at the agent's peril. All the saxophonists of that world were honkers, Illinois, Gator, Big Jay, Jug, the great sounds of our day. Ethnic historians, actors, priests of the unconscious. That stance spread like fire thru the cabarets and joints of the black cities, so that the sound itself became a basis for thought, and the innovators searched for uglier modes. Illinois would leap and twist his head, scream when he wasn't playing. Gator would strut up and down the stage, dancing for emphasis, shaking his long gassed hair in his face and coolly mopping it back. Jug, the beautiful horn, would wave back and forth so high we all envied him his connection, or he'd stomp softly to the edge of the stage whispering those raucous threats. Jay first turned the mark around, opened the way further for the completely [293/294] nihilistic act. McNeeley, the first Dada coon of the age, jumped and stomped and yowled and finally sensed the only other space that form allowed. He fell first on his knees, never releasing the horn, and walked that way across the stage. We hunched together drowning any sound, relying on Jay's contorted face for evidence that there was still music, though none of us needed it now. And then he fell backwards, flat on his back, with both feet stuck up high in the air, and he kicked and thrashed and the horn spat enraged sociologies.

That was the night Hip Charlie, the Baxter Terrace Romeo, got wasted right in front of the place. Snake and four friends mashed him up and left him for the ofays to identify. Also the night I had the grey bells and sat in the Chinese restaurant all night to show them off. Jay had set a social form for the poor, just as Bird and Dizzy proposed it for the middle class. On his back screaming was the Mona Lisa with the mustache, as crude and simple. Jo Stafford could not do it. Bird took the language, and we woke up one Saturday whispering Ornithology. Blank verse.

And Newark always had a bad reputation, I mean, everybody could pop their fingers. Was hip. Had walks. Knew all about The Apple. So I suppose when the word got to Lynn what Big Jay had done, he knew all the little down cats were waiting to see him in this town. He knew he had to cook. And he blasted all night, crawled and leaped, then stood at the side of the stand, and watched us while he fixed his sky, wiped his face. Watched us to see how far he'd gone, but he was tired and we weren't, which was not where it was. The girls rocked slowly against the silence of the horns, and big hats pushed each other or made plans for murder. We had not completely come. All sufficiently eaten by Jay's memory, "on his back, kicking his feet in the air, Ga-ud Dam!" So he moved cautiously to the edge of the stage, and the gritty muslims he played with gathered close. It was some mean honking blues, and he made no attempt to hide his intentions. He was breaking bad. "Okay, baby," we all thought, "Go for yourself". I was standing at the back of the hall with one arm behind my back, so the overcoat could hang over in that casual gesture of fashion. Lynn was moving, and the camel walkers were moving in the corners. The fast dancers and practicers making the whole hall dangerous. "Off my suedes, motherfucker." Lynn was trying to move us, and even I did the one step I knew, safe at the back of the hall. The [294/295] hippies ran for girls. Ugly girls danced with each other. Skippy, who ran the lights, made them move faster in that circle on the ceiling, and darkness raced around the hall. Then Lynn got his riff, that rhythmic figure we knew he would repeat, the honked note that would be his personal evaluation of the world. And he screamed it so the veins in his face stood out like neon. "Uhh, yeh, Uhh, yeh, Uhh, yeh", we all screamed to push him further. So he opened his eyes for a second, and really made his move. He looked over his shoulder at the other turbans, then marched in time with his riff, on his toes across the stage. They followed; he marched across to the other side, repeated, then finally he descended, still screaming, into the crowd, and as the sidemen followed, we made a path for them around the hall. They were strutting, and all their horns held very high, and they were only playing that one scary note. They moved near the back of the hall, chanting and swaying, and passed right in front of me. I had a little cup full of wine a murderer friend of mine made me drink, so I drank it and tossed the cup in the air, then fell in line behind the last wild horn man, strutting like the rest of them. Bubbles and Rogie followed me, and four eyed Moselle Boyd. And we strutted back and forth pumping our arms, repeating with Lynn Hope, "Yeh, Uhh, Yeh, Uhh". Then everybody fell in behind us, yelling still. There was confusion and stumbling, but there were no real fights. The thing they wanted was right there and easily accessible. No one could stop you from getting in that line. "It's too crowded. It's too many people on the line!" some people yelled. So Lynn thought further, and made to destroy the ghetto. We went out into the lobby and in perfect rhythm down the marble steps. Some musicians laughed, but Lynn and some others kept the note, till the others fell back in. Five or six hundred hopped up woogies tumbled out into Belmont Avenue. Lynn marched right in the center of the street. Sunday night traffic stopped, and honked. Big Red yelled at a bus driver, "Hey, baby, honk that horn in time or shut it off!" The bus driver cooled it. We screamed and screamed at the clear image of ourselves as we should always be. Ecstatic, completed, involved in a secret communal expression. It would be the form of the sweetest revolution, to hucklebuck into the fallen capitol, and let the oppressors lindy hop out. We marched all the way to Spruce, weaving among the stalled cars, laughing at the dazed white men who sat behind the wheels. Then Lynn turned and we strutted [295/296] back towards the hall. The late show at the National was turning out, and all the big hats there jumped right in our line.

Then the Nabs came, and with them, the fire engines. What was it a labor riot? Anarchists? A nigger strike? The paddy wagons and cruisers pulled in from both sides, and sticks and billies started flying, heavy streams of water splattering the marchers up and down the street. America's responsible immigrants were doing her light work again. The knives came out, the razors, all the Biggers who would not be bent, counterattacked or came up behind the civil servants smashing at them with coke bottles and aerials. Belmont writhed under the dead economy and splivs floated in the gutters, disappearing under cars. But for awhile, before the war had reached its peak, Lynn and his musicians, a few other fools, and I, still marched, screaming thru the maddened crowd. Onto the sidewalk, into the lobby, half-way up the stairs, then we all broke our different ways, to save whatever it was each of us thought we loved. [296]

Questions for Study, Discussion, and Writing

I. PERSPECTIVES

Millgate: *American Novelists and American Society.* What is the basic reason for the differences between American and English novelists in their conceptions of society? Why have the American novelists lacked assurance in their treatment of society? Why does the American tend to regard the novel as a political instrument? What does Millgate mean by the "moral fable"? What is his attitude toward the attempts of Dos Passos and Wolfe, among others, to encompass the whole of American experience? Compare his statements of these two authors with what Commager says of them at the conclusion of his article. How does the American writer seem to obfuscate the task demanded of the writer: "to define and illuminate the human predicament"? Why has America never favored the novelist of manners? In the American novel of manners why is the person who is opposed to society usually portrayed as the hero? Why have American novelists failed to succeed in the picaresque novel? In what two ways have American writers found that they could cope with the "peculiar difficulties" found in the American social structure?

Commager: *The Literature of Revolt.* What is the dominant attitude, according to Commager, of serious writers toward the American economic system? What were the reasons for the writers' repudiation of the economic system? What is Commager's objection to the protest literature of the twenties? What are the differences between Lewis' and Howells' critical approaches toward American life? What are the reasons for the failure of their separate satirical works? Explain the significance of the statement: "It explains nothing to say that they were out of touch with reality: they had taken out a patent on realism." What explanation can account for the fact that the American writers were objecting to the economic system at the moment when the masses were accepting the system? What is De Voto's objection to the American writer's insistence on criticizing his society? What is Dos Passos' answer to what the American writer seeks? What is the final optimistic note of Thomas Wolfe? In what ways do Millgate and Commager agree and disagree in their evaluation of American writing?

Bourne: *For Radicals.* What is the reason for Bourne's optimism about the possibilities for social reform? Tie this argument in with what Commager has to say about these possibilities. What kind of ideal social order does Bourne have in mind? What are some of the things the "radical" is critical of? In what ways do most "men of position" conform? What does Bourne think of efficiency? What is Bourne looking for in people and in the concept of success? What does the liberally educated student realize about the institutions around him? What is the implication in the task the young radical has set for himself, that of "plunging into its [the world's] activity and attempting to subjugate it to one's ideals"? What is the necessity for self-cultivation for the young radical? How should a radical use prestige? What is the role of the radical? In what ways should any of us be allowed to compromise? In what ways not? What is the difference in tone between Bourne's message and that of Rexroth?

Aaron: *The Rebels.* What does the author say about the young artist-rebels' ancestry? Why was Emerson and later Whitman considered important in the tradition? How can transcendentalism be explained as an ancestor of social idealism? Give reasons for the left writers' objections to Puritanism. What were the enemies of freedom to the young intellectuals? According to Brooks what were some bad effects resulting from the European influence on American writing? What was the significance of Brooks' attack on American culture? Compare this version of the background of leftist writing with Freeman's version.

A Backward Glance: What were some reasons for many writers' disillusionment with the Communist party? Why did the writers first join the party? In what ways did the party help writers? In what ways did it harm them? What was expected of the party writer? What is the author's final evaluation of the value of the party to writers and to American literature? Compare Aaron's version of the value of the party with Freeman's.

Freeman: *The Tradition of American Revolutionary Literature.* How does Freeman define and identify the bourgeois revolution? What makes the literature in the bourgeois period a "class" literature? What was the relationship between art and the ego and what suggestion is here about what the relationship should be? What were some of the philosophies and social movements behind the doctrines of Marx and Engels? What was the political and social orientation of *The Comrade* and what importance does Freeman say it held for American writers? What significance did the Russian revolution have for American writers? What kind of socialist literary heritage did the writer of the twenties find? What were the central tasks for the writers of the twenties? Discuss Freeman's change in tone in his final paragraph. What does the final poem do to the work itself?

Mills: *On the New Left.* What are Mills' definitions of the following terms: end-of-ideology, liberalism, the liberal rhetoric? What is his objection to the political formula of the liberal-rhetoric school? Mills uses four descriptive points to identify the ideology of the end-of-ideology school: (1) it is an ideology of "political complacency . . . to justify the status quo"; (2) it has no orienting theories of society and history; (3) the agency of change for this school is the "going institution"; (4) it denies the possibility of political and human ideals. Why does he find these points objectionable? What group can best answer these four points of criticism? What is his definition of political "right" and "left"? Where do the possibilities for heroism lie open for men today? How do critics attack Mills' position today? What is the advantage of the utopian position today? Compare Mill's "radical of the new left" to Bourne's radical, and Mills' argument with that of Joseph Freeman.

King: *Love, Law and Civil Disobedience.* What are the two forces now opposing each other in the Negroes' fight for social justice? Why is the Negro now determined to fight? What are some of the ways in which oppressed people can deal with their oppression? Why must nonviolent resistance have the philosophy that the means must be as pure as the end. What is King's definition of the ethic of love? How does the ethic of love affect the participant's reaction to an unjust social system? What is the conception of man accepted by the participants of the civil rights struggle? How can a person justify disobeying a law? When one cannot accept morality as the basis for law, what can he use as a definition of an unjust law? How does King use history to prove his theory of the necessity and propriety of civil disobedience?

Rexroth: *The Students Take Over.* What does the author say about the morality of our society? What does Rexroth mean by "immoralism"? What are some of the "immoral" acts the student today is asked to accept? What place does Rexroth give the social rebel? Give the background of the sentence: "Modern society is too complex and too delicate to afford social and political Darwinism any more." Show the relationship that exists among Thoreau, Martin Luther King, and Rexroth in their attitudes toward morality. What is the value of individual action today? Why shouldn't one act or become a hero? What significance did Bayard Rustin's revolt have? What achievements can be traced to the Montgomery bus boycott? What does the author say about the exurbanite young versus the college student involved in social action? What did Rexroth find so remarkable about the sit-ins? In what ways was Chessman a symbol for the young? Why don't the students' activities take the form of a political conflict?

Widmer: *The Diogenes Style.* In what ways have modern literary rebels been influenced by the Judaic prophetic tradition? In what ways does the modern rebel reject this tradition? What are the similarities between the Cynic and the popular impression of the beatnik? What were the reasons for the cynics' obscenity and crudeness? How can one describe Diogenes: his dress, his way of life, etc.? Why did Diogenes live this way? What were some of the parts in his program for reform? In what ways were Diogenes' positions extreme? What is the rebel's attitude toward art and why does he hold this attitude? What are some of the main principles of the rebels? What does the work ethic have to do with society's attitude toward the rebel? What are the author's arguments in support of the statement that society should tolerate the literary rebel? In what ways does Widmer's argument represent a narrow view of the rebel's place and function in society?

Sisk: *Beatniks and Tradition.* What is the importance of the beat writer? What is the meaning of the subversive tradition? What is Sisk's description of the Enemy? Compare this to the one described by Rexroth. What are the characteristics of the writers named as ancestors of the beat writers? What dialectic is at work between the writer and his generation? What are some of the examples of this dialectic? What is dangerous about the habit of equating "literature with opposition to orthodoxy"? In what ways are the beat writers committed to their culture? Why are Americans in general permissive toward its writers in the subversive tradition? What arguments are there to reveal society's fear? Why does the subversive writer have to take an extreme position in his writing and actions? Why is the beat writer likened to a poet? In what ways is the beat writer underlining "traditionally sacred American patterns of thought and action"? Why does the American society need the beat writer?

Carmichael and Hamilton: *The Concept of Black Power.* What will the adoption of black power do for the black people? What is the premise of black power? What is the importance to the authors of the "ethnic basis of American politics"? Discuss the authors' comparison of black power and racism. Of black power and nonviolence. Why do the authors reject civil rights movements? Why do they reject integration as an answer? What are the basic differences between their arguments and the arguments of Martin Luther King?

II. THE SUBVERSIVE TRADITION

Franklin: *The Speech of Polly Baker*. With what two laws is Polly Baker concerned in her plea? What arguments does she advance to support her case for upholding one law and for violating the other? How does she define the duties of a good citizen? Why does she believe herself to be one? What significant point does she make about the nature of man's laws? Discuss the effectiveness of Franklin's couching his arguments in this form rather than in a formal essay about the hypocrisy encouraged by a double standard of morality. Does this selection bear out Mencken's contention in "The Iconoclast" about the relative effectiveness of the horse laugh and the syllogism?

Woolman: *A Plain Way of Living*. How was the decision of Jeremiah a model for Woolman? What did Woolman know that he must sacrifice? Why did he wish to decrease his business activities? To what features of his own trade did he object? What was the reason for his objection? What was his objection to credit purchases? Why, according to Woolman's reasoning, does "the too liberal use of spirituous liquors" lead to increased drinking? What principle should dictate the actions and desires of men? How does the neglect of this principle lead to "manifold confusions in the world"? What, according to Woolman, should be the guiding rule for businessmen?

Hawthorne: *The Maypole of Merry Mount*. Widmer, in "The Diogenes Style," characterizes what he calls "the archetypal rebel." In what ways do the Merry Mounters conform to this characterization: in their motivations, their appearance, their actions, their attitudes toward society, their social and personal values? In what ways do they differ? How do the attitudes and actions of the Puritans, as described by Hawthorne, conform to the standard response of "official society" toward the rebel as discussed by Widmer? Discuss the story as it symbolically characterizes two contrasting views of life. Note especially the connotative values suggested by the maypole, the whipping post, the sword, the falling roses, and the garland of flowers. What, according to Hawthorne, was the principal weakness of the Merry Mounters' way of life? How do they attempt to thwart the inevitable realities of life? Do Hawthorne's sympathies lie with the Merry Mounters or the Puritans? How does he reveal his sympathies? Discuss the implications of the resolution of the story.

Emerson: *Ode Inscribed to W. H. Channing.* In this poem Emerson explains to his friend William Henry Channing, a minister and humanitarian, the reasons for his aloofness from personal involvement in the humanitarian movements of his day, particularly the antislavery issue and the Mexican war. What, according to Emerson, is the work that he is best fitted for? What will happen if he ignores this work and bends his energies to other purposes? What are his objections to political reformers? (Note that Contoocook is a river in New Hampshire; Agiochook is the Indian name for the White Mountains.) What purpose, according to Emerson, would the secession of the North from the South, on the issue of slavery, ultimately serve? What is Emerson's principal criticism of American society in the poem? What purpose should laws serve—property rights or human rights? What is Emerson's hope for the resolution of the political issue? (See Judges 14:9 for the allusion to "honey/Out of the lion.")

Whitman: From *Song of Myself.* Whitman's break with the past can be seen in several aspects of his long poem *Song of Myself* (the first edition of which appeared on July 4, 1855): its strophic, rather than stanzaic, verse paragraphs; its free verse lines—lack of regular patterns of meter and rhyme; but most of all in its subject matter and statements about man. What statements are especially inclined to shock or challenge an American society with a firm belief in the duality of man's nature, in the distrust of physical or sensual pleasure, in the authority of tradition, and in the positive values of humility, work, and productivity? Against what other values of American society does the poem "beat the gong of revolt" (section 23)? What does Whitman mean by "myself"? Discuss whether his pronoun denotes personal egotism or faith in the significance, even divinity, of the "common man."

Dreiser: *Sister Carrie: The Pursuit of Dreams.* A farm girl from Wisconsin, Carrie Meeber arrives almost penniless in Chicago to live with her sister and her family. Their drab life and Carrie's dismal experiences at a factory eventually drive her to become the mistress of a salesman, Drouet, who promises marriage. Later she is deceived by Hurstwood in a false marriage ceremony and lives with him in New York. As Hurstwood's fortunes decline, she finds work as a chorus girl and leaves him. She becomes a well-known actress, with the admirers, wealth, and luxuries that she had dreamed of from the beginning. The first of the two passages relates Carrie's conflicting views of herself after she takes up with Drouet; the second passage concludes the novel. As much a victim as a rebel, Carrie challenges conventional morality in her search for the glittering world of her dreams. What is the specific nature of the conflict in Carrie's mind after she becomes Drouet's mistress? Does Dreiser make a moral judgment of Carrie? What is his attitude toward her? To what does he attribute her dispiriting thoughts in the first passage? How does he object to conventional explanations of immoral behavior in the concluding passage?

Mark Twain: *The War Prayer.* Mark Twain was a close observer of the wars that occurred near the turn of the century, particularly the Spanish-American war and the ensuing occupation of the Philippines. Among other notable figures, Mark Twain denounced the war as imperialistic. "The War Prayer" is one of his many satires of imperialism and the intense nationalistic fervor that often accompanies it. How does he employ the contrast of emotionalism and rationalism to emphasize his message? Does he suggest merely that emotional oratory deludes the congregation, or that the congregation wishes to be deluded? Since the explicit statement of the implied meaning of the prayer is so clearly stated and undeniable, what comment does Twain make on the audience in the final sentence?

Lewis: *The Red Swede.* In *Main Street,* Carol Kennicott, a college-educated librarian from Minneapolis, comes to Gopher Prairie, a small midwestern town of the early twentieth century, as the wife of the village doctor. She is appalled by what Lewis calls the "Village Virus," an intellectual and cultural sterility, a complacency and barbarism that is "Dullness made God." The social life of the town is characterized by the group known as the Jolly Seventeen, the intellectual life by the Thanatopsis Club. The village rebel, Bjornstam, is one of the few people of the town sympathetic with Carol's attitudes and her efforts to raise the town's cultural level. Against what conventional attitudes is Bjornstam in rebellion? How do his manner of life and his opinions of the town's institutions express his rebellious stance? In what form of rebellion does he believe? Why does he lack faith in the foreman's plans for reform? What does he feel to be basically at fault with Gopher Prairie?

Dos Passos: *In the Treadmill.* The three soldiers of Dos Passos' novel about World War I are Fuselli, who quickly loses his ambition to rise in the army as its impersonality crushes him; Chrisfield, a farm boy who is driven to murder by the senseless inhumanity of his military experiences; and John Andrews, a sensitive musician who eventually deserts with Chrisfield. He comes back, however, to face his punishment, but after the armistice, when he can see no reason for staying in uniform, he deserts again. The present passage is the conclusion of "Under the Wheels," the last section of the novel. How does the contrast between the mechanistic and natural imagery in the selection reinforce its comment? What is Geneviève Rod's attitude toward Andrews and his desertion? If she represents the authoritarian, ruling aspects of society, what does her relationship with Andrews suggest about the role of the artist in society? What is Andrews attempting to express through his desertion and through his musical composition? What does Dos Passos symbolically suggest at the end of the book to be the ultimate destruction caused by the war?

Mencken: *Duty* and *The Iconoclast.* What reasons does Mencken give to justify the neglect of "duty"? Why is it unimportant, according to him, for each man to conform to the values of society? What is his attitude toward the nonconformist. What is the value of the rebel to society? What is the etymology of the word *iconoclast?* What social institutions are the particular objects of Menken's attack in the paragraph on the iconoclast? What attitudes of Mencken toward these institutions are expressed in both of the selections? What does Mencken reveal about his attitude toward the American mind when he says that "one horse-laugh is worth ten thousand syllogisms"? Why should it be more effective as well as more intelligent?

Anderson: *Over the Threshold.* Although Anderson's account of his departure from his paint business in Elyria, Ohio, is fictionalized, it dramatizes a typical gesture of revolt by the artist. What is it that Anderson, as an artist, finds objectionable in American commercial and industrial society? What is the purpose of his account of the early ideals of America, a section of his narrative that he calls a digression? What is it, according to him, that "went wrong in the beginning" with America? What does he say is the principal aspiration of America if it is not money? What had he wished to accomplish as the president of his company? Would all of these attainments have been merely fulfillments of ambitions thrust upon him by society? Why did he find them unsatisfying, and even impossible? In what way was Anderson prostituting his life? What, ultimately, is the reason for his rebellion?

Baldwin: *Notes of a Native Son.* What was the effect of his father's death on Baldwin? How had he viewed his father and his father's beliefs? How had the father responded to his color? How had it affected his relationship with his family? Does Baldwin suggest a causal relationship between his father's color and his paranoia? What was Baldwin's attitude as a child toward white people? Why did Baldwin despise his father for his behavior when the teacher came to the house? Why had the year before his father's death been important to Baldwin? What had he learned about himself in New Jersey? In the light of his father's mental illness, is it significant that Baldwin describes his new feelings as a disease? What attitudes and responses of the white people prompted Baldwin's act of rebellion on his last night in Trenton? What does he mean by saying that his *real* life was in danger from the hatred he bore in his own heart?

Ginsberg: *America.* What are the specific features of American social attitudes and traditions that are the objects of Ginsberg's criticisms in the poem? What does he feel that America has done to him? How do his responses compare with those of other artists (Andrews in *Three Soldiers* and Sherwood Anderson) in this section? Does the America he suggests bear any resemblance to the one Anderson describes in his *Story Teller's Story* before "something went wrong"? Does his view of himself as a person suggest in any way Whitman's comments about his "self"? What does he imply in the statement "America the plum blossoms are falling"? What is the purpose of the baby talk and movie-Indian language in the poem? What human and social values are implied in the poem?

III. RADICALS AND REFORMERS

Jefferson: *A Little Rebellion.* Under what three forms of government do societies exist? Why does Jefferson prefer the government "wherein the will of every one has a just influence"? What does he mean by "rebellion"? What kind of government is necessary to allow a rebellion of this kind?

In the second letter, why does Jefferson say that "no society [should] make . . . a perpetual law"? Why are laws so difficult to repeal? What are Jefferson's ideas about laws of inheritance for people and institutions? In what ways is Jefferson's thesis in these two letters radical? In what way not?

Thoreau: *Civil Disobedience.* Does Thoreau think it possible that there could be no government at all? What is his real point in saying that the best government is no government at all? Does he equate "people" with their government? According to Thoreau, what *is* the government and what strength does it have? By what means, majorities or by conscience, does Thoreau say that governments should govern, and what are the full implications of his conclusions? What does Thoreau think of soldiers? Of legislators, heroes, and patriots? What is the relationship between the state and the hero? Why was Thoreau opposed to the American government at the time he was writing? When will most men recognize the right of revolution? Where should reform begin? In what ways can we show our protest to a government? What relationship between the individual and the state is similar to that between the state and the federal government? How does this fit the analogy of John Brown and the State of Virginia? In what way is "action from principle" revolutionary? Why did Thoreau pick on the taxpayer as the one he should confront with his rebellion? What is Thoreau's attitude toward the jail and his imprisonment? In what way is the State superior to the Man? Why did he change his attitude toward his neighbors after his imprisonment? How does Thoreau judge the Constitution and the government? In what way does he seem naive about governments—in respect to the dangers inherent in their power, for instance? What final statement does he make about the importance of an individual toward his government?

Thoreau: *A Plea for John Brown.* What crime is the government guilty of in taking the life of Brown? How is Thoreau allowing Brown to be the heroic embodiment of what he had expressed in "Civil Disobedience"? What is the secret of the eloquence in Brown's works? This talk was given on the day of Brown's execution. Discuss the ironies in Brown's prophecy of the Civil War, in the fact of his own rebellion in the light of the larger rebellion that was to occur a few months later. Compare the speech to the brief speech of Vanzetti's recorded in the excerpt from Sinclair's *Boston.*

Bellamy: *Return to Chaos.* What does the author accomplish by the dream technique? What is there about the headlines that betray the direction of Bellamy's criticism? What is the author's criticism of advertising? Of the presence of the stores? Of the banks? Of working conditions in the manufacturing establishments? About efficiency in capitalism? What dangers to a democratic form of government are there in Bellamy's comparison of the organization of an army and the commercial structure of Boston when he wrote the book? Why was the company at his fiancée's house so scandalized by his statements? What effect is gained on the reader by the reverse awakening to the year 2000? What would Thoreau think of Bellamy's arguments?

London: *A Night with the Philomaths.* Jack London's novel *The Iron Heel,* written in the form of a diary by Ernest Everhard's wife, Avis, describes fictitious events that take place from 1912 to 1932. In what respect does the novel seem dated (tone of the novel, description of society, etc.)? In what ways did London's Darwinian conception of nature and man influence this work? How do the ideas about class structure and the inevitablity of class warfare in the novel reflect the intellectual current of the times? Discuss the conception of "power" as London conceives it and compare it with the conception in Commager's article (in "Perspectives"). The last part of the novel described in detail scenes of bloodshed and destruction resulting from the socialists' uprising in what London referred to as the "second revolt." How does London's description of the debate anticipate his ending of the novel? What does he suggest here about the possibilities and extremes of human action? In what ways have the events in the past few decades borne out his predictions? In what respects can this novel be considered modern?

Dos Passos: *Lover of Mankind.* What is the author's comment about the worker and his allegiance to Debs? In what way is this criticism of the worker a criticism of America's middle class attitude? Why were people afraid of Debs? In what way can he be described as a social rebel?

Dos Passos: *Joe Hill.* How does Joe Hill fit into a rebel tradition? What is the author's feeling about his story of Joe Hill? List the ingredients in the story that make it appealing enough to be made into a legend.

Halper: *The Workers Take Over.* In what tradition of literature would you place this particular story? What is the author's point? What kind of social rebel is Heitman? What does this story say about trade unionism? What does the story say about the work ethic? Would you call this story an argument in favor of socialism? Compare Heitman and Joe Hill as rebels.

Sinclair: *Sacco and Vanzetti.* Nicola Sacco and Bartolemeo Vanzetti, one a shoe worker and the other a fish peddler, both immigrants and professed anarchists, were accused in 1920 of a payroll robbery and murder in South Braintree, Massachusetts, and after a lengthy period of trials, delays and investigations were executed August 23, 1927. It was widely believed that the two men were convicted because they were anarchists rather than for any proved guilt. Why did the story arouse such a reaction from the liberals of the time? What is the reason that Vanzetti's speech has such an appeal? Compare it with Sinclair's eulogistic praise of the speech. What criticism does Sinclair make of the Boston merchant and why does he make this criticism? What kind of propaganda is this writing of Sinclair's? What is Sinclair's moral tone? What comment does Sinclair make about labor? About the liberal intellectuals?

Freeman: *From Bohemia to Russia.* This excerpt is a family portrait, but the family description serves a social purpose. What is this purpose? What does the story say about the American family? What comment does it make about success? About the middle class consciousness of the workingman's problems? What is Freeman's most serious criticism of capitalism? What general mood is established in this story? On what note does he end the story?

Steinbeck: *A Truce in the Battle. In Dubious Battle* is a story of two labor organizers, Mac and Jim, often referred to in the book as "reds," who initiate a farm-workers' strike in a California apple-growing valley. What picture of the strikers do we get in this scene? Of the apple growers? What kind of picture of heroism does this sketch reveal? What kind of literature is this? How successful is it as literature? As propaganda?

IV. A MAJORITY OF ONE

Emerson: *The Transcendentalist.* What distinctions does Emerson make between idealists and materialists? What is his meaning in saying that "Every materialist will be an idealist; but an idealist can never go backward to be a materialist"? What is the source of the idealist's knowledge? How is this source at the center of the idealist's ethical system? How does this ethical system put him at odds with society and its conventions? Why do the Transcendentalists object to work? To what sort of work do they object? What is the source of the Transcendentalist's loneliness? Why does he reject social companionship? What does he expect of his fellow man? What is the basis of the objections of "the philanthropists" to the Transcendentalists? Why do the Transcendentalists object to participation in "causes"? What reforms do they seek? What is Emerson's judgment of them? What is the cause of their frustration, of their compromise with life, of their optimism? What is the value, according to Emerson, of the Transcendentalists? What do they have to offer society? What view of them should society take?

Thoreau: *Where I Lived, and What I Lived For.* Read the first two paragraphs with particular attention to the words "price," "possession," "rich," and "poverty." How do the meanings implied by Thoreau differ from the more usual meanings? What did he find attractive about the Hollowell farm? What does it have in common with his residence at Walden? What was Thoreau's purpose in going to Walden? The chapter develops a contrast between *actual* time and *real* time, and between *actual* place and *real* place. (What parallels are there to Emerson's distinction between idealists and materialists?) What was the real time at Walden? What was the real location of Walden? What does Thoreau imply when he states that "earth is not continent but insular"? What does Thoreau see to be the purpose of life? What is his principal criticism of society? By referring to a dictionary, explain the pun about "sleepers" in his discussion of railroads. Compare Thoreau's statement about the railroad riding "upon us" with Emerson's criticism of "things" in his "Ode to Channing." What are Thoreau's specific comments about work and news? What contrast does Thoreau make between *time* and *eternity?* Which of these concepts, to Thoreau, *is,* and which *appears* to be?

Melville: From *Moby-Dick.* These are the first and twenty-third chapters of the novel. What were Ishmael's initial motives for wishing to go to sea? What was his state of mind when he felt it "high time to get to sea" quickly? What does he mean when he says his "hypos" had gotten the upper hand of him? Does Melville's attention to the lure of water suggest that the water has a symbolic value for mankind? If so, of what is it a symbol? Why did Ishmael choose to go to sea as a common sailor? What social values does he express by this choice of roles? What conventional values of society does he challenge in his discussion of the social levels aboard ship? What does the great whale signify to Ishmael? What comments of Ishmael's especially mark him as a rebel, unable to be satisfied with conventional life? What conflict does Melville suggest in the brief chapter about Bulkington? What does Bulkington sacrifice in his endless voyages? What, according to Melville, does he gain?

Dickinson: *Three Poems.* Compare the remarks about conformity in the first of the poems with those by Thoreau in his plea for John Brown, by Twain in "The War Prayer," and by Anderson in "Over the Threshold." What does Emily Dickinson mean by the phrase "divine majority" in the second poem? Does the reference to the soul limit the application of the poem to spiritual "society," that is, religious beliefs? Can the poem be read as a statement of intense individualism? What is the source of imagery of the second stanza? How does this stanza employ social contrasts? Is the valve and stone imagery in the last two lines appropriate and successful? How does the verse form (especially the two-accent lines in the first two stanzas and the one-accent lines in the final stanza) reinforce the ideas in the poem? In the third poem, how does Emily Dickinson's attitude toward the Calvinistic Puritanism of her townspeople compare with Whitman's remarks about religion? Do they agree about the immediacy of divine revelation through nature? What aspects of nature are emphasized in the poem as manifestations of the divine spirit? Do they seem appropriate images for the poetry of a New England spinster? Would Whitman's images have served as well?

Cowley: *The Story of a Suicide.* Why does Harry Crosby's life interest Cowley? What themes seen elsewhere in this volume does it illustrate (see particularly Cowley's sixth paragraph)? Crosby's suicide, says Cowley, "was the last term of a syllogism." What does Cowley mean by this statement? What would be the other terms of the syllogism? What was the effect of Crosby's experience in the hills of Verdun? Did Crosby understand what had happened to him? What was Crosby's state of mind after the war? For what was he seeking? (How does he compare and contrast in his personality and his search with Kerouac's Dean Moriarty?) Why did Crosby turn to books? How did the "religion of art" serve as a means of escape from what Crosby found repugnant in life? To what aspects of society did he most clearly object? What were the effects of Crosby's reading on him? What did the sun symbolize for Crosby? What is Cowley's attitude toward Crosby? Does he portray Crosby as a victim of his experiences and his society? Does he suggest that Crosby's violent rejection of conventional society led him into, or close to, actual insanity?

Miller: *Epidaurus.* Epidaurus, one of the most important seaports of ancient Greece, is the site of a huge amphitheater, the outstanding example in existence today of a Greek theater. On the plain beyond is the Temple of Esculapius, the god of healing, to which invalids flocked during the annual festivals in his honor in search of a divine cure. How does Miller characterize the peace he found at Epidaurus? What was it about Epidaurus that contributed to this feeling? What fault does Miller find with what society regards as progress? What does he believe to be the faults of society? How does he suggest that these faults can be corrected? What type of rebellion or revolution does he advocate? Compare Miller's essay with the remarks of Thoreau in "Where I Lived, and What I Lived For." How do these authors agree in their idea of what life should be and how its goals may be attained? What parallels can be drawn between Epidaurus as Miller describes it and the residence at Walden in Thoreau's essay?

Mailer: *The Patron Saint of MacDougal Alley.* In a prefatory note to the story, Mailer says that "it is about a Beatnik who arrived too early to know his name" (Mailer wrote the story in 1951). What characteristics of the beatniks as described by John P. Sisk in his essay can be seen in the character, attitudes, and actions of Pierrot? What are his dominant traits? What is he seeking? What is suggested by his lack of awareness of time? How does his inability or unwillingness to exist with reference to time compare with Thoreau in "Where I Lived, and What I lived For"? What is Mailer's (or the narrator's) attitude toward him? Does he view Pierrot with understanding and sympathy? Does he see him as only an idiotic bungler incapable of living a conventional life? What does the title signify.

Kerouac: *Dean Moriarty.* Why did Dean go to New York? What was he seeking? What qualities of Dean are of particular interest to the narrator, Sal Paradise? What does he represent for Sal? In what way is Dean a rebel? How does he differ from the "intellectuals"? What does Sal mean when he says that Dean's "criminality" was "a wild yea-saying outburst of American joy"? What features of Dean's character are illustrated by the description of his work as a parking lot attendant? How does the presentation of Dean in the concluding selection differ from that in the opening? How has he changed?

Compare the description of Dean's visit with the Los Angeles family with Anderson's remarks about his visits with strangers. Are the reactions of Dean and Anderson similar? What is it they both hope to find in strangers? How does Dean compare as a friend with Remi? How do their values differ? What is Sal's attitude toward Remi? What does Dean ultimately symbolize for Sal? Is his symbolic value to Sal supported by what Sal says of him—of his character and his way of life?

Jones: *The Screamers.* Who are the two groups of patrons at the Graham? Whom does the narrator refer to by "us"? How is this group separated from the other? What does the music from Lynn Hope's horn do for the two groups? What is it about his music that appeals to the listeners? What does it represent for them? How does the narrator contrast Hope's music with popular songs? What social implication does this contrast have? What features of American society does the narrator rebel against? As the patrons follow Hope from the Graham, what are their feelings toward each other? What is the effect of Hope's music on them at this time? What are the motives of the dancers in going out into the street? What precipitates their actions into a riot? What does the narrator suggest would be the "sweetest revolution"? Who are the "oppressors" in the story? Is there irony in the last sentence? What is meant by the phrase "whatever it was each of us thought we loved"? What is the meaning of the title—who are "the screamers"?

Topics for Longer Papers

The questions on the individual selections may serve as the basis for topics for short papers, often comparative or contrastive essays or analyses of individual works. Longer papers, supported either by the selections in this volume or by works mentioned in the "Suggestions for Further Reading," may be based on the following considerations:

1. The attitudes of the rebel toward laws and concepts of justice with which he is in disagreement.
2. The attitudes of society toward the rebel.
3. The value of social rebellion and the constructive role of the rebel.
4. The attitudes of the rebel toward tradition, including religion.
5. The Christian as rebel.
6. The rebellion against the double standard of morality.
7. The rebel against the economic aspects of capitalism.
8. The rebel against the moral aspects of capitalism.
9. The expatriate as rebel.
10. The rebellion of the beat generation.
11. A comparison of Caryl Chessman and Dean Moriarty. (See Rexroth's essay.)
12. Whitman or Thoreau as beatnik.
13. Emerson's or Thoreau's influence on American social rebellion.
14. Martin Luther King's debt to Thoreau.
15. The social rebellion expressed in the works of a selected writer or of a single book by an appropriate writer.
16. Differences between the rebel and the reformer.
17. Proletarian idealism in the works (or a work) of a selected writer.
18. John Brown as the prototype of the American social rebel in literature.
19. The rebellion of youth in the twentieth century.

20. The artist as rebel in American literature.
21. The village rebel in American literature.
22. The rebel as bohemian.
23. The poetry (or fiction) of the beat generation.
24. The literature of the hippies of the 1960's.
25. The rebellion of the "lost generation."
26. The literature of the rebellion of the Negro.
27. The radical and the beatnik.
28. Social morality. (See Thoreau, Rexroth, and King.)
29. The cynic as rebel.
30. The hipster as a modern hero.

Suggestions for Further Reading

The first literature of protest in the United States was political, a category outside of the concern of this anthology. In the early 1800's the spokesmen for the Transcendentalist movement, influenced as they were by European and English transcendental philosophies, by American frontier and agrarian concepts, and by the democratic ideas embodied in the Declaration of Independence and the Constitution, created an image of individualism which directed the first important literature of social protest outside of the political writings. The protest movement in the name of the individual took two directions: the moral claim and the artist's claim, both of these claims, or justifications, deriving their primary sanction from ideas in essays of Ralph Waldo Emerson. An important assumption from Emerson's essay "Nature" is that any individual, but in particular the Poet or Seer or Transcendentalist, is capable of perceiving spiritual and moral beauties and intellectual truths, and therefore may assert claims on the basis of the truths gained by means of his perceptions —claims, however, that quite possibly will place the individual at odds with his society. In most of his essays Emerson elaborates on this assumption, but of particular importance in this connection are his early essays, "The American Scholar" (1837), "Divinity School Address" (1838), "Self-Reliance" (1841), and "New England Reformers" (1844), in these works suggesting truly radical ways of viewing education, religion, and man's relation to government and society. Emerson describes his ideal individual in his essays "The Transcendentalist" (1843), an essay included in another section of this anthology, and "The Poet" (1844).

Emerson's friend and disciple, Henry David Thoreau, is concrete and explicit in his description of the confrontation possibility existing between man and his society in "Life Without Principle" (1863), in this essay justifying man's individualistic demands on the fact of his moral intelligence. In *Walden* (1854) Thoreau presents a dramatic demonstration of man's self-sufficiency and therefore his independence of society. Emily Dickinson in many of her poems asserts the validity of the poet's truths over the claims of the world outside. There is a long jump chronologically to the realistic writers of the twentieth century, the gap in time to be explained partially from the fact that the art-for-art's sake writers were minor in this period and the better and more serious novelists were primarily concerned with social issues. The first important writer in the twentieth century to give a serious treatment of the artist-individual was Theodore Dreiser, who presents a case for this artist-hero in *The "Genius"* (1915); Sherwood Anderson's writer-hero of *Winesburg, Ohio* (1919) casts judgment on a midwest small town, as do the artist and craftsmen heroes and heroines of Sinclair Lewis's *Main Street* (1920), *Arrowsmith* (1925), and *Dodsworth* (1929); Willa Cather's heroes and heroines in *Song of the Lark* (1915), *One of Ours* (1922), and *The Professor's House* (1925), and in many of her early short stories reject the uglier features of their American environment for reasons attributable to the incompatibility between artistic, or moral, and social demands. F. Scott Fitzgerald's Jay Gatsby in *The Great Gatsby* (1925), although more of an outlaw than a social rebel, reveals an artist's sensibility in his Platonic conception of himself, and comments are thereby made by Fitzgerald about both the artist and the world of wealth. John Dos Passos in *Three Soldiers* (1921) creates an artist victimized by his antagonist stand. In most of Ernest Hemingway's work the individual code is at variance with social forms. During the Depression, when most writers were concerned more with economic and social matters, Thomas Wolfe and Henry Miller were somewhat isolated in their fictional concerns with the individual's problems in a conformist world. After World War II a series of artist-heroes emerged in the work of most of the major writers, in the writing of Carson McCullers, Truman Capote, Tennessee Williams, Saul Bellow, Bernard Malamud, John Updike, J. D. Salinger, to name only a few. Norman Mailer and the entire beat and hip movement use rationalizations similar to those used by the artist to explain their rejection of middle class values.

Several American writers have been influential in modifying moral codes or changing conventional social attitudes either in statements of their own or by means of fictional examples. Herman Melville in *Pierre* (1852) describes a highly unconventional family relationship, anticipating a thesis that would not reappear until the next century;

Hester Prynne of *The Scarlet Letter* (1850) is Nathaniel Hawthorne's best example of one who violated the moral code of a specific society. Walt Whitman was a true revolutionary in his insistence on a more candid attitude about sex and sex relations. Mark Twain created a classic example of a rebel in *Huckleberry Finn* (1884), and in some of his later works, particularly "The Man That Corrupted Hadleyburg" (1900) and *The Mysterious Stranger* (1916), sought to uncover the immorality of certain current Puritan "moral" attitudes. William Dean Howells in *A Modern Instance* (1881) discussed the forbidden topic of divorce and Stephen Crane's first novel, *Maggie: A Girl of the Streets* (1893), introduced the topic of prostitution without stamping the conventional moral judgment on the prostitute. Frank Norris gave an unorthodox, unsentimental treatment of marriage in *McTeague* (1899). In his open and candid treatment of marriage and sex relationships, again without the conventional moral judgment, Theodore Dreiser in *Sister Carrie* (1900), *Jennie Gerhardt* (1911), *The "Genius"* (1915), and *An American Tragedy* (1925) did much to create a more realistic approach to the problems existing between the sexes. Sherwood Anderson in *Winesburg, Ohio* (1919), *Dark Laughter* (1925), and in other of his short stories, novels, and essays sought to change prevailing attitudes about sex. Because of the pioneering work of these and other writers, the war against Puritan restrictions in the matter of using sex as literary subject matter was largely won by the 1920's, and writers since then have been able to work in a reasonably liberal setting.

The next most important body of protest literature is that which was concerned with the economic structure of the country, specifically the institution of capitalism. Before capitalism became a perceptible power and threat in the social world, a few writers registered objections to the materialistic morality that accompanied a commercial culture. John Woolman in his *Journal* (1774) was one of the first to mention a specific objection to commercial values. Emerson in his earlier essays presented objections to commercial attitudes as part of his Transcendentalist message, and in his later works, particularly in the essays in *The Conduct of Life* (1860), was more explicit in his criticism of the materialistic trend he detected in American culture. Following the Civil War a more general consciousness of the economic imbalance created by early capitalistic practices caused many writers to examine more closely the capitalistic economic structure and rationale. Henry George's *Progress and Poverty* (1878), the dissemination of the ideas of Marx and Engels, and in the last two decades of the nineteenth century the labor turmoil, depressions, and agrarian unrest resulted in several bodies of literature critical of capitalism. Among the most popular of the fictional criticisms were the socialist utopian novels, the most notable being Edward Everette Hale's *Sybaris and Other Homes* (1869), Edward Bellamy's *Looking Backward, 2000–1887* (1888), the most famous of all, and *Equality* (1897), Ignatius Donnelly's *Caesar's Column: A Story of the Twentieth Century* (1891), and two by William Dean Howells, *A Traveler from Altruria* (1894) and *Through the Eye of the Needle* (1907). Two of these authors described social rebels in other novels: Bellamy in *The Duke of Stockbridge* (1879) and Howells in *A Hazard of New Fortunes* (1890).

The muckraking movement, which lasted from about 1902 to 1916, numbered among its novelists Robert Herrick, whose books, *The Common Lot* (1904), *The Master of the Inn* (1908), *A Life for a Life* (1910), and *Clark's Field* (1914) fit into the tradition; David Graham Phillips, with the novels *The Cost* (1904), *The Deluge* (1905), *The Plum Tree* (1905), and *Light-Fingered Gentry* (1907), exposed corruption in Wall Street, politics, and business. Other works of this movement are included in the bibliography of the social protest novels.

During the same period of time other literature described the social rebel in fictional representation. Jack London in *Martin Eden* (1909) presented a hero who rejected the American middle class ideals of his time and in *The Iron Heel* (1908) a hero of the future fighting the oligarchy which had assumed rule of the country. There are few social rebels in much of the social protest fiction written during this time, the fiction primarily exposés of corruption in some activity in business, government, or politics, or illustrations of the victimization that occurs in a factory or that arises from a speculation situation. Social protest novels are included in this bibliography under the assumption that the writers of the novels are fulfilling a social-rebel role in the writing of the work. One of the first novels making this kind of protest was a study of factory conditions in *The Silent Partner* (1871) by Elizabeth Stuart Phelps Ward. Western land speculation was described in *The Gilded Age* (1873) by Mark Twain and Charles Dudley Warner and in Edward Eggleston's *The Mystery of Metropolisville* (1873); mining and oil fraud and speculation in John F. Swift's *Robert Greathouse* (1876) and Josiah G. Holland's *Sevenoaks: A Story of Today* (1875); and political corruption in *Democracy* (1879) by Henry Adams. Charles Bellamy describes a strike in *The Breton Mills* (1879). Corruption in factories and government was described in Thomas S. Denison's *An Iron Crown* (1885), Hamlin Garland's *A Member of the Third House* (1892) and Ignatius Donnelly's *The Golden Bottle* (1892).

A full bibliography of the social protest, or radical, novels from 1900 to 1954 may be found in *The Radical Novel in the United States*

1900–1954 (1956), by Walter Rideout, Appendix, pp. 292–300. Among the many authors listed are I. K. Friedman, Upton Sinclair, Ernest Poole, Edward Dahlberg, Michael Gold, Jack Conroy, Robert Cantwell, Waldo Frank, Albert Halper, Albert Maltz, Joseph Freeman, Willard Motley, James T. Farrell, Richard Wright, Nelson Algren, and Howard Fast. Most of the novels of these writers listed will fit into the social protest tradition. An anthology of short fiction and poems to be included here is *Proletarian Literature in the United States,* edited by Granville Hicks, *et al.* (1935).

A selected bibliography of secondary works about the social rebel or about the tradition of social rebellion in American literature follows:

Aaron, Daniel, *Writers on the Left* (1961).

Aldridge, John W., *In Search of Heresy: American Literature in an Age of Conformity* (1956).

Bode, Carl, ed., *The Young Rebel in American Literature* (1960).

Clark, James J., and Robert H. Woodward, eds., *Success in America* (1966).

Cowley Malcolm, *After the Genteel Tradition: American Writers 1910–1930* (rev. ed., 1964).

―――― *Exile's Return: A Literary Odyssey of the 1920's* (rev. ed. 1951).

Finkelstein, Sidney, *Existentialism and Alienation in American Literature* (1965).

French, Warren, *The Social Novel at the End of an Era* (1966).

Geismar, Maxwell, *Rebels and Ancestors* (1954).

Hahn, Emily, *Romantic Rebels: An Informal History of Bohemianism in America* (1966).

Hassan, Ihab, *Radical Innocence: The Contemporary American Novel* (1961).

Hicks, Granville, *The Great Tradition* (rev. ed., 1935).

Kaul, A. N., *The American Vision: Actual and Ideal Society in Nineteenth-Century Fiction* (1963).

Klein, Marcus, *After Alienation: American Novels in Mid-Century* (1964).

Knight, Grant C., *The Strenuous Age in American Literature, 1900–1910* (1954).

Millgate, Michael, *American Social Fiction: James to Cozzens* (1964).

O'Connor, William Van, *An Age of Criticism, 1900–1950* (1952).

Parkinson, Thomas, ed., *A Casebook on the Beat* (1961).

Parrington, Vernon L., *American Dreams: A Study of American Utopias* (1947).

Parry, Albert, *Garrets and Pretenders: A History of Bohemianism in America* (1933, 1960).

Regier, C. C., *The Era of the Muckrakers* (1932).

Rideout, Walter, *The Radical Novel in the United States 1900–1954* (1956).

Seaver, Richard, Terry Southern, and Alexander Trocchi, eds., *Writers in Revolt, An Anthology* (1963).

Taylor, Walter F., *The Economic Novel in America* (1942).

Walker, Robert H., *The Poet and the Gilded Age: Social Themes in Late Nineteenth Century Verse* (1963).

Widmer, Kingsley, *The Literary Rebel* (1965).

Ziff, Larzer, *The American 1890's: Life and Times of a Lost Generation* (1966).

Students interested in further material on the social rebel should consult the standard bibliographies, in particular the following: Volume III of *Literary History of the United States* by Robert Spiller *et al.* (1948) and *Supplement* (1959); *Eight American Authors: A Review of Research and Criticism,* ed. Floyd Stovall (1963), for studies of Poe, Emerson, Hawthorne, Thoreau, Melville, Whitman, Twain, and James; periodical articles in each of the quarterly issues of *American Literature* and in Lewis Leary's *Articles on American Literature Appearing in Current Periodicals, 1900–1950* (1954); books and articles in "American Bibliography" in *PMLA,* issued annually since 1922; articles in *Abstracts of English Studies* (articles have been abstracted in this publication since January 1958); and *American Literary Scholarship* (issued annually since 1963), edited by James Woodress.

Notes

on the Authors

DANIEL AARON (b. 1912): Professor of English language and literature at Smith College, Aaron has made a special study of the leftist literature of the thirties. His writings include *Men of Good Hope: A Story of American Progressives* (1951) and *Writers on the Left* (1961). He has edited *America in Crisis* (1952), *Emerson: A Modern Anthology* (with Alfred Kazin, 1958), Paul Elmer More's *Shelburne Essays* 1963), and *American Pantheon* (1966).

SHERWOOD ANDERSON (1876–1941): However much Anderson may have romanticized the details of his break with the world of commerce, his personal rejection of commercial and industrial society underscores the major criticism he makes in many of his writings. His best-known work, *Winesburg, Ohio* (1919), for example, dramatizes the devastating effects on the human psyche of life in a small town in the transitional stage between agrarianism and industrialization. An earlier novel, *Marching Men* (1917), describes the oppressive treatment of Pennsylvania coal miners; and *Poor White* (1920) chronicles the spiritual demise of a town after the arrival of the machine. Even so, though his writings sympathetically portray the underprivileged, Anderson was not primarily a writer dominated by social purpose. In 1936 he wrote, "It seems to me that the story-teller is one thing, and the thinker, the political economist, the reformer another. The business of the story-teller is with life, in his own time, life as he feels it, smells it, tastes it. Not for him surely the making of the revolution."

JAMES BALDWIN (b. 1924): As novelist, essayist, and playwright, Baldwin has focused his considerable literary talent on the problems of the Negro in a predominantly white society. He is the author of three novels—*Go Tell It on the Mountain* (1953), *Giovanni's Room* (1956), and *Another Country* (1962); several plays, including *Blues for Mr. Charley,* first produced in 1964; and a collection of his short stories, *Going to Meet the*

Man (1965). It is in his essays, however, that he has reached his widest audience. So far three collections have appeared: *Notes of a Native Son* (1955), *Nobody Knows My Name* (1961), and *The Fire Next Time* (1963). In these works Baldwin has become a highly articulate spokesman for the resentments and frustrations of the American Negro.

EDWARD BELLAMY (1850–1898): "According to the best of my recollections," wrote Bellamy, "it was in the fall or winter of 1886 that I sat down to my desk with the definite purpose of trying to reason out a method of economic organization by which the republic might guarantee the livelihood and material welfare of its citizens on a basis of equality corresponding to and supplementing their political equality." Published in 1887, *Looking Backward* within a few years sold over a million copies, inspired the formation of the Nationalist party, and had direct influence on the Populists, Progressives, and Technocrats. Except for *The Duke of Stockbridge* (published in 1900 but begun in 1879), a sympathetic account of Shays' Rebellion, and *Equality* (1897), another utopian romance, Bellamy's writings were in the tradition of Hawthorne, with whom he was compared. Bellamy died of tuberculosis in his native town of Chicopee Falls, Massachusetts.

RANDOLPH BOURNE (1886–1918): Handicapped throughout his short life by a deformed back, Bourne graduated from Columbia University in 1913 to become a forceful literary critic and social commentator. He opposed the ethics of big business, America's participation in World War I, and sentimental literature. In addition to *Youth and Life* (1913), his first book, he published *The Gary Schools* (1916) and *Education and Living* (1917) and compiled *Toward an Enduring Peace* (1916). A posthumous volume, *Untimely Papers*, was published in 1919.

STOKELY CARMICHAEL (b. 1941?): The coiner of the black-power slogan, Carmichael was born in Trinidad and grew up there, in New York City, and in Washington, D.C. While attending Howard University, from which he was graduated in 1964, he was active in student government and in local civil rights activities. He has been affiliated with the Student Non-violent Coordinating Committee almost from its beginning in 1960 and was elected chairman in May 1966. One of the foremost of the angry young leaders of the black people in America, he has been arrested more than fifteen times for his participation in demonstrations in several Southern states and New York.

HENRY STEELE COMMAGER (b. 1902): Professor of History at Columbia University from 1938 to 1956 and at Amherst College since 1956, Commager has lectured and taught throughout the United States and in several foreign countries. Born in Pittsburgh in 1902, he received his education at the University of Chicago and was awarded the Ph.D. in 1928. His voluminous list of books, a reflection of the breadth of his interests, includes *Growth of the American Republic* (1930), *Documents of American History* (seven editions from 1934 to 1963), a biography of Theodore Parker (1936), *The Heritage of America* (1939), *Majority Rule and Minority Rights* (1943), *Freedom, Loyalty, Dissent* (1954), and *The Era of Reform* (1960). *The American Mind* (1950) is a study of American thought since the 1880's.

MALCOLM COWLEY (b. 1898): A member of Harry Crosby's generation, Cowley was born in Pennsylvania and was educated at Harvard, which he left in 1917 to join the American Field Service in France. His *Exile's Return* (1934, 1951) is an analytical study, based on personal observations and experiences, of the expatriate life of his generation during the 1920's. A critic and former editor of the *New Republic*, he has written extensively on contemporary American literary figures, notably F. Scott Fitzgerald, Ernest Hemingway, and William Faulkner. Among his books are *After the Genteel Tradition* (1937), *The Literary Situation* (1954), and (with Robert Cowley) *Fitzgerald and the Jazz Age* (1966).

EMILY DICKINSON (1830–1886): Granddaughter of a founder of Amherst College and daughter of one of its trustees, Miss Dickinson lived her outwardly uneventful years within the confines of Amherst, Massachusetts, where the stern vestiges of New England's Calvinistic Puritanism maintained a stronghold. Of her lawyer father she wrote in 1862, "He buys me many books, but begs me not to read them, because he fears they joggle the mind." Miss Dickinson did not need books, however, to provoke her naturally rebellious spirit. Her withdrawal into a private world following the death or removal of men whom she admired or loved paralleled her withdrawal in spirit from the rigid conventionalities of New England social and religious life that much of her poetry expresses. During her lifetime she released only a handful of poems for publication, maintaining that "Publication is the auction/Of the mind of man"; a three-volume collection of her poetry, edited by Thomas H. Johnson, was published in 1955.

JOHN DOS PASSOS (b. 1896): The writings of Dos Passos (born in Chicago) have consistently been on the side of individual rights in the face of a society deteriorating, as he describes it, because of the dehumanization resulting from materialistic values. His first success was *Three Soldiers* (1921), but his most notable contribution has been the trilogy *U.S.A.* (1938), combining *The 42nd Parallel* (1930), *Nineteen Nineteen* (1932), and *The Big Money* (1936). In his defense of the individual he has remained steady, he says, while the forces tyrannizing over the individual have moved from the extreme right to the extreme left. Because he now writes of Thomas Jefferson rather than of Sacco and Vanzetti, he has been termed a "reformed rebel," a label with which he does not concur.

THEODORE DREISER (1871–1945): The poverty of the Indiana childhood of Dreiser, stemming from the economic failure of his father, impressed upon him a social philosophy combining Darwinism and Nietzscheanism as the means for obtaining the comforts and necessities of the world. It taught him, too, a distrust of the moral codes of polite society, for in a time of particular need for his family it was the mistress of his elder brother, herself the madame of a brothel, who came to their aid. Dreiser's sympathy for the victim of the American social system can be seen in many of his novels other than *Sister Carrie* (1900), notably *Jennie Gerhardt* (1911) and *An American Tragedy* (1925).

RALPH WALDO EMERSON (1803–1882): In his lectures, essays, and poems, Emerson evidenced a determined rebellion against outworn creeds, traditions, and intellectual fashions. Licensed in 1826 to preach, he became disillusioned with the doctrines and rites of Christianity and resigned his Unitarian pastorate after three years at the Second Church of Boston. His first book, *Nature* (1836), established the credo of the New England Transcendentalists. His "The American Scholar" address, delivered at Harvard in 1837, was called by Oliver Wendell Holmes "our intellectual Declaration of Independence"; and his "Divinity School Address," also delivered at Harvard, alienated him in 1838 from religious conservatives by placing the authority of individual intuition and inspiration above that of the rational and authoritarian interpretation of the Scriptures. Emerson was not invited back to Harvard, his alma mater, for thirty years. In his writings and in his life Emerson rebelled against authoritarianism and encouraged the individual's independence from the past, from society, and from materialistic values and advocated reliance on private resources and the sacredness of one's own integrity.

BENJAMIN FRANKLIN (1706–1790): A less fiery rebel than his contemporary Thomas Paine, Franklin was no less outspoken and had no less political and social influence. He is the only American whose name appears on the four great documents connected with American independence: the Declaration of Independence, the treaties with France and Great Britain, and the Constitution. His skill as a literary satirist can be seen in several works that span his long career: a number of the *Dogood Papers* (1722), "Rules by Which a Great Empire May be Reduced to a Small One," and "An Edict by the King of Prussia" (both 1773).

JOSEPH FREEMAN (b. 1897): Born in the Ukraine, Freeman came to the United States in 1904 and grew up in the Brooklyn slums. At seventeen he became a Socialist. Following his graduation from Columbia University in 1919, he became a journalist and during the next two decades worked at a number of tasks associated with the Socialist cause. For some time he edited the *New Masses;* he wrote an unproduced screenplay, *Soviet,* for M.G.M.; he wrote a critical introduction for the volume *Proletarian Literature in the United States* (1935); and he produced an autobiography, *An American Testament* (1935), that was selected by the Writer's Congress as the best autobiography of the year. In 1939 he severed his connections with leftist publications and began freelancing. His first novel, *Never Call Retreat*, appeared in 1943. A second, *The Long Pursuit*, was published in 1947.

ALLEN GINSBERG (b. 1926): Born in Newark, New Jersey, Ginsberg attended high school in Paterson, was dismissed from Columbia University in 1945 after two years of study, but he was readmitted and graduated in 1949. The publication of *Howl and Other Poems* (1956), the subject of a highly publicized obscenity trial, made him the best known of the "beat" poets. His poems take potshots at diverse aspects of contemporary American civilization—materialism, authoritarianism, militarism—but their fundamental objection is not so clearly defined. "My poetry," Ginsberg has said, "is Angelical ravings, and has nothing to do with dull materialistic vagaries about who should shoot who. The secrets of individual imagination are of no use to this world, except perhaps to make it shut its trap . . ." (*Evergreen Review*, November–December 1959). Ginsberg's other books include *Empty Mirror; Early Poems* (1961), *Kaddish and Other Poems* (1961), *Reality Sandwiches, 1953–60* (1963), and *The Yage Letters* (with William Burroughs, 1963). In 1966 he was awarded a Guggenheim fellowship in poetry.

ALBERT HALPER (b. 1904): Born in the Chicago slums, Halper drifted from job to job for seven years following graduation from high school. But in 1928 he left his clerkship in the post office to devote himself to writing. His novels—*Union Square* (1933), *The Foundry* (1934), *The Chute* (1937), *Sons of the Fathers* (1940), *The Little People* (1942), *Only an Inch from Glory* (1943), and *The Golden Watch* (1953)—reflect the hopes and frustrations of the poor and support his contention that "any writer who considers himself a serious workman must have a 'message' or he is not worth his salt." It is his sympathy with the underprivileged in his novels, rather than a propagandistic quality, that constitutes their message and their value.

CHARLES V. HAMILTON: Chairman of the Department of Political Science at Roosevelt University in Chicago, Professor Hamilton has also taught at Tuskegee Institute, Albany State College in Georgia, Rutgers University, and Lincoln University. He holds a baccalaureate degree from Roosevelt University, a law degree from Loyola University, and both a master's degree and a doctorate from the University of Chicago. He is the author of a monograph, *Minority Politics in Black Belt Alabama*, and has published articles on constitutional law and civil rights in the *Wisconsin Law Review*, *Phylon*, and the *Journal of Negro Education*.

NATHANIEL HAWTHORNE (1804–1864): Great-grandson of a judge at the Salem witchcraft trials and descendant of generations of Puritans, Hawthorne took both personal and artistic interest in the Puritan definitions of morality and social responsibility. His first successful novel, *The Scarlet Letter* (1850), he called a "hell-fired book"; the more conservative of its readers labeled it a contribution to "the brothel library," but it pleased a wide audience of readers who championed Hester Prynne's fore-shadowings of moral emancipation. More an observer of society than an active participant in its affairs, Hawthorne did contribute money to the experiment in communal living at Brook Farm and resided and worked there for several months in 1841. His fictional account of his experiences, *The Blithedale Romance* (1852), is critical of reformers and utopias. In some of his short tales and sketches—"Earth's Holocaust" and "The Celestial Railroad," for example—he is a particularly keen, though sometimes veiled, critic of the American scene.

THOMAS JEFFERSON (1743–1826): The principal author of the document that serves today as the model statement of political independence for newly emerging nations, Jefferson (1743–1826) devoted his energies throughout his life to the cause of individual freedom. His epitaph, which he wrote, summarizes the attainments of which he was most proud: "Here Was Buried Thomas Jefferson, Author of the Declaration of Independence, the Statute of Virginia for Religious Freedom, and Father of the University of Virginia." Distrusted by conservatives, he asserted that "a little rebellion, now and then, is a good thing, and as necessary in the political world as storms in the physical."

LEROI JONES (b. 1934): Born in Newark, New Jersey, Jones attended several universities, including Rutgers and Columbia, and earned the M.A. degree in German literature. He has published several volumes, including poetry, *Preface to a Twenty Volume Suicide Note* (1961) and *The Dead Lecturer* (1964); a sociological study, *Blues People: Negro Music in America* (1963); and a novel, *The System of Dante's Hell* (1965). He has also written several widely performed plays: *The Toilet, Dutchman*, and *The Slave*. He is the most versatile of the young Negro writers and does not restrict his writings to studies of racial relationships.

JACK KEROUAC (b. 1922): A highly controversial writer, Kerouac has been praised for the spontaneity of his prose of the generation for which he is a leading spokesman but has been condemned by critics and readers who view the novel as an art form. Born in Lowell, Massachusetts, he drifted about, served in the Navy and Merchant Marine, and traveled in the United States and Mexico before establishing himself as a writer. Fame came with the publication of his second novel, *On the Road* (1957), which he reportedly wrote in three weeks. Books of his fiction or poetry have since been published annually. He claims to have coined the term "beat," saying that it means "beatific," and has defined the beat generation as "mainly, . . . a new literary movement aimed at freer expression of highly personal responses, and . . . , in that sense, modern individualistic romance for all it's worth."

MARTIN LUTHER KING, JR. (1929–1968): An advocate of the passive resistance tactics of Thoreau and Mahatma Gandhi, Dr. King emerged in 1958 as a national leader of the Negro nonviolent resistance to racial inequities when he led the Negroes of Montgomery, Alabama, in the year-long boycott of local bus companies that led to the desegregation of the buses. Born in Atlanta, he was educated in Atlanta, was graduated from Crozier Theological Seminary in Chester, Pennsylvania, and received a Ph.D. from Boston University in 1955. In August, 1963, he was one of the organizers of the civil rights march on Washington, D.C. He received the Nobel Prize for Peace in 1964. A forceful and eloquent speaker, he wrote the story of the Montgomery boycott in *Strive Toward Freedom* (1958), which Perry Miller has compared in its restraint to the *Journal* of John Woolman, and another volume, *Why We Can't Wait* (1964). In his last public address he told his followers, "I've seen the promised land," and added prophetically, "I may not get there with you." The next day, April 4, 1968, he was killed by an assassin's bullet in Memphis.

SINCLAIR LEWIS (1885–1951): The first American to win the Nobel Prize for Literature (in 1930), Lewis in his life and writings gave full expression to the rebellious spirit of the period following World War I. In the Gopher Prairie of *Main Street* (1920) he satirically portrayed the middle class life not only of his native Sauk Center, Minnesota, but of small towns throughout America. In his next success, *Babbitt* (1922), he criticized American business ethics and the booster spirit of large towns. When the Pulitzer Prize was offered to him for *Arrowsmith* (1925), he refused it as a protest against the criteria for the award, saying that its intent was to make writers "safe, polite, obedient, and sterile." The attack on sham, pretension, and hypocrisy in numerous facets of American life became his stock in trade as a writer.

JACK LONDON (1876–1916): Born an illegitimate child in San Francisco, London received no schooling until the age of ten, worked among waterfront toughs in Oakland, led a boys' gang, and by seventeen was, as he later described himself, "a drunken bum." After a cruise on a whaling ship, he joined Kelley's "Army of Protest" in 1894, only to desert to become a tramp. Largely self-taught, he left the University of California after one semester to begin what was eventually a fabulously successful writing career. His admirations included Darwin and Spencer, whose evolutionary ideas influenced the strong, individualistic heroes of *The Sea-Wolf* (1904) and *Martin Eden* (1909), as well as the writings of Karl Marx. His sympathy with the proletariat can be seen in *People of the Abyss* (1902) and *The Iron Heel* (1907), which chronicles an unsuccessful Socialist revolution. A member of the Socialist party, he resigned from it in March, 1916, eight months before his death, because of "its loss of emphasis on the class struggle."

NORMAN MAILER (b. 1923): Born in Long Branch, New Jersey, Mailer grew up in Brooklyn, entered Harvard at the age of sixteen, and won an award from *Story Magazine* in 1941. His first novel, *The Naked and the Dead* (1948), reflects his own experiences as a rifleman in the Pacific in World War II and dramatizes the conflict between the individual and society. Mailer's admiration for the person who seeks independence is obvious in this and later books, such as his second novel, *Barbary Shore* (1951), and his first book-length essay, *The White Negro* (1957). His critical observations on American society inform his most recent novels, *An American Dream* (1965) and *Why Are We in Vietnam?* (1967), as well as the collections of his writings that he has personally edited: *Advertisements for Myself* (1959), *Death for the Ladies and Other Disasters* (1962), *The Presidential Papers of Norman Mailer* (1963), and *Cannibals and Christians* (1966).

HERMAN MELVILLE (1819–1891): Following a brief periof of school teaching near Pittsfield, Massachusetts, Melville went to sea in 1839 as a deck hand. His experiences before the mast provided the substance for his earliest books—*Typee* (1846), *Omoo* (1847), *Mardi* and *Redburn* (1849), and *White-Jacket* (1850)—in which, much to his profit but to the occasional consternation of prudish readers, he wrote with obvious approval of the sexual freedom of the natives on the island of Typee, criticized Christian missionaries, and laid bare the cruelty and inhumanity aboard both American merchant and naval ships. The restlessness that had driven him to sea in the first place still pursued him, however, and in *Moby-Dick* (1851) he used a whaling-ship setting to investigate the nature of ultimate reality and truth. Though now regarded as a masterpiece, the novel was poorly received by readers and critics of the day. Like his own Ahab, Melville sought the unknowable for the remainder of his years. In 1856 his friend Hawthorne wrote of him: "He can neither believe, nor be comfortable in his unbelief; and he is too honest and courageous not to try to do one or the other . . . he has a very high and noble nature."

H. L. MENCKEN (1880–1956): "So many young men," wrote Ernest Hemingway in *The Sun Also Rises*, "get their likes and dislikes from Mencken." Through his editorial positions on the *Smart Set*, beginning in 1908, and on the *American Mercury*, starting in 1914, Mencken attacked pretension, hypocrisy, and middle class conventions in all areas of life— politics, morality, religion, as well as literature. His indictments, first published in periodicals and newspapers, were collected between 1919 and 1927 in six volumes with a revealing title, *Prejudices*. The title of his published notebooks, *Minority Report* (1956), is equally denotative. Much of his work is timely and thus ephemeral; but in *The American Language*, first published in 1919 and supplemented as late as 1948, he made a lasting contribution to American culture.

HENRY MILLER (b. 1891): Born in Brooklyn, Miller moved in the 1920's to Paris, where his first books, extravagant recreations of his early life in New York City, were published. The first, *Tropic of Cancer*, appeared in 1934; the second, *Tropic of Capricorn*, in 1939. Banned in the United States and all English-speaking countries, they were not published in this country until 1961. Meanwhile, Miller had returned to America to live at Big Sur, California, and to continue the writing that was recognized by his election to the American Institute of Arts and Letters in 1958. He has acknowledged his indebtedness to a number of American literary rebels —Emerson, Thoreau, Whitman, Twain, Mencken, for example. *Tropic of Cancer,* significantly, has as its motto a statement by Emerson: "These novels will give way, by and by, to diaries or autobiographies—captivating books, if only a man knew how to choose among what he calls experiences that which is really his experience, and how to record truth truly."

MICHAEL MILLGATE (b. 1905): A British scholar, Millgate has specialized in the study of American fiction. In addition to *American Social Fiction* (1964), he has published two studies of William Faulkner, in 1961 and 1966, and in 1965 edited *Transatlantic Dialogue,* an edition of Sir Edmund Gosse's correspondence with several American authors, and an edition of Theodore Dreiser's *Sister Carrie.*

C. WRIGHT MILLS (1916–1962): A member of the sociology faculty of Columbia University from 1945 to his death, Mills also taught for brief period at Maryland and Chicago, at Brandeis University, and as a Fulbright professor at the University of Copenhagen. His books—among which are *The New Men of Power* (1948), *White Collar* (1951), *The Power Elite* (1956), and *The Sociological Imagination* (1959)—have been extremely influential though controversial studies of American society. He is regarded by some as the intellectual father of the "new left" movement.

KENNETH REXROTH: Widely acclaimed for his translations from the Japanese, Chinese, Greek, and Latin, Rexroth is largely self-educated. Born in South Bend, Indiana, he now resides in San Francisco, where he is a close observer of social and intellectual movements. His first volume of poetry, *In What Hour* (1940), received the California Literature Silver Medal Award for poetry in 1941, and his second volume, *The Phoenix and the Tortoise* (1944) in 1945. He has edited or written over twenty volumes of poetry, essays, and fiction, and has held several one-man shows of his abstract paintings, including one in Paris. His autobiography, *An Autobiographical Novel,* was published in 1966. He is a regular contributor to the San Francisco *Chronicle-Examiner* and to *Saturday Review.*

UPTON SINCLAIR (b. 1878): Author of over seventy volumes, Sinclair, who was born in Baltimore, has in all but his first few books expressed a biting indictment of such diverse facets of American society as the meatpacking industry (*The Jungle,* 1906, which influenced the first Pure Food legislation), labor–management struggles (*King Coal,* 1917, written on behalf of the Colorado coal miners), journalism (*The Brass Check,* 1919), and government (*Oil!,* 1927, portraying the scandals of the Harding administration). A candidate for the governorship of California in 1934, he campaigned on an antipoverty platform (the "EPIC" plan), won the Democratic nomination but was defeated. In 1940 he began the publication of the "Lanny Budd" series of novels, a comprehensive chronicle of contemporary history.

JOHN P. SISK (b. 1914): A member of the English faculty of Gonzaga University in his native Spokane, Washington, since 1938, Sisk is especially interested in the modern novel and in English and American literature since the Renaissance. He is a regular contributor to *Commonweal* and has published numerous essays in *America, Ramparts,* and *Prairie Schooner.* He is the author of a novel, *A Trial of Strength* (1961), which won the Carl Forman Award in an international contest.

JOHN STEINBECK (b. 1902): Born in Salinas, California, in 1902, Steinbeck has drawn from his intimate knowledge of working people—the fruit pickers, paisanos, small ranchers—in this and closely neighboring areas for the novels that earned him the Nobel Prize for Literature in 1962. "I am completely partisan," he has confessed. "Every effort I can bring to bear is and has been at the call of the common working-people to the end that they may eat what they raise, wear what they weave, use what they produce." His partisanship can be most clearly seen in the three novels set in Monterey—*Tortilla Flat* (1935), *Cannery Row* (1945), and *Sweet Thursday* (1954); *In Dubious Battle* (1936), the story of an unsuccessful Communist-organized strike of fruit pickers; *Of Mice and Men* (1937), which tells of two farm laborers who yearn for land of their own; and *Grapes of Wrath* (1939), which chronicles the exodus of the dispossessed farmers of the Dust Bowl to California during the 1930's.

HENRY DAVID THOREAU (1817–1862): From July 4, 1845, to early September 1847, Thoreau lived quietly on the shores of Walden Pond, near his native Concord, Massachusetts, closely observing the natural world about him, reading deeply, keeping a journal, and attempting to learn to live deliberately, fronting only the essential facts of life. In *Walden* (1854) he said of his motives: "I did not wish to live what was not life, living is so dear; nor did I wish to practise resignation, unless it was quite necessary." Though not a recluse, Thoreau valued the meditative life of the poet and nature lover. Yet his commitment to the cause of individual liberty led him into a headlong assault against society. In 1849, in "Civil Disobedience," he advocated the practice of passive resistance to unjust laws, and at the time of the trial of John Brown, whom he had assisted, he spoke eloquently of Brown's cause and the injustice of the laws which could destroy a man for adhering to the dictates of a pure conscience.

MARK TWAIN (SAMUEL L. CLEMENS) (1835–1910): So sensitively attuned to his times that he could satirize their excesses and foibles at the same time that he fell prey to them himself, Mark Twain wrote the devastating indictments of society seen in *The Gilded Age* (1873) and *Huckleberry Finn* (1884) while investing in schemes to amass a fortune. Through Huckleberry Finn he unforgettably dramatized the conflict of the person whose "sound heart" is at odds with his "deformed conscience"—in other words, whose intuitive sense of justice and human rights makes him rebel against the conventions and laws of his society. In such later works as *Pudd'nhead Wilson* (1894), "The Man That Corrupted Hadleyburg" (1898), and *The Mysterious Stranger* (1916), Twain gave imaginative expression to the attitude that he expressed at the time of the Boer war: "My idea of our civilization is that it is a shoddy, poor thing & full of cruelties, vanities, arrogancies, meannesses, & hypocrisies." Twain's need for the applause of the society he criticized, however, prevented him from following in the footsteps of Huck Finn, who was able to "light out for the Territory" and escape a society whose values he could not accept.

WALT WHITMAN (1819–1892): From his earliest days as a New York City journalist, Whitman was an interested commentator on social problems. He espoused reform movements and opposed slavery and in 1842 published an artless temperance novel, *Franklin Evans; or, the Inebriate.* It was with *Leaves of Grass* (1855), however, that he first found the voice to express his exultant faith in the common man—a faith in his superiority over creeds, traditions, conventions. Whitman's book of poems, enlarged and revised through nine editions up to the year before his death, was praised by Emerson but was received with hostility by the genteel critics who saw only obscenity in its celebration of the body and its candid sexual allusions. After the Civil War, during which Whitman served as a volunteer nurse in Washington hospitals, the publication of *Drum-Taps* (1865) made Whitman more acceptable to the public and helped to change his image from that of a "dandy" to that of "the good, gray poet."

KINGSLEY WIDMER (b. 1925): Raised in the midwest, Widmer was born in Minneapolis and has taught literature at the universities of Minnesota, Washington, California, and Tel-Aviv and at Reed College, and since 1956 has been on the English faculty of San Diego State College. A specialist in the study of literary rebels, he has published critical studies of D. H. Lawrence—*The Art of Perversity* (1962)—and Henry Miller (1963). He has also edited *Literary Censorship: Principles, Cases, Problems* (1961).

JOHN WOOLMAN (1720–1772): Born in New Jersey, a child of Quaker parents, Woolman began preaching at the age of twenty-one. As a young clerk the next year, he refused to make out a bill of sale for a Negro slave. His life was devoted to preaching throughout the colonies to settlements of Friends. The burden of his sermons and writings, a protest against the excesses and evils of secular life, is illustrated by the brief selection in this volume. He died before his journal, which Whittier called "a classic of the inner life," was published.